Ius Gentium: Comparative Perspectives on Law and Justice

Volume 48

More information about this series at http://www.springer.com/series/7888

Colin B. Picker • Guy I. Seidman
Editors

The Dynamism of Civil Procedure - Global Trends and Developments

Springer

Editors
Colin B. Picker
Law Faculty, University of New South Wales
Sydney, Australia

Guy I. Seidman
The Interdisciplinary Center
The Radzyner School of Law
Herzliya, Israel

ISSN 1534-6781 ISSN 2214-9902 (electronic)
Ius Gentium: Comparative Perspectives on Law and Justice
ISBN 978-3-319-21980-6 ISBN 978-3-319-21981-3 (eBook)
DOI 10.1007/978-3-319-21981-3

Library of Congress Control Number: 2015951722

Springer Cham Heidelberg New York Dordrecht London

Printed on acid-free paper

Springer International Publishing AG Switzerland is part of Springer Science+Business Media (www.springer.com)

Preface

This book explores the surprising dynamism of the field of civil procedure – that civil procedure is not static, that it is ever changing. This book provides a series of chapters that explore a cross selection of recent developments in civil procedure from around the world. In doing so, the collection conveys the dynamism and innovations of modern civil procedure – by field, method, and system.

In addition, the introductory chapters lay out the context within which the other examinations fit. That context is comparative, with the introductory chapters providing detailed expositions of the world of comparative civil procedure. The substantive chapters thereafter build on that theoretical framework, with the result that this book provides a consideration of dynamism in civil procedure in comparative perspective.

Sydney, Australia — Colin B. Picker
Herzliya, Israel — Guy I. Seidman

Contents

About the Authors

Loïc Cadiet Loïc Cadiet is a Professor at the Sorbonne Law School (University Paris I), where he teaches general theory of litigation, judicial systems, civil procedure, and ADR. Loïc Cadiet is also the President of the International Association of Procedural Law, the Co-Editor-in-Chief of the *International Journal of Procedural Law*, and a senior member of the Institut Universitaire de France (Chaire Systèmes de justice et droit du procès).

Andrew Higgins Dr. Andrew Higgins is an Associate Professor of Civil Procedure at Faculty of Law, University of Oxford, and a Fellow in law at Mansfield College. He teaches civil procedure on Oxford's BCL/Mjur course and has published widely on procedural issues including case management, costs, and collective redress. He has recently published a book *Legal Professional Privilege for Corporations: A Guide to Four Major Common Law Jurisdictions* (Oxford University Press 2014). He is currently the General Editor of *Civil Justice Quarterly* and a practicing Australian barrister specializing in mass tort litigation.

Michael Legg Associate Professor Michael Legg specializes in civil procedure, class actions, litigation funding, and regulatory and commercial litigation. He is the author of *Case Management and Complex Civil Litigation* (Federation Press, 2011), co-author of *Principles of Civil Procedure in New South Wales* (Thomson Reuters, 2012) and *Annotated Class Actions Legislation* (LexisNexis, 2014), and Editor of *The Future of Dispute Resolution* (LexisNexis, 2013). His research has been cited by a number of Australian courts and law reform commissions. He is a member of the Law Council of Australia's Class Actions Committee and a Board Member of the National Pro Bono Resource Centre. He is admitted as a solicitor before the Supreme Court of New South Wales and as an attorney in New York.

James R. Maxeiner Professor James R. Maxeiner is the Ius Gentium Series Editor. He holds a J.D. from Cornell, an LL.M. from Georgetown, and Ph.D. in Law (Dr. jur.) from the Ludwig Maximilian University (Munich, Germany). He is also Associate Director, Center for International and Comparative Law, University of

Baltimore. He is a member of numerous international law associations, including International Academy of Comparative Law; American Law Institute; American Foreign Law Association (Vice President); American Society for Comparative Law; Gesellschaft für Rechtsvergleichung; International Association of Procedural Law; American Bar Association; and the Deutscher Anwaltverein. He is a former Fellow of the Alexander von Humboldt Foundation, Max Planck Society, and German Academic Exchange Service.

Colin B. Picker Colin Picker is a Professor and the Associate Dean (International) at the University of New South Wales (UNSW) in Sydney, Australia. He has a Ph.D. from UNSW, a J.D. from the Yale Law School, and an A.B (summa cum laude) from Bowdoin College, Maine (Political Science and Russian). He teaches and researches in the areas of international economic law (IEL), public international law, and comparative law. Recent projects have included legal cultural analyses of different aspects and fields within IEL, often with a specific focus on China's legal culture and involvement in and with IEL. Prior to joining UNSW in 2010, Colin Picker was the Daniel L. Brenner/UMKC Scholar and Professor of Law at the University of Missouri – Kansas City School of Law. He entered academia in 2000, after practicing in the Washington, D.C., law firm Wilmer, Cutler & Pickering. His practice included transnational and trade litigation, international transactions, and international congressional policy work. He was one of the founders and was the founding Executive Vice President of the Society of International Economic Law from 2008 to 2014.

Guy I. Seidman Guy I. Seidman is a Law Professor at the Law Faculty at the Interdisciplinary Center, Herzliya, since 1999. He was trained in Israel (LL.B., LL.M., Tel Aviv University) and the United States (LL.M., S.J.D., Northwestern University, Chicago). Professor Seidman specializes in administrative and comparative law, and has researched, published, and taught in Israel, Europe, and the United States.

Elisabetta Silvestri Elisabetta Silvestri is an Associate Professor of Italian civil procedure and comparative civil procedure at the Department of Law, University of Pavia, Italy. She was educated at the University of Pavia, Faculty of Law and at Cornell Law School. She has been a Visiting Scholar at Yale Law School and at the London School of Economics. She is Scientific Director of the postgraduate program for the training of mediators and ADR professionals, University of Pavia and is a Co-Director of the Public and Private Justice seminar at the Inter-University Centre, Dubrovnik, Croatia.

Lang Thai Lang Thai is a Lecturer in the School of Law, Deakin University in Melbourne, Australia. She holds an LL.M. (Monash), Grad DipEd (Melbourne), combined B.Sc. and LL.B. (Monash), and she has also been awarded a scholarship from the Methodist Ladies College, an elite private school in Melbourne during her senior years of school for her academic achievements. She is a qualified Australian lawyer and a qualified secondary school teacher and has practiced law both in Singapore and Australia. She has been Visiting Scholar at the University of Hong Kong Law Faculty (2001 and 2006) and Visiting Scholar at the University of Oxford Law Faculty (2009). Many of her refereed articles have been published in leading high-quality journals in the areas of corporate law and commercial law. Her articles have been cited favorably in court judgments. She has a keen interest in comparative corporate law.

Jeffrey E. Thomas Jeffrey E. Thomas is Associate Dean for International Programs and is the Daniel L. Brenner Faculty Scholar, and Professor of Law at the University of Missouri – Kansas City. His research focuses on the interaction between law and culture, the rule of law, and insurance law. A number of his recent works use a comparative law perspective. He has been a Fulbright Fellow at Immanuel Kant Baltic Federal University in Kaliningrad, Russia (2010), and at Nankai University in Tianjin, China (1999–2000). He is an elected member of the American Law Institute. Before joining the faculty at University of Missouri – Kansas City, he was a Bigelow Teaching Fellow at the University of Chicago. He earned his B.A. in Political Science from Loyola Marymount University, and his J.D. from University of California, Berkeley.

Kristie Thomas Dr. Kristie Thomas is currently a Lecturer in Business Law and Director of Executive MBA Programmes at Nottingham University Business School. She also gained her Ph.D. from Nottingham University in 2008; her doctoral research concerned the intellectual property system in China following its WTO accession in 2001, which incorporated surveys and interviews with a variety of respondents, including business and legal professionals in China. Her current research interests reflect her interests in comparative law, international trade, and business practice more generally. She has a particular interest in Asia, having spent 2 years based at the University's China campus from 2004 to 2006 and having previously also lived in Taiwan for 2 years.

Brenda Tronson Brenda Tronson is a Barrister at Level 22 Chambers, Sydney, Australia, practicing in public law and commercial law and appearing in a range of courts and tribunals. She completed her undergraduate degrees at the University of New South Wales, Australia, and then the B.C.L. and M.Phil in Law at Oxford University. Brenda has worked as an associate to Justice Crennan at the High Court of Australia and for Freehills, now Herbert Smith Freehills. She is a Sessional Lecturer in civil procedure at the University of New South Wales.

Teresa Arruda Alvim Wambier Teresa Arruda Alvim Wambier is a Professor at Pontifícia Universidade Católica de São Paulo, and holds LL.D. and LL.M. She is the Coordinator of the Centre for Post Graduate Studies of Civil Procedure at the same University. She is also President of the Instituto Brasileiro de Direito Processual, Vice President of Instituto Ibero Americano de Derecho Procesal, and a member of the Board of the International Association of Procedural Law. She is also a member of the Instituto Panamericano de Derecho Procesal, of the Portuguese Institute of Procedural Law. Since 1983, she has served as the Editor-in-Chief of the Brazilian Revista de Processo. She was most recently the General "Rapporteuse" of the Committee in change of drawing up a Bill for a new Brazilian Civil Procedural Code.

Margaret Woo Margaret Woo is Professor of Law at Northeastern University School of Law. In 1997, she was named the law school's Distinguished Professor of Public Policy. She is also a Faculty Director for the law school's Program on Human Rights and the Global Economy and a Co-Editor for the *Journal of Legal Education*, the premier journal on legal education with the Association of American Law Schools. Professor Woo has published and spoken widely on the role of courts in economic development and democracy. A specialist on Chinese legal reform, she is a former Fellow of the Bunting Institute (Radcliffe College) and is presently an associate of the East Asian Legal Studies Program at Harvard University. She has received prestigious grants from a variety of organizations, including the National Science Foundation and the Ford Foundation and was on the Senior Scholar Roster for the Fulbright Scholars Program. Her books include *East Asian Law: Universal Norms and Local Culture* (Routledge, 2003) and *Chinese Justice: Civil Dispute Resolution in Contemporary China* (Cambridge University Press, 2011). She is also co-author of *Litigating in America: Civil Procedure in Context* (Aspen Publishing, 2006). Professor Woo is an elected member of the prestigious American Law Institute and the International Association of Procedural Law, and is a Fellow with the American Bar Foundation. She previously served on the Board of Directors for the Law and Society Association and chaired the civil procedure section of the Association of American Law Schools. A graduate of Brown University, Professor Woo received her law degree from New York University School of Law.

Part I
The Context

Chapter 1
Comparative Civil Procedure

Guy I. Seidman

1.1 Introduction and Definitions

As suggested in the title of this edited volume, there are interesting global trends and developments in the field of comparative civil procedure – that it is indeed a dynamic system.[1] These involve the development of procedures and remedies alongside an expanding number of jurisdictions that now make major contributions to the field. But before we come to speak of the new in this book, in order to set the context and to highlight how this book contributes to our understandings of comparative civil procedure, this chapter aims to bring readers up to speed regarding the current state of comparative civil procedure.

As the name indicates, the field surveyed in this chapter is a cross between two more general fields: one is *civil procedure* and the other is *comparative law*. That is we are dealing with the issues covered when civil procedure and comparative law are juxtaposed, creating a third, distinct and independent (sub)field of study. This is not to say that the territory covered by the juxtaposition of these two fields is small. Quite to the contrary. But it is to say that of the vast fields that are covered when we come to study *the law*, as it applies in the entire world, what is of concern here is a somewhat more specific area. Defining it more clearly, at least in formal terms:

[1] Dynamic is defined as "always active or changing". See Merrian-Webster online at http://www.merriam-webster.com/dictionary/dynamic. While dynamism is defined as "a dynamic or expansionist quality". See http://www.merriam-webster.com/dictionary/dynamism.

G.I. Seidman (✉)
The Radzyner School of Law, The Interdisciplinary Center,
POB 167, Natan Alterman St., Herzliya 46150, Israel
e-mail: gseidman@idc.ac.il

C.B. Picker, G.I. Seidman (eds.), *The Dynamism of Civil Procedure - Global Trends and Developments*, Ius Gentium: Comparative Perspectives on Law and Justice 48, DOI 10.1007/978-3-319-21981-3_1

Firstly, as for Comparative law: this field, in a nutshell, is perhaps best explained as "a *special method* within jurisprudence."[2] It's maim aims are both *academic* – broadening juridical knowledge – and *practical* – helping jurists understand and interpret their own laws, providing lessons where legal reform is considered and finally "comparative studies may serve as a *means to transnational unification or harmonization* of law."[3] In addition, some now consider Comparative Law to be a field in its own right. As we shall see, one of the main driving forces in comparative law is the debate over the relationship between the two major Western legal families – common and civil law,[4] and one of the typical ways of thinking about how comparative law functions *in fact* is by looking at the role of legal practitioners in both legal systems.[5] As widely employed as it is, nonetheless Comparative Law, both as a methodology and as a separate field, has been criticized: it does not have a clear, 'scientific' methodology and it is not, for the most part, a branch of positive national law, which means it does not have the binding force of law and it is not an essential tool in the routine work of most legal practitioners. At the same time, as this book indicates, the interest in- and study of- comparative law is flourishing. Not only is it a field of great intellectual interest to academics but in an age of globalism, of increased interconnectivity of people, goods and finances, the need to learn 'foreign' law and the efforts to harmonize national laws make comparative law very relevant indeed.[6]

---

[2] *See*: Peter Gottwald "Comparative Civil Procedure" 22 *Ritsumeikan L. Rev*. 23 (2005). Also see: Catherine Valcke "Comparative Law as Comparative Jurisprudence – the Comparability of Legal Systems" 52 *Am. J. Comp. L*. 713 (2004).

[3] *See*: Gottwald, 22 *Ritsumeikan L. Rev*. 23, id. at 24. See, more generally: George A. Bermann, Patrick Glenn, Kim Lane Scheppele, Amr Shalakany, David V. Snyder & Elisabeth Zoller "Comparative Law: Problems and Prospects" 26 *Am. U. Int'l L. Rev*. 935 (2011). On the concept of functionalism in comparative law see: Jaakko Husa "Metamorphosis of Functionalism – or Back to Basics?" 18(4) Maastricht J. of Europ. & Comp. L. 548 (2011). Also see: Robert Wyness Millar "The Mechanism of Fact-Discovery: A Study in Comparative Civil Procedure" 32 *Ill. L. Rev*. 261 (1937–1938).

[4] "Comparatists fall into one of three Camps. First, there are those who see legal systems as differing so greatly in fundamental respects that each is essentially unique…. A second camp is comprised of those comparatists who believe that our rapidly shrinking world is moving inexorably towards convergence…. Finally, there are those who take the position that neither uniqueness nor convergence… characterize[s] nonlocal law." *See*: Arthur T. von Mehren "The Rise of Transnational Legal Practice and the Task of Comparative Law" 75 *Tul. L. Rev*. 1215 (2001).

[5] Markesinis makes the following interesting argument: he suggests "that in their history the two systems often converged only to diverge again later. It is a sub-thesis of this essay then that the convergences occurred when practitioners took the lead in the law-shaping process of both countries and was weakened whenever 'theoreticians' obtained the upper hand. This is the thesis of a comparative lawyer, not a legal historian; and it is put forward tentatively for the sake of further consideration." *See*: Sir Basil Markesinis "French System Builders and English Problem Solvers: Missed and Emerging Opportunities for Convergence of French and English Law" 40 *Tex. Int'l L.J*. 663, 664 (2005).

[6] For an example of the comparativist's malaise *see*: Mathias M. Siems "The End of Comparative Law" 2 *J. of Comp. L*. 133 (2007); for a more optimistic view *see*: Oliver Brand "Conceptual

Secondly, civil procedure: as most readers will know, *civil procedure* is commonly defined in the common law[7] as the body of law governing the methods and practices used in civil litigation. More specifically, it is part of the law known as *procedural law* – *i.e.*, the rules prescribing the steps for having a right or duty judicially enforced or considered, as opposed to *substantive law*, such as contracts, property or corporate law, that define the actual rights or duties themselves. Furthermore, it is a specific part of the body of procedural law – the part dealing with civil or private rights, as opposed to the part dealing with criminal or administrative procedures, *i.e.*, the rules governing the mechanisms under which crimes are investigated, prosecuted, adjudicated, and punished for the former, or the procedures used before administrative agencies or used before courts to make agencies accountable, for the latter.

These definitions help us more clearly understand what civil procedure is all about. If we go back in history, it is quite clear, As Pollock & Maitland observed, that *civil* procedure "substitutes a litigatory procedure for the rude justice of revenge."[8] And some would say that this is its prime directive. "It seems reasonably safe to say… that the earliest purpose of civil litigation was to provide an alternative to self-help and to the violence to which it may give rise."[9] Civil procedure developed to include a vast array of procedures and processes that are meant to allow private parties – actual persons, single or plural, corporations, sometimes even the government – to bring legal action against others to validate, uphold and enforce their substantive private law rights against any perceived attempt to injure them.[10]

Not only is civil procedure the bedrock on which much of social structure is based – but the field of *comparative* civil procedure, the study of the state sanctioned process by which private rights are upheld, is one of the oldest established

Comparisons: Towards a Coherent Methodology of Comparative Legal Studies" 32 Brook. J. Int'l L. 405 (2007); Russell A. Miller "Remarks at the Opening of the Symposium Celebrating the 10th Anniversary of the Geraman Law Journal – The German Law Journal As 'Lived' Comparative Law" 10 *German L.J.* 1309 (2009).

[7] We use in this chapter common law definitions from Black's Law Dictionary, (9th ed., 2009); for more detailed discussion of common and civil law definitions *cf.*: J.A. Jolowicz "Civil Litigation: What's it for?" 67(3) *Cambridge L. J.* 508, 508–509 (2008).

[8] *See*: Frederick Pollock & Frederick William Maitland *The History of English Law before the Time of Edward I* (Cambridge, 1968, vol. 2) 574; also *see*: Jolowicz, *Cambridge*, id. at pp. 509–510 and *cf.* J.A. Jolowicz "Adversarial and Inquisitorial Models of Civil Procedure" 52(2) *In'tl & Comp. L. Q.* 281, a.

[9] *See*: Jolowicz, *Cambridge*, id. at p. 510.

[10] Comparisons of civil procedure systems can, of course, be made at many degrees of depth. For example, one can analyze the relationship between the system of rights and remedies administrated through judicial system and the system of administrative rights and remedies conducted through the social 'safety net' or the relationship between a procedural system and the structure of authority in the regime in which it is embedded, from strong hierarchical central regimes to decentralized systems. For the former analysis *see*: Geoffrey C. Hazard, Jr. "Civil Procedure in Comparative Perspective" 49 *Sup. Ct. L. Rev*. 2d Ser. (Canada) 657 (2010); for the latter *see*: Mirjan Damaška "*The Common law/Civil Law Divide*: *Residual Truth of a Misleading Distinctions*," *in* J. Walker & O. Chase eds., Common Law Civil Law and the Future of Categories 3 (2010).

areas of comparative law. A prominent example for both points is the Roman *Law of the Twelve Tables* of ca. 450 BC, the earliest Roman attempt at a legal code. Scholars believe that this ancient legal code was the result of a comparative law effort and was written following a visit by a Roman delegation to Greek cities. While not all of this code has survived to our times, what we know is that the first table dealt with civil procedure: specifically with summons before the magistrate (which was left up to the plaintiff to achieve), with dispute settlement and resolution left to the magistrate at trial.[11]

It seems almost intuitive to suggest – as Prof. Dodson does, that "[t]here is little doubt that comparative law- and even comparative procedure specifically- has the potential to be an important study." Among the explanations – that studying alternative legal regimes helps one understand and critically appraise one's own domestic law; that transnational litigation is becoming more common, requiring knowledge of foreign law and advising legal harmonization; familiarity with foreign laws may bring about the willingness to adopt legal solutions.[12] And yet, there are counterarguments or opposing forces, which fall under two main categories. *One*, concerns the disinterest and disinclination in some nations towards comparative law in general: this is especially the case in the United-States, where "exceptionalism is deeply entrenched both in American legal tradition and systems, and in the larger American culture" and where "proceduralists are notoriously parochial."[13] A *second* is the argument that there is something inherent in *procedure* that makes it less acceptable for nations to draw lessons about it from other countries: *i.e.*, that nations are more likely to adopt *substantive* foreign law than they are to admit *procedural* law. Authors suggest that "procedure is different because of its broad interconnectivity. Procedure is tied to a legal system's fundamental organizing principles and norms, making it resistant to change and difficult to understand out of context" and that "court procedures reflect the fundamental values, sensibilities, and beliefs (the

[11] On this and the relevance of ancient legal codes *see*: Ernest Metzger "Roman Judges, case Law, and Principles of Procedure" 22 *Law & Hist. Rev.* 243 (2004); S. Stuart Madden "Integrating Comparative Law Concepts into the First Year Curriculum: Torts" 56 *J. Leg. Ed.* 560 (2006); on earlier legal traditions see: J. Russell VerSteeg "Legal Procedure and the Law of Evidence in Ancient Egypt" 9 Tul. J. Int'l & Comp. L. 233 (2001) & Martha T. Roth "Mesopotamian Legal Traditions and the Law of Hammurabi" 71 Chi.-Kent L. Rev. (1995) 13.

[12] *See*: Scott Dodson "The Challenge of Comparative Civil Procedure: Civil Litigation in Comparative Context, by Oscar G. Chase, Helen Hsershkoff, Linda Silberman, Yashuei Taniguchi, Vincezo Varano & Adrian Zuckerman, 2007 St. Paul, Minn.: West Group, p. 607" 60 *Ala. L. Rev.* 133, 138–139 (2008).

[13] Dodson, *Ala. L. Rev.* id. at pp. 141–142. It is useful to remind the readers of the now classics debate that took place in the 1980s between Prof. John H. Langbein, who extolled the virtues of German civil procedure, which he found superior that of the United States, and Prof. Ron J. Allen, who questioned this view. For a useful overview of the debate and description of the German civil procedure *see*: Michael Bohlander "The German Advantage Revisited: An Inside View of German Civil Procedure in the Nineties" 13 *Tul. Eur. & Civ. L.F.* 25 (1998). For more on the debate see: Bradley Bryan "Justice and Advantage in Civil Procedure: Langbein's Conceptions of Comparative Law and Procedural Justice in Question" 11 *Tulsa J. Comp. & Int'l L.* 521 (2004).

'culture') of the collectivity that employs them."[14] In 1974, the great Anglo-German comparativist *Otto Kahn-Freund* argued, even more broadly, that some

> [M]ay say that procedural law is tough law. All that concerns the technique of legal practice is likely to resist change. In most respects the organisation of the courts and of the legal profession, the law of procedure and the law of evidence help to allocate power, and belong, in Montesquieu's sense, to the *lois politiques*. Comparative law has far greater utility in substantive law than in the law of procedure, and the attempt to use foreign models of judicial organisation and procedure may lead to frustration and may thus be a misuse of the comparative method.[15]

It is difficult to understand or explain why nations would be more accepting of foreign *substantive* norms than practices that serve to validate them. Perhaps cultures are more attached to their customs than their norms, perhaps professors are more interested (or more persuasive) about the benefits of adopting substantive rather than procedural law. I would join Professor Gottwald in rejecting such claims and in saying that "I do not see that there is something different in procedural law.... If this opinion were true civil procedure would be the only branch of law not open for comparative studies,"[16] and this is clearly not the case.

Nonetheless, comparative civil procedure may have been slower to develop than many other fields of comparative law, and it is fair to say that there are several specific problems unique to comparative procedural law. Professor Gottwald points to four issues: *firstly*, that even where a transnational case arises, national courts typically apply, at most, *substantive* foreign law and operate according to their domestic procedures; only rarely are foreign procedures at issue (the 'lex fori' principle); *secondly*, foreign procedures can be relevant in such specific instances as where the legal case may be filed in more than one jurisdiction ('forum shopping'); *thirdly*, for comparativists who seek to compare not the law in the books but the 'law in action' it is very difficult to compare civil procedure because the actual practice among individual judges and courts tend to diverge significantly; *finally*, at the end of the day, civil procedure is a tool for achieving justice among litigants; any serious evaluation of the success of legal systems in achieving this goal and any comparison among them must go well beyond procedure and look at their substantive law in general, the level of recognition and protection of fundamental rights, and the status of courts generally in each nation.[17]

---

[14] For the former see: Dodson, *Ala. L. Rev.* id. at p. 140 & fns. 38–39; for the latter see: Oscar G. Chase, "American 'Exceptionalism' and Comparative Procedure" 50 *Am. J. Comp. L.* 277, 278 (2002) (using the United States as an example he shows "how the well-documented idiosyncrasies of American culture are reflected in the procedural rules that govern civil litigation.") Also see: John D. Jackson, "Playing the Culture Card in Resisting Cross-Jurisdictional Transplants: A Comment on 'Legal Processes and National Culture'" 5 *Cardozo J. Int'l and Comp. L.* 51 (1997).

[15] *See*: Otto Kahn-Freund "On Uses and Misuses of Comparative Law" 37 *Modern L. Rev.* 1, 20 (1974). Also see: John W. Cairns "Watson, Walton, and the History of Legal Transplants" 41 *Ga. J. Int'l & Comp. L.* 637, 664–665 (2013).

[16] *See*: Gottwald, 22 *Ritsumeikan L. Rev.* 23, id. at 24–25.

[17] *See*: Gottwald, 22 *Ritsumeikan L. Rev.* 23, id. at 26–28.

All of this is not to say that comparative civil procedure is unimportant or that it receives no academic attention. Far from it: comparative civil procedure's goals, including the potential for change and reform "hold promise, even for American proceduralists."[18]

With the burgeoning of comparative law in recent years, so has the interest in comparative civil procedure. There is a well-established community of scholars interested in comparative civil procedure: founded in 1950, the International Association of Procedural Law (http://www.iaplaw.org/) is probably the most established and active institution in this field: it has held its 2014 annual conference in Seoul, Korea and is set to hold its 15th World Congress of Procedural Law in 2015 in Istanbul, Turkey. The scholars active in IAPL and the many who join them from adjacent fields have produced a large volume of literature.

1.2 Learning by Differentiating: Divergence within the Duopoly

Two of the main features of traditional comparative law were that it focused on the study of the two main Western legal systems, common and civil law, and that it drew many lessons from the direct comparison of the two. The two were portrayed as contrasting, apposite models. An author would typically present the models, then explain which of the two her national legal system resembled most and what there was to learn from this 'study in contrasts'.[19]

But why are common and civil law different in the area of civil procedure? If we look for one catch-phrase to answer this question while presenting common and civil law as two contrasting models, it would be this: "in common law the remedy is said to precede the right, *ubi remedium, ibi ius*; where in the civil law right is said to precede the remedy, *ibi remedium*."[20] Indeed, the (substantive) common law developed within a procedural framework of causes of action. As the late Professor Glenn noted, "[i]n contemporary language the common law was… a law of procedure; whatever substantive law existed was hidden by it, 'secreted' in its 'interstices'."[21]

What this means is that there is a significant difference in the attitude of common and civil law jurists regarding civil procedure, which is, when all is said and done,

---

[18] Dodson, *Ala. L. Rev.* id. at p. 143.

[19] For a recent example of this kind – dealing with the divergence but also considering the convergence of the common and civil law civil procedure – see: Stephen Stewart & Annik Bouche "Civil court case management in England & Wales and Belgium: philosophy and efficiency" 28(2) *C.J.Q.* 206 (2009).

[20] *See*: Helge Dedek "From Norms to Facts: The Realization of Rights in Common and Civil Private Law" 56(1) *McGill L. J.* 77, 79–80 (cite), 82 (2010) also see: William Tetley "Mixed Jurisdictions: Common Law V. Civil Law" (Codified and Uncodified) 60 *La. L. Rev.* 677, 707 (2000); and Markesinis, 40 *Tex. Int'l L.J.*, id. at 673 (noting that the development of early English law through the writ system displays all the procedural hallmarks of classic Roman Law).

[21] H. Patrick Glenn, Legal Traditions of the World (Oxford UP, 4th edition. 2010) p. 243 & fn. 23.

the main avenue to attain the remedy and secure the substantive right. Common law lawyers took procedures much more seriously as part of their pragmatist, less academic approach. In contrast, civilian lawyers, the more academically inclined, were more interested in doctrinal theorization and less in civil procedure. The overall and somewhat unfortunate result (for us as academics) is, as one of our distinguished colleagues has written and seems to be mostly referring to – "[i]n many countries civil procedure is considered a subject hardly lending itself for scholarly investigations."[22]

But, as is noted in Chap. 2 of this collection this binary view, the civilian versus the common law approaches, has somewhat changed in recent decades. This traditional form of analysis sometimes referred to as 'the divergence model,' which had a strong hold on the study of comparative law including that of comparative civil procedure has started to give way. We now speak of a narrowing of the gap between common and civil law, sometimes referred to as 'the convergence model'; we take note of mixed jurisdictions, that do not comfortably fall within the common-civil law bifurcation and non-Western legal traditions. Nonetheless, the study of 'the other' legal system remains the backbone of comparativism. Consider how the eminent Professor Hein Kötz presented matters in a 2002 lecture:

> It is indeed a routine business meeting an American lawyer will believe he is attending when he is led into a German courtroom. What is most likely to strike him is the fact that mainly the court conducts the interrogation of witnesses….[I]n an ordinary case there is relatively little questioning by counsel for the parties, at least by common law standards….
>
> Civil procedure in Germany and in other civil law jurisdictions differs from the American system by making the judge responsible for the selection of expert witnesses, for the examination-in-chief of both fact and expert witnesses, and for creating the record based on those examinations. The judge's conspicuous role in the actual taking of evidence, especially in the taking of witness testimony, has led common lawyers to label Continental civil procedure as "inquisitorial" or "non-adversarial"….
>
> One salient characteristic of European civil procedure lies indeed in the fact that it is wholly unfamiliar with, and knows nothing of, the idea of a "trial" as a single, temporally continuous presentation in which all materials are made available to the adjudicator…. Procedure in the common law jurisdictions, on the other hand, has been deeply influenced by the institution of the jury.[23]

---

[22] The article reports on both common and civil law nations. The author's thesis, however, is that this was not always the case – see: C. H. van Rhee "Civil Procedure: A European *Ius Commune*?" 4 *Eur. Rev. of Private Rights* 589 (2000). Another continental proceduralist wrote – "civil procedure has traditionally been considered a very technical branch of the law – the technical branch *par excellence*; and as a mere technique it has usually been studied and taught. Only too rarely have its ideological foundations, its background, its socio-political impact been analyzed." *See*: Mauro Cappelletti "Social and Political Aspects of Civil Procedure – Reforms and Trends in Western and Eastern Europe" 69 *Mich. L. Rev*. 847, 881 (1970–1971).

[23] *See*: Hein Kötz "Civil Justice Systems in Europe and the United States" 13 *Duke J. Comp. & Int'l L.* 61 at 63, 66 & 72 (2003). In fairness, Kötz does also note similarities between the systems, reaching the conclusion that "in their own ways both the German and American systems are adversary systems of civil procedure." (id. at p.67).

Many commentators have followed suit, making detailed observations of the differences between the common and civil law models of civil procedures. Most authors point to about a dozen main points of difference between the systems.[24] I have grouped them into four main groups: (1) matters concerning judges; (2) matters concerning entry into court; (3) matters concerning the functioning of the trial; (4) social and cultural aspects.

1.2.1 On Judges

The first and most important of the three issues we discuss in this section concerns the role and function of judges in civil proceedings. More specifically – "the traditional differentiation between the civil and common law systems is the difference in the responsibilities of judges and lawyers."[25] Scholars have long divided the world's two main procedural systems into an *adversarial* (common law) camp and an *inquisitorial* (civil law) camp, and while this division "turns on categories that are imperfect at best" these labels are still said to "serve as a convenient shorthand, so long as we recall their limitations."[26]

As will see later, these limitations are quite significant. Yet as late as 1975, a federal judge could describe the American system as one that "does not allow much room for effective or just intervention by the trial judge in the adversary fight about the facts. The judge views the case from a peak of Olympian ignorance."[27] What this meant was that the judge was essentially a passive umpire, a neutral arbiter, tasked with the narrow role of determining issues of law and giving instructions to the jury. The judge is not a fact-finder. The animating value in the American legal system was the concept of *adversariness*, where it is the parties' counsel who had the primary responsibility for shaping the case and moving it forward.

In civil law countries, the model of the *inquisitorial*judge is very different: a professional judge, who received extensive specialized training before appointment, the civil law judge is the fact-finder, an active participant in legal proceedings and the ruler on issues of law. She is the dominant figure in the trial, responsible for determining the law, examining the witnesses, discovering the truth, and seeing that justice is done.[28] Where does this leave civil advocates? The traditional description

---

[24] On this *see* most notably in this section: Linda S. Mullenix "Lessons from Abroad: Complexity and Convergence" 46 *Vill. L. Rev.* 1, 5–12 (2002) and the sources cited in the following fns.

[25] *See*: Geoffrey C. Hazard & Angelo Dondi "Responsibilities of Judges and Advocates in Civil and Common Law: Some Lingering Misconceptions Concerning Civil Lawsuits" 39 *Cornell Int'l L. J.* 59, 60–61 (2006).

[26] Chase, 50 *Am. J. Comp. L.*, id. at 283.

[27] *See*: Marvin E. Frankel "The Search for Truth: An Umpireal View" 123 *U. Pa. L. Rev.* 1031, 1042 (1975).

[28] *See*: Edward F. Sherman "Transnational Perspectives Regarding the Federal Rules of Civil Procedure" 56 *J. Legal Educ.* (2006) 510, 511; also *see*: Dodson, *Ala. L. Rev.* id. at pp. 148.

of a dominant civil law judge leaves civil lawyers with a residual role – they can make suggestions concerning the evidence, propose issues to be examined or questions to be asked at hearings, or submit comments concerning the legal basis of the dispute.[29]

A second issue concerns the effect of the judicial decision. Common law nations such as the United States, apply doctrines such as *res judicata*. In the United States, issue and claim preclusion is governed by an elaborate body of decisional law that operates to prevent relitigation of claims and issues that could have, or should have, been asserted in a prior proceeding against parties and their privies. In contrast, most civil law countries do not recognize the doctrine of res judicata, or the 'binding effect' of prior legal decisions.

Finally, is the judge the sole decision maker in court proceedings? *Theright to trial by jury* in many civil actions is guaranteed in the United States by the 7th Amendment of the Constitution, but in most civil law countries, there is no right to a trial by jury. In England jury trial for civil cases was the only form of trial until the mid-nineteenth century; from that time on English enthusiasm for the jury trial has waned mostly because it was not being asked for; now, this practice is almost unknown in England.[30] Damaška and Hazard note that the use of juries reflects a distinctive allocation of authority: it reflects the localization of the judicial establishment, since juries are made up of an *ad hoc* group of local citizens, rarely trained in law. This contrasts sharply with the practice in civil law countries such as France, Germany or Italy, where a professional in law is required to have diverse geographical experience – and also with the practice in England where most of the judiciary is centered in London.[31]

1.2.2 Entry into Court: Money and Standing

One preliminary issue is *standing*: in the United States, standing to sue in federal courts is a constitutional requirement. While there is much debate on this issue – authorities suggest that Congress is constitutionally limited in its ability to confer standing to sue in American civil litigation. In contrast, many civil law systems statutorily confer standing to sue on individuals, groups and associations.[32] The Court of Justice of the European Union has taken a restrictive approach when

[29] *See*: Hazard & Dondi, id. at p. 60–61.

[30] *See*: Mullenix, *Vill. L. Rev*, id. at p. 5; Richard L. Marcus "Putting American Procedural Exceptionalism into a Globalized Context" 53 *Am. J. Comp. L.* 709, 712–713 (2005).

[31] See fn. 4, id. For a more detailed discussion of the procedural virtues and deficiencies of the jury system *see*: Geoffrey C. Jr. Hazard "Jury Trial and the Principles of Transnational Civil Procedure" 25 *Penn St. Int'l L. Rev*. 499 (2006–2007).

[32] For the practical (and comparative) implications *see*: M.J. Leeming & G.J. Tolhurst "'When You Got Nothing, You Got Nothing to Lose': Assignment of Choses of Action and Standing in the United States Supreme Court" 8(2) *Ox. U. Commonwealth L. J.* 237 (2008); and *cf.* Tom Zwart "Standing to raise constitutional issues in the Netherlands" 6(4) *Elec. J. Comp. L.* (2002).

interpreting the standing requirements of private parties wanting to challenge EU law measures. The Lisbon Treaty (2009) introduced some change, but commentators argue that access to the Court remains overly restricted to private parties.[33]

Of more general interest is the issue of *the financing of litigationandattorney's fees* – that is the financial incentives surrounding litigation. There are several issues of relevance here:

- The 'American Rule' that applies in the United States, holds that each side of the litigation bears its own litigation costs, expenses and attorney fees (with some statutory fee-shifting exceptions). The result is that attorney's fees are, by far, the largest expense for American litigants. Contingency fee contracts are permissible and even usual in certain types of litigation, most notably in personal injury and other tort litigation. In addition, plaintiffs' attorneys are permitted to front the costs of contingent litigation. In contrast, civil law countries and the United-Kingdom follow the 'English rule' or the 'loser pays' rule. Civil law countries prohibit contingency fee contracts, and do not permit attorneys to front the costs of litigation.[34]
- The American legal system has fostered and encouraged the so-called '*entrepreneurial' lawyer* who, with a vested interest in the litigation, pursues and vindicates client claims. This system of entrepreneurial lawyering is incompatible with civil law systems.[35]
- Most civil law countries do not recognize *punitive damage* claims. In those countries, punitive damages simply are not available – and many of them even refuse to enforce a foreign judgment for punitive damages. Most common law countries allow for but significantly constrain punitive damages. In the United States most states and the federal courts recognize punitive damage claims, and with far less restrictions.[36]

---

[33] On this and for a comparison of standing requires in the European court with other regional supranational courts see: Mariolina Eliantonio & Haakon Roer-Eide "Regional Court and Locus standi for Private Parties: can the CJEU Learn Something from the Others?" 13(1) *The Law & Practice of Int'l Courts and Tribunals* 27 (2014); also see: Henry Onoroa "Locus standi of individuals and non-state entities before regional economic integration judicial bodies in Africa" 18(2) *African J. of Int'l & Comp. L.* 143 (2010).

[34] *See*: Mullenix, *Vill. L. Rev*, id. at p. 6; Edward F. Sherman, id. at pp. 522–523. Also see: Alessandra De Luca "Cost and fee allocation in Italian civil procedure" 29(4) *C.J.Q.* (2010) 428; James Maxeiner "Cost and Fee Allocation in Civil Procedure" 58 *Am. J. Comp. L.* (2010)195. For a comparative economic analysis of the 'American' and 'English' rules see: Amy Sedgwick "There are more ways than one to allocate legal costs" 32(2) *C.J.Q.* 300 (2013).

[35] *See*: Mullenix, *Vill. L. Rev*, id. at p. 6–7; Samuel Issacharoff & Geoffrey P. Miller "Will Aggregate Litigation Come to Europe" 62 *Vand. L. Rev*. 179, 180 (2009) (reporting of European reformer's hope that "that collective actions, representative actions, group actions, and a host of other aggregative arrangements can bring all the benefits of fair and efficient resolution to disputes without the dreaded world of American entrepreneurial lawyering.")

[36] *See*: Mullenix, *Vill. L. Rev*, id. at p. 7; Dodson, *Ala. L. Rev*. id. at p. 146.

- In the United States, courts have recognized the ability to award *aggregate tort damages*. Civil law countries do not recognize the ability to award aggregate personal injury tort damages.[37]
- The Federal Rules of Civil Procedure (FRCP) – and most States – provide for *class action litigation*. Almost all civil law countries, as well as England (a common law country), did not traditionally have a class action procedure.[38]
- Handling *Pro Se Litigants*: the U.S. procedure is designed for represented parties. Yet in the twenty-first century American litigants often act without lawyers: while some choose to do so, most of those appearing without counsel simply cannot afford professional representation. The response of the legal system has been patchy. They included efforts to help parties attain legal representation, paid or unpaid, and giving pro se litigants some litigation instructions. Some courts have tried to adapt the American adversary system to the needs of pro se litigants, for example by setting obligations on courts to notify litigants of their rights. This raised concerns that a court acting this way could compromise its' impartiality. Civil law countries, such as Germany, have found both similar and different solutions: Germany reduces the frequency of pro se litigation by requiring representation in district court cases and by providing extensive legal aid. This is done at a very significant cost – second only to England and much greater than the expenditure in America. That said, attorneys are paid 'legal aid' rates and if they win the case this is supplemented by the costs imposed on the losing side. In addition, a non-attorney consultant is allowed to assist the pro se litigant and judges' obligation to clarify matters to the litigants is more stringently observed when a party is unrepresented.[39]

1.2.3 The Actual Civil Procedure

There are numerous differences between the *common* and *civil law* civil procedures.

- *The trial as a single, live event*: two of the classic differences between common and civil law are that the American trial – especially when held before a jury – is a *single, live,* event; witnesses and evidence are presented seriatim in a continuous proceeding and the witnesses are examined, live, before the jury. In contrast, the civil law trial is traditionally segmented. Evidence is collected over time by an 'investigating magistrate,' who questions the witnesses and prepares a written dossier. When completed, the written file is brought as evidence before the judges for judicial decision.[40]

[37] *See*: Mullenix, *Vill. L. Rev*, id. at p. 7.

[38] *See*: Mullenix, *Vill. L. Rev*, id. at p. 7.

[39] *See*: Richard L. Marcus, id. at 725–729.

[40] *See*: Edward F. Sherman, id. at pp. 513–514.

- *Evidentiary Standards and Allocation of Burdens of Proof*: trial procedure and the admissibility of evidence are governed in the United States by the Federal Rules of Evidence, which circumscribe the ability to adduce proofs. In contrast, most civil law countries, do not recognize or apply evidentiary rules as stringently as the United States, their law courts often allow various forms of evidence and testimony. In addition, while in the United States the plaintiff carries the burden of production and proof – civil law countries sometimes shift the allocation of burdens of production and proof in civil cases to the defendant.[41]
- *Civil Discovery and Pleadings*: the American FRCP provide extensively for discovery of factual information and expert testimony prior to trial. Since 1938, the provision for liberal discovery in the Federal Rules (which was a significant change from the code pleading system that it replaced) has been considered a necessary adjunct to the regime of notice pleading. Most countries require plaintiffs to provide, in their initial pleadings, substantial factual arguments and some evidence to support their legal claim. This is the case even in civil law countries such as Germany, Japan and Italy. Yet these civil law jurisdictions do not provide for American-style liberal discovery or severely restrict discovery by 'blocking statutes.' "At any rate, no other country in the world has any system of discovery approaching that provided for in the Federal Rules of Civil Procedure."[42]
- *The appointment of expert witnesses*: where judges and lawyers are faced with complex professional and scientific questions which cannot be resolved without the help of specialists, it may be necessary for an expert witness to be called in. The essential problems here are *cost*, since the time and attention of genuine experts is expensive, and *bias*, because an expert may be somewhat influenced by the identity of the compensator. In the United States each party may hire its expert witness who then informs the court or the jury. In civil law countries the tradition is that expert testimony should come from experts appointed by the court and civil procedural codes have empowered judges to appoint experts at will and often even against the will of the parties. The background to this rule is that it is the duty of the civil law court to establish the facts truthfully. The court appointed expert is considered a neutral auxiliary of the court who serves the court, not the parties to the case. That is why the continental term is 'expert' – rather than 'expert witness': the expert, contrary to the witness, is also appointed to draw conclusions on the basis of the available and relevant facts.[43]

---

[41] *See*: Mullenix, *Vill. L. Rev*, id. at p. 8.

[42] *See*: Mullenix, *Vill. L. Rev*, id. at p. 5–6 (cite: p. 6); Dodson, *Ala. L. Rev*. id. at p. 144; and see, in more detail: Scott Dodson & James M. Klebba "Global Civil Procedure Trends in the Twenty-First Century" 34 *B.C. Int'l & Comp. L. Rev*. 1, 3–8 (2011). For a historical and comparative analysis of pleadings in the United States and Australia *see*: Elizabeth Thornburg, Camille Cameron "Defining Civil Disputes: Lessons from Two Jurisdictions" 35 *Melb. U. L. Rev*. (2011) 208.

[43] *See*: Remme Verkerk "Comparative aspects of expert evidence in civil litigation" 13 *Int'l J. of Evidence & Proof* 167 (2009) (focusing on Austrian law); Hazard, 49 *Sup. Ct. L. Rev*., id. at p. 662.

1.2.4 Social and Cultural Issues

There are many differences between the legal cultures present in civil and common law systems, many of them reflect, or are even embedded in their procedural practices. To mention but a few[44]:

- One major issue is *legal education*: in the United-States (but not in most other common law jurisdictions) legal education is a post-graduate course of study and (as is the case in all common law jurisdictions) it is a separate academic degree. In many civil law countries, legal education is part of an integrated undergraduate course of study, with specialized training for a professionalized judiciary and other legal functions.
- A second issue concerns the legal authority of *case law* and the importance of *academic writings*: both common and civil law and common law accept the primary legal authority of constitutions, statutes and regulations. This is the common denominator. Beyond this – in civil law the opinions of legal scholars provide the most authoritative source for determining the law, while in common law such sources have, at best, a persuasive role as secondary sources; and common law nations and common law jurisdictions accept court decisions (typically that of the highest courts) as generally binding, through the doctrines of *stare decisis*, binding precedent and res judicata, while civil law countries generally do not formally recognize these doctrines, limiting the scope of court decisions to the particular parties to the decision, though jurisprudence constant and de facto employment of precedent play an increasing role in civil law systems.
- A third issue concerns the *annexation* of civil claims to criminal proceedings. In the United States, criminal, civil and administrative law proceedings are separate. A civil proceeding may follow (or precede) a criminal action – but they are not conjoined. Each proceeding entails a different burden of production and proof and is conducted through a different procedure. Yet in many civil law countries it is possible to 'annex' a civil claim to a criminal proceeding and to seek civil remedies in the context of a criminal proceeding. The combined criminal-civil proceedings enable a civil claimant to use the resources of the prosecutor's office to pursue civil relief.
- Finally, it is said, at least according to critics, that a culture of grievance, rights-talk and 'litigiousness' that exists in the United States encourages citizens to resolve any and every complaint through litigation. In civil law countries, by contrast, no such culture of litigiousness exists, and is indeed alien to societal norms.
- As Professor Mullenix notes this short discussion is quite incomplete. It does not include, for example, generalizations about the vast differences in social and political systems that also have an effect on legal culture. It does not describe

[44] *See*: Mullenix, *Vill. L. Rev*, id. at pp. 9–13.

differences in legal structures or institutions. But this survey does provide some sense "of how the legal academy thinks about and teaches comparative civil procedure, an exercise in difference that is profoundly pervasive and entrenched."[45]

While common and civil law remain the two prevailing legal cultures within Western legal systems, at least two major developments have taken place in recent years have called into question this orthodox method of studying and teaching these two models. They do so in two different ways, that we will aim to explore in Chap. 2 of this collection:

In fairness, many scholars have long doubted the accuracy of the common and civil law models, especially in view of the differences between nations that were member of the same family – bear in mind the vast differences between the United-States, England and New-Zealand who are all common law nations; while Germany, Japan and Brazil, each radically different, are all civil law nations.[46] But now there is doubt whether the two formal models of common and civil law – if they ever existed in their 'pure', theoretic form – still exist. What researchers are showing are processes of learning and the cooperation among Western nations that bring about a process termed 'convergence' of the two, as if the tectonic plates upon which the two 'continents' of common and civil law, which have long been oceans apart, are drifting closer, possibly on their way to create some 'super continent'. On this topic, and its effects on the study of comparative civil procedure, see Chap. 2, *infra*.

A second issue concerns the reduced focus on formal legal study of the national legal systems of states that are member of the two mainstay Western legal traditions. Going beyond tradition, researchers now look at procedures on a transnational level, consider the legal systems of non-Western nations – some but not all former colonies and study more deeply the history, sociology and economics of law; on these topics as they apply to the study of comparative civil procedure, see Chap. 2, *infra*.

1.3 Conclusion

As shown in the other chapters in this collection, civil procedure today is both highly varied and exceptionally dynamic. By the same token, the field of comparative civil procedure has matured to become an integral and mainstream part of legal

---

[45] *See*: Mullenix, *Vill. L. Rev*, id. at p. 11.

[46] Describing the deliberations that led to the ALI/Unidroit Principles (discussed below) in which he took part, Prof. Neil Andrews says that "[i]t was apparent throughout the drafting group's discussion that there were radical differences between the USA and English systems, and between the various civil law jurisdictions represented around the table. These differences make a nonsense of both the glib phrase 'Anglo-American procedure' and the crude expression 'civilian procedure'." *See*: Neil Andrews "Chapter 2: Principles of Civil Justices" 10 IUS Gentium 25, 41 (2012).

scholarship. While significant differences in approaches and style will be easily apparent from the different chapters, one constant reflected throughout is the fact that context is critical, be it the historical, substantive, political, cultural or economic context. As such, the comparative analyses of legal system's civil procedure systems places comparative civil procedure as a foundational part of one's understanding of a legal system, regardless of the specific system – civil or common law based.

Chapter 2
The New Comparative Civil Procedure

Guy I. Seidman

2.1 Introduction

Like all fields, comparative civil procedure must adapt to developments within its field and should continuously challenge the conventional wisdom that may dominate the field. Both these tasks are connected to each other and may be mutually reinforcing. Thus, changes within civil procedure around the world, the sort of changes discussed in many of the contributions to this volume, may force a reappraisal of conventional comparative understandings and approaches. Likewise, new approaches or understandings may themselves then feed into change to the underlying procedural systems as domestic employ them in crafting new procedures.

While much of this book concerns the procedural systems of different countries and legal systems, this chapter will consider the two primary classical comparative law approaches and examine their continuing validity and vitality. This chapter will present the perspective that comparative civil procedure today has moved beyond the traditional binary classification reflected by the archetypes supposedly present in Civil or Common law system, but now includes coherent procedural approaches present in hybrids and trans-systemic procedural systems.

G.I. Seidman (✉)
The Radzyner School of Law, The Interdisciplinary Center,
POB 167, Natan Alterman St., Herzliya 46150, Israel
e-mail: gseidman@idc.ac.il

C.B. Picker, G.I. Seidman (eds.), *The Dynamism of Civil Procedure - Global Trends and Developments*, Ius Gentium: Comparative Perspectives on Law and Justice 48, DOI 10.1007/978-3-319-21981-3_2

2.2 A first Reality Check: A Civil/Common Law Division May No Longer Be Valid

There is significant agreement that for all parts of comparative law, including comparative civil procedure, the two arch-models of common and civil law are drawing closer, which is a departure from the classic conception of comparative law – as studied and taught for decades, and as generally assumed to be correct by legal scholars that are not comparatists. Most comparatists now agree that this phenomenon, referred to as '*convergence*', is really taking place, although the matter, and the details, is still subject to academic debate.[1]

There are several ways by which comparatists explain (and perhaps themselves facilitate) the convergence phenomenon:

First, reevaluation: some commentators look back and raise doubts as to the validity of the original common and civil law models. Some doubt whether the models ever accurately described the law, suggesting that they portrayed common and civil law as more different than they really were; others note the vast variance among the national legal systems of the many countries that are members of the two primary law families, and doubt whether the model ascribed to each legal system really applies in any of them.

Second, legal study and reform: it seems fair to argue that the vast comparative work carried out by academics and the study of and experience in foreign legal systems carried out by many jurists, including judges, over the past century has changed national laws: whether through gradual evolution or explicit legal reforms. Such examinations have brought the existence of 'foreign' solutions to domestic problems to the attention of national decision makers (even in the 'exceptional' United States of America). Looking at, considering and sometimes choosing legal solutions from the 'other' legal family surely draws nations – and systems – a little closer together.[2]

Third, active convergence: with the rise of international and supranational regimes, most notably the *European Union*, conscious efforts are made to minimize the differences between legal systems in order to *harmonize* national laws. If some 'remodeling' is required to the classic approaches of common and civil law to enable their cohabitation and for the streamlining of their legal orders, it now seems a fair and worthwhile price to pay.

---

[1] For classic discussions of these issues *see*: John Henry Merryman "On the Convergence (and Divergence) of the Civil Law and the Common Law" 7 *Stan. J. Int'l L.* 357 (1981); Mathias Reimann "The Progress and Failure of Comparative Law in the Second Half of the Twentieth Century" 50(4) *Am. J. Comp. L.* 671 (2002); *cf.*: Pierre Legrand "European Legal Systems Are Not Converging" 45(1) *Int'l & Comp. L. Q.* (1996).

[2] *Cf.*: *See*: Arthur T. von Mehren "The Rise of Transnational Legal Practice and the Task of Comparative Law" 75 *Tul. L. Rev.* 1215 (2001); Antonios Platsas "Comparative law as the ideal means of convergence of the national financial systems in the world of globalization" 7(2) *Coventry L. J.* 53 (2002).

Professor Örücü termed this process "the growing *ius commune novum*" and noted that it "certainly includes England", arguing that "[t]he path leads towards an integrated Europe. Integration will be in many fields. It will extend far beyond the limited number of fields of private law."[3] Indeed, many commentators have argued that convergence has and is taking place in many more areas of law – from constitutional law, corporate law and healthcare law to labor law – although there are different degrees of convergence, specific to each legal field.[4] This also applies in comparative civil procedure, where authors have been pointing to increasing similarities between common and civil law.

In an example of a reevaluation of classic terms Professor Jolowicz takes on one of the defining distinctions between common and civil law – where the former is termed 'adversarial' and the latter 'inquisitorial' – and suggests that –[5]

> Contrary to popular belief… French civil procedure as set out in the code of 1806 was not 'inquisitorial'. True, it was not 'adversary' in the full common law sense, but it was 'accusatory'…. [I]t was for the parties to control the procedure, and it was for the parties to put their allegations, their proofs and their arguments before the court. The role of the court was passive and was no more than to decide between rival cases of the parties. Throughout the 19th Century and the first half of the 20th, control of the proceedings was… 'abandoned to the parties'.

As Jolowicz explained elsewhere, the French judges' role, as originally instituted and confirmed by the Code of Civil Procedure of 1806 "had nothing of the inquisitorial about it. The Court's role was essentially passive and was not more than to decide between the rival contentions of the parties." It was only a 1965 decree that instituted a more effective judge with real power, who can make orders binding on the parties and impose sanctions.[6] There is evidence of similar notions elsewhere in civil law: for example *Verkerk* similarly argues that continental procedure does not embrace a model of an 'inquisitorial' and 'authoritarian' judiciary. He notes that the drafter of the 1895 Austrian Code of Civil Procedure believed that both parties and the court should actively cooperate in order to establish the facts: "[t]he ideal embraced in most Continental systems is not that of an inquisitorial or adversarial

---

[3] *See*: Esin Örücü "Looking at Convergence through the Eyes of a Comparative Lawyer" 9(2) *Elec. J. Comp. L.* (2005). [http://www.ejcl.org/92/art92-1.html#par23].

[4] *See*: Nathan Cortez "International Health Care Convergence: The Benefits and Burdens of Market-Driven Standardization" 26 Wis. Int'l L.J. 646, 649 & fns. 5–6 (2008); Sjef van Erp "Different Degrees of Convergence: A Comparison of Tort Law (Example: Fairchild v. Glenhaven Funeral Services) and Property Law" 6(3) *Elec. J. Comp. L.* (2002)[http://www.ejcl.org/63/art63-4.html]("In tort law, sometimes a strong degree of convergence can be found, whereas in property law it is much more difficult to find even a limited degree of convergence. Still, also in the area of property law civil and common law show more resemblances than might seem at first glance."); also *see*: Fernanda G. Nicola "Family Law Exceptionalism in Comparative Law" 58 Am. J. Comp. L. 777 (2010)(noting that "[t]oday, family law is, to a surprising degree, at the center of comparative law inquiries committed to legal unification.").

[5] *See*: J.A. Jolowicz "Civil Litigation: What's it for?" 67(3) *Cambridge L. J.* 508 (2008) at p. 513 and fn. 15 (citing French Prof. René Morel).

[6] *See*: J.A. Jolowicz "Adversarial and Inquisitorial Models of Civil Procedure" 52(2) *In'tl & Comp. L. Q.* 281 (2003) at p. 286.

model, but that of cooperation between an active judge and the parties."[7] Professor Glenn suggests that a better, non-pejorative, term for the common and civil law's procedure would be accusatorial (instead of adversarial) and investigative (instead of inquisitorial).[8]

Another shibboleth concerns the influence of Roman law: Roman law is credited with furnishing continental Europe's legal systems as a whole with a set of terms of motions, while the English common law grew independently and apart from civil law. Modern scholarship shows that Roman law has, in fact, penetrated English law much more deeply that is commonly known and it has also shown that much of French law is not fully based on Roman law but rather on the work of local jurists who adapted (or even changed) Roman law to meet French requirements.[9]

Moreover: the rise of modern civil procedure is, in terms of legal history, relatively recent: both common and civil law procedures harp back to the eleventh to thirteenth century, but they were significantly revised and reformed in the eighteenth and nineteenth centuries. For example, the origins of continental civil procedure are in Roman law, starting with the discovery and study of the Justinian code and then turning, in the Middle Ages into the *jus commune* procedure – "adopted by the ecclesiastical and imperial courts; defined and refined by the learned *doctors* at the School of Bologna and all the other Schools in Italy and elsewhere which followed the Bolognese model" – yet that system was very different from the modern one, as revised since the French revolution.[10] Markesinis comes close to suggesting that were it not for cultural reasons and the interests of legal practitioners of both English and French law – the law of these nations could have met in some middle ground, and not turned to two opposing models.[11]

Yet even where the gaps between common and civil law models cannot be re-defined away, researchers argue that the gaps that have existed between common

[7] *See*: Remme Verkerk "Comparative aspects of expert evidence in civil litigation" 13 *Int'l J. of Evidence & Proof* 167 (2009), at p. 176.

[8] *See*: H. Patrick Glenn, Legal Traditions of the World (Oxford UP, 4th edition. 2010), at p. 144 & fn. 47. On the pejorative sense of the term see: Cullen Murphy "God's Jury: the Inquisition and the Making of the Modern World" (Mariner Books, 2012) (established by the Catholic Church in 1231, the Inquisition continued in one form or another for almost seven hundred years. Although mostly associated with the persecution of heretics and Jews and with burning at the stake the targets of Inquisitions were more numerous and its techniques more ambitious. The Inquisition pioneered surveillance, censorship, and "scientific" interrogation.)

[9] *See*: Sir Basil Markesinis "French System Builders and English Problem Solvers: Missed and Emerging Opportunities for Convergence of French and English Law" 40 *Tex. Int'l L.J.* 663 (2005), at p. 666.

[10] Among the unique characteristics of *jus commune* civil procedure, some of them are still reflected in current civil practice – that it attributed a monopoly to the written elements, that it discouraged any direct contact between the adjudicating body and the parties and that it unfolded piecemeal resulting in cases of enormously long duration – civil proceeding lasting several decades were not unusual. *See*: Mauro Cappelletti "Social and Political Aspects of Civil Procedure – Reforms and Trends in Western and Eastern Europe" 69 *Mich. L. Rev.* 847 (1970–1971), at 847–850 (cite from p. 847).

[11] *See*: Markesinis, 40 Tex. Int'l L.J., id. at p. 675 et seq. (Part III).

and civil law procedures are narrowing. This is the result of the second and third processes noted above: both extensive cross-system studies and exchanges and the result of real life needs and pressures of inter- and transnational legal developments. Estimates Professor Mullenix –

> In the next millennium... as a consequence of the globalization of complex legal disputes, the differences in American and civil law procedure may well converge in interesting ways. It may turn out that the litany of comparative differences that comparative scholars enumerate does not consist of as great a chasm as they suggest. Moreover, the convergence of American procedural law with civil adjective law has already begun in many aspects of complex civil litigation... [where] this convergence is nascent, if not already evident.[12]

She is not alone in her analysis and assessment, and we now discuss the issue in more detail.

2.3 Growing Similarity between Civil and Common Law Civil Procedures

In discussing the growing *similarities* between the civil procedures of common and civil law we will use most of the groupings that we employed in discussing the *differences* between the two in Chap. 1 of this collection, specifically: (1) matters concerning judges; (2) matters concerning entry into court; and (3) matters concerning the functioning of the trial.

2.3.1 On Judges

First: A good starting point to discuss the changes in common and civil law in recent decades are the legal effects of the judicial process. French authors used the term '*Praetorian law*' to indicate the judge-made case law nature of English law – which stood in contrast to the statutory nature of French law. This contrasting description, however, is no longer accurate: on the civil law side – "not only are important parts of French law largely created by judicial decisions--administrative law is the obvious example--but existing, statute-based law has also been substantially enriched, and even transformed, by judicial decisions," while on the common law side it is now the case that "vast swathes of English law stem from statute, which is often--but not always--fleshed out by decisions."[13] Some academics would go a little further: Professor Kidane argues that there is no principled reason why the basic tenets of the continental inquisitorial system cannot be adopted to improve the

---

[12] *See*: Linda S. Mullenix "Lessons from Abroad: Complexity and Convergence" 46 *Vill. L. Rev.* 1 (2002), at p. 12.

[13] *See*: Markesinis, 40 Tex. Int'l L.J., id. at pp. 664–665.

existing system of deportation proceedings in the United-States. Noting that judicial procedures often reflect society's fundamental values and sensitivities, she stops there and does not recommend the transplantation of the entire inquisitorial system.[14]

Second: a more significant change concerns the role and function of judges in both common and civil law court. While some of the scholarly literature still discusses the differences between the American judge and the civil law 'inquisitorial' judge, it seems that these traditional paradigms have somewhat changed, even if significant differences remain between civil law and common law jurisdictions as to the roles of judges and counsel.

In common law systems, as has typically been the case for small claims courts or in magistrate courts, more judges are now directly involved in shaping and managing cases. Indeed, it is said that it is now the case – particularly in the realm of complex litigation – that the American 'managerial judge' "has undertaken roles that are indeed converging with the civil law inquisitorial judge. In many respects, then, it is difficult to differentiate between the American judge and his or her civil law counterpart as they deal with complex cases."[15] Professor Mullenix explains that while American judges are still not fact finders (or more accurately – fact investigators), it is difficult not to take note of the increasing managerial involvement of judges in the resolution of complex cases, often verging on functions such as fact-finding/investigating. Indeed, the Manual for Complex Litigation now authorizes and encourages increased judicial involvement in resolving complex litigation. The convergence of the judicial function with investigative fact-finding in complex litigation has been most evident in the expansive use of court-appointed expert witnesses, science panels and special masters, that Judges employed to find facts, frame legal conclusions and administer remedies.[16]

---

[14] *See*: Won Kidane "The Inquisitorial advantage in Removal Proceedings" 45 *Akron L. Rev*. 647, 654 (2011–2012).

[15] *See*: Mullenix, *Vill. L. Rev*, id. at 13; also: Edward F. Sherman, "Transnational Perspectives Regarding the Federal Rules of Civil Procedure" 56 *J. Legal Educ*. (2006) 510, at pp. 511–512. For a plethora of similar statements to this effect see: Thomas D. Rowe. Jr. "Authorized Managerialism Under the Federal Rules – and the extend of Convergence with Civil-Law Judging" 36 *We. U. L. Rev*. 191 (2007–2008) at p. 203 et seq.; On the English case, where the English courts not possess extensive 'case management' powers *see*: Neil Andrews "Chapter 16: Case Management and Procedural Discipline in England &Wales: Fundamentals of an Essential New Technique" 31 *IUS Gentium* 335 (2014); also: Kenneth M. Vorrasi "Note: England's Reform to Alleviate the Problems of Civil Process: A Comparison of Judicial Case Management in England and the United States" 30 J. Legis. 361 (2004). On possible application of the 'managerial judge' model in common law jurisdictions *see*: James Fowkes "Civil Procedure in Public Interest Litigation: Tradition, Collaboration and the Managerial Judge" 1(3) *Camb. J. In'tl & Comp. L*. 235 (2012).

[16] *See*: Mullenix, *Vill. L. Rev*, id. at 14–19; see, similarly, Thomas D. Rowe. Jr., id. at 210–211; Scott Dodson "The Challenge of Comparative Civil Procedure: Civil Litigation in Comparative Context, by Oscar G. Chase, Helen Hsershkoff, Linda Silberman, Yashuei Taniguchi, Vincezo Varano & Adrian Zuckerman, 2007 St. Paul, Minn.: West Group, p. 607" 60 *Ala. L. Rev*. 133 (2008), id. at pp. 148–149.

An example of a change in the United States that appeared with the American managerial judging is the judicial promotion of settlement and Alternative Dispute Resolution (ADR) such as early neutral evaluation, court-annexed mediation or arbitration, which is not prescribed in the federal rules of civil procedure. The success of ADR has also prompted much criticism: some criticize the idea of judicial promotion of settlement as contrary to the very purpose of having courts while others are worried about 'privatizing' dispute resolution. That said, ADR and settlement promotion have also long been institutionalized tradition in France and such procedures have also existed or are in being added in many other civil law jurisdictions as well as in England.[17]

In civil law systems too things are somewhat different than the inquisitorial prototype suggests. Attorneys now play a central role in civil law proceedings going well beyond the traditional role and often collaborating with the judge as to such matters as exchange of information and taking of evidence. For example, the judge in the modern German system is not as aggressive as imagined by some: true, the German judge in considerably more activist than her American counterpart, but she does not have an inquisitorial responsibility to determine the truth and it is the parties who control the issues presented for decision and select the evidence to be considered.[18] French law recognizes and protects the parties' ability to define the litigation through statements of the claim, defense, and desired remedy, but the parties do not exclusively control the evidence that comes before the court for its decision; similar rules apply in Spain.[19]

Hazard & Dondi suggest broad functional similarities between common and civil law lawyers. They note that commercial lawyers of both legal systems have a primary role in defining the disputes as well as their legal and factual bases. The lawyers select the forum and formulate the claims and defenses and counterclaims to be considered. They suggest that in both common and civil law "the best metaphor for the roles of judge and advocates in modern commercial litigation in both civil and common law system is that of a committee in which there are representatives for each different interest (the advocates) and a chairperson (the judge) responsible for the orderly exploration and resolution of the controversy."[20]

---

[17] *See*: Thomas D. Rowe. Jr., id. at 209–210; Richard L. Marcus "Putting American Procedural Exceptionalism into a Globalized Context" 53 *Am. J. Comp. L.* 709 (2005), at pp. 729–731. Also see: Peter L. Murray "Privatization of Civil Justice" 15 *Willamette J. Int'l L. & Disp. Resol.* 133 (2007); M. Henry Martuscello II "The State of the ADR Movement in Italy: the Advancement of Mediation in the Shadows of the Stagnation of Arbitration" 24 *N.Y. Int'l L. Rev.* 49 (2011). On the imposition of legal costs on litigants who have refused a reasonable offer as leverage to contain costs and expedite the resolution of civil dispute *see*: Pablo Cortés "A comparative review of offers to settle – would an emerging settlement culture pave the way for their adoption in continental Europe?" 32(1) *C.J.Q.* 2013, 42.

[18] *See*: Edward F. Sherman, id. at p. 512; Richard L. Marcus, id. at 723.

[19] *See*: Thomas D. Rowe. Jr., id. at 207.

[20] *See*: Geoffrey C. Hazard & Angelo Dondi "Responsibilities of Judges and Advocates in Civil and Common Law: Some Lingering Misconceptions Concerning Civil Lawsuits" 39 *Cornell Int'l L. J.* 59 (2006), pp. 62–64 (cite: p. 62).

Finally: as for the *rightto a jury trial*: Civil jury trials have been almost completely extinguished in most common law jurisdictions. The United States is the lone holdout, often because the right to a civil jury trial is protected in the federal and state constitutions. Nonetheless, that protection is not always absolute. Thus, although the Seventh Amendment of the U.S. Constitution guarantees the right to trial by jury for traditional causes of action, a right that litigating attorneys hold sacrosanct, it is a waivable right if not invoked and may not exist for modern federal statutory causes of action. In practice, most federal cases are typically resolved without recourse to a jury trial. In the fiscal year ending September 30, 2013 the first tier and trial instance of the federal judiciary the U.S. District court completed 346,766 civil and criminal cases while 375,870 new cases where filed. The number of civil cases completed that year was 5027, and of them 2025 were civil jury trials. As a result, debates over the right to a jury trial, especially in complex litigation, are now largely an academic exercise.[21]

2.3.2 *Entry into Court: Money and Standing*

- *Cost and Fee Allocation*: clearly it is still the case, in both common and civil law jurisdictions, that the financial burdens of litigation impacts the decision whether to go to court and any associated litigation strategy. Recent years have seen major reforms on this topic in a range of European civil law nations as well as in the United Kingdom, a common law legal system. Discussion of this issue typically revolved around two issues: one is the dichotomy between the "American rule" where each sides bears its litigation costs and "the English rule" whereby the losing litigants pays for costs (this is referred to as "costs follow the event" or as a shifting of the winner's litigation costs to the loser.); the second is the matter of contingency fee – permitted in the United States but not in civil law systems. Researchers suggest in the financing of litigation and attorney's fees we can observe some measure of convergence between common and civil law systems. Analyzing recent studies, Professor Reimann calls the basic dichotomy – between shifting and non-shifting of costs –

  > [H]opelessly simplistic as well as virtually useless. It is hopelessly simplistic because the reality is much more complex: no system makes the winner completely whole… and even in the United States. Some costs are shifted to the loser… most jurisdictions operate somewhere in between. The usual dichotomy is virtually useless because what basic principle a legal system proclaims says little about which costs (and which amounts) are actually shifted to the loser: some jurisdictions announcing the "loser pays" rule arguably charge the loser for no more than in the United States.[22]

---

[21] *See*: Mullenix, *Vill. L. Rev*, id. at pp. 20–22; http://www.uscourts.gov/Statistics/JudicialBusiness/2013/us-district-courts.aspx. For an interesting discussion of the decline of the civil jury trail in America *see*: Anthony J. Scirica, Chief Judge "Judge's Response to Professors Hazard and Truffo" 25 *Penn St. Int'l L. Rev*. 519, 527–530 (2006).

[22] *See*: Mathias Reimann "Chapter 1: Cost and Fee Allocation in Civil Procedure: A Synthesis" 11 *IUS Gentium* 3, 9 & fn. 24 (2012).

Professor Reimann suggests that we think of cost and fee allocation and the question of shifting expenses (which typically includes court costs, attorney's fees and expenses incurred in collection of evidence) in civil procedure as part of a *broad spectrum*. At one end of the range are legal systems that shift nearly all of the winner's litigation expenses to the loser ("major shifting"); perhaps surprisingly, England is not in this category but rather "Germanic" jurisdictions such as Austria, Germany and the Netherlands but also many other nations: from Poland to Finland to Turkey. In the middle we find jurisdictions that shift substantial parts – but not nearly the whole – of the litigation costs on to the loser ("partial shifting"); this group includes nations of the British commonwealth traditions such as England, Australia and Canada and East Asian countries such as Japan but also such nations as France and Mexico. At the other end of the range we find nations where only a fraction of the winner's costs are recoverable form the losing side ("minor shifting"). The only country squarely in this group is the United States.[23]

Professor Mullenix makes several interesting observations on this topic. *Firstly*, she too notes that one must look carefully not only at the cost shifting rule that a jurisdiction *claims* to have but to what happens in *practice*, and she too paints a more nuanced and complicated picture. For example, some civil law and common law systems, such as that of the United Kingdom, have legal aid programs that subsidize plaintiffs' costs for pursuing aggregate relief. This allows for pooling of public and private resources in order to pursue aggregate relief. Finland and Sweden have proposed class litigation statutes that would publicly finance aggregate litigation. *Secondly*, she notes that even the American rule, as applied in the United States, is, in practice, subject to numerous exceptions such as fee-shifting statutes, the common fund doctrine and lodestar formulas for calculating attorney fees. She notes that in class action litigation, Americans courts oversee fee petitions and approve, modify or reject fee petitions, and that defendants usually pay attorney's fees, which is the 'loser pays' rule without the concomitant obligation that the plaintiff pay the defendant's fees if the plaintiff loses. But Federal Rule of Civil Procedure 68, the 'Offer of Judgment' rule, effectively holds a plaintiff liable for the defendant's post-offer costs if the plaintiff rejects an offer and then subsequently recovers less than the offer. The result is the despite the 'American rule' each side rarely pays its own fees in complex litigation. *Thirdly*, it is noteworthy that state attorneys general, allied with private attorneys, have created a new model for structuring and financing complex litigation in the United States. Pioneered in the late 1990s in suits against the tobacco companies, it allows private and public cooperation under contractual fee agreements to pursue aggregate litigation against corporate defendants. This model shows a high degree of convergence with European common law and civil law systems that already have some degree of combined public and private financing of complex litigation.[24]

[23] *See*: Mathias Reimann, *IUS Gentium*, id. at pp. 8–16.

[24] *See*: Mullenix, *Vill. L. Rev*, id. at pp. 26–28.

- *Punitive Damages*: here too we see some measure of common and civil law convergence: in the United-States, where punitive damages have a long history of acceptance with little restrictions, it is now the case that most states have enacted caps or rations or both to constrain punitive damage awards. In addition, the U.S. Supreme Court has imposed limits on the amount of punitive damages and these apply even in the states that have not enacted their own restrictions. Professor Dodson concludes "that unfettered and individualized damage award, at least in the context of punitive damages, may be moving toward the rest of the world."[25] Moreover, while it is true that newspapers often report enormous punitive damages awards and that American tort lawyers are unlikely to accept a system without punitive damages – the fact is that punitive damages are not a significant factor, at least in most large-scale complex litigation which are mostly settled without any punitive damages. In addition, punitive damage classes are rarely certified by American courts.[26]
- *Class or Group Litigation*: As Professor Baumgartner noted – "[c]lass actions have gone global." For decades class action litigation was limited to the United States and few other countries – mostly common law jurisdictions such as Australia and England, but also Sweden and Brazil – in terms of both scholarly interest and practical effects. Yet more recently, class action litigation has captured the attention of foreign academics and law reformers. In fact, some foreign jurisdictions have already adopted some group litigation devices inspired by the FRCP representative litigation devices. In addition, Americans are beginning to take interest in the international landscape of group litigation, especially taking note of the reasons why some countries reject American-style class actions.[27] The result is a vigorous debate on the advantages and disadvantages of class action and group litigation.[28] As matters now stand, the majority of European Union Member states have, in recent years, either introduced or seriously considered introducing some form of collective redress. These include Denmark, England, Finland, France, Germany, Hungary, Italy, the Netherlands, Norway, Poland, Portugal, Spain and Sweden. Furthermore – the European Commission is now looking into finding a coherent European Union Approach to collective redress.[29] The trend, however, goes much beyond Europe (it includes, for example

---

[25] *See*: Dodson, *Ala. L. Rev*. id. at p. 146.

[26] *See*: Mullenix, *Vill. L. Rev*, id. at pp. 22–24.

[27] *See*: Samuel P. Baumgartner "Class Action and Group Litigation in Switzerland" 27 *Nw. J. Int'l L. & Bus*. 301, 308–309 (2007) (cite: p. 301). Also: Antonio Gidi "Class Actions in Brazil – A Model for Civil Law Countries" 51 Am. J. Comp. L. 311 (2003).

[28] For example, Samuel Issacharoff & Geoffrey P. Miller examine the European aversion of American style class action, and wonder whether the concerns are, at the end of the day, mostly cultural and if so, will Europe fail to ward off class action, as it failed against Starbucks and Macdonald's? See: Samuel Issacharoff & Geoffrey P. Miller "Will Aggregate Litigation Come to Europe" 62 Vand. L. Rev. 179, 180–181 (2009).

[29] *See*: Csongor István Nagy "Comparative Collective Redress from A Law and Economic Perspective: Without Risk There is No Reward!" *Colum. J. Eur. L*. 469 (2013); also: Stefano M. Grace "Strengthening Investor Confidence in Europe: U.S.-Style Securities Class Actions and

Argentina, Brazil and Mexico) and not all nations considering adoption of aggregative litigation procedures end up adopting them. For example, in Japan, Austria, Belgium and Switzerland, the idea of introducing class action was met with considerable opposition.[30]

2.3.3 The Functioning of the Trial

There are many signs of a narrowing of the gaps between common and civil trial practices:

- *The trial as a single, live event*: changes were made in German civil procedure since 1977 for a "concentrated trial" – a final, single event trial, where witnesses would be heard. Germany – and more recently Austria as well – has also moved away from the concept of a "documentary curtain" whereby a hearing judge takes the evidence and prepares a written summary for a different judge who hears arguments and decides the case. Other civil law nations such as Italy and Spain have also undertaken reforms toward more adversarial practices. On the American side, there is growing realization of the shortcomings of the live, oral testimony given at trial: to mention just two of the problems: such testimony is rarely entirely spontaneous at trial, at least because discovery devices such as depositions permit sides to question opposing witnesses long before the trial; in addition, trial often take place years after the events to which witnesses testify, raising concerns regarding the accuracy of their testimony. "American trial practice has been moving towards accepting more testimony in written form" such as depositions and summaries or in video recording instead of live testimony, especially from expert witnesses.[31]
- *Civil Discovery and Pleadings*: Commentators suggest changes imposing heightened pleading on plaintiffs in the United-States by statute and Supreme Court decisions, but these "changes do not necessarily reflect a willingness to alter the American pleading system generally. And even these specific changes are still far from the kind of fact-pleading, evidentiary-based system, that for, example,

The Acquis Communautaire" 15 J. Transnat'l L. & Pol'y 281 (2006); Roald Nashi "Note: Italy's Class Action Experiment" 43 *Cornell Int'l L.J.* (2010) 147. On the internal EU debate until 2010 see: Christopher Hodges "Collective redress in Europe: the new model" 29(3) *C.J.Q.* 370 (2010).

[30] *See*: Mark A. Behrens, Gregory L. Fowler & Silvia Kim "Global Litigation Trends" 17 *Mich. St. J. Int'l L.* 165, 172–173 (2009). On the Japanese alternative to the class action – the Representative Action *see*: Carl F. Goodman "Japan's New Civil Procedure Code: Has it Fostered A Rule of Law Dispute Resolution Mechanism?" 29 *Brook. J. Int'l L.* 511, 589–592 (2004).

[31] *See*: Edward F. Sherman, id. at p. 514–515 (cite: from p. 514); Scott Dodson & James M. Klebba "Global Civil Procedure Trends in the Twenty-First Century" 34 *B.C. Int'l & Comp. L. Rev.* 1 (2011), at pp. 15 16.

Germany has."[32] Yet it seems that the United States is shifting away from the "notice-based exceptionalism towards a fact-based model more akin to the pleading standards in the rest of the world."[33] In the discovery area, the trend seems clear: since the FRCP came into place in 1938 "every reform of the discovery rules has been to require more frank and early disclosure, and has been intended to circumscribe discovery abuse." The reforms in discovery law came as a result of the realization that the FRCP more often impede the fact-finding process rather than enhance it.[34]

- *The appointment of expert witnesses*: there are difficulties with both civil and common law models. For example, civil courts often have difficulty attaining the services of expert witnesses because they are too expensive or too remote, and settle for the available and neutral, albeit perhaps not very expert, witness. In common law experts are often chosen on the basis of their theatrical ability, and the side with the deeper pocket has an advantage in hiring experts. Civil law systems are considering such reforms as the sides jointly appointing an expert, or having a court appointed expert in addition to experts appointed by the parties. That said, even in common law countries, it is in the best interest of the expert to do her utmost to sound fair and unbiased, when appearing before a judge or a jury.[35]

2.4 A Second Reality Check: Looking beyond Traditions: Hybrids and Trans-systemic Approaches

There is a whiff of change in the air – in part a direct response to the erosion in acceptance of the accuracy of a clear division between common and civil law systems. Thus, there may be more to comparative law than the common and civil law convergence-divergence debate. A series of factors have had three interlinked effects: *first*, they have turned the convergence of common and civil law systems, across many fields including civil procedure, from a theory to an almost universally agreed upon reality. This we described to sufficient effect in the parts above; *Second*, real life economic, social and political demands have taken comparativism away from the exclusive domain of academics and into real-politik, influencing previously immune fields such as international trade and litigation and supranational governance structures, such as the European Union. *Finally*, these factors have also diminished the importance of individual nation states, especially that of some of the founding members of the common and civil law families – possibly with the

---

[32] *See*: Dodson, *Ala. L. Rev*. id. at pp. 144–145 (cite: p. 145); also *See*: Mullenix, *Vill. L. Rev*, id. at pp. 24–26.

[33] *See*: Dodson & Klebba, id. at p. 8.

[34] *See*: Mullenix, *Vill. L. Rev*, id. at pp. 24–25 (cite: p. 24).

[35] *See*: Geoffrey C. Hazard, Jr. "Civil Procedure in Comparative Perspective" 49 *Sup. Ct. L. Rev*. 2d Ser. (Canada) 657 (2010), at pp. 662–663.

exception of the exceptional United States – and brought more attention to legal systems outside of the group of Western-developed nations.

In this section we present an overview of three of these issues and factors: (1) *Mixed jurisdictions* that call into question the common-civil law distinction and the purity of the models. (2) Stepping outside the domestic legal regimes we ask: what model does *transnational litigation* follow? (3) We observe concerted efforts to blur common-civil law differences across regional and international systems: we note, in particular, *model codes* and the unique case of the *European Union*.

2.4.1 *Mixed Jurisdictions: Does One Plus One Make* Three?

There are at least 16 jurisdictions around the world, 12 of them independent nation states, "where common law and civil law coexist and commingle and constitute the basic materials of the legal order." These jurisdictions are, in alphabetical order: Israel, Lesotho, Louisiana, Malta, Mauritius, Namibia, the Philippines, Puerto Rico, Quebec, Scotland, South-Africa, Seychelles, Sri Lanka, St. Lucia, Swaziland, and Zimbabwe. All were all governed by more than one European nation of settlers or colonial powers, and each adopted, at different periods in their individual histories, both civil and common law. What is special about these jurisdictions is that: *first*, they did not choose to reject those foreign legal systems outright and develop (or revert to) an independent legal system – perhaps tribal or religious law – but have rather retained significant elements of European law in their domestic legal system; *second*, they have retained elements from both major European families and so, while their legal systems may resemble common or civil law, they do not resemble them in full; the result, at least by some accounts, is that each of these jurisdictions cannot clearly by pigeonholed as *common* or *civil law* and so, some would argue, these jurisdictions have a difficulty finding their legal 'home'.

This is why they are grouped, by some, into a third group, one that Professor Palmer calls (in the introduction to his classic edited volume, now in its second edition) "*mixed jurisdictions*".[36] When the first edition came out in 2000, each one of these jurisdictions (covering among them a population of over 150 million and a territory the size of a subcontinent) "lived in physical and intellectual isolation, cut from family members around the world, each was born one of a kind.... [s]ituated at the four corners of the earth."[37] While aware of the dramatic differences between

---

[36] Vernon Valentine Palmer (ed.) Mixed Jurisdictions Worldwide: The Third Legal Family (Cambridge UP, 2nd edition, 2012) at pp. xiii (cite), 625–631.

[37] Palmer, id. at pp. 3–5 (cite: p. 3). Perhaps the number of mixed jurisdictions is actually higher: Palmer observes that "[t]he prevailing perceptions of lawyers and judges, for example, help to explain why today Texas and California are not regarded as mixed jurisdictions in the classical sense. They are called common law states, yet they were once Spanish possessions in which Spanish law fully applied. Even now, they still retain important parts of this civilian heritage in their trial procedure, property and land titles, water law, matrimonial systems, and so forth." *See*: Vernon Valentine Palmer "Quebec and Her Sisters in the Third Legal Family" 54 *McGill L.J.* 321, 342 (2009). On the background to the creation of mixed jurisdictions *see*: William Tetley, id.

these jurisdictions, Palmer's work has considered whether "mixed jurisdictions, despite very obvious diversities in terms of their peoples, cultures, religions and languages, have closely related legal systems." His intuition was that there were numerous similarities and shared tendencies among such jurisdictions.[38]

In fairness, the concept of mixed jurisdictions has intrigued researchers well before Palmer's book, and a precise definition for the term is hard to come by. Palmer's book deals with nations that reflect a classic definition, now well over a hundred years old, which defines mixed jurisdictions as "legal systems in which the Romano-Germanic tradition has become suffused to some degree by Anglo-American law."[39] But one could easily consider a more inclusive definition, such as the one suggested by Tetley:

> A mixed legal system is one in which the law in force is derived from more than one legal tradition or legal family. For example, in the Quebec legal system, the basic private law is derived partly from the civil law tradition and partly from the common law tradition. Another example is the Egyptian legal system, in which the basic private law is derived partly from the civil law tradition and partly from Moslem or other religiously-based legal traditions.[40]

Perhaps with this in mind, an earlier book, published in 1996, looked at other nations and territories as potential mixed-jurisdictions. These included the Basque country in Spain, Turkey, the Russian Federation, Hong-Kong, Algeria, Japan, Slovenia, post-Unification Germany and even the European Community, as a "mega mix".[41] If we follow this route, one could widen the definition almost to abstraction: since there is "no shared understanding of what this term means. In one sense, all jurisdictions can, in one way or another, be said to be mixed, because all are constructed from a variety of different influences."[42] Indeed, serious questions may be raised over the precise nature of the mixed – or some might say hybrid, or

---

[38] Palmer, id. at p. xiv; also see p. 4.

[39] *See*: Maurice Tancelin, Introduction, in F.P. Walton, The Scope and Interpretation of the Civil Code 1 (Wilson & Lafleur Ltee, 1907, reprinted by Butterworths, 1980), and in more detail: William Tetley "Mixed Jurisdictions: Common Law V. Civil Law (Codified and Uncodified)" 60 *La. L. Rev*. 677 (2000), at pp. 679–680.

[40] *See*: William Tetley, id. at pp. 684.

[41] *See*: Esin Örücü, Elspeth Attwooll & Sean Coyle, eds. Studies in Legal Systems: Mixed and Mixing (Kluwer, 1996).

[42] *See*: Daniel Visser "Book Review: Mixed Jurisdictions Worldwide: The Third Legal Family. By Veron Valentine Palmer (Ed.). Cambridge University Press, 2001." 78 *Tul. L. Rev*. 2329 (2004) also Palmer, id. at p. 11 & fn. 28. This realization that arguably no legal system is 'pure' from foreign influences means that a jurisdiction becomes a 'mixed' one at a hard-to-determine point, when the level of contribution from a second legal family raises doubts as to its identity as belonging to the first family. As a jurist from Israel I am aware that my country is often described as one of the 'mixed jurisdictions' but am of the opinion that the common law traditions in Israeli law are dominant enough to comfortably leave us within the purview of that legal family. *See*: Vernon Valentine Palmer "Mixed Legal Systems ... and the Myth of Pure Laws" 67 *La. L. Rev*. 1205, 1208–1209 (2007); Eliezer Rivlin "Israel as a Mixed Jurisdiction" 57 McGill L.J. 781 (2012).

composite – legal systems.[43] What is quite clear is that since the turn of the millennium, there is growing academic interest in mixed-jurisdictions: in 2002, the First Worldwide Congress on Mixed Jurisdictions convened in New Orleans, and the World Society of Mixed Jurisdiction Jurists (WSMJJ) was formed, accompanied by extensive academic literature. The Fourth Worldwide Congress of the WSMJJ will be held in Montreal in 2015.[44]

One lesson that can be drawn is that it is less important whether mixed jurisdictions do or do not form a cohesive group, one that can be seen as a third legal family – what is important is that the classic duopoly in comparative law no longer holds. As Palmer says –

> By speaking of a third legal family, I do not wish to imply that there are no other families beyond common law, civil law, and mixed jurisdictions. To the contrary, I believe that only the limits of our present knowledge and our basic Eurocentric lack of curiosity have kept us from discovering many more.[45]

A second lesson is that there is a great potential to the study of mixed jurisdictions. In terms of comparative civil procedure, the legal literature coming out of jurisdictions that we think to be 'mixed' in some degree could be very interesting: these are jurisdictions that have internalized the idea of synthetizing law from two or more legal families and where rules and principles from two or more legal systems are not merely of academic interest or of practical importance for political and commercial reasons – they are part of *the law*, part of the domestic legal tradition. Studying such jurisdictions can provide crucial insights into the actual results of legal mixology, to be carefully watched before any jurisdiction – one that views itself as clearly related to a single, specific legal tradition – ventures into comparative law experiments. After all, as Professor Gottwald notes "[m]ost modern *codifications* or greater amendments are the *result of comparative studies*, even if the legislator did not reveal how and where he found his ideas."[46]

Palmer notes, briefly, that "Everywhere in the mixed jurisdiction world, civil procedure is adversarial along Anglo-American lines. The emphasis of that procedure is upon the remedy rather than the right, and this has left a visible imprint on substantive civil law, which emphasizes the right rather than the remedy."[47] But this seems a little too simple and inclusive – and much more detailed research into the precise workings and makeup of civil procedure in mixed jurisdictions is called for. Professor Picker raises these questions in more detail. Noting that most mixed

[43] For such a discussion *see*: Esin Örücü, Introduction in: Esin Örücü, ed. Mixed Legal Systems at New Frontiers (Wildy, Simmonds & Hill Publishing, 2010) pp. 1–8.

[44] *See*: Esin Örücü, Preface & Introduction in: Esin Örücü, ed. Mixed Legal Systems, id. at pp. vii, 8; http://www.mixedjurisdiction.org/; also see: Maria Otero "Bibliography: Mixed Jurisdictions" 39 *Int'l J. Legal Info*. 73 (2011).

[45] *See*: Palmer, McGill L.J., id. at p. 342 (2009).

[46] *See*: Peter Gottwald "Comparative Civil Procedure" 22 *Ritsumeikan L. Rev*. 23 (2005)(*Italics* – in the original).

[47] *See*: Palmer, McGill L.J., id. at p. 343 (2009).

jurisdictions began as civil law systems and were later suffused with common law elements, he finds it an interesting question whether there is a pattern to their reception of common law: "[h]ave only specific parts of the common law tradition been adopted, *e.g.*, its civil procedure but not its contract law, and have common law elements tended to appear only within certain areas of the original civil law system?"[48]

Picker notes, and I clearly agree, that the substance of civil procedure in mixed jurisdictions is an issue that bears consideration in its own right. One can only imagine, he notes "the consequences that result from substantive civil law flowing through a common law procedural system!"[49] His observations so far are that –

> Elements of common law procedure commonly found in mixed jurisdictions include adversarial proceedings (with a larger role for attorneys than traditionally found in civil law systems), cross-examination of witnesses, the finality of the first instance judgment, the limited role of appeals courts, the "various writs," and, of course, the ever-present jury – whether or not it is actually employed. Each of the mixed jurisdictions employs these and other common law procedural devices to varying extents due to the different histories of the systems – the penetration or reception of common law procedural mechanisms depends on the system's stage of development when subjected to common law influences, e.g., conquest by a common law colonial power.[50]

These mixed systems, as well as the very many other forms of mixed systems in the world (not just comprised of civil and common law parts, but also religious and other legal system components) are important and different legal systems that suggest there is much to be considered outside the traditional common and civil law classifications.

2.4.2 *Transnational Litigation*

Business people need to have their disputes tried, decided and executed in a fair and efficient manner. They are willing to pay for it too. Thus, commercial litigation has always been one of the main driving forces in the development of law – both procedural and substantive. This has been the case not only in national – but also in international law: national states and functioning court systems are relatively new, while the law merchant is much older. This substantive law, the *lex mercatoria* could be defined as an amalgam of trade practice, focused according to the needs of

---

48 *See*: Colin Picker "International Law's Mixed Heritage: A Common/Civil Law Jurisdiction" 41 *Vand. J. Transnat'l L.* 1083, 1126 (2008).

49 *See*: Picker, id. at p. 1127.

50 *See*: Picker, id. at p. 1128. Also see: David Parratt "Tales of the Unexpected: Procedural Rule Change and Their (Unintended) Consequences" 12(1) *Elec. J. Comp. L.* (2008)(arguing that changes to Scottish civil procedure in the 19th century pushed Scots law away from its Civilian heritage and in the direction of common law).

international business, creating a *ius commune* among commercial merchants.[51] In its somewhat romanticized version, the law merchant –

> [I]s not subject to the territorial jurisdiction of local authorities, but functions as a self-regulating regime run by transnational merchant judges and set apart from domestic law and local rulers. Its court system--the embodiment of the Law Merchant at work--satisfied the transregional interests of itinerant merchants, who traveled with their goods and wares from port to port, fair to fair, and market to market.[52]

It is not surprising that there is extensive renewed interest in this ancient law: it is clear that the ancient instrument of the law merchant foreshadowed the needs of modern trade and commerce. The difficulty is that despite increased globalization and interdependence of world economic processes it is still sovereign states that make up the territory of the world, devising laws and establishing courts. Merchants are no longer left to devise their own solutions – laws, procedures, and courts – and are not comfortable with leaving it up to nation states. Explains one commentator:

> In an increasingly borderless and multijurisdictional international business environment, parties seek certainty and predictability in the resolution of cross-border commercial disputes. The legal risk associated with doing business on a multinational level must be kept to a minimum. When disputes do arise and self-help remedies are non-viable, parties want to rely on an efficient and effective dispute resolution system. Unfortunately, the divergent nature of procedural law in the different judicial systems throughout the world means businesses face extra costs and greater uncertainty when engaging in domestic litigation in a foreign jurisdiction.[53]

More clearly put, transnational civil procedure is a pertinent issue in the growing class of civil cases that transcend national borders, *i.e.*, include a transnational (procedural) element, such as a foreign party or evidence located abroad.[54] We will not detail here all the issues that may be categorized under transnational civil procedure – but will say that they are very diverse. Two examples include the growing

---

[51] *See*: Richard A. Epstein "Reflection on the Historical Origins and Economic Structure of the Law Merchant" 5 *Chi. J. Int'l L.* 1 (2004); Charles Donahue, Jr. "Medieval and Early Modern Lex Mercatoria: An Attempt at the Probatio Diabolica" 5 *Chi. J. Int'l L.* 21 (2004); Michael Douglas "The Lex Mercatoria and the Culture of Transnational Industry" 13 *U. Miami Int'l & Comp. L. Rev*. 367, 370–371 (2006).

[52] *See*, for a critical view: Leon E. Trakman "the Twenty-First-Century Law Merchant" 48 *Am. Bus. L.J.* 775 (2011). On the meaning of transnational law see: Roger Cotterrell "What is Transnational Law?" 37 *L. & Soc. Inquiry* 500 (2012).

[53] *See*: Stephen McAuley "Achieving the Harmonization of Transnational Civil Procedure: Will the ALI/Unidroit Project Succeed?" 15 *Am. Rev. Int'l Arb.* (2004) 231. Also: Leon E. Trakman "From the Medieval Law Merchant to E-Merchant Law" 53 *U. Toronto L.J.* 265 (2003); "From St. Ives to Cyberspace: The Modern Distortions of the Medieval" 'Law Merchant' 21 *Am. U. Int'l L. Rev*. 685 (2006).

[54] *See*: Samuel P. Baumgartner "Is Transnational Litigation Different?" 25 *U. Pa. J. Int'l Econ. L.* 1297, 1300 (2004); also Samuel P. Baumgartner "Book Review: Transnational Litigation in the United States: The Emergence of a New Field of Law (Reviewing Gary B. Born & Peter B. Rutledge, International Civil Litigation in the United States," (Wolters Kluwer, 4th ed. 2007)) 55 *Am. J. Comp. L.* 793 (2007) On what transnational law means, generally, *see*: Reza Dibadj "Panglossian Transnationalism" 44 *Stan. J. Int'l L.* 253 (2008).

number of class actions that are filed in the United States with foreign class members (these are alternatively known as global, multinational, international, or transnational class actions)[55] but also to the recognition of judgments, especially transnational ones, in foreign countries.[56]

These difficulties focused the attention on the need to harmonize transnational civil procedure. Two entities – The American Law Institute ("ALI") and the International Institute for the Unification of Private Law ("UNIDROIT") – have joined forces to developed the Principles and Rules of Transnational Civil Procedure ("PRTCP").[57] The final draft of the PRTCP was approved by both bodies in 2004 and published in 2006. The PRTCP was not the first attempt to bridge common and civil law procedures but it is considered to be "the most detailed identification of points of common ground" and it is very likely that it will "assist greatly in the intellectual mapping of civil justice and that it will influence policy-makers."[58] The drafting team, of which Professor Andrews was a member, included seven civil lawyers but only two common law representatives. As a result "[e]verywhere the restraining hand of the Civil Law is visible, and robust Common Law tendencies (American and English) are curbed."[59]

Andrews explains that the PRTCP offers a balanced distillation of best practice, especially in the sphere of transnational commercial litigation, and, moreover, that they are not restricted to the "largely uncontroversial 'high terrain' of constitutional guarantees of due process,"[60] but also operate in three additional levels of importance:

The first level, that of quasi-constitutional procedural guarantees secures judicial competence, independence and impartiality, procedural equality, due notice, publicity, prompt justice, right to assistance by professional and independent counsel and both attorney-client privilege and the privilege against self-incrimination.

The second level, that of major guidelines concerning the style and course of procedure, includes a long list of topics such as party initiation of proceedings and definition of scope of proceedings; pleadings and allocation of burden and nature

[55] The increase in their number can be attributed to a growing global presence of multinational corporations, combined with the broad reach of American class action attorneys. *See*: Antonio Gidi "The Recognition of U.S. Class Action Judgments Abroad: the Case of Latin America" 37 *Brook. J. Int'l L.* 893, 894 (2012); also: Tanya J. Monestier "Transnational Class Actions and the Illusory Search for Res Judicata" 86 *Tul. L. Rev.* 1 (2011).

[56] *See*: Madeleine Tolani "U.S. Punitive Damages before German Courts: A Comparative Analysis with Respect to the Ordre Public" 17 *Ann. Surv. Int'l & Comp. L.* 185 (2011) also Gidi, Brook. J., id.

[57] *See*: http://www.unidroit.org/instruments/transnational-civil-procedure; http://www.ali.org/index.cfm?fuseaction=publications.ppage&node_id=76.

[58] *See*: Neil Andrews "The Three Paths of Justice Court Proceedings, Arbitration, and Mediation in England; Chapter 2: Principles of Civil Justice" 10 *IUS Gentium* 25 (2012) ('Chapter 2') at p. 42–43 (cite: p. 43).

[59] *See*: Neil Andrews, Chapter 2, id. at p. 41.

[60] *See*: Neil Andrews, Chapter 2, id. at p. 41.

of standard of proof; judicial initiative in evidential matters and management of proceedings and encouragement of settlement; parties' duty to cooperate, act fairly and promote efficient and speedy proceedings; parties' right to discontinue or settle proceedings; a basic costs shifting rule; finality of decisions; appeal mechanisms and effective enforcement.

The third level, concerning points of important detail includes such matters like protection of parties lacking capacity; security for costs; expedited forms of communication; non-party submissions and making of judicial 'suggestions'.[61]

2.4.2.1 What Impact Will the PRTCP Have at the National Level?

These are, still, early days. But some lessons can already be suggested. In a 2005 lecture delivered in Jakarta, Indonesia on the topic of "Principles of Transnational Civil Procedure," Australian Federal Court Justice James Allsop described the PRTCP project as one that had begun "by distinguished American and European professors" with the vision "to develop a body of principles for transnational cases which could apply in national courts and in so doing replace domestic procedural rules whenever the parties to litigation involved nationals of different states or where the case could otherwise be described as international." He then explained to his listeners why this project is pertinent to him – and them:

> Transnational litigation is growing. It is growing in particular in this region. That fact is simply a by-product of the vast economic development occurring in this region and its transnational so-called "globalised" character. As part of that, there will grow a number of centres of commercial litigation. However, it is vital to the economic development of the region that there develop comprehensively and broadly, in as many legal systems and centres as possible, a recognition of the importance of resolving disputes, in particular commercial disputes, by reference to recognised and accepted world standards of procedure and method. Arbitration plays and will continue to play a central role. But not all commercial disputes can be settled by an agreed arbitral forum.[62]

What seems to me to be an achievement of the PRTCP is the effort to be inclusive of both civil and common law civil procedures, where possible, allowing practitioners of both legal families to find 'acceptance' in this code.

If we move back closer to the originators of the PRTCP: we can see US Federal Judge Scirica noting that in practice, the American discovery "is still broader than that contemplated by the Transnational Principles and Rules. *But at least in theory, the basic standards are similar*."[63] On discovery, Professor Sherman suggests that the PRTCP "take a middle ground, although occasionally borrowing from American practice"[64] and Prof. Mullenix would go even further, arguing that provisions in the

---

[61] *See*: Neil Andrews, Chapter 2, id. at pp. 41–42.

[62] *See*: http://www.austlii.edu.au/au/journals/FedJSchol/2005/17.html.

[63] *See*: Anthony J. Scirica, id. at p. 522 (*Italics* – added). Also *see*: Stephen McAuley, id. at pp. 249–249.

[64] *See*: Edward F. Sherman, id. at pp. 517.

PRTCP "would effectively level the discovery playing field among civil and common law jurisdictions."[65]

What about jury trials? One of the main proponents of PRTCP, Professor Geoffrey Hazard, is of the opinion that the principles of transnational civil procedure are compatible with *both* civil jury trials – as in the American common law system – and with nonjury trial procedures as in other common law systems and in the civil law systems.[66] But it has to be said that the PRTCP does, in fact, adopt of model of a trier of facts that substantially corresponds to the civil law model and is based on a non- jury type of court composed of one or more professional judges.[67]

What about experts? American Judge Anthony Scirica suggests that this depends on how the PRTCP are implemented in practice: this could end up as "a system similar to ours, which relies heavily on party-appointed experts, or similar to a civil law systems, which relies heavily on court-appointed experts."[68]

Similarly we can see American law Professor Edward F. Sherman noting that the PRTCP, which seeks "to identify certain fundamental principles for transnational commercial litigation," sees strengths and weaknesses in both common and civil law approaches to the judges' role in court. The PRTCP therefore adopts a rule that permits *either* approach, provided that "a person giving testimony may be questioned first by the court or the party seeking the testimony," and "all parties then… have opportunity to ask supplemental questions."[69]

This, however, is not always the case: for example, the FRCP adopts notice pleading standards, which stands in contrast to the requirement in most other countries of a fuller statement of the facts and evidence supporting the claim. The *PRTCP* rejects notice pleading, requiring that "[t]he statement of facts must, so far as reasonably practicable, set forth detail as to time, place, participants, and events."[70]

If we return to the United-States, the shining beacon of exceptionalism, where "American proceduralists have not been comparativists",[71] it is interesting to note that recent decades have seen a debate over the potential for change and adjustment with foreign practices. It is done in the context of the question whether transnational litigation is a separate field, that needs its own, distinct, procedural law or whether the domestic American procedural rules, written with mainly domestic litigation in mind, are appropriate even in transnational litigation. There is clearly, as noted in

---

[65] *See*: Mullenix, *Vill. L. Rev*, id. at p. 24.

[66] *See*: Geoffrey Hazard, *Penn St. Int'l L. Rev.*, id. at p. 499 et seq.

[67] See: Michele Taruffo "Principles and Rules of Transnational Civil Procedure: An Evidentiary Epistemology" 25 *Penn St. Int'l L. Rev*. 509 (2006–2007).

[68] *See*: Anthony J. Scirica, id. at p. 527.

[69] *See*: ALI/UNIDROIT, Principles of Transnational Civil Procedure, Rule 29–4, at 144 (Cambridge University Press, 2006); Edward F. Sherman, id. at pp. 512.

[70] *See*: ALI/UNIDROIT, Principles, id. at Rule 12.3, at 111; Edward F. Sherman, id. at pp. 515.

[71] *See*: Richard L. Marcus, id. at 709. Also see: James R. Maxeiner "Pleading and Access to Civil Procedure: Historical and Comparative Reflections of Iqbal, A Day in Court and A Decision According to Law" 114 *Penn. St. L. Rev*. 1257, 1264–1265 (2010).

this chapter, an academic interest in the comparative study of transnational civil procedure – and even in legal practice, transnational dispute resolution is considered by many as a distinct specialty. But is it possible to forecast –

> [F]rom this set of national and international trends a movement toward transnationalism and comparativism in American procedural law, at least for cases with an international dimension, how confident should we be in this forecast? Two or three decades from today, will the American civil procedure and conflict-of-law rules applicable to transnational disputes be noticeably different from those that govern garden-variety domestic cases? Or will differences between the international and the domestic be differences at the margin, as traditionally has been so?...
>
> Nearly two decades have passed since this debate began. In that time, has the procedural law applied by American courts to adjudicate international disputes become noticeably autonomous from that which governs wholly domestic disputes?[72]

Professor Marcus suggests that while the PRTCP "seeks to accommodate the jury trial, its embrace of stricter pleading standards and less aggressive discovery provisions are flashpoints in view of this cultural aspect of American litigation, which distinguished the U.S. from most or all of the rest of the world," but he is somewhat optimistic, saying that "it may be over time American exceptionalism of this sort can be relaxed."[73]

Dubinsky offers a somewhat disheartening view, at least of the current situation, *i.e.*, what American courts *are actually doing*. He argues that when American courts are confronted with disputes with a transnational dimension, they reach for their familiar toolbox, the one with the tools for fixing domestic problems and that they extrapolate from their experience with familiar domestic litigation, especially interstate litigation.[74]

One final comment: the rationale behind the PRTCP was one of harmonization or approximation, noting that "the costs and distress resulting from legal conflict can be mitigated by reducing differences in legal systems, so that the same or similar 'rules of the game' apply no matter where the participants may find themselves."[75] The same logic can apply to efforts to narrow down the gaps between the major legal systems in other more specific areas relating to civil procedure. For example, despite the unsuccessful attempt by the Hague Conference to devise an international convention on jurisdiction and recognition and enforcement of judgments, Professor Simona Grossi retraces the debate between the common and civil law delegations on their jurisdictional laws and suggests that there are analytic ways to uncover symmetries between the two systems and unify their approach to jurisdictional law

---

[72] *See*: Paul R. Dubinsky "Is Transnational Litigation a Distinct Field? The Persistence of Exceptionalism in American Procedural Law" 44 *Stan. J. Int'l L.* 301, 302–306 (cite: pp. 303 & 306 (2008)).

[73] *See*: Richard L. Marcus, id. at p. 738.

[74] *See*: Dubinsky, id. at p. 306 also see pp. 356–357. Also see: Thomas O. Main "The Word Commons and Foreign Laws" 46 *Cornell Int'l L.J.* 219 (2013).

[75] *See*: Geoffrey C. Hazard, Jr., Michele Taruffo, Rolf Sturner, Antonio Gidi "Introduction to the Principles and Rules of Transnational Civil Procedure" 33 *N.Y.U. J. Int'l L. & Pol.* 769 (2001).

and choice of law rules. Grossi argues that "conflict of laws rules governing civil and commercial matters should be harmonized and that such harmonization is feasible and worth pursuing." Therefore, she suggests the adoption of an international convention on conflict of laws rules, to apply to litigation on civil and commercial matters.[76]

2.4.3 *The European Union's Effects*

2.4.3.1 Is There a European Law of Civil Procedure?

There are several interesting ways to think about this question.

At one level one could say that as long as Europe is made up of several dozen independent sovereign nations, each applying its own internal, domestic, national law, a European law of civil procedure would consist of whatever rules and principles are found to be common to these national laws.[77]

If we look for legal instruments formalizing and unifying European commitment in the field of civil procedure than there is one that stands out: it is the *European Convention on Human Rights*. The European Court of Human Rights in Strasbourg oversees the implementation and secures compliance with of the Convention by the 47 member states of the *Council of Europe*. This is a diverse group that includes, besides the members of the European Union, such nations as Russia, Switzerland and Turkey and covers well over 800 million persons.[78]

Article 6(1) the Convention, essentially a constitutional codification of the right to a fair trial, provides that:

> In the determination of his civil rights and obligations or of any criminal charge against him, everyone is entitled to a fair and public hearing within a reasonable time by an independent and impartial tribunal established by law. Judgment shall be pronounced publicly but the press and public may be excluded from all or part of the trial in the interest of morals, public order or national security in a democratic society, where the interests of juveniles or the protection of the private life of the parties so require, or the extent strictly necessary in the opinion of the court in special circumstances where publicity would prejudice the interests of justice.[79]

Article 6(1) is of great important, but at the end of the day it is mostly a constitutional level guarantee of national procedural conduct, and it recognizes internationally expected norms of good conduct. It is not, strictly speaking, a

[76] *See*: Simona Grossi "Rethinking the Harmonization of Jurisdictional Rules" 86 *Tul. L. Rev*. 623 (2012).

[77] *See*: Peter Gottwald "The European Law of Civil Procedure" 22 *Ritsumeikan L. Rev*. 37 (2005).

[78] For example, in England, The Human Rights Act 1998, which took effect in October 2000 made the European Convention on Human Rights *directly applicable in English Court. See*: Gottwald, 22 *Ritsumeikan L. Rev*. 37, id. at p. 37; *See*: Neil Andrews, Chapter 2, id. at pp. 25–26; http://human-rights-convention.org/.

[79] *See*: http://human-rights-convention.org/; for analysis *see*: Neil Andrews, Chapter 2, id. at pp. 26–40.

breakthrough in comparative civil procedure. For this, we need to look at a unique instrument of supranational cooperation: the *European Union*.

The first step taken within the European community to create a unified law of civil procedure was the Brussels convention on Jurisdiction and the Recognition and Enforcement of Judgments in Civil and Commercial Matters of September 1968 which has been in force since 1973.[80] At first blush, this looked like a conventional treaty between the then six member states of the European Communities –

> But only after a short time after this treaty came into operation, it was realized that it contained not just recognition rules but in the first part unified rules of jurisdiction which might prove as a core of a unified European Civil procedure to come.[81]

And so it became common to speak of a European civil procedure when dealing with the Brussels convention.[82] Several major occurred since the late 1990s:

Firstly, in the Amsterdam Treaty of 1997 civil procedure was switched from the so-called 'third column' of EU law, *i.e.*, intergovernmental cooperation, to the 'first column', *i.e.*, a direct competence of the Union itself. Article 65 of the EC treaty now gave the power to legislate in the field of judicial cooperation in civil matters with cross-border implications including the elimination of "obstacles to the good functioning of civil proceedings, if necessary by promoting the compatibility of the rules on civil procedure applicable in the Member States." This, writes Prof. Wagner, was "a major step forward towards 'real' harmonization, or rather unification." And in the years 2000–2008, the European Council together with the European Parliament published a long set of *European Regulations* which are directly binding within the then 25 member states (including the relatively new members from Eastern and Southern Europe, with only Denmark excluded).[83]

Secondly, another layer of European civil procedure results from the European Council's decision in Tampere, Finland in 1999, for a program on the transformation of the principle of mutual recognition of judicial decisions in civil and commercial matters. This program became concrete in 2001 and comprises common rules for simplified and accelerated cross-border judicial proceedings for claims of consumers or merchants with regard to small claims, to maintenance or to uncontested claims.

Thirdly, in addition to the regulations there are *directives* with procedural content, such as a January 2009 European council directive to improve access to justice

---

[80] Known as the Brussels I Convention; http://en.wikipedia.org/wiki/Brussels_Regime. *See*: Gottwald, 22 *Ritsumeikan L. Rev*. 37, id. at p. 37; Gerhard Wagner "Harmonization of European Civil Procedure – Policy Perspectives" in: X. E. Kramer and C. H. van Rhee (eds.) Civil Litigation in a Globalising World (Asser Press, The Netherlands, 2012) 93 at p. 94 (also available at SSRN: http://ssrn.com/abstract=1777233); http://curia.europa.eu/common/recdoc/convention/fr/c-textes/_brux-textes.htm.

[81] *See*: Gottwald, 22 *Ritsumeikan L. Rev*. 37, id. at pp. 37–38; Gerhard Wagner, id. at p. 95.

[82] And after 1988 – with the parallel Lugano Convention which was concluded with the EFTA states of that time. *See*: Gottwald, 22 *Ritsumeikan L. Rev*. 37, id. at p. 38.

[83] *See*: Gerhard Wagner, id. at pp. 95–96 (cite: p. 95); Gottwald, 22 *Ritsumeikan L. Rev*. 37, id. at p. 38.

in cross border disputes by establishing minimum common rules regarding legal aid or other financial aspects of civil proceedings.

Fourthly, a December 2002 decision by the European council established the so-called *European judicial net in civil matters*: an administrative network to ease the exchange of information between member states and to solve problems in the cooperation on concrete cases. Gottwald's evaluation is that "[t]he European Civil procedure is not a settled matter but a dynamic one as there is the political intention to improve the judicial cooperation."[84]

Since 2005 matters have advanced even further. The Lisbon Treaty of 2009 "did nothing to alter, expand or scale back the power of the EU in the field of civil procedure," and Article 65 of the EC treaty was transformed more of less intact in Article 81 of the Treaty on the Functioning of the European Union (TFEU).[85] The conclusion, as measured by the numbers of directives and regulations churned out by the European Commission over the past decade might have been that European Civil Procedure is a rapidly growing field. That is not quite the case since "the practical impact of legislative acts passed… remains very limited. These measures of 'horizontal harmonisation' create uniform rules for disputes of every kind, *yet they remain confined to cross-border cases*."[86] In the EU supranational legal order (not unlike the American federal order) "the judicial system of dispute resolution and private enforcement of EU rights remains largely decentralized, taking place before member states' courts."[87] In practice, member states' procedural regimes are considerably divergent – even though most of them are part of one family, civil law. The result is that EU institutions are trying to intervene, more and more often, in member states' national civil procedures so as to ensure that EU law is effectively enforced in a similar manner across the EU. As the European Commission moved beyond issues of international jurisdiction and enforcement of foreign judgments, "it placed European institutions alongside the national ones, which continued to govern domestic disputes. This results in duplicative sets of procedural rules which place a heavy burden on the judges who have to work with them."[88] The steady extension "of EU competence in the area of civil justice, traditionally regarded as the bastion of state sovereignty, has met member states' hesitation and resentment and to the desirability and feasibility of EU institutions designing civil procedure rules."[89]

[84] *See*: Gottwald, 22 *Ritsumeikan L. Rev*. 37, id. at pp. 38–39 (cite: at p. 39).

[85] *See*: Gerhard Wagner, id. at p. 96.

[86] *See*: Gerhard Wagner, id. 93 (*Italics* – added).

[87] *See*: Zampia Vernadaki "Civil Procedure Harmonization in the EU: Unravelling the Policy Considerations" 9(2) *J. of Contempt. E. Res*. 297, 298 (2013).

[88] *See*: Gerhard Wagner, id. 93.

[89] See: Zampia Vernadaki, id. at p. 299. Also see: Eva Storskrubb "Civil Procedure and EU Law – A Policy Area Uncovered" (Oxford Studies in European Law, 2008); *Cf.* http://ec.europa.eu/justice/civil/commercial/eu-procedures/index_en.htm.

Furthermore, Vernadaki argues that EU intervention in member states' procedural systems happened so far in a fragmented and incoherent way – lacking a systematic planning and clearly set objectives[90] – so it is likely that the development of such policies will be a significant challenge the EU will face in coming years.

A final word: it is interesting to note that the European Law Institute (ELI) and the International Institute for the Unification of Private Law (UNIDROIT) have started cooperating in late 2013 on a joint project of "European Rules of Civil Procedure." This cooperation is aimed at adapting the ALI-UNIDROIT Principles from a European perspective in order to develop European Rules of Civil Procedure.[91]

2.5 Conclusion

As noted above, the traditional discussions in comparative civil procedure have historically and too often focused on the black letter law of civil procedure in common and civil law countries. This may perhaps have made sense in the past. This is what business believed it required. It is in the commercial interests of both the parties to the litigation and their lawyers that there be as clear as possible rules to the game called 'the legal process', and at least until recent years, most of this business was conducted in Western/developed countries. But, the reality as discussed above is that the division was never particularly meaningful and in any event has undergone significant convergence in any case. Furthermore, as discussed above, there are now alternatives to tradition or state-centered approaches with just as much vitality and applicability.

In this conclusion two last points will be raised to further show the new directions and the ongoing dynamism that exists within comparative civil procedure – both of which reflect that there are many ways to look at comparative civil procedure beyond the traditional one.

The first is *interdisciplinary study*. This is the application of methods from other academically recognized disciplines in an effort to shed a light on the law and provide greater insight, even if it does not necessarily help to win a legal argument or case. One of the first extra-legal disciplines to enter mainstream legal research was history. Its value seems clear: norms are not created in an instant and do not appear out of nowhere. There is a background to the law, and it needs to be studied and understood in order for us to be able to evaluate the current – and future – position of the law. Comparative civil procedure is no different and valuable insights may be gleaned from an historical approach.

---

[90] See: Zampia Vernadaki, id. at p. 299.

[91] *See*: http://conflictoflaws.net/2013/the-eli-unidroit-project-from-transnational-principles-to-european-rules-of-civil-procedure-1st-exploratory-workshop/; http://www.europeanlawinstitute.eu/projects/current-projects-contd/article/from-transnational-principles-to-european-rules-of-civil-procedure/?tx_ttnews%5BbackPid%5D=137874&cHash=30981e5bc9618fbff47b45f915163642.

One such useful example of a *historical* study of civil procedure is by Professor C.H. van Rhee who argues that while this field was considered an academic discipline worthy of scholarly attention up the period of codification in Europe, from the second part of the eighteenth century, national codification resulted in a decline in the significance of both legal history and comparative law in the context of civil procedure. "[T]he importance of knowledge regarding the differences and similarities between national and foreign procedural law was less evident to an attorney in the period after codification."[92] Another useful application of an historical approach to the study of comparative civil procedure looks at the history and success of 'legal transplants' of civil procedure – reflecting one of the most dynamic manifestations of comparative law.[93] For a third example we turn to David Parratt, who argues that changes to civil procedure effected Scotland both historically and recently, pushing this legal system – considered a mixed jurisdiction – away from civil law heritage in the direction of the common law.[94]

A second discipline that has entered mainstream legal scholarship more recently with very dominant effect is *economics*. Law and economics has a lot to say on civil procedure – including in its comparative aspects: after all, a major purpose of civil procedure is to resolve disputes efficiently as well as fairly and professionally. So, it is not surprising to see articles focusing on the economic problems of the German civil procedure – particularly costs and delays – and discussing possible solutions for them.[95] In 1997 Professor Geoffrey P. Miller noted that at that time comparative civil procedure had not drawn extensively on the literature of the economic analysis of procedural rules and methods. He suggested that this body of theory had much to offer the procedural comparativist, studying dispute-resolution systems in different jurisdictions. He noted that economic analysis that had focused, for the most part, on rules in the Anglo-American legal world could usefully be applied, with appropriate modifications, to Continental and other procedural systems.[96] Some – but not nearly enough – scholars have heeded that call.

There are many other disciplines of the social sciences that have an interesting if less immediately pertinent input into civil procedure. Sociology explains each nation's customs regarding dispute resolution: how litigious are the people? Do they choose courts or ADR? Psychology explains the mindset of litigants, the likelihood of reaching a compromise and many other issues. All of these issues are especially relevant in comparative perspective.

In sum, as shown in this Chapter, comparative civil procedure is clearly both dynamic in substantive terms, procedures changing and mutating, but is also dynamic in its methodologies and approaches.

---

[92] *See*: C. H. van Rhee "Civil Procedure: A European *Ius Commune*?", id. at pp. 589, 597 (cite).

[93] *See*: John W. Cairns, id. at pp. 664–665, 694–695.

[94] *See*: Parratt, id. at p. 1.

[95] *See*: Marianne Roth "Towards procedural economy: reduction of duration and costs of civil litigation in Germany" 20 *C.J.Q.* 102 (2001).

[96] *See*: Geoffrey P. Miller "The Legal-Economic Analysis of Comparative Civil Procedure" 45 *Am. J. Comp. L.* 905 (1997).

Chapter 3
Comparative Law as an Engine of Change for Civil Procedure

Colin B. Picker

3.1 Introduction

The title of this book suggests that it constitutes an examination of the dynamism within civil procedure across different legal systems and civil procedure devices. This may have struck civil procedure experts as strange in light of the fact that dynamism may be defined as "vigorous activity and progress".[1] Historically those are qualities that may not have been the first to spring to mind when thinking about civil procedure. Nonetheless, activity, vigour and progress form the themes throughout the contributions to this book, and arguably characterize modern civil procedure.[2]

In this book the presence of dynamism is explored in different legal systems, including that of the European Union, France, the United States, Brazil, Australia, the United Kingdom and China. So too is that dynamism found in the analyses and discussions of the changes or need for change of specific aspects of civil procedure including litigation costs, class actions, derivative actions, pleadings, and res judicata. While most of the individual contributions may be considered on their own to be comparative analyses of their respective subjects, there is no doubt that, when considered as a whole, the book presents the dynamism of civil procedure in comparative perspective. Those comparative analyses permit us to better understand the dynamism in civil procedure – for change in the abstract can be less visible or hard to discern and its significance and impact less evident.

---

[1] *See* http://www.oxforddictionaries.com/definition/english/dynamism (last checked 19 March, 2015).

[2] *See* M. Woo, Chapter 7 at footnote 1.

C.B. Picker (✉)
UNSW Law, University of New South Wales, Sydney, NSW 2052, Australia
e-mail: c.picker@unsw.edu.au

C.B. Picker, G.I. Seidman (eds.), *The Dynamism of Civil Procedure - Global Trends and Developments*, Ius Gentium: Comparative Perspectives on Law and Justice 48, DOI 10.1007/978-3-319-21981-3_3

In addition, those comparative analyses play an instrumental role as well. They also can illuminate the need for change with respect to specific civil procedural systems or the particular procedural devices found within those systems. While we may have come to similar conclusions by examining those systems or devices in isolation, employing comparative analytic methods can provide a richer analysis. That need for change, which is a very common and pertinent call that we find in virtually all legal systems in recent years, is correspondingly advanced. Furthermore, if a comparative critique leads to the conclusion that change is necessary then that same comparative law may provide pertinent examples for such change – as well as methodologies for successfully transplanting any such changes. In other words, comparative law may itself usefully contribute to change in civil procedure. This has long been a raison d'être of comparative law and in this particular time and field of study, we find that it is very likely to achieve its lofty promise.

This last introductory chapter will therefore explore the relationship between comparative analysis and dynamism within civil procedure – what in this chapter will be called "comparative law-led change". This chapter will briefly explore the relationship between comparative law and a dynamic civil procedure, though, it will do so unanchored to any one legal system and its civil procedure. Rather, the elemental concepts and characteristics of civil procedure found across the many different legal systems of the world will form the fabric against which the relationship between comparative law and civil procedure's dynamism will be considered. As relevant, reference back to the materials in the other chapters in this book, which span a respectable cross section of the world's primary forms of legal systems and devices, will be employed to illuminate the points made below.

3.2 Civil Procedure's Inertia

Traditionally, civil procedure has not been associated with dynamism in the law. Perhaps, it may even have been the case that civil procedure may have been among the last of the legal fields to be considered full of vigour and energy. Indeed, Tronson's chapter in this book even opens with a famous quote from a nineteenth century novel by Charles Dickens that captures the conservatism that surrounded litigation proceedings.[3] But today, despite the many obstacles to change in civil procedure discussed below, it appears as though there is a new dynamism in the field across the world, or at the very least a clear realization of the need for improvement and reform, potentially coupled with a willingness to look across borders for solutions. An excellent example is associated with Wambier's chapter on the new Brazilian Civil Procedure in which she examines what was during drafting a proposed new law of procedure, but that now been enacted during the production of this

[3] *See* Tronson, Chapter 9 (the quote is from *Bleak House*).

book.[4] Nonetheless, bringing about change in civil procedure is very often an uphill battle. For dowdiness or conservatisms within the field runs deep. It is almost as though there was a latent inertia existing within civil procedure that stands in the way of change.

Sources of such an inertia to change in civil procedure may come from a number of sources, but due to the length constraints of a simple chapter in an edited collection, this chapter will focus on just a two types of inertial sources. The first set of sources examined here concern the natures of civil procedure and how those natures may contribute to an inertia. The second set of inertial sources are connected to the legal participants and their resistance to change in civil procedure.

As an initial matter, the natures of civil procedure themselves may be thought of as possessing innate inertia that makes law slow to change. While some of the reasons for that inertia relate to the legal cultures and attitudes of legal participants, as discussed below, it may be that law, at an axiomatic level, must possess that resistance to change – for without it, it is not law! For law that is insufficiently stable, at a practical and perhaps even theoretical level, undermines the certainty and predictability that is one of the cornerstones of the Rule of Law. After all, as a practical matter, members of society cannot be expected to keep up, follow, conform and adhere to law that changes too often, perhaps even more so with procedural law that governs the "rules of the road" in litigation. When the law changes too much, participants that fail to keep up would then effectively be operating outside the law (though not quite "outlaws"). This does not mean the law must be static, though some non-western approaches to law may support such a view.[5] Rather, that change should be slow, certainly by today's digital age standards, so that the law's development and operation (often directly connected to law's development) must be organic, evolutionary and deliberate. In fact, this is how, outside of revolutionary contexts, we see the law develop. After all, that the law is slow to develop and to operate and moves with the speed of a snail is a well-worn legal trope. For example, carved in stone on the Yale Law School building there is one small, usually unnoticed, carving of a snail – showing the speed of the law![6]

Within the law, however, civil procedure may be one of the fields more innately resistant to change. Just a few of the reasons for that inertia will be discussed here. As an initial matter procedure is so tied up with the behaviours, responsibilities and responses of both the private and public participants, and the balances across them in trials or proceedings that it cannot easily be changed without that balance being thrown off to the detriment of some party – be it private, public, claimant or respondent. While those sorts of balances may appear in other fields, they do not impact as varied a group as in procedure. While changes to tort or contract impact one private

[4] *See* Código de Processo Civil, Lei No. 13.105, 16 March 2015 (available at http://www.planalto.gov.br/ccivil_03/_Ato2015-2018/2015/Lei/L13105.htm, last checked 20 March 2015).

[5] *See, e.g.*, Harold J. Berman, Law and Revolution: The Formation of the Western Legal Tradition 7–10 (1983) (one of the characteristics of the Western law is that growth and change of law is part of its pattern of development)

[6] http://www.thenewjournalatyale.com/2009/12/if-these-stone-walls-could-talk/.

party or another, and public law changes impact public or private parties, change to procedure impacts all litigants across all civil relationships – private and public, as well as all relationships involving any associated institutions that make use of the civil law dispute resolution system. After all, when other parts of the law are the subject of disputes then the dispute will be subject to civil procedure and when other parts of the law need to be judicially interpreted that too brings civil procedure to the fore. This is not the case for contract law or for family law or for constitutional law.[7] Therefore, change to civil procedure may have significant knock-on effects through the entire civil law. Therefore, because civil procedure is a foundational part of the legal system and changes to it will impact significant aspects of the rest of the legal system, change must be carefully considered. This must necessarily slow down change, for all proposed change will then be subject to critique and scrutiny from the entire civil side of the law, and not just from civil procedure experts.

The second set of sources for the inertia may be driven by those civil procedure experts. Civil procedure lawyers and the judges who administer it might be more inward looking or less open to foreign legal approaches than lawyers or legal participants of other fields. For example, in studies of Mixed Jurisdictions,[8] it was found that common law legal participants were particularly attached to their civil procedure, with an "emotional, almost religious attachment"[9] which would stand in the way of change. Another reason for the attachment, and hence resistance to change, may be due to the fact that so much civil procedure is judge and litigator made or driven, compared with substantive legal fields which are increasingly created by the legislature or the administrative state and its civil service. While the legislature may not always be reform-minded (especially if conservatives are in power), and certainly few would describe civil servants as revolutionary (though if driven by political appointees they may in fact be radical), they will have a detachment from the law for which they are responsible for, and hence more willing to change it. In contrast, it is likely that the judiciary and litigators, the ones involved in the daily life of the civil procedure, will fear the uncertainty that would come with change.

Furthermore, those mostly responsible for the development of civil procedure, especially in the common law systems, the lawyers and judges, are by their nature

[7] Though changes to a constitution may also impact large parts of the legal system too, but that is part of the reason that the process for changes to constitutions is so difficult.

[8] Mixed Jurisdictions are "legal systems in which the Romano-Germanic tradition has become suffused to some degree by Anglo-American law." William Tetley, *Mixed Jurisdictions: Common Law v. Civil Law (Codified and Uncodified)*, 60 La. L. Rev. 677, 679 (2000); *see generally* Vernon Valentine Palmer, *Introduction to the Mixed Jurisdictions*, in Mixed Jurisdictions Worldwide: The Third Legal Family (Vernon Valentine Palmer ed., 2001).

[9] Stephen Goldstein, *The Odd Couple: Common Law Procedure and Civilian Substantive Law*, 78 Tul. L. Rev. 291, 293 (2003); Vivian Grosswald Curran, *Romantic Common Law, Enlightened Civil Law: Legal Uniformity and the Homogenization of the European Union*, 7 Colum. J. Eur. L. 63, 78–79 (2001) (arguing that procedure is central to the common law worldview).

risk averse and conservative,[10] being professionals in a field that places great value on predictability and certainty – two of the central tenets of the Rule of Law. As such, that part of the law left in their hand may be less likely to be changed than that which is within the domain of the legislature. Even scholars of civil procedure, the ones often responsible for change in civil law systems, may be more conservative than scholars of other legal fields, for they are more likely to have come out of practice, or have immersed themselves within the conservative legal culture of practice, and hence may be more conservative than their academic colleagues working in the substantive law fields.

Another factor that may contribute to conservatism among civil procedure scholars, litigators and judges is that procedure, unlike many substantive fields of law, is less amenable to ideological or cultural shifts among the population or even within legislatures. This is because procedure, at least where it is perceived to be generally fair and efficient, may be more value- or normatively- neutral, and less often betray its intrinsic biases – after all, it does not immediately concern rights and liabilities to the same extent as substantive fields.[11] It 'merely' deals with the complex dance between litigants and the court where the substantive fields are litigated. Hence, ideological or political disputes among civil procedure experts, disputes which then lead to change, may be less common. Though for sure, there will be disputes – but perhaps driven more by the internal issues that arise within civil procedure, as opposed to reflecting external political or ideological values and conflicts.[12] Furthermore, as views change across generations, civil procedure is less likely to be buffeted by those winds of change and less likely to have to undergo change to conform to a new normative context. This does not mean it is immune, as the chapters in this collection clearly show. Certainly, the chapters on Chinese civil procedure show incredible dynamism – ones driven by significant internal normative changes.[13]

---

[10] *See, e.g.*, Richard Tromans, *Challenging the Conflict Culture: Mediation's Struggle for Acceptance in Europe*, 68 Euro. Law 19–23 (2007).

[11] Min Zhou, *A Comparative Analysis of Contemporary Constitutional Procedure*, 30 Case W. Res. J. Int'l L. 149, 158–159 (1998) ("The separation of law into procedural and substantive categories began early in the history of legal study, a separation originally proposed in the academic community by Jeremy Bentham. According to Bentham, substantive law is the law that creates, defines, and regulates the rights and duties of the parties, while procedural law prescribes methods for enforcing rights or obtaining redress for their invasion" citing Jeremy Bentham, A Treatise on Judicial Evidence, and Principles of Judicial Procedure XI (Baldwin, Cradock & Joy) (1825)). This is not to say that civil procedure has no impact on rights and liabilities – for the consequence of civil procedure rules may extinguish rights or expose liabilities – but civil procedure has traditionally not been conceived as creating rights and liabilities.

[12] For example, Legg and Higgin's chapter's comparison of overriding "purpose requirements" for civil procedure notes the greater presence and recognition of politics in the United States on this issue, than is the case in the relatively similar legal systems of England or Australia. M. Legg & A. Higgins, Chapter 8.

[13] *See, e.g.*, K. Thomas, Chapter 6 and M. Woo, Chapter 7. Normativity may be ubiquitous, and hence more present in civil procedure reform, in those systems undergoing substantial societal and

Before leaving the issue of civil procedure's inertia, one last extension of the metaphor may also be insightful with respect to civil procedure (and law in general). The metaphor is loosely derived from Newton's First law of Motion: "[w]hen viewed in an inertial reference frame, an object either remains at rest or continues to move at a constant velocity, unless acted upon by an external force".[14] The discussion above has just focused on the resistance to change from a static position – in other words changing from a state of rest. But might the rest of the metaphor be applicable – that once change has started the internal inertia also operates to keep the law changing? There may in fact be some validity to the extension of the metaphor in both the general law and the more specific civil procedure context. For example, consider the ongoing change in law that inevitably follows a revolution, during which there will be many years of change until the system settles back down again – perhaps slowed down by the inevitable forces of reaction and conservatism that we have seen appear after the first few tumultuous post revolution years, that 'friction' slowing it down until complete standstill is reached.[15] The metaphor may even apply in the more prosaic period that follows the enactment of a new law. In that case, change continues as the many different participants to that new law struggle to understand, interpret and apply the law in many different contexts, creating large numbers of contradictory findings and rulings. That change may only be brought to a rest by the final force of the highest court handing down definitive interpretations or through the legislature or other such bodies re-entering the field to clarify the new rule. With civil procedure being so very pervasive across the legal system, we can expect it would be considered and interpreted differently across so many more fora as a result of the centrality of civil procedure to all disputes. But then it should be brought to rest sooner, the change slowed down and halted, for the more widespread confusion and chaos would more quickly come to the attention of the highest courts or legislatures.

But, returning to the obstacles discussed above, clearly they can all be overcome, for we know civil procedure changes. Certainly, so many of the chapters in this book, such as those concerning the Brazilian and Chinese civil procedure show that inertia has been overcome. But it can be a slow process, though eventually a tipping point may be reached, after which change will take place. As the remainder of this chapter will show, civil procedure experts can move the system towards that tipping point through, among other approaches, employing comparative critiques that both show how things are done elsewhere and provide guidance as to what change could be successfully instituted.

---

governmental transitions – for the civil procedure will like all aspects of the law be impacted by the changing private and public relationships that arise in such transitions.

[14] *See* Newton's First Law, Wikipedia at http://en.wikipedia.org/wiki/Newton%27s_laws_of_motion (last checked 17 March, 2015).

[15] *See, e.g.*, Mary Ann Glendon, Paolo G. Carozza & Colin B. Picker, Comparative Legal Traditions: Texts, Materials And Cases On Western Law, 4th Edition (Thomson West Publishing 2015) at 74–75 (discussing the law change following the French Revolution).

3.3 Comparative Law-Led Change

Despite the above obstacles, civil procedure has undergone and is undergoing change. The contributions to this book are testament to civil procedure's periodic and occasional dynamism. The question is then what mechanisms or forces can overcome those obstacles to ensure that change can take place as needed, and not be unnecessarily delayed or stymied.

There are many different types of forces, stimulations, mechanisms and approaches that can encourage change. Change may also be driven by many different legal participants, including legislators, think tanks, governments, litigators, associations of lawyers, international conventions or institutes. Those participants may push for change or be persuaded to support change through scholarly papers, lobbying, and through litigation. Those participants may have decided change was necessary when confronted or impacted by changes in values, demographics, economics, competition, and even technology.[16] The result for civil procedure of all these forces, participants and changed contexts may be new rules, understandings and behaviours, statutes, codes, judicial interpretations and other sources of new civil procedure.

Each of these may result in different types of change. For example, technology driven change may be less likely to lead to fundamental or axiomatic change. Thus, while e-discovery has created tremendous challenges for civil procedure systems, the fundamental approach is not typically under threat. Similarly, change introduced by the judiciary in court decisions should also be less fundamental due to the conservatism that may typically be associated with the judiciary as discussed above. Though there are many examples of fundamental civil procedural change driven by judicial determinations, such as was the case with the *Erie* doctrine.[17] In contrast, change driven by scholars, the executive or legislatures may be revolutionary (perhaps reflecting their position away from the fray of the court room). Change that is reflected in a code, especially of the continental law tradition variety, may have immediate wide spread impact, sometimes even extending to foreign legal systems. Change driven by competition, such as that presented by private dispute settlement mechanisms, may be transient in the many cases where the benefits of the competitor's approach prove ephemeral. Judicial opinion change may be less certain or legitimate – easily over-ridden by a later case or even by the legislature (if not constitutional).

Across all of these mechanisms there will be a methodological approach to the determination that the change is necessary – the research methods that leads to the conclusions.[18] The research methodology employed may include one of the primary

[16] *See, e.g.*, L. Cadiet Chapter 4 at part IIB.

[17] *Erie Railroad Co. v. Tompkins*, 304 U.S. 64 (1938) (finding that the US constitution requires a federal court sitting in diversity jurisdiction, handling a state common law based civil action, to apply state law and not federal common law to the claim).

[18] In this chapter the focus is on the research methodologies, and not on the theoretical frameworks. The two will often overlap, with the one driving the other. But they should not be confused – though that confusion is endemic.

research methodologies: doctrinal ("doctrinal research is aimed at the systematisation and critique of a defined body of positive law",[19] *e.g.*, research largely confined to the existing law – cases, statutes, legislative history, regulations and so on[20]); empirical (*e.g.*, data driven legal research[21]); socio-legal (research of legal issues through sociological analyses and perspectives[22]) and, of direct relevance to this book and chapter, comparative analyses (at its most basic – research that considers and compares domestic and foreign legal systems).[23] But, among the many different methodologies for change leading to dynamic civil procedure systems noted here, perhaps the most common is that achieved through comparison with other civil procedure systems.

The "other" system providing the comparison, however, can cover many different "systems". The chapters in this book provide many excellent examples. Maxeiner, for example, directly challenges one of America's "conventional wisdoms" about its civil procedure – that it is exceptional – through the traditional direct comparative critique with other legal systems.[24] But, the comparison does not have to be with another national legal system's civil procedure – Cadiet explores the evolution of French civil procedure against the backdrop influence of the European Union and Council of Europe.[25] Similarly, the comparisons can take place within a federal or federation context as is the case for Silvestri's consideration of the European union approach to mass claims – all the while having to take into account the many issues raised by the existence of sovereign member states and their approaches and implementations. Sometimes the legal system's comparative analysis is drawn from its own domestic historic influences, which continue under new conditions – providing a point of comparison against which to measure the new

[19] Roux, Theunis Robert, *Judging the Quality of Legal Research: A Qualified Response to the Demand for Greater Methodological Rigour*, (2014) 24 Legal Educ. Rev. (forthcoming). Available at SSRN: http://ssrn.com/abstract=2499258.

[20] Doctrinal research has been and continues to be the primary form of legal research. *See, e.g.* Terry Hutchinson & Nigel Duncan, *Defining and Describing What We Do: Doctrinal Legal Research*, 17 Deakin L. Rev. 83 (2012).

[21] *See* Michael Heise, *The Past, Present, and Future of Empirical Legal Scholarship: Judicial Decision Making and the New Empiricism*, 2002 U. Illinois L. Rev. 819 (2002). An example applied to civil procedure was a study employing data on civil disputes that then suggested they are taking too long. Michael Heise, *Justice Delayed?: An Empirical Analysis of Civil Case Disposition Time*, 50 Case W. Res. L. Rev. 813 (2000).

[22] See Banakar, Reza & Travers, Max, *Introduction to Theory and Method in Socio-Legal Research* in Theory and Method in Social-Legal Research (R. Banakar, M. Travers, eds.) (Oxford, Hart, 2005). Available at SSRN: http://ssrn.com/abstract=1511112. For an example of a sociological analysis in civil procedure, concerning under-claiming and over-claiming, *see* Sachin S. Pandya & Peter Siegelman, *Underclaiming and Overclaiming*, 38 Law & Soc. Inquiry 836 (2013).

[23] Other significant research methodologies may include ones that rely on historical sources and data or on economic materials.

[24] J. Maxeiner, Chapter 5.

[25] L. Cadiet, Chapter 4, Part IB.

issue.[26] The same comparative role of history is found in Thai's discussion of the evolution of the Australian derivative action and in Thomas' analysis of U.S. pleading standards. Sometimes, the implicit comparator is in fact an ideological opposite – thus Woo's analysis of the modern Chinese procedure posits the Chinese values in comparison with that of the "standard" civil procedure of western liberal systems – in China's new procedure "order over freedom, duty over rights, collective over individual interests."[27] Finally, presentation and analysis of a system that is foreign to the author/analyst with no direct comparators also has value – for it is viewed through the prism of the analyst's knowledge and experience of her own original legal system. As such the analyst's emphases and conclusions will all, to some extent, reflect the home legal system of the analyst. It may also permit insights about the foreign system that might be denied a local expert who may be too close to the system to see what the foreigner can see. This collection has no pure examples of that genre, though this author has engaged in versions of that form before.[28]

In addition to analyses of a foreign system, learning about and examining other civil procedure systems very often permits a greater understanding of one's own system's inadequacies. Through comparison those features of one's own system that are by comparison more effective can be identified and bolstered and strengthened as necessary, while inadequacies may also be identified and then can be the subject of reform, perhaps even based on the foreign system's approaches. But despite an apparently obvious utility and deceivingly non-complex methodology, the employment of comparative law is frought with difficulties and obstacles. As an initial matter, it should be noted that comparative analysis is itself rife with traps for the unwary or narrow minded and even if successfully carried out, any lessons that may be considered applicable for one's home legal system may often face resistance.

Perhaps before embarking on long and complex comparative analyses any opposition to the results of the research must first be understood – for perhaps by keeping those in mind the research may be structured, without compromising its integrity, so as to overcome future opposition to its role in law reform. As an initial matter, in some legal systems in particular there are concerns about the legitimacy of comparative law-led change. In the United States, for example, the use of comparative law to drive change is contentious and a flash point for some, though more often the opposition is in the constitutional law arena.[29] Furthermore, there may be some that

[26] It has been said, after all that "[t]he past is a foreign country; they do things differently there." L. P. Hartley, The Go-Between, 9 (1953).

[27] See Woo Chapter 7.

[28] *See, e.g.*, Colin B. Picker, *China's Legal Cultural Relationship to IEL: Multiple and Conflicting Paradigms* in China in the New International Economic Order: New Directions and Changing Paradigms (Cambridge Univ. Press, 2015) (Lisa Toohey, Colin Picker & Jonathan Greenacre, eds.) (2015) at 62–76.

[29] *See, e.g.*, *Roper v. Simmons*, 125 S.Ct. 1183 at 1198 (2005) (Explaining that the issue is decided under the 8th Amendment of the U.S. Constitution, and other countries' stance on the issue is merely instructive and not binding) compared to Roper, at 1215–16 (O'Connor, J., dissenting) ("T]his Nation's evolving understanding of human dignity certainly is neither wholly isolated from, nor inherently at odds with, the values prevailing in other countries."); *see also id.* at 1216 ("[A]n

will simply view some foreign systems negatively – as less able and sophisticated and hence expect little to be learned from those systems. This is not to say that all systems are comparable, rather that wholesale or inaccurate discrimination is often what is taking place.[30] Sometimes what may be going on in the background is a result of a conflation of a distaste for the other state's culture or politics with the parent state's legal approaches and hence an unwillingness to even consider the potential benefits of comparative analyses involving the legal system of those states. In other cases, misplaced concerns about comparability between very different systems may lead to missed opportunities where the civil procedure within an alien system is actually less alien than the rest of the system – especially where it is, as with all civil procedure systems, simply seeking to regulate an efficient, fair and practical dispute settlement system.[31]

But would not globalization force the civil procedure experts to become more open to comparative law-led change? It may – but that impact may be offset by some countervailing effects. Of course, we should expect that the exposure to matters foreign in transnational disputes will inexorably introduce foreign legal concepts – or more critically help to reduce native hostility or suspicion of foreign approaches, eventually creating the fertile ground upon which foreign civil procedural approaches may take root. But, offsetting that effect is that while globalization is leading to more transnational litigations and the challenges posed by them, less often is it the case that in a transnational dispute there will be a need to consider foreign civil procedure law. The reason is that while the litigants may have to consider aspects of foreign substantive law, they will not typically have to consider foreign civil procedural laws because the usual rule is that the law of the forum determines the procedure, even if the substantive law, through choice of law, ends up resulting in application of foreign substantive law.[32] Of course, to the extent foreign discovery, service of process or enforcement of judgment are introduced then the domestic lawyer must consider foreign law – but typically only within its own

---

international consensus …can serve to confirm the reasonableness of a consonant and genuine American consensus."); *but see Atkins v. Virginia*, 536 U.S 304, 347–48 (2002) (Scalia, J., dissenting) ("Equally irrelevant [to the disposition of the case] are the practices of the 'world community,' whose notions of justice are (thankfully) not always those of our people."). *See also*, Steven G. Calabresi, "*A Shining City on a Hill*": *American Exceptionalism and the Supreme Court's Practice of Relying on Foreign Law*, 86 Bos. Univ. L. Rev. 1335 (2006) (contrasting the use of foreign law by the judiciary and legal elites compared with political and popular legal culture's opposition to that use).

[30] While the author is certainly not chauvinistic, he presents well many of these, and other, issues. *See* Sir Basil Markesinis, *Understanding American Law by Looking at it Through Foreign Eyes: Towards a Wider Theory for the Study and Use of Foreign Law*, 81 Tul. L. Rev. 123 (2006). The author also specifically discusses when systems are not suitable. *Id.* at 176–78.

[31] A perfect example of the error of those views is provided in Maxeiner's contribution to this book, in which he debunks the America view that its civil procedure is "exceptional". *See* J. Maxeiner, Chapter 5.

[32] "A court usually applies its own local law rules prescribing how litigation shall be conducted even when it applies the local law rules of another state to resolve other issues in the case." Restatement (Second) Conflict of Laws §122 (1971).

jurisdiction, and increasingly resolved through convention, following which transnational litigation experts are likely to be called in to handle those international issues. Nonetheless, the slow and inexorable exposure to international and foreign legal participants and ideas must eventually transform even the civil procedure experts and participants into global lawyers – conversant and open to foreign law, including foreign approaches to civil procedure.

Other opposition to comparative law may be related to the many bad comparative analyses that exist and to the failed efforts to transplant law following faulty analyses – such efforts tainting the entire methodology. It is thus critical that it is done correctly. Of course, and as noted above, comparative critiques can be difficult. Common mistakes include: failure to properly assess the functions of the compared legal issues; failure to take into account all the relevant contexts – legal or otherwise; analysis clouded by ethnocentrism, parochialism or ignorance; and insufficient critique of - or too much deference to - either the foreign or domestic legal issue. Transplantation of civil procedure rules is particularly problematic:

> Thus, for example, the failure to take into account the existence and role of safeguards. A safeguard is a legal device related to a legal device that ameliorates the harmful side effects that emanate from the original legal issue. Safeguards are not always immediately obvious, often coming into existence or operation in ad hoc and pragmatic fashion. Hence they are not always there by design, especially in the common law legal systems. An example is the safeguard function of the rules of evidence that offsets some of the failings of the jury system. Relatedly, and more obviously, are the safeguard abilities of a judge to overturn a jury verdict or reduce damages in civil cases in the United States. Thus, the civil jury system in the United States cannot be adequately subject to a comparative analysis without taking into account those safeguards.[33]

So, comparative law can be remarkably difficult to employ, often requiring the analysts to have spent decades learning about the different legal systems to ensure context, function and other demands are suitably taken into account.

But, despite these negatives there is little question that insights from analysis of foreign countries' legal systems may still be useful even if the insights are the product of difficult or even imperfect flawed analyses. This is because insights such as those are akin to ones derived from pure thought exercises – ones loosely tied or even unanchored to reality – that may still retain utility. This is especially true given that it may be impossible to perform a 'perfect' comparative analysis, for there are simply too many contexts for them all to be taken into account. All comparatists perforce engage in generalizations and simplifications and hence all are inaccurate at some level, yet still provide insights that may be useful. Furthermore, comparative analysis will always be highly personal, reflecting the particular knowledge and experience of the analyst – for law is not a science. Indeed, in this collection there are three sets of examples of analyses that overlap – yet with different approaches

---

[33] Colin B. Picker, *Comparative Civil Procedure: Opportunities and Pitfalls*, in THE FUTURE OF DISPUTE RESOLUTION (Michael Legg, ed.) (Lexis Publ.) (2012) at 254. *See, also*, John H. Langbein, *The Criminal Trial Before the Lawyers*, 45 U. CHI. L. REV. 263, 273 (1978); Shaun P. Martin, *Rationalizing the Irrational: The Treatment of Untenable Federal Civil Jury Verdicts*, 28 CREIGHTON L. REV. 683, 688–89 (1995).

and insights – truly showing the power of comparative analyses. One set considers China's civil procedure system,[34] another set overlaps somewhat on the issue of litigation costs,[35] and the last considers group or class actions – albeit in different legal systems.[36]

Another way to ensure the analysis is done properly is to ensure that what is being compared is in fact comparable – comparative analysis is most productive when applied to things that are in fact comparable. Comparability is related to, among other things, functions and contexts – the bases of the functionalist and contextualist methodologies in comparative law.[37] Using a classic idiom of comparability "they are alike as apples and oranges" the basic concepts of elementary comparative analysis can be illuminated.[38] So – are apples and oranges comparable? Well, depending on the relevant function or context, what we use them for and within what environment, apples and oranges may or may not be comparable. For example, functionally as a healthy snack for children's lunches, or as typical fruit juices available all over the world – they fulfil a similar role and are comparable. But for pie making or for preservatives – apples and oranges are clearly different and are not comparable the way rhubarb and apples may be for making pies and oranges and limes for making marmalade. Similarly, contextually, for example, they may be comparable as fruits sold in a supermarket, especially at this era when seasonal concerns are overcome by the triumph of trade and logistics, but for purposes of agriculture, the actual growing of them, they may not be – how can one compare apples thriving in Tasmania versus Oranges flourishing in Israel. But then, as far as science is concerned, apples and oranges are almost indistinguishable.[39]

Applying this concept to civil procedure leads to the question of whether civil procedure systems are functionally and contextually comparable. Viewed up close, at the micro level, they all appear to be very different from each other. Civil procedure systems can be very legal system specific, including such technical issues as the way documents must be submitted and the order of proceedings to larger contextual issues such as the role of the judge and counsel. In some cases the legal cultural context will substantially impact the procedure (arguably the existence and hence large impact of the civil jury in the United States is a function of American legal culture[40]). Indeed, the value of local counsel may sometimes be associated

[34] Compare K. Thomas with M. Woo., Chapters 6 and 7.

[35] Compare M. Legg & A. Higgins with B. Tronson, Chapters 8 and 9 (Legg & Higgins consider cost as part of their discussion of the overriding purpose for civil procedure discussions).

[36] Compare E. Silvestri and L. Thai, Chapters 10 and 11.

[37] *See* Oliver Brand, *Conceptual Comparisons: Towards a Coherent Methodology of Comparative Legal Studies*, 32 Brook. J. Int'l L. 405, 415 (2007).

[38] *See, e.g.*, Catherine Valcke, *Comparative Law as Comparative Jurisprudence--The Comparability of Legal Systems*, 52 Am. J. Comp. L. 713, 720 (2004).

[39] *See* Scott A. Sanford, *Apples and Oranges--A Comparison*, 1 Annals of Improbable Research, May/June 1995, available at http://www.improbable.com/airchives/paperair/volume1/v1i3/air-1-3-apples.html (scientifically "apples and oranges are very similar").

[40] Oscar G. Chase, *American "Exceptionalism" and Comparative Procedure*, 50 Am. J. Comp. L. 277, 288–92 (2002).

with their expertise in managing the at-times very complex and not always transparent local rules of procedure. Compliance with the local rules of civil procedure are so critical that deviation from the proscribed rules is dangerous and hence rare. Often, in common law systems in particular, the rules are only challenged when compliance was not possible and the only avenue to save the action is to challenge the very rule itself.

But, despite the uniqueness of procedural devices, there are certain common approaches, needs and characteristics of procedural systems around the world. Procedure must provide the "rules of the road" for dispute settlement systems, letting litigants understand the demands placed on them by the court and by the other parties, as well as ensuring litigants understand their rights before, during and after litigation. Those common issues cover service of process, discovery, evidence presentation and authentication, witness management before and during the trial, the roles of the judges and lawyers and jurors (in those rare systems employing civil law juries) and so on. Furthermore, all procedural systems must balance similar competing demands and limitations, including balancing the costs, access, and timing issues that relate to all participants in the civil litigation context including plaintiffs, defendants, witnesses, judges and counsel. In other words, the fundamental contexts and functions will largely be similar across all systems. Whether this amenability to comparative analysis is greater than other legal fields is not really relevant for the thesis here, though it may be that legal fields with greater normative content, which may be local or unique, may prove to be less easily or visibly comparable and hence are less amenable to comparative critique and comparative law driven change. In contrast, civil procedure would appear to be ideally suited to comparative critiques and hence amenable to comparative law driven change.

3.4 Conclusion

Despite the obstacles and difficulties in employing comparative law, and despite the inertia of civil procedure, we can expect to see more and more comparative law-led change. This is not just because of globalization, though that is a very strong factor, but also because comparative critiques are an innate form of analysis and hence intuitively easily understood and accepted. From early in human development we engage in comparisons – mother versus father, big brother versus littler brother, energetic friends versus placid friends, safe versus unsafe food, dangerous versus harmless animals and so on. We innately even understand that comparisons must be made in context and with different functions taken into account – the two basic approaches to comparative law analysis: functionalism and contextualism discussed above.

Furthermore, while we do see a certain homogeneity to civil procedural systems, given that there are more than two hundred-plus national and regional legal systems in the world there is therefore a large store of comparative examples to support the many different types of comparative examinations desired. Even if they only differ in small amount to each other, the large number of systems will provide a large pool of ideas for the development of civil procedure. Indeed, the different legal systems and traditions may be viewed as laboratories, especially powerful ones when systems are otherwise alike. For example, Wambier's contribution to this book, about res judicata in the new Brazilian Civil Procedure, employs comparisons across a wide range of other civilian systems, including the Spanish and Japanese, and even considers how the common law approaches the issue.[41] As Brazil was considering how to reform their civil procedure they were thus able to draw upon numerous examples and to consider how effective they were before even considering their relevance in a Brazilian context.

But, the mere existence of multiple examples for comparative analyses is insufficient to ensure the methodology is employed. Civil procedure participants and experts must be open to its use. Fortunately, we live in a time in which employment of comparative law is complemented by a rapidly increasingly internationalized profession and field. The globalization of legal education, academia and the legal profession combined with greater penetration of legal systems by international and regional obligations has provided a great deal of exposure to foreign law and approaches. While much of that exposure impacts substantive laws, it, as noted above, must also eventually impact procedure too – in domestic, regional and transnational fora. In some ways the normative neutrality of procedure should make such penetration easier, though as has been seen in the mixed jurisdictions, procedure is one of the fields of law held dear by legal participants.

Thus, change even in civil procedure, both comparative law-led and otherwise, may be unstoppable in light of globalization, convergence and internationalization within legal systems. As other chapters have noted, convergence and the forces of globalization, reflected primarily through greater incidence and penetration in transnational litigation or domestic litigations with some foreign nexus, have increasingly challenged traditionally domestically focused forms of procedure. Where those new procedures have resulted in increased efficiencies and better outcomes and can then be applied in purely domestic contexts they are eventually impounded in them. Given these forces and trends, it may almost be the case that comparative law and critique, and hence comparative law-led change, may become so normalized as to not even be noticed – if indeed that has not already happened.

But, because civil procedure forms one of the basic structures of legal systems, with all other fields being forced through its operations, great care and thought must be employed before tinkering with the system, for it will have impacts throughout the legal system. Rule of law with its concomitant demands for predictability and certainty demands that in this field above all else, care be taken when altering it. Because of that very high threshold, comparative law-led change, when done properly (truly taking care to avoid transplantation errors) may be among the safest for civil procedure - for ideas and mechanisms that are "imported" or against which domestic procedure is compared will themselves have been tested in their own

[41] T. Wambier, Chapter 14.

system and should therefore carry with them greater legitimacy. As a result, greater confidence can be accorded comparative law-led change in civil procedure.

Given the power and legitimacy of comparative law-led change it behoves everyone to ensure it is properly understood. The examples of such quality comparative analyses as are found in this collection are consequently worth studying both for their specific contributions to civil procedure and also for those that would consider employing comparative law as a vehicle for change in their civil procedure.

Part II
Dynamism of Specific Countries & Regions

Chapter 4
Sources and Destiny of French Civil Procedure in a Globalized World

Loïc Cadiet

As the means for obtaining judicial enforcement of the rights that persons may assert, civil procedure is fundamentally the law governing judicial resolution of disputes within civil society. More technically, it may be defined as the set of legal rules and judicial practice regulating the organization and functioning of the courts of law competent for settling disputes affecting private interests.

Do we deal with "private judicial law" (*droit judiciaire privé* in French) or with "civil procedure" (*procédure civile* in French)? This is an appropriate issue because both expressions co-exist in French law, which can itself be puzzling to a reader unfamiliar with the subject.[1] The traditional title of the field is civil procedure. This tradition goes back to the reign of Louis XIV, and more precisely to the civil ordinance of April 1667 "concerning the reform of justice."[2] The first commentators on this text dealt, in regard to it, with "civil procedure". The tradition lingered on and, under the Code of Civil Procedure of 1806, one of the Napoleonic codes, the teaching of civil procedure was nothing more than the teaching of the Code. The title did not raise any difficulty until the end of the nineteenth century, at which time there was added to the study of procedure in the official *curricula* of university education also the study of judicial organization, procedural rules and enforcement. The term civil *procedure* thus appeared too narrow, and thus inaccurate. Therefore, some authors preferred to speak, at the beginning of the 1940s, of "private judicial law" (*droit judiciaire privé*). Private judicial law thus denotes both the law of civil *justice*

Professeur à l'Ecole de droit de la Sorbonne – Université Paris 1- President of the International Association of Procedural Law.

[1] See L. Cadiet, E. Jeuland, *Droit judiciaire privé*, Paris, LexisNexis, 2013, No 11.

[2] See N. Picardi, A. Giuliani, *Code Louis*, t. I, *Ordonnance civile*, 1667, Giuffrè ed., Milano, 1996.

L. Cadiet (✉)
Law School, Université Paris 1, 12, place du Panthéon, Paris Cedex 05, 75231, France
e-mail: Loic.cadiet@univ-paris1.fr

C.B. Picker, G.I. Seidman (eds.), *The Dynamism of Civil Procedure - Global Trends and Developments*, Ius Gentium: Comparative Perspectives on Law and Justice 48, DOI 10.1007/978-3-319-21981-3_4

(judicial organization and competence of the courts) and the law of the civil *trial* (the lawsuit, the proceedings, appeals and enforcement procedures). There was another signification of this evolution, *id est* the idea that civil procedure is not only a matter for practitioners; it is really a matter of law and we may say a matter of fundamental law.[3]

This semantic observation is the background of my paper which will successively deal with the sources (Sect. 4.1) and the destiny (Sect. 4.2) of French civil procedure. We have to pay great attention to History; it is generally the key of intelligent reform of law, and procedural law is no exception.

4.1 Sources

Sources of French civil procedure are mainly *domestic* and depend, in the major part, on the Government ruling, and not on the Parliament ruling.[4] However one must also consider the part and the role of *international* sources.[5]

The question of the international sources of civil procedure has elicited interest from French jurists only in fairly recent times. This is clear from reading works on French civil procedure. The question of international sources for civil procedure is envisaged only by contemporary authors, and does not appear in older works.

That significant change occurred with the founding of the Fifth Republic, when General De Gaulle arrived in power in 1958. This coincided with the building of a united Europe, based on the Treaty of Rome of March 25th, 1957. So it might be asserted that the international sources of French civil procedure are mainly, but not entirely, European. Specifically this evolution was permitted by Article 55 of the new 1958 French Constitution which lays down the superiority of international treaties over domestic law in general.[6] This article states: "Treaties or agreements duly ratified or approved shall, upon publication, prevail over Acts of Parliament, subject, with respect to each agreement or treaty, to its application by the other party." For what we are concerned, French legislators and judges must therefore take into account international treaties containing procedural provisions. There are several of these. Most of them have provisions governing international disputes.[7] They are bilateral or multilateral international agreements for judicial co-operation, such as

[3] Something similar occurred in England and Wales for some decades. The development of a procedural *doctrine* is strengthened by the reform of civil procedural rules at the end of the 1990s.

[4] See L. Cadiet, E. Jeuland, *op. cit.*, No 15–28. *Adde* Ph. Théry, « La question des sources », *in* L. Cadiet et G. Canivet (eds), *1806–1976–2006 – De la commémoration d'un code à l'autre : 200 ans de procédure civile en France*, LexisNexis, 2006, p. 261 & ff.

[5] See L. Cadiet, "Les sources internationales de la procédure civile française", *in Mélanges Hélène Gaudemet-Tallon*, Paris, Dalloz, 2008, p. 209–227.

[6] See now Art. 88–1 to 88–5, French Constitution of 1958 specifically for EU law.

[7] See . B. Sturlèse, *V°* « Coopération judiciaire internationale », *in* L. Cadiet (ed.), *Dictionnaire de la justice*, Paris, Presses universitaires de France, 2004.

The Hague Conventions, or the EU regulations, which provide mainly for court jurisdiction, notification of acts, rules of evidence or the effect of judgements.[8] For all these provisions, the international nature of the sources is simply explained by the international nature of the dispute. However, there are also international instruments directly applicable to purely domestic disputes and not just to international ones, such as the European Convention on Human Rights, especially Article 6 § 1 which lays down the right to a fair trial (*droit à un procès équitable*). Here the international nature of the source takes on another dimension since the international provisions must prevail over the domestic law on procedure. This may lead to conflicts between rules, between international and domestic rules, in which the French judge is the arbiter. The result should normally be that the international rule prevails.[9]

One thing these various sources have in common is that they are *direct normative sources* of French civil procedure. However, that does not mean that they are the only sources of French procedural law, nor that they are as recent as they appear.

Indirect sources must also be taken into account. That means that the study of foreign law, jurisprudence or even case law may be a secondary source, of inspiration, for domestic legislators, and French law is no exception. These discreet sources are very old. Without exaggerating, it can be said that they go back to the discovery of Roman law by the Italian glossators of the School of Bologna at the start of the second millennium, when that prodigiously fecund seat of legal learning spread knowledge throughout Europe, not least France – mainly in Montpellier and at the Sorbonne in Paris. It seems that this intellectual migration began in 1234, with the publication of the treatise written by Tancredus, under the title *Ordo Judiciarius*, translated into French which had a great influence in France, where the jurists followed the Italian example with, for instance, the *Judicial Mirror*, by Guillaume Durand, a Provencal native who read law in Bologna and taught it in Modena before returning to France.[10]

These introductory observations are useful in order to understand the way the evolution of French civil procedure followed, as I will present according to a chronological order. This order is based on the codifications that structured the development of French judicial law, and more particularly the Code of Civil Procedure dated 1975. I will thus distinguish the international sources of French civil procedure before the New Code of Civil Procedure of 1975 (Sect. 4.1.1) from those following it (Sect. 4.1.2).

---

[8] See all these provisions *in* L. Cadiet (ed.), *Code de procédure civile*, Paris, LexisNexis, 34th ed., 2015, "Droit européen et international".

[9] See L. Cadiet, « Les conflits de légalité procédurale dans le procès civil », *in Mélanges en l'honneur de Jacques Boré*, Paris, Dalloz, 2007, p. 57 & ff.

[10] See E. Glasson, *Les sources de la procédure civile française*, Paris, L. Larose et Forcel, 1882, p. 21–22. Concerning G. Durand (Durantie), see F. Roumy, *V°* « Durand », in P. Abareyre, J.-L. Halpérin, J. Krynen (eds), *Dictionnaire historique des juristes français, XII*^{e} *– XX*^{e} *siècle*, Paris, Presses universitaires de France, 2nd ed., 2013.

4.1.1 The International Sources of French Civil Procedure Before the New Code of Civil Procedure of 1975

Before the new French Code of Civil Procedure of 1975, the question of international sources of French civil procedure was not envisaged as such. It is clear that neither the legislator, nor case law, nor academic doctrine ever raised the notion in these terms. Yet French civil procedural law is made up by rules based on various sources, in which the domestic aspect has always existed side by side with outside sources. It was the case for the building of French civil procedural law before the Napoleonic code of civil procedure was drawn up in 1806 (Sect. 4.1.1.1). It was also the case for the development of French civil procedural law until the new Code of Civil Procedure was adopted in 1975 (Sect. 4.1.1.2).

4.1.1.1 The Napoleonic Code of Civil Procedure (1806)

At first view, international sources for procedure cannot be discerned for the period preceding the drafting of the Code of Civil Procedure of 1806. This code is commonly presented by most observers as a sort of copy of an older law, the great Royal Ordinance of 1667 on civil procedure, drawn up by Colbert, who was Louis XIV's main minister.[11] The 1806 Code not only kept the title of the 1667 Ordinance; it also repeated many of its rules. The drafters of the Napoleonic Code of Civil Procedure, who were judges and lawyers from the *Ancien Régime*, found themselves incapable of departing completely from the old law; they tended to reproduce many of its features, which explain the comment from the nineteenth-century authors that the 1806 Code was "already old when it was born."[12]

But that opinion is not quite true.

The Napoleonic law did not reproduce all the provisions of the old law. The 1806 Code is rather a mixture of the old legal tradition and some innovations of the French Revolution that brought in the local justice characterized by an oral and adversarial procedure, and laid down the principles of giving grounds for a judgement and publicising it. It also instituted justices of the peace (*justices de paix, juges de paix*) and created a procedure for settling out of court before any judgement in the case (*conciliation*).

Above all, this opinion critically fails to highlight the extraordinary work that led up to the civil ordinance of 1667.

When Ernest Glasson, who was one of the great masters of French judicial law in the late nineteenth century, wrote a book devoted to the sources of French

[11] On the process to drafting this ordinance, also called *Code Louis*, see J. Krynen, *L'Etat de justice – France, XIIIe-XXe siècle*, vol. I : L'idéologie de la magistrature ancienne, Paris, Editions gallimard, 2009, p. 191 & ff.

[12] E. Glasson, A. Tissier and R. Morel, *Traité théorique et pratique d'organisation judiciaire, de compétence et de procédure civile*, Sirey, 3rd edition, t. I, No 25, p. 65.

civil procedure,[13] he certainly did not examine the question of international sources as such, in the way that authors would today. His purpose was to deal with the historical sources that he intended to describe from the beginnings of the French State when the monarchy became established in the eleventh century. He wished to show how French procedure was built up from the feudal procedures, and indeed contrary to them, forming a blend of two different sources: Canon law, and the royal ordinances. Then he showed how a national procedure that was encapsulated in the 1667 Ordinance, and later in the Napoleonic code, came into existence.

However, from a modern point of view, two of these sources could, to some extent, be considered as international sources since the original feudal source was identified as the *Germanic source* of French law, and the later Canon law source as the *Roman source* of French law. But, in their day, while nation-States did not exist, these elements were considered not as foreign elements since France itself was the fruit of this Roman-Germanic blend, with its mixture of codified law in the Roman provinces of the south and the customary law of the northern provinces of France.[14] As Glasson wrote in another of his studies into the relationships between French and German law, Roman law "was for us virtually French law".[15] It was only with the emergence of the nation-States in the late nineteenth century that the question of international sources of law was first asked. In this meaning, it is a modern question which began to be discussed long before 1958, as becomes clear when we turn to the period leading up to the Code of Civil Procedure of 1806 and the drafting of the new Code in 1975.

4.1.1.2 The New Code of Civil Procedure (1975)

The great change of political system brought about in France in 1958, from a parliamentary to a semi-presidentialist system, made it possible to draft a new Code of Civil Procedure, together with the reform of the judiciary.[16] The main change consisted in transferring the competence for drafting civil procedure from Parliament to Government.[17] I will not go into the details of how this important code was drafted.

---

[13] E. Glasson, *Les sources de la procédure civile française*, *op. cit.*

[14] Variations on this theme are many and diverse, even outside the legal field. See e.g. J.-L. Amselle, « Le multiculturalisme à la Française », *in Universalia 2003*, Encyclopaedia Universalis, p. 119–124, especially p. 120, which refers to the « *schème mental* » which, since the XVIIIth century, tends to oppose the double origin Frankish (coming from « Germanie ») and Gaulish (and then romanised) within the French people.

[15] E. Glasson, *Les rapports du droit français et du droit allemand*, Paris, especially p. 7.

[16] As to the details of how this code was drafted, see especially Cour de cassation, *Le nouveau Code de procédure civile : vingt ans après*, Paris, La documentation française, 1998. – J. Foyer and C. Puigelier (eds), *Le nouveau Code de procédure civile (1975–2005)*, Paris, Economica, 2005. – L. Cadiet and G. Canivet (eds.), *1806–1976–2006 – De la commémoration d'un code à l'autre : 200 ans de procédure civile en France*, Paris, LexisNexis, 2006.

[17] See Art. 34 and 37 French Constitution 1958. Jean Foyer played a role in this shift: see L. Cadiet, *V°* "Foyer", *in* P. Abareyre, J.-L. Halpérin, J. Krynen (eds), *Dictionnaire historique des juristes français, XII*ᵉ *– XX*ᵉ *siècle*, *op. cit.*

I would just like to highlight the role of international sources in this creation. Although they are not the most important sources, they nevertheless play a role. They are both direct and indirect: they can be presented as both direct with regards to normative sources (section "Normative sources"), and indirect when considering intellectual influences (section "Academic doctrine").

Normative Sources

Normative sources are the result of the tumultuous history of France and Germany during the nineteenth and early twentieth centuries. First, the French Code of Civil Procedure of 1806 was applied for some time in the Western parts of Germany as a result of the Napoleonic conquests, and these French rules were influential when the German codes were being drafted. I may say the same with regards to the codes in Switzerland, Austria and Italy.[18] Afterwards, some German procedures were applied locally in Alsace and Moselle, which became part of the German Empire by the 1870 war until the First World War. From 1871 onwards, the legal organisation of this French region was changed, the judicial professions were reformed and the Napoleonic Code was replaced by the new Imperial Code, the Ordinance for civil trials (ZPO, *Zivilprozess Ordnung*). The interesting thing is that, despite the return of Alsace-Moselle to France at the end of the First World War, some aspects of German civil procedure continued to be applied in the form of local law, traces of which still remain. The New Code of Civil Procedure is indeed completed by "an appendix relating to its application in the Bas-Rhin, Haut-Rhin and Moselle", whose Article 1 provides that: "The New Code of Civil Procedure shall be applicable in the Bas-Rhin, Haut-Rhin and Moselle, subject to any unrepealed specific provision and the following permanent provisions".[19]

The most amazing aspect of this is that while the New Code has in principle been applicable in Alsace-Moselle since January 1st, 1977, some of the local institutions were taken into account when the New Code [1975?] was drawn up.[20] There was, therefore, a kind of exchange, between the local law and the new National code. Thus it was that the New Code borrowed a number of rules from local law, itself a product of German procedural law. Some examples are the form of appeal, which is by declaration to the clerk of the court and not by writ of summons, the statement of lapse when the term of the procedural period has been reached, or the proceedings

---

[18] See R. van Rhee, « The influence of the French Code de procédure civile (1806) in 19th Century Europe », *in* L. Cadiet et G. Canivet (eds), *1806–1976–2006 – De la commémoration d'un code à l'autre : 200 ans de procédure civile en France*, *op.cit.*, p. 129 & ff.

[19] See G. Wiederkehr, *Jurisclasseur de procédure civile*, Fascicule N°63. – J.-L. Vallens, *V°* « Alsace-Moselle », *in* L. Cadiet (ed.), *Dictionnaire de la justice*, Paris, Presses Universitaires de France, 2004.

[20] See J. Foyer, « Le nouveau Code et l'unification du droit de la procédure », *in* J. Foyer et C. Puigelier (eds), *Le nouveau Code de procédure civile (1975–2005)*, *op.cit.*, p. 17 & ff. – P. Haegel, « L'harmonisation avec le droit local alsacien-Mosellan », *in* Cour de cassation, *Le nouveau Code de procédure civile : vingt ans après*, *op. cit.*, p. 35 & ff.

in non-contentious matters. These are clear examples of how foreign rules have become integrated into French law, after having been naturalised when Alsace-Moselle returned to France. As one may see there is a European history of civil procedure and this history is a circular one.

However, foreign contributions to French law are not just limited to this. We must also take account of the mutual influence between French doctrine and certain foreign ideas, conceptions or theories of procedure, and the effect this may have had indirectly on the creation of the New Code of Civil Procedure.

Academic Doctrine

The idea of reforming the Napoleonic Code of Civil Procedure emerged early on, although no political possibility to do it appeared until the 1958 Constitution. A commission charged with preparing a reform was created as early as 1862. It was followed by others, the work of which led to proposals for a revision, and even bills that never succeeded. However, it is interesting to note that these attempts led to great debates where for the first time, comparative procedural law began to be examined.[21] Even more interesting is the role played by Austrian law in this comparison, insofar as the Austrian Code of civil procedure was reformed in 1895 under the influence of Franz Klein (1854–1926). That influence can be seen quite clearly in the remarkable writings of Albert Tissier (1862–1925), a professor of the Faculty of Law of Paris[22] and author of one of the two great French books on civil procedure at the late nineteenth and early twentieth centuries.[23] In the years following the centenary of the French Code of Civil procedure, Albert Tissier expressed and defended the concept of a modern civil procedure that gave the judge an active role and increased its managing powers in the procedure.[24] This re-alignment of the judge's role went along with the new conception of the civil procedure, since the judge then took on a social active role, totally incompatible with the idea of the parties alone having a role to play in the proceedings.[25] It was partly in reference to Austrian law, which he often quoted, that Albert Tissier developed this thesis repeated subsequently by many equally eminent authors such as René Morel and Henry Vizioz.

---

[21] See A. Wijffels, « Le destin du Code de procédure civile (1806) en France », *in* L. Cadiet et G. Canivet (eds), *1806–1976–2006 – De la commémoration d'un code à l'autre : 200 ans de procédure civile en France*, *op. cit.*, p. 199 & ff.

[22] See J.-L. Halpérin, *V°* « Tissier Albert », *in* P. Abareyre, J.-L. Halpérin et J. Krynen (eds), *Dictionnaire historique des juristes français, XIIe – XXe siècle*, *op. cit.* – L. Cadiet, « Albert Tissier (1862–1925) A contribution to a European history of civil procedure », *in Festschrift für Rolf Stürner zum 70. Geburtstag*, München, Mohr Siebeck, 2013, p. 909–916.

[23] See E. Glasson, A. Tissier and R. Morel, *Traité théorique et pratique d'organisation judiciaire, de compétence et de procédure civile*, *op. cit.*

[24] See A. Tissier, « Le centenaire du Code de procédure et les projets de réforme », *Revue trimestrielle de droit civil* 1906, p. 625 & ff.

[25] See A. Tissier, « « Le rôle social et économique des règles de la procédure civile », *in* F. Larnaude *et alii*, *Les méthodes juridiques*, Paris, V. Giard & E. Brière, 1911, p. 105 & ff.

René Morel, in the 30s and 40s of the twentieth century, is the most obvious descendant of Albert Tissier. He is no doubt the person who coined the expression "private judicial law" when referring to civil procedure, meaning that civil procedure is not merely a practice, a collection of recipes, but law itself, comprising fundamental rules, as worthy of in-depth theoretical study as any other rule in substantive law.[26] He is also the probable inventor of the expression "guiding principles for trial" (*principes directeurs du procès*) by which today the New CPC [1975?] begins, in Articles 1–24.[27] Maybe the very expression "guiding principles for trial" comes from the German notion of *grund prinzipien*, through an illustrious American comparative law specialist of the early twentieth century, Robert W. Millar, and his "formative principles of civil procedure",[28] adopted as "guiding principles of French procedure" by René Morel[29] and subsequently by Henry Vizioz.[30] Although this genealogy is not absolutely certain, what is certain is that the notion of guiding principles for trial was then taken up by Henry Motulsky,[31] Jean Foyer and Gérard Cornu[32] who were the "Fathers" of the new French Code of Civil Procedure. When you realise that Henry Motulsky (1905–1971), who was a German Jew who fled the Nazi regime in 1933, completed his academic studies in Germany and had practised law in Germany before arriving in France, it becomes clear that the intellectual communications from country to country must undoubtedly have influenced the French civil procedure.[33] Not only that: Henry Vizioz brought into France the work

[26] René Morel suggested the expression « *Civil judicial Law* » : *Traité élémentaire de procédure civile*, Sirey, 1ère éd. 1932, No 4. It was Henry Solus who popularized the expression « *Private judicial law* » : Private judicial law course worksheets, Faculté de droit de Paris, 1940–1941.

[27] L. Cadiet, « Et les principes directeurs des autres procès ? Jalons pour une théorie des principes directeurs du procès », *in Mélanges Jacques Normand*, Paris, Litec, 2003, p. 71 & ff. – G. Cornu, « Les principes directeurs du procès civil par eux-mêmes, fragment d'un état des questions », *in Mélanges Pierre Bellet*, Paris, Litec, 1991, p. 83 & ff.

[28] See G . Rouhette, « L'influence en France de la science allemande du procès civil et du code de procédure civile allemand », *in Das Deutsche zivilprozessrecht und seine ausstrahlung auf andere rechtsordnungen*, Gieseking-Verlag, Bielefeld, 1991, p. 159–199, especially No 19–20.

[29] See R. Morel, *Traité élémentaire de procédure civile*, Sirey, 1st ed. 1932; 2nd ed. 1949, No 424–427.

[30] See H. Vizioz (1886–1948), *Etudes de procédures*, Bordeaux, Editions Brière, 1956, p. 441.

[31] See H. Motulsky, « Prolégomènes pour un futur Code de procédure civile : la consécration des principes directeurs du procès civil par le décret du 9 septembre 1971 », *Recueil Dalloz* 1972, p. 91 & ff. Concerning H. Motulsky, see G. Bolard, *V°* « Motulsky (Henri) », *in* L. Cadiet (ed.), *Dictionnaire de la justice*, Paris, PUF, 2004. – L. Cadiet, *V°* « Motulsky », *in* P. Abareyre, J.-L. Halpérin, J. Krynen (eds), *Dictionnaire historique des juristes français, XIIe – XXe siècle*, *op. cit.* – *Adde* C. Bléry et L. Raschel (eds), *Qu'est devenue la pensée d'Henri Motulsky ? Procédures* 2012, dossier 1 & ff.

[32] See G. Cornu and J. Foyer, *Procédure civile*, Paris, Presses Universitaires de France, 1st ed. 1958; 3rd ed. 1996, No 96. Concerning G. Cornu and J. Foyer, see L. Cadiet, *V's* « Cornu » and « Foyer », *in* P. Abareyre, J.-L. Halpérin, J. Krynen (eds), *Dictionnaire historique des juristes français, XIIe – XXe siècle*, *op. cit. Adde* B. Beignier, *V°* « Foyer », *in* L. Cadiet (ed.), *Dictionnaire de la justice*, *op. cit.*

[33] See F. Ferrand, "L'influence de la procedure civile allemande sur la doctrine de Henri Motulsky », *in* C. Bléry et L. Raschel (eds), *Qu'est devenue la pensée d'Henri Motulsky ?*, *op. cit.*, art. 10.

of Italian doctrine, not least that of Giuseppe Chiovenda, and Chiovenda on his side had been influenced by the Austrian codes of the late nineteenth century because this code was implemented in the north of Italia.[34]

It is therefore clear that although international sources, be they normative or doctrinal, direct or indirect, were not the main factor in reforming French civil procedure of the late twentieth century, they had a significant influence in the drafting of the New Code of Civil Procedure of 1975. The same can be said for the subsequent period. Indeed, French civil procedure has drawn even more from international sources since the adoption of the 1975 Code.

4.1.2 *The International Sources of French Civil Procedure Since the New Code of Civil Procedure of 1975*

When one looks at the international sources of French civil procedure since the Code of Civil Procedure was adopted, the most obvious feature is of course the procedural approximation within Europe. However, it is not completely homogeneous; it has different forms depending on whether we look at the European Union or the Council of Europe (Sect. 4.1.2.1). Furthermore, it is not exclusive. As in former times, the international nature of the sources of French civil procedure is not just due to normative harmonisation; the more indirect form of internationalisation, I mean cultural adaptation, must also be taken into account (Sect. 4.1.2.2).

4.1.2.1 Approximation

Within Europe, procedure may be harmonised in two ways, depending on whether it depends on the European Union (section "Harmonisation within the European union") or on the Council of Europe (section "Harmonisation within the council of Europe").

Harmonisation Within the European Union

The European Union has been built up by gradual enlargement since the Treaty of Rome in 1957; it is now a set of 28 countries (with Croatia). Within the European Union, procedure has been harmonised directly but only in parts.[35]

---

[34] See G. Chiovenda, *Principii di diritto processuale civile*, 3rd ed. 1923, Ristampa inalterata con prefazione del Prof. Virgilio Andrioli, Napoli, Casa editrice Dott. Eugenio Jovene, 1965, especially p. 18–25, who refers to A. Tissier, « Le centenaire du Code de procédure et les projets de réforme », *op. cit.* On Chiovenda, see H. Vizioz, *Etudes de procédures*, *op.cit.*, p. 169 & ff.

[35] See L. Cadiet, E. Jeuland, S. Amrani-Mekki, *Droit processuel civil de l'Union européenne*, Paris, LexisNexis, 2011.

The harmonisation has been direct insofar as it consists of rules applicable in domestic law without it being necessary to subordinate such application to legislative reception or transposition. For a long time, these rules were the result of international conventions concluded between the member States of the European Community. The most famous is the Brussels convention of 1968 on jurisdiction and the enforcement of judgments in civil and commercial matters.[36] Then European integration went one step further with the Amsterdam Treaty, which made relevant civil procedure the same throughout the EC, meaning that the harmonisation of that civil procedure takes the form of European regulations which are like laws directly applicable in the member States of the EU as soon as they have been published in the *Official Journal of the European Union*.[37] The European Court of Justice, whose seat is in Luxembourg, enforces them, and its decisions are binding upon all the national courts.[38]

Nevertheless, the European rules that were created since 1999 do not cover all civil procedure. They are limited in two ways.

First, the European rules do not apply to purely domestic disputes; they only apply to disputes involving at least two EU countries.

Furthermore, not all civil procedure is covered by these European rules, but only certain aspects, such as: jurisdiction and the enforcement of judgments in civil or commercial matters[39]; jurisdiction and the recognition and enforcement of judgments in matrimonial matters and the matters of parental responsibility[40]; service of judicial and extrajudicial documents in civil or commercial matters[41]; cooperation

[36] See especially P. Gothot et D. Holleaux, *La convention de Bruxelles du 27 septembre 1968 – Compétence judiciaire et effets des jugements dans la CEE*, préf. H. Batiffol, Paris, Editions Jupiter, 1985, and then H. Gaudemet-Tallon, *Les Conventions de Bruxelles et de Lugano*, Paris, LGDJ, 1993, which became *Compétence et exécution des jugements en Europe – Règlement No 44/2002, Conventions de Bruxelles et de Lugano*, Paris, LGDJ, 4th ed. 2010.

[37] http://eur-lex.europa.eu. See J. Normand, « Le rapprochement des procédures civiles dans l'Union européenne », *in* Cour de cassation, *Le Nouveau Code de procédure civile : vingt ans après*, *op.cit.*, p. 265 & ff. – See also Y. Gautier, *V°* « Espace judiciaire européen », *in* L. Cadiet (ed.), *Dictionnaire de la justice*, *op.cit.*

[38] http://curia.europa.eu.

[39] (EC) Regulation No 44/2001 European Council, 22 December 2000, on jurisdiction, recognition and enforcement of civil and commercial judgements, replaced by (EU) Regulation No 1215/2012 European Council, 12 December 2012 on jurisdiction, recognition and enforcement of civil and commercial judgements.

[40] (EC) Regulation No 2201/2003 of 27 November 2003 concerning jurisdiction and the recognition and enforcement of judgments in matrimonial matters and the matters of parental responsibility.

[41] (EC) Regulation No 1393/2007 of the European Parliament and of the Council of 13 November 2007 on the service in the Member States of judicial and extrajudicial documents in civil or commercial matters (service of documents).

between the courts of the Member States in the taking of evidence[42]; insolvency proceedings[43]; enforcement order for uncontested claims[44]; small claims procedure[45]; jurisdiction, applicable law, recognition and enforcement of decisions and cooperation in matters relating to maintenance obligations[46]; and jurisdiction, applicable law, recognition and enforcement of decisions and acceptance and enforcement of authentic instruments in matters of succession.[47]

We are still a long way away from a European judicial Code, the idea of which was mooted some years ago by the commission created and chaired by Marcel Storme.[48] However, the developments have not finished yet.[49] New European regulations are being drafted, especially on the creation of a European bank account preservation order[50]; it may be that the question of harmonising some internal civil procedures will be raised.[51] Indeed, the European Law Institute is going to explore the possibility of drafting European principles of civil procedure.[52]

Anyway, at the moment, approximation of national procedures applicable to domestic disputes, and not to international ones, is reached within the scope of the Council of Europe which is another international organisation.

---

[42] (EC) Regulation No 1206/2001 Council of Europe, 28 May 2001, on cooperation between the courts of member States in the matter of evidence in civil and commercial cases.

[43] (EC) Regulation 29 May 2000, on insolvency proceedings.

[44] (EC) Regulation No 805/2004 European Parliament and Council of Europe, 21 April 2004, on creation of a European enforcement order for uncontested claims.

[45] Regulation (EC) No 861/2007 of the European Parliament and of the Council of 11 July 2007 establishing a European small claims procedure.

[46] Council Regulation (EC) No 4/2009 of 18 December 2008 on jurisdiction, applicable law, recognition and enforcement of decisions and cooperation in matters relating to maintenance obligations.

[47] Regulation (EU) No 650/2012 of the European Parliament and of the Council of 4 July 2012 on jurisdiction, applicable law, recognition and enforcement of decisions and acceptance and enforcement of authentic instruments in matters of succession and on the creation of a European Certificate of Succession.

[48] M. Storme (ed.), *Rapprochement du droit judiciaire de l'Union européenne, Approximation of Judiciary Law in the European Union*, Dordrecht, Kluwer & Martinus Nijhoff, 1994.

[49] See S. Bollée, L. Cadiet, E. Jeuland, E. Pataut (eds), *Les nouvelles formes de coordination des justices étatiques*, Paris, IRJS Editions, 2013. – L. Cadiet, E. Jeuland, S. Amrani-Mekki, *Droit processuel civil de l'Union européenne*, *op. cit. Adde*, previously, A.-M. Leroyer et E. Jeuland (eds), *Quelle cohérence pour l'espace judiciaire européen* ? Paris, Dalloz, 2004.

[50] See Regulation (EU) No 655/2014 of the European parliament and of the Council of 15 may 2014 establishing a European Account Preservation Order procedure to facilitate cross-border debt recovery in civil and commercial matters.

[51] See e.g. F. Frattini, "European area of Civil Justice – Has the community reached the limits ?" *Zeitschrf. für Europ. Privatrecht*, 2006, p. 225 & ff. – Cf. M.-L. Niboyet, « 2005 : la coopération judiciaire européenne prend sa vitesse de croisière », *Droit & Patrimoine*, 2006, No 145, p. 110 & ff., especially p. 111–112.

[52] ELI-UNIDROIT Project: From Transnational Principles to European Rules of Civil Procedure.

Harmonisation Within the Council of Europe

The Council of Europe currently includes 47 countries, including countries such as Russia and Turkey which are Euro-Asian countries. In this frame of course, normative integration is much less important than in the European Union. The procedural approximation operates here at the level of very general procedural principles, based on the European Convention for the Protection of Human Rights and Fundamental Freedoms, which is a regional application of the 1948 Universal Declaration of Human Rights.

This Convention, updated regularly,[53] was signed in Rome in 1950 and ratified by France in the early 1970s. However, it took full effect in French law only in 1981, when France accepted that individuals have the right to stand before the European Court of Human Rights (Conv. EDH, art. 34), which is unique in that it is the "only true supranational court of appeal in international law".[54] In this system, French claimants may ask the French judges to enforce the Convention since, under Article 55 of the French Constitution, the French judge must apply the Convention. It is only where they do not obtain satisfaction before French courts, after the final appeal in the national system has failed, that they may appeal to the European Court of Human Rights. It means that the intervention of the European Court of Human Rights is thus subsidiary.[55]

French citizens may thus appeal to the European Court of Human Rights in Strasbourg.[56] This referral may lead to a declaration that the Convention has been violated and the Defendant State may find itself ordered to provide a "just satisfaction" to the injured party (Conv. EDH, art. 41). The effect of the European Convention on Human Rights may go further, at least in criminal cases, for which there is a procedure for re-examination of the national judgement violating the Convention.[57]

[53] *Via* protocol No 11 dated 11 May 1994, on restructuring of the control mechanism set up by the convention. See V. Berger *et alii*, *La procédure devant la nouvelle Cour européenne des droits de l'homme après le Protocole No 11*, Brussels, Bruylant, 1999. – J.-F. Renucci, « Le protocole n° 14 amendant le système de contrôle de la Convention européenne des droits de l'homme », *Gazette du Palais* 11–13 July 2010, p. 15 & ff.

[54] J.-F. Flauss, *V°* « Cour européenne des droits de l'homme », *in* L. Cadiet (ed.), *Dictionnaire de la justice*, *op.cit.*

[55] Conv. EDH, art. 35 : « *La Cour ne peut être saisie qu'après l'épuisement des voies de recours internes* » / « *Referral to this court shall be only after every internal recourse has been tried...* ». See J. Normand, « La subsidiarité de la Convention européenne des droits de l'homme devant la Cour de cassation », *in Mélanges Jean Buffet*, *Petites affiches* 2004, p. 357 & ff.

[56] http://www.echr.coe.int.

[57] For the time being this reexamination is not opened in civil and administrative matters: see Cour de cassation, chambre sociale, 30 Sept. 2005, *Bulletin des arrêts civils de la Cour de cassation*, V, No 279. – Conseil d'Etat 11 Feb.2004, *Mme Chevrol*, *Recueil* Dalloz 2004, p. 1414, conclusions Schwartz; Conseil d'Etat 4 October 2012, *Baumet*, No 328502, *Gazette du Palais* 24–25 October 2012, 19, comment Guyomar.

As a consequence of this European mechanism, the Convention is often invoked and applied by the French courts and we may say that the French rules of civil procedure have gradually been tested against the requirements for a fair trial.[58]

It is Article 6 of the European Convention on Human Rights which provides for a fair trial, and it is itself based on Article 10 of the 1948 Universal Declaration of Human Rights,[59] of which the European Convention on Human Rights is a regional application. Article 6, Paragraph one, states *in limine* that:

> *In the determination of his civil rights and obligations or of any criminal charge against him, everyone is entitled to a fair and public hearing within a reasonable time by an independent and impartial tribunal established by law. Judgment shall be pronounced publicly,* but the press and public may be excluded from all or part of the trial in the interests of morals, public order or national security in a democratic society, where the interests of juveniles or the protection of the private life of the parties so require, or to the extent strictly necessary in the opinion of the court in special circumstances where publicity would prejudice the interests of justice.

However, the principles for a fair trial are to be found not just in Article 6 § 1 of the Convention; there is also the prolific case law of the European Court in Strasbourg and the guarantees it has built up in the course of its rulings: mainly, the respect of hearing both parties (*principe de la contradiction*), the principle of equality of arms, the obligation for judges to give grounds for their judgement or the right to an effective enforcement of the judgement.[60] These principles are doubtless the basis of minimum procedural legality, common to all type of trials and to all European countries, whatever their legal tradition, only subject to the margin of appreciation left to each State to allow it to take account of the core of its national specificities. Thus the litigation, be it civil, criminal or administrative, and the various national laws, based on Common Law or Roman and Germanic law, are gradually drawing closer.[61] In other words, beyond the procedural approximation arising both from the European Convention on Human Rights and the European Union on the basis of common procedural principles and mutual recognition, a regional procedural law system is gradually and subtly moving into place. France and French procedural law are naturally a part of that.[62]

But there is something more.

A further step is taken with the mutual acculturation of European countries, even worldwide countries in some aspects.

---

[58] See L. Cadiet, « La légalité procédurale en matière civile », *Bulletin d'information de la Cour de cassation*, No 636, 15 March 2006, especially No 15, 27–28 and 31.

[59] « *All persons have the equal right to have their case heard fairly and publicly by an independent, impartial court, which shall decide either their rights and obligations or recognise that any criminal accusation against them is proved* » (Paris, 10 December 1948).

[60] See F. Ferrand, *V°* « Procès équitable », *in* L. Cadiet (ed.), *Dictionnaire de la justice*, *op. cit.*

[61] See M. Delmas-Marty, H. Muir Watt and H. Ruiz Fabri (ed.), *Variations autour d'un droit commun*, Société de législation comparée, 2002, especially p. 23 & ff: « L'émergence d'une conception commune du procès équitable ».

[62] See *infra* 4.2.1

4.1.2.2 Mutual Acculturation

Procedural harmonisation concerns legal regulation. Cultural adaptation concerns practice (section "Cultural adaptation via court practices") and ideas (section "Acclimatisation via academic law").

Cultural Adaptation via Court Practices

A good example of procedural acculturation is given by the application of the European Union procedural rules. As I mentioned earlier, the procedural rules in the European Union apply only to transnational disputes involving EU member countries. They are not applicable to internal disputes, since these disputes fall under *lex fori* alone.

However, the secondary effect or indirect effect of this situation merits attention. Inevitably, they are the same judges that will apply national rules of procedure in domestic cases and in European procedural rules in the others, even though they are foreign to their legal tradition.

One example. Under regulation n° 1206/2001 dated 28th May 2001 on cooperation between the courts of member States in the matter of evidence, French judges may be directly asked by a court in another EU country to execute an order to investigate in the special forms provided by the law of the referring court (Art. 10, 3°), and representatives of that referring court may even be present when the French court implements the measure of investigation (Art. 12, 1°). For instance, a French judge may be led to order disclosure or cross-examination at the request of an English court, may be in the presence of an English judge, even though these tools do not exist at all in French civil procedure. These occurrences may be of considerable pedagogical value for the judges involved, since they give them experience in foreign procedural techniques. These techniques are so to speak acclimated and that leads to gradual harmonisation of court practices, by mutual adaptation.[63] Transnational disputes may thus become testing grounds for international exchanges of court practices, and thus acclimatisation to new procedures, and ultimately, this cultural adaptation will gradually lead to harmonisation of national procedural rules.

There is another path for acclimatisation; it's academic law if I can use the expression to translate *droit savant* into English.

Acclimatisation via Academic Law

Ideas are another vector of procedural adaptation. The advantage of ideas is that they are free -in the sense that they are covered by academic freedom – and freedom is all the easier to express or write for a scholar, who, contrary to a French judge, has

[63] See D. Lebeau and M.-L Niboyet, « Regards croisés du processualiste et de l'internationaliste sur le règlement CE du 28 mai 2001 relatif à l'obtention des preuves civiles à l'étranger », *Gazette du Palais*, 19–20 February 2003, p. 6–19, especially p. 2.

no duty of courtesy. Ideas circulate freely, more freely than court procedures which, on principle, are limited by State sovereignty.

Today, as in the past, academic doctrine is therefore an indirect source of civil procedure, since scholars undertake critical analysis of their legal system, not least by comparing it to those in other countries. Comparative law here plays a traditional role in the making of laws and regulations, but it also – and this is more recent – helps judges make leading decisions. For some years, the French Cour de Cassation does not hesitate to use comparative law as a basis for its more important judgments.[64]

In addition to comparative law, academic doctrine also includes soft law which could ultimately become a sort of new *jus commune* of civil procedure, comparable to the work done in contract law. The work drafted by the Storme Commission, which I mentioned earlier, could be quoted in this respect. In recent years, major work has been done by UNIDROIT with its *Principles of transnational civil procedure*.[65] It was a great challenge, since it concerned the legal regulation of economic globalization[66]; the result is as great as the challenge. I will not go into the content of these principles here. I will merely say that they have been made possible by the gradual alignment of the procedural law in the various legal systems over the past few years, according to comparable economic and social necessity. The increased access to justice has entailed diversification and rationalization of courts' responses in most legal systems.[67] The drafting of the principles has given rise to several major discussions in France, involving most French specialists of civil procedure and international law.[68] The discussions naturally led to systematic comparison between these principles and French solutions in order to determine whether they were compatible or not.[69] This brought to the fore the trend in French civil procedure of encouraging a phase of case preparation at the start of the proceedings, grouping all

[64] See G. Canivet, "The Use of Comparative Law Before the French Private Law Courts", *in* G. Canivet, M. Andenas et D. Fairgrieve (ed.), *Comparative Law before the Courts, The British Institute of International and Comparative Law*, p. 181 & ff.

[65] ALI/UNIDROIT, *Principles of Transnational Civil Procedure*, Cambridge University Press, 2006.

[66] See E. Loquin, *V°* « Mondialisation », *in* L. Cadiet (ed.), *Dictionnaire de la justice*, *op. cit.* – C. Kessedjian, E. Loquin (eds), *La mondialisation du droit*, Paris, Litec, 2000, especially C. Kessedjian, « La modélisation procédurale », p. 236 & ff. And for a general overview M. Delmas-Marty, « De la mondialisation du droit », *in Mireille Delmas-Marty et les années UMR*, Paris, Société de législation comparée, 2005, p. 333 & ff.

[67] See F. Ferrand, « La conception du procès civil hors de France », *in* L. Cadiet, G. Canivet, *1806–1976–2006, de la commémoration d'un code à l'autre : 200 ans de procédure civile en France*, *op. cit.*, p. 277 & ff.

[68] See Ph. Fouchard (ed.), *Vers un procès civil universel ? Les règles transnationales de procédure civile de l'*American Law Institute, Paris, éd. Panthéon-Assas, 2001. – F. Ferrand (ed.), *La procédure civile mondiale modélisée*, Paris, Editions juridiques et techniques, 2004. – See also M.-L. Niboyet, « Ebauche d'un droit judiciaire transnational », *in* Ph. Fouchard and L. Vogel (ed.), *L'actualité de la pensée de Berthold Goldman*, Paris, Ed. Panthéon-Assas, 2004, p. 47 & ff.

[69] See F. Ferrand, « Le nouveau Code de procédure civile français et les Principes ALI-UNIDROIT de procédure civile transnationale : Regard comparatif », *in* J. Foyer and C. Puigelier (ed.), *Le nouveau Code de procédure civile (1975–2005)*, Paris, Economica, 2006, p. 439 & ff.

the interlocutory issues and deciding procedural incidents before the hearing (*principe de concentration*), so that only the relevant issues are presented in court.[70] It is another matter to suggest that the UNIDROIT principles could be turned into rules with the possibility of "contractualizing" their application in international disputes (subject to national law). This is currently being discussed. If it were admitted, it would in a way be an alliance between the doctrine and practice in creating civil procedure, a kind of return to the methods of the medieval School of Bologna. *Nova et vetera*. It is a guide for the evaluation of the destiny of French procedural law.

4.2 Destiny

I will not deal here with the future of civil procedure in the common sense. I just want to stress that the French law of civil procedure is faced with an evolution, which is not unique to it, but may be found in varying degrees in other countries.[71] Civil procedure is becoming more and more open to international issues. As an illustration of this destiny, I just wish to highlight the conception of civil procedure revealed by this evolution.[72] Maybe I will be provocative by saying that the traditional distinction between *commonlaw/civil law* no longer expresses an absolute reality. It seems to me outdated in the macro-comparative view of systems of justice (Sect. 4.2.1) as well as in a micro-comparative view of dispute resolution (Sect. 4.2.2).

4.2.1 In the Macro-comparative Framework of Justice Systems

On the macro-comparative field of justice systems, the *genealogical* distinction between common law and civil law is losing its historical sense.

Nowadays, the geographic proximity overrides progressively the diverse genealogy of national systems. I understand that the leaves of a tree never falls far from its roots, but I also know that we are different people from our parents, the result of a different genetic combination as well as of a different emotional and social story. In the Bible, it is written: "My neighbor beside better than my brother off.[73]" What the

---

[70] See especially S. Amrani-Mekki, E. Jeuland, Y.-M. Serinet and L. Cadiet, « Le procès civil français à son point de déséquilibre ? Décret No 2005–1678 du 28 décembre 2005 », *Juris-classeur périodique* (*Semaine Juridique*) 2006, I, 146.

[71] See J. Walker & O. G. Chase (eds), *Common Law, Civil Law, the Future of categories*, Toronto, LexisNexis, 2010, especially L. Cadiet, "Avenir des catégories, catégories de l'avenir: perspectives", p. 635–655.

[72] See F. Ferrand, « La procédure civile internationale et la procédure civile transnationale : l'incidence de l'intégration économique régionale », *Uniform Law Review/Revue de droit uniforme*, 2003–1/2, NS – Vol. VIII, p. 397–436.

[73] Salomon, *Le livre des proverbes*, XXVII, 10.

geopolitical evolutions in the world show today is the "structuration" of regional spaces for common development, economic and cultural, even political and social. I agree with Jürgen Basedow when he expresses the opinion that the increasing number of regional institutions seems to announce the shifting of global legislation from the international level to an interregional level.[74] The European construction is from this point of view well enough advanced in the field of integration and things will progress more with the accession by the European Union to the European Convention for Human Rights.[75] There are some other various attempts of this type, but they are not numerous and do not present the same degree of development, in West Africa,[76] South America[77] and, even less, in Eurasia.[78] Anyway we may applaud here the important work accomplished in Africa within the OHADA system and in Latin America by the Ibero-American Institute for Procedural Law. I am convinced that these regional regroupings are the way of the future. These regional organizations, it is particularly true in Europe, make up original systems of justice transcending the national systems of justice coming from different traditions. This new ensemble is something other than the sum of these juxtaposed parts. It is a new common law, not in the Anglo-American sense, but in the sense of *jus commune*.[79] The national courts are moving towards a dialog amongst themselves and the national courts are also discussing with regional courts, where they exist. Harmonization, hybridization, and coordination are the master words of this new manner of justice thinking, not in terms of family but in terms of space, for which my French colleague Mireille Delmas-Marty makes reference through the notion of

---

[74] J. Basedow, « Vie universelle, droit mondial ? A propos de la globalisation du droit », *in Mélanges Xavier Blanc- Jouvan*, Paris, Société de législation comparée, 2005, p. 223–238, who judiciously observes: « *l'augmentation du nombre d'institutions à caractère régional semble annoncer un déplacement de la législation mondiale du plan international vers le plan interrégional* » (p. 237).

[75] Traité UE (*EU Treaty*), Art. 6, consolidated that appeared *in Journal official de l'Union européenne*, No C 115 *in* 9 May 2008. The *Traité de Lisbonne* dated 13 December 2007 (*EUOJ* No C 306, 17 December 2007) includes a Protocol to be annexed to the EU Treaty which indicates the conditions for accession, notably to guarantee that the recourse formed by the non-member States and the individual recourse would be directed correctly against the member States and/or the Union, according to the case.

[76] Especially with the OHADA, treaty on the harmonisation of business law in Africa: http://www.ohada.com.

[77] MERCOSUR is not so well organized (http://www.mercosur.int), but a remarkable work is emphasized in the legal field by the Instituto Iberoamaericano de derecho procesal (IIDP): http://iibdp.org.

[78] See V. Yarkov and *alii*, « Harmonisation of civil procedural law in Eurasia », *in* D. Maleshin (ed), *Civil Procedure in cross-cultural dialogue*: *Eurasia Context*, Moscow, Statut Publishiong House, especially p. 335 & ff.

[79] See M.-F. Renoux-Zagamé, *V°* « *Jus commune* », *in* L. Cadiet (ed.), *Dictionnaire de la justice*, *op. cit.*

ordered pluralism,[80] that expresses the unity in the diversity, this unity from which Albert Camus said that it's not the crushing of differences but harmony of contrasts.

The European judicial space is thus a new frame of thinking which must be considered by itself, with its normative rulings and its jurisdictional practices, and not by reference to the genealogy of legal and judicial national systems that compose it. In order to reinforce their mutual acculturation, this unity is favored by the complementary putting into place at the heart of these regional ensembles, of networks connecting practitioners of all the State members, like in Europe with the European Judicial Network in criminal, civil and commercial matters (*Réseau judiciaire européen*)[81] and the European Judicial Training Network (*Réseau européen de formation judiciaire*).[82] Today more than yesterday and tomorrow more than today, the attorney, the judge and the professor of law must be attorney, judge and professor of law before being a national attorney, a national judge and a national professor of law. But I know that it is a long way. Guy Canivet, former chief Justice of the *Cour de cassation*, and currently judge at the Constitutional Court (*Conseil constitutionnel*), is right when he says that "judiciary power is by nature non-national, in the measure where it is less linked to a territory than to principles".[83] In the new social fights in favor of the protection of the environment, consumers, workers' rights and that of small investors, progress may be better expected from international activity of judges than from the long and difficult international negotiations between states.[84] A new form of management for transnational disputes is perfectly conforming to the regulatory role which falls to the state courts in the emerging new world order.[85] For example, from the procedural point of view, the development of international group actions marks a reinforcing of the social role of civil justice that appeared at the end of the nineteenth century in Europe, but until then confined to the frame of national judicial systems and in the traditional field of individual disputes.[86]

It is still necessary beyond these general considerations to pass from the macro-comparative level to the micro-comparative level and to attempt to qualify the new model, which emerges in the field of dispute resolution.

---

[80] See M. Delmas-Marty, *Pour un droit commun*, Paris, Editions du Seuil, 1994; *Les forces imaginantes du droit*, Paris, Editions du Seuil, II. Le pluralisme ordonné, 2006.

[81] See http://www.ejn-crimjust.europa.eu and http://ec.europa.eu/civiljustice/index_en.htm.

[82] See http://www.ejtn.net.

[83] G. Canivet, « La convergence des systèmes juridiques par l'action du juge », *in Mélanges Xavier Blanc-Jouvan*, Paris, Société de législation comparée, 2005, p. 11–23, especially No 27.

[84] See L. Cadiet, « Justice, économie et droits de l'homme », *in* L. Boy, J.-B. Racine & F. Siiriainen (eds), *Economie et droits de l'homme*, Bruxelles, Larcier, 2009, p. 537–567.

[85] See H. Muir Watt, « Régulation de l'économie globale et l'émergence de compétences déléguées : sur le droit international privé des actions de groupe », *Revue critique de droit international privé* 2008, p. 581 & ff, especially No 14.

[86] See L. Cadiet, « D'un code à l'autre : de fondations en refondation », *in* L. Cadiet, G. Canivet (eds), *1806–1976–2006, de la commémoration d'un code à l'autre : 200 ans de procédure civile en France*, *op. cit.*, p. 3–17.

4.2.2 *In the Micro-comparative Framework of Procedural Models*

In the micro-comparative framework of procedural models, the classical distinction between the inquisitorial procedure and the adversarial one does not take into account the contemporary procedural realities, just as the distinction between common law and civil law does not represent the current legal systems.

(a) The *reasons* that push us to progressively nuance this distinction are of a technical, economic and legal order and all refer to globalization. The conferences of the International Association of Procedural Law during these ten past years have often dealt with these issues.[87] Maybe we have not enough considered how scientific and technical progress, which knows no borders, models judicial procedures and make them move toward an international process that will leave less room to national singularities. Whatever our value judgment on this evolution, a revolution of paradigmatic type which is taking place, leading to a "deritualization", even a "delocalization" of justice, whereas traditional rites expressed the significance of local legal cultures. For instance, the desk judge, according to Judith Resnik's terms,[88] a judge of a computerized procedure, does not need a court house, which puts into question the fundamental principles of democratic justice, to begin with the publicity of justice. The technical norm models the legal rule. Giuseppe Tarzia, who was an eminent Italian comparativist, had not missed this point when he observed ten years ago that "the technical evolution imposes the fixation of common rules for the admissibility of the new means of proof, especially the electronic evidence. One is in the technical sector where the diversity of historical traditions cannot block the formation of a common law".[89] Computerization puts also into question the traditional distinction

[87] See L. Cadiet & O. G. Chase, 'Culture et administration judiciaire de la preuve', Rapport général au XIIème *congrès de l'Association internationale de droit judiciaire*, Mexico, 22–25 Sept. 2003, *in* C. Gomez Lara y M. Storme, *XII Congreso Mundial de Derecho Procesal*, PUAM, t. I, 2005. – See H. Rüssmann, 'The Challenge of information society : application of advanced technologies in civil litigation and other procedures', *in* W. Rechberger (ed), *Procedural Law on the Threshold of a New Millennium*, XI World Congress on Procedural Law, Wien, ManzscheVerlags- und Universitätsbuchhandlung, 2002, p. 205–249. – See J. Walker, G. Watson, E. Jeuland & A. Landoni Sosa, 'Information technology on litigation', *in* A. Pellegrini Grinover, P. Calmon (eds), *Direito Processual Comparado*, XIII World Congress on Procedural Law, Rio de Janeiro, Ed. Forense, 2007, p. 119–197. – See spec. S. Amrani-Mekki, 'El impacto de las nuevas tecnologías sobre la forma del proceso civil', *in* F. Carpi, M. Ortells Ramos (eds), *Oralidad y escritura en un proceso civil eficiente*, Universitat de València, 2008, vol. I, p. 93–133. – M. . Kengyel, Z. Nemessányi (Eds), *Electronic Technology and Civil Procedure. New Paths to Justice from Around the World*, Ius Gentium: Comparative Perspectives on Law and Justice, Dorndrecht, Heidelberg, New York and London, Springer, 2012, XV.

[88] J. Resnik, "Managerial Judges, Jeremy Bentham and the Privatization of Adjudication", *in* J. Walker & O. G. Chase (eds), *Common Law, Civil Law, the Future of categories*, Toronto, LexisNexis, 2010, p. 205–224.

[89] G. Tarzia, "Harmonisation ou unification transnationale de la procédure civile", *Rivista di diritto internazionale privato e processuale*, 2001–4, p. 869–884.

of oral and written proceedings to which the new technology cannot be reduced.[90] It favors the cooperation of the judge and the lawyers, in the measure where it supposes the definition and it puts into place common protocols of data exchange in contributing to the rationalization of the functioning of courts and procedures. Thus computerization appears as an important tool of judicial management, which translates itself into the emergence of a new economic culture of procedure.[91] In some way, economy rejoins science from which it shares assuredly a quantitative culture. Justice and procedure are captured by technology and by economy that may subject them to their own categories. Procedural efficiency has become a major challenge for legislative reforms and a main principle of the civil trial or, to say it in the English manner, an "overriding objective" (Civil Rules Procedure, Part. 1). This objective is not absent from French procedural law. For instance, since the start of the 1970s, French CPC limits the judge in his case management "to what is sufficient to resolve the case, in choosing measures that are the most simple and least onerous" (Art. 147 CPC). In this wake, an academic proposal to reform the Italian CPC, presented by Professor Andrea Proto Pisani, contains in its preliminary provisions some "*Principî fondamentali dei processi guiridizionali*", and especially an Article 0.8, entitled "*Efficienza del processo civile*".[92] Therefore, this tendency is certain. But it is also certain and important to underline that neither science nor economy are not an end in themselves. The only goal of procedure is a just solution of the case and before observing justice in the sentence itself, fairness must first characterize the procedure which drives to it. If a fair procedure does not protect necessarily against unjust results, there is little chance that an unfair procedure leads to fair results. Procedural efficiency cannot be achieved to the detriment of a fair trial. A justice of quality is a justice which succeeds to combine these two logics.[93] This quest is at the heart of the mission of evaluate European judicial systems confided to the European Commission for Efficiency of Justice.[94]

(b) Still it is necessary to precise identify *what is going to replace the traditional distinctions between the adversarial model and inquisitorial model* of procedure. My opinion is that the main stream of contemporary evolution in work is the emergence of a cooperative model of procedure within a plural justice system.

---

[90] See S. Amrani-Mekki, "El impacto de las nuevas tecnologías sobre la forma del proceso civil", *op. cit.*

[91] See L. Cadiet, "Le procès civil à l'épreuve des nouvelles technologies", *Procédures* 2010, Dossier, art. 8; "La théorie du procès et le nouveau management de la justice : processus et procédure", *in* B. Frydman, E. Jeuland (eds), *Le nouveau management de la justice et l'indépendance des juges*, Paris, Dalloz, 2011, p. 111–129.

[92] A. Proto Pisani, *Per un nuovo codice di procedura civile*, Il Foro italiano, gennaio 2009, V, 1 (estratto).

[93] See L. Cadiet, « Efficience *versus* équité ? » *in Mélanges Jacques van Compernolle*, Bruxelles, Bruylant, 2004, p. 25–46.

[94] www.coe.int/cepej.

The *cooperativemodelof procedure* expresses the idea that the trial is not the property of parties ("chose des parties") nor the property of the judge ("chose du juge") but both belongs to the parties and to the judge because parties and judge are necessarily led to cooperate in order to reach, in a reasonable time, the fair and efficient resolution of the dispute. The idea of judicial case management takes into account this idea and translates this idea into to an increase in powers of the judge in the respect of rights of the parties. Admittedly, the judge decides on private matters, but he decides in the respect of the law and in order to assure social peace. Moreover the referral to the judge puts into work a State institution whose financing by the national revenue cannot depend only on private initiative. This cooperative model of procedure is at the base of the main guiding principles for trial consecrated by the French CPC in 1975. It also gives its base to the reform of English procedural rules in 1998.[95] It is finally consecrated by the European Courts,[96] as well as by the UNIDROIT Principles of transnational civil procedure, especially in Article 11.2 which states that "The parties share with the court the responsibility to promote a fair, efficient, and reasonably speedy resolution of the proceeding".[97] A lot is said in this remarkable provision. I just want to add that this cooperative model is intended to be deployed through procedural agreements concluded between the parties, and even between the judge and parties, be it in the framework of each particular case, under the form notably of individual agreements, be it in the framework of general protocols, concluded between the courts and their usual interlocutors, especially the Bar. There are many illustrations of this growing contractualization of procedure and of justice.[98] The English system is not so far from France since the *Woolf* reform has introduced pre-action protocols for some type of litigation.[99]

This cooperative dimension of contemporary procedure is also reflected in a *plural system of justice*. By this I mean by this that dispute resolution is not limited to the solution of disputes by a court instituted by the law. Rather, the referral to the judge must not be conceived as a first recourse but as a final recourse, which must be used only when it is not possible to settle the dispute in another way. It is necessary to have exhausted all the possible avenues of dialog before going to a judge. It is a civic duty and a social responsibility for citizens to first exhaust other dispute resolution approaches. Speaking of a plural justice system aims to express the idea that for each case there must be applied the mode of resolution which is the most appropriate to it and that the law must facilitate provided that these methods present

[95] See J. Bell, « L'Angleterre: à l'aube d'une réforme radicale de la procédure civile », *Revue générale des procédures* 1999, p. 307–319.

[96] See e.g. CEDH, 2nd section, 3 Feb. 2009, *Poelmans c/ Belgium*, No 44807/06, *Procédures* 2009, No 81, obs. Fricero.

[97] ALI/UNIDROIT, *Principles and Rules of Transnational Civil Procedure*, *op. cit.*

[98] See L. Cadiet, J. Normand, S. Amrani-Mekki, *Théorie générale du procès*, Paris, Presses universitaires de France, 2nd ed. 2013, No 118–137.

[99] See A. Binet-Grosclaude, C. Foulquier, L. Cadiet, J.-P. Jean et H. Pauliat, *Mieux administrer la justice en interne et dans les pays du Conseil de l'Europe pour mieux juger*, Rapport pour l'Agence nationale de la recherche, Limoges-Paris-Poitiers, June 2012.

the same guarantees of good justice. For instance the right to a fair conciliation must respond to the right for a fair trial.[100] Of course it is necessary to insert in this panorama the independent public authorities especially the agencies for regulating the markets, when they have the mission to adjudicate disputes or to conciliate the parties, without forgetting the role played by the collective funds of guarantee in matters of torts, especially in traffic accidents and medical litigation that are contemporary forms of distributive justice located in the interstices of substantial law and procedural law. In all these forms of plural justice, their evolution invites us to consider that procedure cannot be thought as simply "ready-to-wear" but of "made-to-measure".[101]

Concerning the jurisdictional procedure it means that the system of justice must offer to each sort of case the type of procedure suited to it, be it summary or not, quick or not, adversarial or not. It must also be possible to pass easily from one type of procedure to another by means of "passageways" which permit a reorientation of the procedure without having to start from the beginning of the proceedings, according to the evolution of the case, that can become simpler or, to the contrary, more complex. This diversity, flexibility and reactivity are a good response to the complexity of contemporary societies, leading to the abandonment of the conception of a static and standard procedure, based on a rigid division of work between the judge and the parties, regulated by the legislation, to the benefit of a dynamic and diversified conception of procedure, resting to the contrary on a constant cooperation of the judge and parties, able to turn to agreements already evoked as a tool of procedural management.

Consultation, negotiation, agreement, convention and even contract are the keywords of the destiny of the French civil procedure as tools of a democratic justice based on the cooperation of citizens and State.

---

[100] See L. Cadiet, « Procès équitable et modes alternatifs de règlement des conflits », *in* M. Delmas-Marty, H. Muir-Watt & H. Ruiz-Fabri (eds), *Variations autour d'un droit commun – Premières rencontres de l'UMR de droit* comparé de Paris, Paris, Société de législation comparée, 2002, p. 89–109.

[101] See L. Cadiet, « Le procès civil à l'épreuve de la complexité », *in Mélanges Bruno Oppetit*, Paris, Litec, 2010, p. 73–94; « La justice face aux défis du nombre et de la complexité », *Les Cahiers de la Justice*, 2010/1, Ecole nationale de la magistrature et Dalloz, p. 13–35.

Chapter 5
The United States Federal Rules at 75: Dispute Resolution, Private Enforcement or Decisions According to Law?

James R. Maxeiner

5.1 Introduction

The Federal Rules of Civil Procedure were introduced in 1938 to provide procedure to decide cases on their merits. The Rules were designed to replace decisions under the "sporting theory of justice" with decisions according to law. By 1976, at midlife, it was clear that they were not achieving their goal. America's proceduralists split into two sides about what to do.

One side promotes rules that control and conclude litigation: e.g., plausibility pleading, case management, limited discovery, cost indemnity for discovery, and summary judgment ("dispute resolution"). The other side defends rules that open litigation to investigation of possible rights: e.g., notice pleading, open and free discovery, and limited summary judgment ("private enforcement").

Both sides focus on process. They overlook the essential goal of civil justice the world over: "to apply the applicable substantive law to the established facts in an impartial manner, and pronounce fair and accurate judgments."[1] They forget decisions according to law. Abroad we can see systems of civil justice that work, if only we

 Associate Professor of Law, University of Baltimore School of Law. J.D. Cornell; LL.M. Georgetown; Ph. D. in Law (Dr. jur.) Munich. I would like to thank for support and encouragement Philip K. Howard, President of Common Good and author of *The Rule of Nobody: Saving America from Dead Laws and Broken Government* (2014). I also acknowledge the support of a University of Baltimore School of Law summer research stipend. This essay originally appeared in 30 Ga. St. L. Rev. 983 (2014).

[1] Alan Uzelac, Goals of Civil Justice and Civil Procedure in Contemporary Judicial Systems 3 (Ius Gentium, vol. 34, 2014).

J.R. Maxeiner (✉)
Center for International and Comparative Law, University of Baltimore School of Law,
1420 N Charles St, Baltimore, MD 22101, USA
e-mail: jmaxeiner@ubalt.edu

C.B. Picker, G.I. Seidman (eds.), *The Dynamism of Civil Procedure - Global Trends and Developments*, Ius Gentium: Comparative Perspectives on Law and Justice 48, DOI 10.1007/978-3-319-21981-3_5

would look. Whereas the heroes of American civil justice, David Dudley Field, Jr., Roscoe Pound, Edmund C. Clark, and Edson D. Sunderland, looked abroad for solutions, today's proceduralists from the private enforcement side tell us to avert our eyes from foreign systems. Why? Supposedly our system in its goals is exceptional. In fact, it is not. We could and should learn from others.

The U.S. Federal Rules of Civil Procedure of 1938 outfitted American civil justice with tools to apply law to facts. They were an attempt to banish overly contentious litigation (the "sporting theory of justice").[2] Applying law to facts is fundamental to civil justice. Civil lawsuits resolve disputes between parties by determining legal rights and duties. By enforcing law, they make civil life possible in mass society.

The Federal Rules were not, however, a comprehensive reform of civil justice. They were limited to rules of court.[3] Although they bestowed on courts new power and authority to apply law to facts, they left key aspects of civil justice (e.g., court organization, jurisdiction, costs, appeals) unaltered.[4] They created no new institutions, such as a ministry of justice, which might have helped to make reform reality. They were accompanied by no codification of substantive law, such as David Dudley Field, Jr. sought when he led America's last major attempt to rationalize procedure.[5] Old ways persisted.

When the Federal Rules went into effect September 16, 1938, judges and lawyers did not change their practices.[6] Although judges had new powers and authority to formulate issues, they did not make much use of them. Although lawyers had new powers and authority to reach together the real issues between the parties, they rarely cooperated to do that. When eventually lawyers did use their new powers and authority, they acted not to streamline trials, but to unearth new causes and to conduct pretrial inquiries.[7] Applying law to fact receded as a goal of the Rules. Parties settled, not because the merits were against them, but because process costs and risks were too great.[8] Trials vanished.

---

[2] Robert G. Bone, *Improving Rule 1: A Master Rule for the Federal Rules*, 87 Denv. U. L. Rev. 287, 290 (2010).

[3] *See* James R. Maxeiner, *Pleading and Access to Civil Procedure: Historical and Comparative Reflections on* Iqbal, *a Day in Court and a Decision According to Law*, 114 Penn St. L. Rev. 1257, 1261–62 (2010); Jay S. Goodman, *On the Fiftieth Anniversary of the Federal Rules of Civil Procedure: What Did the Drafters Intend?*, 21 Suffolk U. L. Rev. 351, 360–61 (1987).

[4] Elwood Hutcheson, *The New Federal Rules of Civil Procedure*, 13 Wash. L. Rev. & St. B. J. 198, 198–99 (1938).

[5] David Marcus, *The Past, Present, and Future of Trans-Substantivity in Federal Civil Procedure*, 59 DePaul L. Rev. 371, 389–92 (2010). *Cf.* Jeremy Bentham, Scotch Reform 60 (1808) ("without a body of *substantive* law to stand upon, *a system of pleading is a superstructure without a foundation*") [emphasis in original].

[6] *See* Jack B. Weinstein, *After Fifty Years of the Federal Rules of Civil Procedure: Are the Barriers to Justice Being Raised?*, 137 U. Pa. L. Rev. 1901, 1907–08 (1989).

[7] *See* Rex R. Perschbacher & Debra Lyn Bassett, *The Revolution of 1938 and Its Discontents*, 61 Okla. L. Rev. 275, 286–87 (2008).

[8] *Id.* (identifying the goals of federal litigation as evolving from "deciding cases on the merits to merely disposing of cases as expeditiously as possible").

By 1976, serious problems were apparent.[9] Proceduralists fractured into two sides that continue to this day. One side focuses on resolving disputes[10]; the other focuses on social goals through private enforcement of public law.[11] Debates about revisions of the Federal Rules are about process and not about making decisions according to law. The former side restores the spirit of the sporting theory of justice and rewards zealous advocates[12]; the latter emulates the endless equity proceedings that exhausted estates and benefited only solicitors.[13] Neither side adequately accounts for the interests of litigants.

Neither side addresses the essential goal of the Federal Rules, which is the need of the public: routine application of law to facts to determine rights and resolve disputes. Neither side considers comprehensive reform of civil justice which would overhaul the Rules and reach beyond to restructure the whole system. No wonder that there is again popular dissatisfaction with the administration of civil justice.

The public's goal is stated in Federal Rule 1: "to secure the just, speedy, and inexpensive determination of every action and proceeding."[14] The founders of the nation stated the same goal already in 1776 when they declared everyone "ought to have justice and right, freely without sale, fully without any denial, and speedily without delay, according to the Law of the Land."[15] That declaration forms part of many state constitutions.[16] It is due process in the federal Constitution.[17] It is not a utopian goal but an attainable one. If only we would adopt modern legal methods.

A way to that goal is before our eyes, but we do not look. Abroad we can see systems of civil justice that work. But whereas the heroes of American civil justice, David Dudley Field, Jr., Roscoe Pound, Edmund C. Clark, and Edson D. Sunderland, urged us to look abroad for solutions,[18] today's proceduralists tell us to avert our

---

[9] Stephen N. Subrin, *How Equity Conquered Common Law: The Federal Rules of Civil Procedure in Historical Perspective*, 135 U. Pa. L. Rev. 909, 911–12, 974 (1989) (describing concerns over excessive costs and delays and discovery abuses raised at the 1976 Pound Conference).

[10] Jay Tidmarsh, *Resolving Cases "on the Merits,"* 87 Denv. U. L. Rev. 407, 408 (2010).

[11] Perschbacher & Bassett, *supra* note 7, at 291.

[12] *See* Tidmarsh, *supra* note 10, at 408.

[13] *See* Perschbacher & Bassett, *supra* note 7, at 291.

[14] Fed. R. Civ. P. 1.

[15] Md. Decl. of Rights art. 19. Other states adopted similar declarations. *See, e.g.*, Mass. Const. pt. 1, art. 11 ("Every subject of the commonwealth ··· ought to obtain right and justice freely, and without being obliged to purchase it; completely, and without any denial; promptly, and without delay; conformably to the laws.").

[16] Conn. Const. art. 1, § 10 ("All courts shall be open, and every person, for an injury done to him in his person, property or reputation, shall have remedy by due course of law, and right and justice administered without sale, denial or delay."); R.I. Const. art., 1 § 5 ("Every person ought to obtain right and justice freely, and without purchase, completely and without denial; promptly and without delay; conformably to the laws.").

[17] U.S. Const. amend. V ("No person shall ··· be deprived of life, liberty, or property, without due process of law").

[18] Richard L. Marcus, *Modes of Procedural Reform*, 31 Hastings Int'l & Comp. L. Rev. 157, 164 (2008).

eyes.[19] Why? They assert that our system is exceptional in its goals.[20] This is that story.

Section 5.2 reports dismay at the 75th anniversary commemorations: the Federal Rules do not work to resolve routine cases justly, quickly, and inexpensively.[21] Section 5.3 chronicles where we have been: how the Federal Rules were supposed to turn lawsuits from sporting contests into applications of law to facts to determine rights and how they are turning in a fourth era of civil procedure into dispute resolution.[22] Section 5.4 relates the epic story of the attempt to use the Rules for private enforcement of social goals.[23] Finally, Sect. 5.5 points a way to return to decisions on the merits by stripping away the blinders that keep us from learning from foreign civil systems that work well.[24]

5.2 A Requiem for the Federal Rules at 75?

> [A]fter seventy-five years of these Rules, have the Rules satisfied their own standard [of Rule 1]? … [H]ave the Rules in fact achieved the just, speedy and inexpensive determination of every action? Harold H. Koh (2013)[25]

The Federal Rules of Civil Procedure turned seventy-five in 2013. Judges, lawyers and academics around the country celebrated.[26] Above all, they extolled social uses of the Rules that have made it possible, in their view, for civil litigation to shape America. When the Rules were adopted in 1938, they were intended to govern routine dispute resolution.[27] Today the Rules sometimes are put to work for private enforcement of public law norms, for making public policy, and even for creating

---

[19] *See infra* note 234.

[20] *See, e.g.*, Richard Marcus, *"American Exceptionalism" in Goals for Civil Litigation*, 34 Ius Gentium 123, 139–40 (2014) [hereinafter Marcus, *American Exceptionalism*].

[21] *See infra* Sect. 5.2.

[22] *See infra* Sect. 5.3.

[23] *See infra* Sect. 5.4.

[24] *See infra* Sect. 5.5.

[25] Harold H. Koh, *Keynote Address*: *"The Just, Speedy, and Inexpensive Determination of Every Action?"*, 162 U. Pa. L. Rev. 1525, 1526 (2014).

[26] *See, e.g.*, *Law School Celebrates the 75th Anniversary of the Federal Rules of Civil Procedure*, University of Cincinnati College of Law, http://www.law.uc.edu/news/75th-anniversary-federal-rules-of-civil-procedure (last visited Apr. 24, 2014); *Renowned Scholar Arthur R. Miller and Distinguished Panel to give 18th Annual Pedrick Lecture*, *"Revisiting the Rules: Celebrating 75 years of the Federal Rules of Civil Procedure*," Arizona State University Sandra Day O'Connor College of Law (Feb. 20, 2014), http://www.law.asu.edu/News/CollegeofLawNews/TabId/803/ArtMID/7835/ArticleID/4642.

[27] Fed. R. Civ. P. 1 ("These rules govern the procedure in all civil actions and proceedings in the United States district courts ⋯ . They should be construed, administered, and employed by the court and the parties to secure the just, speedy, and inexpensive determination of every action and proceeding.").

new norms.[28] These social uses are said to define the character of the American system of civil litigation.[29]

Americans engaged in civil litigation either love the Federal Rules or hate them, depending mainly upon how they feel about the Rules' social uses. Members of the profession who live by the rules—judges, lawyers and law professors—largely love them.[30] Business people, who are subject to them, largely hate them.[31] Both sides presume to speak for the public who are neither legal professionals nor businessmen and who encounter the Rules only sporadically. Because civil litigation in state courts is in the mold of the Federal Rules, judgments of the Federal Rules are judgments of civil procedure generally.

For professionals, the social uses of civil procedure are God's work: the oppressed at long last have access to justice and to the levers of power.[32] These social uses give meaning to their lives; they let them work to change society for the better. For businessmen, these "social" uses are the Devil's doing: the clever exasperate the conscientious with frivolous and expensive lawsuits.[33] They confound legitimate commerce.

The two sides demonize each other.[34] One side sees no lawsuit besides those which are frivolous and whose costs are outrageous; it doubts the ethics of anyone who would promote such base behavior.[35] The other side sees no plaintiff's plea that is other than proper and finds no price that is too high to pay for "justice"; it questions the conscience of anyone who would reject such claims of right and put a dollar value on justice.[36] Both sides can point to thousands of cases that fit their respective views.

Neither side, however, addresses the millions of cases that do not fit either viewpoint. These are cases of people who do not vocalize about the Federal Rules. These people are the ninety-nine percent. They have no goal in mind loftier than

---

[28] Stephen B. Burbank, Sean Farhang & Herbert M. Kritzer, *Private Enforcement*, 17 LEWIS & CLARK L. REV. 637, 667 (2013).

[29] STEPHEN N. SUBRIN & MARGARET Y. K. WOO, LITIGATING IN AMERICA: CIVIL PROCEDURE IN CONTEXT 37 (2006).

[30] *See, e.g.*, Carol Rice Andrews, *Thinking About Civil Discovery in Alabama: Using the Federal Rules of Civil Procedure as a Thinking Tool*, 60 ALA. L. REV. 683, 685 (2009).

[31] *See, e.g.*, *About ATRA*, AM. TORT REFORM ASS'N, http://www.atra.org/about/ (last visited Apr. 24, 2014) (describing the costs of civil litigation and the economic impact to business).

[32] *See, e.g.*, James A. Bamberger, *Confirming the Constitutional Right of Meaningful Access to the Courts in Non-Criminal Cases in Washington State*, 4 SEATTLE J. FOR SOC. JUST. 383, 392–94 (2005) (discussing the fundamental right of individuals to have open access to courts).

[33] *See About ATRA*, *supra* note 31.

[34] *See* Stephen C. Yeazell, *Unspoken Truths and Misaligned Interests: Political Parties and the Two Cultures of Civil Litigation*, 60 UCLA L. REV. 1752, 1754 (2013).

[35] *Id.* at 1757–59.

[36] Arthur R. Miller, *Are the Federal Courthouse Doors Closing? What's Happened to the Federal Rules of Civil Procedure?*, 43 TEX. TECH L. REV. 587, 598–99 (2011); *see also How Our Civil Justice System Protects Consumers*, PUBLICCITIZEN (Apr. 29, 2002), http://www.citizen.org/congress/article_redirect.cfm?ID=7545.

routine dispute resolution according to law. They are the people who, when they have a claim against a careless contractor or a cash poor customer, think that the legal system should uphold their rights and return to them their claims without deduction. They are the people who, when they are sued, think that they should have a day in court to voice their views. They are the people who, when they are fired by their employers, think that they should have a chance to challenge the grounds for termination. These people are left out of the conversation altogether. Often, they give up without ever taking their cases to court. These people cast a pall on the revelries of the Federal Rules at seventy-five.

At the Pennsylvania conference, keynote speaker, proceduralist, and internationalist, Professor Harold Koh, asked the uncomfortable question: "Have the Rules achieved the *just*, *speedy* and *inexpensive* determination of *every* action?"[37] Koh, the former diplomat and law school dean, was too polite to say no. He answered his question: only partially.[38] Others were not so gentle. Professor Arthur R. Miller, who for litigators is practically synonymous with the Federal Rules (as joint author of the treatise on the Federal Rules, "Wright & Miller", as former rules reporter for the Advisory Committee for Civil Rules, and as premier proponent of social uses of the rules),[39] gave a less than stellar grade: "at best, B minus, and on an inflated grade curve, that's below the median."[40]

Other participants at other commemorations were less buoyant. At a University of Michigan celebration of Federal Rules Advisory Committee Reporter Ed Cooper, Paul V. Niemeyer, judge on the Fourth Circuit Court of Appeals, and former chairman of the Federal Rules Advisory Committee, despaired: "Unfortunately, any objective evaluation of current federal civil process will inevitably lead to the conclusion that the process is functioning inadequately in its purpose of discharging justice speedily and inexpensively."[41] Professor Burbank, the host of the Pennsylvania celebration, in a joint paper presented concurrently with his party, painted a depressing picture: "[T]he federal courts [are] unattractive to business and inaccessible to the middle class."[42] For the poor, there is no "functioning federal civil legal aid system worthy of the name."[43]

Today Americans doubt whether the Federal Rules can ever achieve the objective of securing "the just, speedy, and inexpensive determination of every action and proceeding." In 2013 the Federal Rules Advisory Committee proposed that Rule 1

---

[37] Koh, *supra* note 26, at 1526.

[38] *Id.* at 1527 ("In sum, even by the Rules' own standard, the interim report card seems decidedly mixed: Is today's civil process just? Sometimes no. Is it speedy? Relatively. Inexpensive? Not really. Are there determinations of every action? Terminations, yes, but not necessarily 'determinations.'")

[39] *Arthur R. Miller, Biography*, New York University Law School, https://its.law.nyu.edu/faculty-profiles/profile.cfm?section=bio&personID=20130 (last visited June 11, 2014).

[40] I was present for both the keynote address and Professor Miller's presentation and report these comments from my memory and notes. The presentation was not published.

[41] Paul V. Niemeyer, *Is Now the Time for Simplified Rules of Civil Procedure?*, 46 U. Mich. J.L. Reform 673, 673 (2013).

[42] Burbank, Farhang & Kritzer, *supra* note 28, at 650.

[43] *Id.* at 653.

be amended to provide, not just that the rules be "interpreted and administered" to achieve these goals, but that they actually be so "*employed by the court and the parties*."[44] Already four years before, the American College of Trial Lawyers counseled ratcheting down Rule 1's goals to seeking "*reasonably prompt, reasonably efficient, reasonably affordable resolution*."[45]

This is not what the public expects. It is not what it expected in 1938 when the Federal Rules took effect. At the time, Arthur T. Vanderbilt, President of the American Bar Association, reported: "If these new Rules are intelligently and liberally administered by the United States District Judges, with a view to promoting the administration of justice *in the interest of litigants*, there will indeed be a new dawn in the judicial history of this country."[46] Lawyers forgot the law and litigants. Dawn has turned to dusk.

5.3 Chronicles of the Federal Rules

> The aim is stated in the deathless prose of Rule 1 of the Federal Rules of Civil Procedure as the achievement of "just, speedy, and inexpensive" resolution of civil disputes. Paul D. Carrington (1995)[47]

5.3.1 Prologue

Most chronicles of the Federal Rules begin in August 1906 when Roscoe Pound, then the Dean of the University of Nebraska College of Law, addressed the annual meeting of the American Bar Association (ABA) on the topic: "The Causes of Popular Dissatisfaction with the Administration of Justice."[48] It is among the most famous addresses ever given to American lawyers.[49] Pound's speech resonated because the public *was* dissatisfied with civil justice.[50]

---

[44] Comm. on Rules of Practice & Procedure of the Judicial Conference of the U.S., Preliminary Draft of Proposed Amendments to the Federal Rules of Bankruptcy and Civil Procedure 281 (2013).

[45] Paul C. Saunders et al., Final Report on the Joint Project of the American College of Trial Lawyers Task Force on Discovery and the Institute for the Advancement of the American Legal System 4 (2009).

[46] Arthur T. Vanderbilt, *Foreword* to *Reports of the Section of Judicial Administration*, 63 Annu. Rep. A.B.A. 500, 519 (1938).

[47] Paul D. Carrington, *In Memoriam*: *Maurice Rosenberg*, 95 Colum. L. Rev. 1897, 1901 (1995).

[48] Roscoe Pound, *The Causes of the Popular Dissatisfaction with the Administration of Justice*, 29 Annu. Rep. A.B.A. 395, 395 (1906).

[49] *See* John H. Wigmore, *Roscoe Pound's St. Paul Address of 1906*: *The Spark That Kindled the White Flame of Progress*, 20 J. Am. Judicature Soc'y 176 (1937).

[50] *See Id.* at 178. For a list of some of the criticisms as they continued through the years, see James R. Maxeiner et al., Failures of American Civil Justice in International Perspective 287–99 (2011).

In his 1906 address, Pound diagnosed causes of dissatisfaction. He did not prescribe cures. But he did not limit his diagnosis to civil procedure: he looked at the legal system and its methods generally. Among the chief causes he counted: (1) private prosecution[51]; (2) the "sporting theory of justice"[52]; (3) judicial supremacy[53]; (4) case law in an era calling for legislation[54]; (5) backward procedure[55]; (6) archaic court organization[56]; and (7) putting courts into politics.[57]

Despite initial opposition, the ABA mounted several programs of reform that responded to Pound's critiques.[58] The reform that eventually led to the Federal Rules sought transfer of authority for making rules of court in cases at law from Congress to the Supreme Court.[59] As broad as was Pound's diagnosis, the ABA program was narrow. Its principal goal was not civil justice or even civil procedure reform. It was the creation of uniform rules for suits at law (not even equity) in federal courts to replace use of state procedure in federal courts.[60] The struggle, nevertheless, took more than twenty years.[61] Through these many years, the debate was about enabling the Supreme Court to issue court rules.[62] Most everyone assumed that the rules created would be good ones.[63]

---

[51] Pound, *supra* note 48, at 403. ("Private prosecution has become obsolete."). Common law methods failed to keep government and public utilities in line. They did not protect employees or consumers; *see* 3 ROSCOE POUND, JURISPRUDENCE 343–44 (1959).

[52] Pound, *supra* note 48, at 405 ("The idea that procedure must of necessity be wholly contentious disfigures our judicial administration at every point."). The question should not be, "[w]hat do substantive law and justice require?," but here it is, "[h]ave the rules of the game been carried out strictly?" *Id.* at 406.

[53] *Id.* at 407. American courts make public policy decisions as incidents of private litigation. *Id.* "[C]ourts are held for what should be the work of the legislature." *Id.* at 408.

[54] *Id.* at 408, 415. Case law, Pound wrote, is inherently uncertain, confusing, incomplete, and bulky. The times called for the development of law through legislation; yet American legislation was crude and unorganized.

[55] *Id.* at 408. American courts decide cases on points of practice leading to "[u]ncertainty, delay and expense, and above all ··· injustice." *Id.*

[56] *Id.* at 411–12. Rigid and yet overlapping jurisdictional lines (e.g., diversity) waste judicial resources and delay decisions of cases on their merits. "It ought to be impossible for a cause to fail because brought in the wrong place." *Id.* at 412. "Even more archaic is our system of concurrent jurisdiction ··· involving diversity of citizenship." *Id.* at 411.

[57] *Id.* at 415 ("Putting courts into politics and compelling judges to become politicians, in many jurisdictions has almost destroyed the traditional respect for the Bench.").

[58] *See generally* Austin W. Scott, *Pound's Influence on Civil Procedure*, 78 HARV. L. REV. 1568 (1965).

[59] *Id.* at 1573.

[60] Stephen B. Burbank, *The Rules Enabling Act of 1934*, 130 U. PA. L. REV. 1015, 1054 (1982).

[61] *Id.* at 1097.

[62] *Id.* at 1078 (describing a debate in the Judiciary Committee where proponents of the Rules defined what powers the Supreme Court would have to make rules regarding practice and procedure).

[63] *See* Richard Marcus, "*Looking Backward*" *to 1938*, 162 U. PA. L. REV. 1691, 1694 (2014).

In 1934, Congress finally adopted the Rules Enabling Act.[64] Pursuant to that Act, the Supreme Court chose Charles E. Clark, Dean of Yale Law School, to head up the project.[65] Clark picked Edson R. Sunderland, professor at the University of Michigan School of Law, as chief assistant.[66] Sunderland was principal draftsmen of the pre-trial provisions that became the most controversial features of the Federal Rules.[67]

In 1934, on the eve of the adoption of the Enabling Act, and before being picked to draft the Federal Rules, Sunderland set out a prescription for reform. Just as Pound *diagnosed* the whole of civil justice, so Sunderland *prescribed* almost as broadly: "the business of the courts," "effectiveness of court organization," and "adequacy of court procedure."[68] Under adequacy of court procedure, Sunderland included proposals for "ascertaining and designing the dispute" and "trying the dispute."[69] Both anticipate Sunderland's work to turn civil procedure toward decisions on the merits and according to law.

5.3.2 *Clark and Sunderland's Goal: Decisions According to Law (1938)*

Dean Clark and Professor Sunderland authored the Federal Rules of Civil Procedure of 1938.[70] The Rules are intended, states Rule 1, "to secure the just, speedy, and inexpensive determination of every action."[71] They were designed, Clark wrote soon after their adoption, to be a "simple and flexible system of procedural steps wherein the merits of the case are at all times stressed."[72] "[T]he rules are good or bad," wrote Sunderland, "in proportion to the contribution which they make to a speedy

---

[64] 28 U.S.C § 2072 (2012).

[65] Fred Rodell, *For Charles E. Clark: A Brief and Belated but Fond Farewell*, 65 Colum. L. Rev. 1323, 1323 (1965).

[66] *See* Stephen N. Subrin, *Fishing Expeditions Allowed: The Historical Background of the 1938 Federal Discovery Rules*, 39 B.C. L. Rev. 691, 714 (1998) [hereinafter Subrin, *Fishing Expeditions*].

[67] *Id.* (identifying Sunderland as the drafter of the provisions on summary judgment and discovery).

[68] Edson R. Sunderland, *Improving the Administration of Civil Justice*, 167 Annals Am. Acad. Pol. & Soci. Sci. 60, 60–70 (1933). Systematization of substantive law was the principal omission from Sunderland's prescription.

[69] *Id.*at 73–80. The other two points—only tangentially included in the Federal Rules—were "obtaining jurisdiction over the defendant" and "obtaining a review."

[70] Charles E. Clark, *Edson Sunderland and the Federal Rules of Civil Procedure*, 58 Mich. L. Rev. 6, 6 (1959).

[71] Fed. R. Civ. P. 1.

[72] Charles E. Clark, *The Nebraska Rules of Civil Procedure*, 21 Neb. L. Rev. 307, 308 (1942); *see also* Peter Julian, *Charles E. Clark and Simple Pleading: Against a "Formalism of Generality,"* 104 Nw. U. L. Rev. 1179, 1196 (2010).

and satisfactory decision on the merits."[73] To decide cases on the merits requires *deciding what to decide*: i.e., what is the applicable law and which facts are material and in dispute. Then can facts be found and law applied.[74] Deciding cases on the merits means making decisions according to law.

5.3.2.1 Pleading: The Old Way of Deciding What to Decide

To facilitate deciding cases on the merits, the Federal Rules had to overcome failures of two prior eras of American civil procedure, i.e., common law pleading and code pleading, in deciding what to decide. Common law pleading as designed, and code pleading as applied, failed because they forced parties to an issue, in the case of the former, or to multiple issues, in the case of the latter, too soon.[75] At the same time, for certain classes of cases, there existed a parallel system of "equity" pleading. It failed because it never got to an issue.[76]

Common law and code pleading expected that parties *by themselves* would come to an issue.[77] Through pleading, parties chose the law to be applied.[78] At trial, parties proved facts that would, in theory, decide rights based on the law agreed and thus would resolve their disputes according to law. In common law pleading, parties were to make a single issue, whether of law, or of fact, determinative.[79] In code pleading, parties had more leeway: they could raise multiple issues of law or fact. But they were to raise all issues in pleading.[80] Clark and Sunderland saw that was too soon.

Clark and Sunderland were pleading's critics par excellence. Pleadings, Clark wrote, "are only a mere step in trying to get to the actual merits of the litigation."[81] They serve, Sunderland explained, "only as preliminary forecasts of the real

---

[73] Edson R. Sunderland, *The Problem of Trying Issues*, 5 Tex. L. Rev. 18, 20 (1926) [hereinafter Sunderland, *Trying Issues*]; *accord* Edson R. Sunderland, *The Machinery of Procedural Reform*, 22 Mich. L. Rev. 293, 296 (1924) [hereinafter Sunderland, *Machinery*]; *cf.* Paul D. Carrington, *Ceremony and Realism: Demise of Appellate Procedure*, 66 A.B.A. J. 860, 860 (1980) ("[J]udges not only make law, they also decide cases—real cases ··· in conformity with law ···.").

[74] Charles E. Clark, Handbook of the Law of Code Pleading 2 (2d ed. 1947) ("Before any dispute can be adjusted or decided it is necessary to ascertain the actual points at issue between the disputants."); Henry John Stephen, A Treatise on the Principles of Pleading in Civil Actions 1 (1867) ("In the course of administering justice between litigating parties, there are two successive objects—to ascertain the subjects for decision, and to decide."); Maxeiner, *supra* note 3, at 1265 n.26 ("The issues of fact and of law must be framed clearly enough so that the tribunal knows what to decide.") (citing Fleming James, Jr. et al., Civil Procedure § 3.1, at 180 (5th ed. 2001)).

[75] *See* Julian, *supra* note 72, at 1184, 1186.

[76] Clark, *supra* note 74, at 16–17.

[77] Julian, *supra* note 72, at 1184, 1186.

[78] *Id.*

[79] *Id.* at 1184.

[80] *See id.* at 1186.

[81] Clark, *supra* note 72, at 312.

issues."[82] It is a truism of lawsuits that no one can predict with certainty what the process will turn up in the way of facts and legal issues. An issue that may not have been apparent at the outset can become central to a decision.

Civil procedure aims at correct application of law to facts. The process starts out with imperfect knowledge of which rules are applicable and of which alleged facts are true. Applying law to facts requires determining rules that are applicable to facts and finding facts that are material to applicable rules.

Determining which rules are applicable and finding which facts are material are *interdependent* inquiries: Until one knows which rules apply, one cannot know which facts are material. Until one knows the facts, one cannot know which rules apply. Settle the applicable rules too soon, and facts may be overlooked that would change the result if other rules applied. Fail to settle the applicable rules soon enough, and the process may detour to find facts that are not material under the rules actually applied and may not even be disputed. "The process of applying law to facts is thus one which requires going back and forth from law to facts and facts to law."[83]

Sunderland identified this back-and-forth process:

> [T]he process of developing issues is one which proceeds in stages,—first and most vaguely in the written pleadings; secondly, and much more explicitly, in the opening statements of counsel, and finally and conclusively in the production of the evidence. By the time the case is ready for the decision of the court or the jury, the real points in dispute are fully revealed.[84]

In the end, common law pleading and code pleading shared the same malady: apply pleading requirements strictly, and decisions are made unjustly without the benefit of all the facts; apply pleading requirements too loosely, and trials go off track or parties are "ambushed" by facts and law not previously disclosed that they are not prepared to meet.[85]

5.3.2.2 Pre-trial: The New Way of Deciding What to Decide

In the Federal Rules of 1938, Clark and Sunderland introduced measures meant to minimize the sporting elements of procedure and to promote deciding cases on their merits.[86] No longer would the parties alone choose the law and designate the material facts; the court would help them identify the legal and factual issues. No longer would the parties identify at the outset the precise facts that they would prove.

---

[82] Sunderland, *Trying Issues*, *supra* note 73, at 18.

[83] Maxeiner et al., *supra* note 50, at 90–91.

[84] Sunderland, *Trying Issues*, *supra* note 73, at 19.

[85] Edson R. Sunderland, *The Provisions Relating to Trial Practice in the New Illinois Civil Practice Act*, 1 U. Chi. L. Rev. 188, 200 (1933).

[86] Alexander Holtzoff, New Federal Procedure and the Courts 6–7 (1940); Sunderland, *supra* note 85, at 200 (stating that a trial should be "a well-organized presentation of the merits of the case instead of a contest in which each party attempts to overwhelm his opponent by unexpected attacks from ambush").

They would present facts, and courts would decide parties' rights under law and justice. Through pleading and pretrial discovery, the parties and the court would formulate the issues. Through summary judgment, trial, jury instructions, and justified judgments (special verdicts, findings of fact, and conclusions of law), courts would apply law and validate their applications of law to fact.[87]

The Federal Rules are most controversially known for relaxing pleading and for creating discovery.[88] These measures avoid premature determination of law and facts, but also were to promote expeditious handling of cases by eliminating false issues.[89] They were to see to it that, unencumbered by fictions and technicalities, parties provided courts with facts.

The Federal Rules are less well-known, and are less favorably known among professionals, for their measures for applying law and validating decisions, e.g., summary judgments, jury instructions, special verdicts, directed verdicts and court findings of fact, and conclusions of law. Just as relaxed pleading and discovery were to assure all the facts came out, these measures were to assure that issues were framed, trials were conducted expeditiously and efficiently, and decisions were reached on the merits.[90] These were to assure that courts correctly gave parties their rights.

The enigma of the Federal Rules was, and is, who shall formulate the issues? In common law and code pleading, lawyers did. The Federal Rules of 1938 offered a change: they authorized, but did not require, courts to formulate issues. That has proved to be a fatal flaw. So what were these tools? [91]

Finding and Presenting Material Facts in Dispute

The Federal Rules created a new system of presenting facts. The Rules were to be "avenues to justice and not dead-end streets without direction or purpose."[92] Under the new system, parties were not required to establish in their pleadings the precise legal ground of their claims. Rule 7, in allowing for only one form of pleading for all cases, eliminated the common law requirement that parties had to choose a form of action and therefore legal ground for recovery.[93] Rule 8, by requiring only "a

---

[87] *See* Maxeiner et al., *supra* note 50, at 200–06.

[88] *See, e.g.*, Holtzoff, *supra* note 86, at 6–7.

[89] Subrin, *Fishing Expeditions*, *supra* note 66, at 716–17.

[90] *See* Maxeiner, *Pleading*, *supra* note 3, at 1278–79.

[91] To avoid confusion with the Rules as amended, the Rules as adopted in 1938 are spoken of in the past tense, even though often the same language is found in the current rules. There are a number of editions of the Rules as adopted in 1938. Here, this article addresses the 1939 Federal Rules of Civil Procedure for the District Courts of the United States. Fed. R. Civ. P. (1939).

[92] Holtzoff, *supra* note 86, at 14–15 n.1 (quoting Laverett v. Cont'l Briar Pipe Co., 25 F. Supp. 80, 81 (E.D.N.Y. 1938)).

[93] Fed. R. Civ. P. 7; Julian, *supra* note 72, at 1184–86.

short and plain statement of the claim showing that the pleader is entitled to relief,"[94] made it impossible to oblige plaintiffs to present precise outlines of facts they would prove to establish their rights.[95]

The new system directed parties toward applying law to facts and away from immaterial matters. So Rule 8(d) provided that failure to deny an averment in a pleading requiring a response (e.g., a complaint) has the effect of an admission.[96] This was to focus parties on disputed points of material fact and expedite decisions.[97] Rule 8(e)(1) provided that averments "shall be simple, concise, and direct. No technical forms of pleading or motions are required."[98] It thus reinforced elimination of the forms of action and abolition of legal fictions that had accompanied them, and worked to produce decisions on the merits.

Rule 8(e)(2) allowed parties to state claims alternatively,[99] thus allowing them to account for the possibility that facts proven might fit different legal claims.[100] Rule 8(f) provided that all pleadings were to be construed so "as to do substantial justice."[101] Rule 9 relieved parties of pleading and proving matters that normally might be assumed to be true (e.g., (a) capacity of parties, (d) genuineness of official documents, and (e) validity of judgments) and assigned these as matters for opposing parties to challenge.[102] At the same time, however, it required that certain matters, i.e., fraud or mistake, be stated with "particularity" and that special damages (e.g., consequential damages or punitive damages), be stated "specifically."[103] Rule 9 thus promoted moving the conflict to material matters likely to be in dispute.

---

[94] FED. R. CIV. P. 8(a)(2).

[95] Clark did not use the term "notice pleading" in the Federal Rules and did not regard Rule 8's requirement as a mere notice, but as a "more *legal* requirement." Charles E. Clark, *Simplified Pleading*, 27 IOWA L. REV. 272, 278 (1942); *accord* HOLTZOFF, *supra* note 86, at 25 ("It suffices to plead conclusions, whether of fact or of law, provided the complaint is sufficiently definite so as to give fair notice to the opposite party of the precise nature of the claim.").

[96] HOLTZOFF, *supra* note 86, at 2627 (setting out Rule 8(d) as adopted in 1938); *see also* FED. R. CIV. P. 8(b)(6) (for the modern version of the Rule).

[97] *But see* HOLTZOFF, *supra* note 86, at 32 ("A statement that the defendant is without knowledge or information sufficient to form a belief as to the truth of certain allegations in the complaint has the effect of a denial. This is the case even if the facts are presumably within the pleader's knowledge.").

[98] *See id.* at 27; *see also* FED. R. CIV. P. 8(d)(1).

[99] HOLTZOFF, *supra* note 86, at 27 (for the Rule as enacted in 1938); *see also* FED. R. CIV. P. 8(d)(2) (for the modern version of the Rule).

[100] HOLTZOFF, *supra* note 86, at 25 ("In view of the fact that the pleader will be awarded that relief to which he is entitled, a pleading may not be dismissed on the ground that a party has misconceived his remedy and his prayer for judgment is not well founded, provided he is entitled to some relief on the facts averred."). "Inconsistent claims may be joined in the same pleading ··· . The pleader is not required to elect as between such claims." *Id.* at 26.

[101] *Id.* at 27.

[102] FED. R. CIV. P. 9(a), (d), (e); *see also* HOLTZOFF, *supra* note 86, at 27–30.

[103] FED. R. CIV. P. 9(b), (g); *see also* HOLTZOFF, *supra* note 86, at 29–30.

Rule 11 followed the precedent of code pleading, which used a requirement of signing pleadings as a way to prevent attorneys from making fictitious claims.[104] It thus authorized judges to strike pleadings that were without good ground or were interposed for delay and permitted them to sanction attorneys for willful violations.[105] Rule 11 would move parties on to matters material and in dispute. Rules 13 and 14 swept away old cramped counterclaim and third-party practice and invited consideration of all issues among all parties.[106]

Formulating Issues

The new system sought to suppress the sporting theory of justice and direct proceedings to issues material under substantive law and in dispute.[107] Rule 12(b) consolidated for early court decision dilatory objections directed to procedural prerequisites, i.e., subject matter jurisdiction, personal jurisdiction, venue, process, service of process, and sufficiency of the complaint.[108] Rule 12(h) required that most of these objections be made immediately or be forever waived.[109] Dispatching these expeditiously from the proceedings permitted the process to move on to decisions on the merits. Rule 12(c) and 12(d) permitted courts to decide cases on the pleadings, where the merits were already clear or failing procedural prerequisites fatal.[110] Rule 12(e) and 12(f) bestowed on courts authority to begin applying law to facts by striking pleadings, defenses, and redundant, immaterial, impertinent, or scandalous matter.[111] To decide cases required party motion; the court could strike pleadings on its own without party motion.[112]

Rule 15 underscored the tentative nature of pleadings as a preliminary step in getting at the material issues between the parties and in dispute.[113] Even at trial, should a party object that evidence presented was outside the pleadings, Rule 15(b) directed the court to freely allow amendment "when the presentation of the merits of the action will be subserved thereby."[114] It authorized the court to grant a continuance to enable the other party to meet the evidence.[115]

---

[104] Fed. R. Civ. P. 11(a), (b); *see also* Holtzoff, *supra* note 86, at 31.

[105] Fed. R. Civ. P. 11(a), (c); *see also* Holtzoff, *supra* note 86, at 32.

[106] *See* Fed. R. Civ. P. 13, 14.

[107] *See* Scott, *supra* note 58, at 1568–68.

[108] Fed. R. Civ. P. 12(b).

[109] Fed. R. Civ. P. 12(h).

[110] Fed. R. Civ. P. 12(c), (d).

[111] Fed. R. Civ. P. 12(e), (f).

[112] *Id.*

[113] Fed. R. Civ. P. 15.

[114] Fed. R. Civ. P. 15(b) (1938).

[115] *Id.*

Rule 16, then titled "Pre-Trial Procedure: Formulating Issues," was the key to making the new system of applying law work.[116] Where common law pleading and code pleading looked to the parties to settle the issues between them, Rule 16 enabled judges to take an active hand.[117]

In the new system, the parties were to use discovery to formulate issues for trial. So George Ragland, who provided the systematic foundation for discovery, wrote:

> [Pleading and discovery] effect a division of labor toward a common end, namely, the formulation of the dispute into a justiciable form by disclosing the material controverted facts and eliminating the uncontroverted and unessential facts in each case prior to its final presentation for decision. Discovery procedure and pleading approach the problem from the same basic standpoint: both are equally in harmony with the traditional Anglo-American doctrine of party-formulation of issues.[118]

Applying Law to Facts

To facilitate getting process to decide real issues between parties, as well as to expedite process, Rule 56 introduced the nearly new device of summary judgment.[119] Rule 56(c) required courts to render judgment "forthwith" if all materials on file and submitted showed that there was "no genuine issue as to any material fact and that the moving party is entitled to a judgment as a matter of law."[120]

The Rules as adopted aimed at trying cases according to substantive law and justice. They included many provisions intended to promote rational determination of law, finding of fact, and applying law to facts. The Rules expected judges to work to help jurors decide according to law. Rule 51 governed judges giving jurors instructions in how to decide.[121] Rule 49 encouraged judges to require juries to explain their verdicts through special verdicts and answers to interrogatories.[122] Rule 48(c) permitted judges to poll jurors to assure their adherence to their verdict.[123] Rule 50 gave judges substantial authority to decide issues or cases as a matter of law, both before and after jury deliberation.[124] Rule 52 required that judges justify their decisions in those cases where juries were not used.[125] Rule 38 provided that juries would be deemed waived if not requested at the outset of proceedings.[126] Perhaps because trials have fallen into disuse, these measures are only occasionally thought of today.

---

[116] Harry D. Nims, *The Cost of Justice: A New Approach*, 39 A.B.A. J. 455, 458, 522–23 (1953); Fed. R. Civ. P. 16.

[117] *Id.*

[118] George Ragland, Jr., Discovery Before Trial 260 (1932).

[119] Fed. R. Civ. P. 56.

[120] Fed. R. Civ. P. 56(c).

[121] Fed. R. Civ. P. 51.

[122] Fed. R. Civ. P. 49.

[123] Fed. R. Civ. P. 48(c).

[124] Fed. R. Civ. P. 50.

[125] Fed. R. Civ. P. 52.

[126] Fed. R. Civ. P. 38.

5.3.3 The Federal Rules Come of Age Lagging Justice (1959)

The Federal Rules came into force September 16, 1938.[127] Theirs was the misfortune that less than a year later, Europe went to war. As a result, the Rules had a stunted childhood. When they turned twenty-one, one of their supporters, Judge Alfred P. Murrah, lamented that "wartime controls and limitations on travel brought a decrease in litigation and there was little opportunity for the new procedures to become firmly rooted."[128] The end of the war did not improve things. "In their struggle to keep pace with [the great tide of postwar litigation], many courts either lacked the time or the interest to delve into what new procedural techniques might be helpful."[129] Events, the judge concluded, "had suppressed development of widespread knowledge of the Federal Rules and of the use of the pre-trial conference."[130]

In their teenage years, the Federal Rules suffered from a judgment common to the gifted young: "not performing up to ability." Already in 1950, addressing civil justice generally, "realist" Judge Jerome Frank let loose his polemic, *Courts on Trial: Myth and Reality in American Justice*.[131] Report cards finding problems with Rules started to appear soon thereafter. Judge Prettyman in 1951 directed his to "non-routine cases."[132] In 1953, Benjamin Kaplan, later first Reporter of the Federal Rules Advisory Committee, thought the conclusion unremarkable that "legal procedure still falls far short of reasonable and reasonably attainable goals."[133] By the mid 1950s, bad report cards were common. "Teachers" called conferences to discuss the shortcomings of civil justice. When the Rules were still but eighteen, in 1956, Attorney General Herbert Brownell, Jr. convened the first Attorney General's Conference on Court Congestion and Delay in Litigation.[134]

The year that the Federal Rules turned twenty, 1958, it might have seemed that just about everybody was dumping on the civil justice system, if not always on the Rules themselves. In February of 1958, Warren E. Burger, then recently appointed D.C. Circuit Judge, who later as Chief Justice would be the Rules' supreme critic, addressed a regional ABA meeting in a talk with a title reminiscent of Judge Frank's

---

[127] *Current Rules of Practice & Procedure*, United States Courts, http://www.uscourts.gov/rulesandpolicies/rules/current-rules.aspx (last visited June 21, 2014).

[128] Alfred P. Murrah, *Pre-Trial Procedure*, 328 Annals Am. Acad. Pol. & Soc. Sci. 70, 73 (1960).

[129] *Id.*

[130] *Id.*

[131] Jerome Frank, Courts on Trial: Myth and Reality in American Justice (1950).

[132] Judicial Conference of the United States, Committee Report on Procedure in Anti-Trust and Other Protracted Cases, 13 F.R.D. 62, 62–63 (1953) *in* Leon R. Yankwich, "*Short Cuts*" *in Long Cases*, 13 F.R.D. 41, 62–84 (1953); *see also* Dennis A. Kendig, *Procedures for Management of Non-Routine Cases*, 3 Hofstra L. Rev. 701, 701–02 (1975).

[133] Benjamin Kaplan & Livingston Hall, *Foreword*, 287 Annals Am. Acad. Pol. & Soc. Sci. vii, vii (1953).

[134] *Conference on Court Congestion and Delay Executive Committee*, J. Am. Judicature Soc. 91, 91 (1956).

polemic, "The Courts on Trial: a Call for Action Against Delay."[135] Chief Justice Warren followed up with a one-two punch of addresses in May at the annual meeting of the American Law Institute and in August at the annual meeting of the American Bar Association.[136] At the latter, the nation's Chief Justice told the group: "[I]nterminable and unjustifiable delays in our courts are today compromising the basic legal rights of countless thousands of Americans and, imperceptibly, corroding the very foundations of constitutional government in the United States."[137] If that was not stern enough correction, interspersed between the two Chief Justice's critiques at the ALI and ABA meetings, Attorney General Brownell's successor, Attorney General William P. Rogers, held the second Attorney General's Conference on Court Congestion and Delay in Civil Litigation.[138] The ABA, as it had to Pound's Address at the 1906 Annual Meeting, responded to Chief Justice Warren's admonitions by establishing a special committee (on Court Congestion), which even published its own monthly newsletter, *Court Congestion*.[139]

When the Federal Rules turned twenty-one, the American Academy of Political and Social Science delivered a rhetorical kick in the pants: a symposium titled *Lagging Justice*.[140] The symposium analyzed the long time it took to get to trial after pleadings were closed.[141] Participants identified the causes of lagging justice, less in the Rules themselves, and more in management, personnel, and, above all, in growth in the number of proceedings without adequate additional judicial manpower.[142] Pretrial discovery was not mentioned as a cause of delay, but failure to make full use of the pretrial conference of Rule 16 was.[143] Drafter, then Judge, Clark was invited to speak up for his offspring and did: Clark claimed that criticism was "overdrawn."[144] The symposium title "Lagging justice," he said, was "not apt."[145] Certainly his Rules had not led to problems: "the general success of the rules has been phenomenal. This is shown not only ··· by the uniform chorus of praise, but also by their adoption

---

[135] Warren E. Burger, *The Courts on Trial: A Call for Action Against Delay*, 44 A.B.A. J. 738, 738 (1958).

[136] Earl Warren, *The Problem of Delay: A Task for Bench and Bar Alike*, 44 A.B.A. J. 1043, 1043 (1958).

[137] *Id.*

[138] Henry P. Chandler, *The Problem of Congestion and Delay in the Federal Courts*, 328 ANNALS AM. ACAD. POL. & SOC. SCI. 144, 152 (1960).

[139] Milton D. Green, *The Situation in 1959*, 328 ANNALS AM. ACAD. POL. & SOC. SCI. 7, 8 (1960).

[140] *See* Glenn R. Winters, *Foreward*, 328 ANNALS AM. ACAD. POL. & SOC. SCI. vii, vii–viii (1960); Harry Kalven, Jr., *The Literature of Judicial Administration: Books*, 43 J. AM. JUDICATURE SOC'Y 210, 210–11.

[141] Kalven, *supra* note 140, at 210.

[142] *See generally* Roger A. Johnsen, *Judicial Manpower Problems*, 328 ANNALS AM. ACAD. POL. & SOC. SCI. 29 (1960) (exploring various ways to more effectively use the undermanned American judiciary).

[143] *See* Murrah, *supra* note 128, at 70.

[144] Charles E. Clark, *Practice and Procedure*, 328 ANNALS AM. ACAD. POL. & SOC. SCI. 61, 61 (1960) [hereinafter Clark, *Practice and Procedure*].

[145] *Id.*

in the states."[146] The Symposium did not consider revision of the Rules or an overhaul of civil justice.[147]

In defending the Rules, Clark held firm to the idea that they worked to decide cases on the merits by facilitating the framing of issues. His new pleading was not some form of notice pleading; it addressed the "very practical need ··· of uncovering the matters really in dispute well in advance of the formal and pretentious full-dress trial."[148] The various pretrial procedures—discovery, summary judgment, and pre-trial conferences—were working towards "uncovering the merits at an early stage."[149] The pre-trial conference was at hand "to settle the issues and admissions of things not questioned and generally to advance the case for trial only on essentials."[150] Clark provided the tools, but his optimistic views of how they would be used were not borne out by experiences.

5.3.4 At Middle Age: Popular Dissatisfaction (Again) (1976)

By the 1970s, it was clear that American civil justice was in trouble. Already in 1971 Maurice Rosenberg, himself a hero of civil procedure, pronounced American civil justice "failing" and lamented that "'Crisis' is the word most commonly used to describe the status of our judicial system."[151] Chief Justice Burger tried to cure the maladies. He called a conference for 1976 to address them.

5.3.4.1 The National Conference on the Causes of the Popular Dissatisfaction with the Administration of Justice ("The Pound Conference") (1976)

In April 1976, just months shy of the 70th anniversary of Pound's famous address in St. Paul, the chief justices of the supreme courts of the American states under the leadership of Warren E. Burger, Chief Justice of the United States, gathered for a

---

[146] *Id.* at 66.

[147] In 1959, Hans Zeisel, Harry Kalven, Jr., and Bernard Buchholz published the first edition of their famous study. HANS ZEISEL, HARRY KALVEN, JR., & BERNARD BUCHHOLZ, DELAY IN THE COURT: AN ANALYSIS OF THE REMEDIES FOR DELAYED JUSTICE (1959). In the Lagging Justice Symposium, they presented the study's results as calling for the most modest of change. Harry Kalven, Jr., *The Bar, the Court, and the Delay*, 328 ANNALS AM. ACAD. POL. & SOC. SCI. 37, 44–45 (1960); Hans Zeisel, *The Jury and the Court Delay*, 328 ANNALS AM. ACAD. POL. & SOC. SCI. 46, 52 (1960). Yet years later, Professor Carrington termed their study "a monstrous empirical assault on the institution of the civil jury." Carrington, *In Memoriam*, *supra* note 47, at 1902.

[148] Clark, *Practice and Procedure*, *supra* note 144, at 62.

[149] *Id.* at 65.

[150] *Id.*

[151] Maurice Rosenberg, *Devising Procedures That Are Civil to Promote Justice That Is Civilized*, 69 MICH. L. REV. 797, 798 (1971).

conference that took its name from Pound's own address: "The National Conference on the Causes of Popular Dissatisfaction with the Administration of Justice."[152] The Chief Justice asked his state counterparts: "[H]ow can we serve the interests of justice with processes more speedy and less expensive?" [153]

The 1976 Pound Conference in St. Paul was Pound's 1906 address redux—right down to the very venue in the Chamber of the Minnesota House. Except, where Pound had been a doctor diagnosing disease, the Chief Justice was less a doctor prescribing cure than a pathologist conducting a post-mortem.[154] Seventy years of law reform had spawned new law reform organizations such as the American Judicature Society, the American Law Institute, and the Federal Judicial Center, but, had not secured the just, speedy, and inexpensive determination of every action.

5.3.4.2 What Went Wrong?

Clark and Sunderland overestimated the likelihood of the bench and bar moving out of historic character.[155] The Federal Rules were to promote cooperation between bench and bar. Judges were to help bring adversary lawyers to issues, which courts would then try.[156] Instead, however, judges were reluctant to interfere with adversaries' control of process.[157] Lawyers declined to define material issues in dispute.[158]

Where Sunderland saw discovery as a way to eliminate undisputed issues, lawyers used the rules to discover new disputes. They used easy pleading and discovery to further their clients' interests "by all means and expedients, and at all hazards and costs to other persons."[159] Notice pleading was fine and discovery was even better. Why settle for an unpredictable jury result when one could use discovery to drive the opponent into the ground?

From lawyers' perspective the Federal Rules gave them tools for mining gold. Plaintiffs' lawyers, particularly those paid on contingent fees, could use discovery to create uncertainty on claims and recovery and thereby garner bigger recoveries and larger fees.[160] Defendants' lawyers, working by the hour, could make money looking under every stone for evidence and taking every precaution to meet every

---

[152] Warren E. Burger, *Preface to* The Pound Conference: Perspectives on Justice in the Future 5, 6 (A. Leo Levin & Russell R. Wheeler, eds., 1979).

[153] *Id.*

[154] *See id.*

[155] Paul D. Carrington, *Virtual Civil Litigation: A Visit to John Bunyan's Celestial City* 98 Colum. L. Rev. 1516, 1518–19 (1998).

[156] *Id.* at 1519.

[157] *Id.*

[158] *Id.*

[159] The quote is from Lord Brougham's famous description of adversary representation. Monroe H. Freedman, *Henry Lord Brougham and Zeal*, 34 Hofstra L. Rev. 1319, 1323 (2006).

[160] Subrin, *Fishing Expeditions*, *supra* note 66, at 741.

conceivable attack.[161] It is no coincidence that hourly billing became the norm when discovery became routine.[162]

Cases were not decided by who was right, but by who played the game better. The Federal Rules were used not to decide what to decide—the long elusive common law goal—but to broaden what to decide. The consequence was predictable: cases were never decided. They were settled.[163]

Even had the Federal Rules been used as intended, it seems unlikely that they would have been fully successful in demolishing sporting justice and substituting decisions according to law. They were procedure reform without court reform or law reform.[164] They did not address indemnity for attorneys' fees, jurisdiction, or appellate review. All three of these contribute to contentious litigation in America. The Federal Rules did not reorganize courts or judicial selection. They were not accompanied by systematization of substantive law.

As a result, the Federal Rules did not end gamesmanship: rather they changed the game from swift checkers to slow chess.[165] Worse, they turned contests into wars of attrition.[166]

5.3.5 The Fourth Era in Civil Procedure

The newest chronicles of the Federal Rules say that today we are in a new, fourth era in civil procedure.[167] The first was common law pleading.[168] The second was code pleading under Field's 1848 code.[169] The third was under the original Federal

---

[161] *Id.*

[162] George B. Shepherd & Morgan Cloud, *Time and Money: Discovery Leads to Hourly Billing*, 1999 U. Ill. L. Rev. 91, 94–95 (1999) (using an economic model to support the premise that liberal discovery rules under the Federal Rules were a "substantial factor" in encouraging the legal profession to move to hourly billing).

[163] *See* Subrin, *Fishing Expeditions*, *supra* note 66, at 706–07.

[164] Roscoe Pound, *A Practical Program of Procedural Reform*, 22 Green Bag 438, 439 (1910) ("It is not too much, indeed, to say that improvement in these three particulars [court organization, bench, and bar] is a necessary precursor of thoroughgoing reform of procedure.").

[165] *Compare* William D. Mitchell, *The New Federal Rules of Civil Procedure*, 61 Ann. Rep. A.B.A. 423, 430 (1936) ("[A] suit is not a mere game of checkers ⋯ ."), *with* William S. Bailey, *Successful Pretrial Motions in 10 Moves*, Trial, Mar. 2009, at 22 (examining pretrial motions as chess moves).

[166] *See, e.g.*, Frederick L. Whitmer, Litigation Is War: Strategy & Tactics for the Litigation Battlefield 1 (2007); Simon H. Rifkind, *Are We Asking Too Much of Our Courts*, 70 F.R.D. 79, 107 (1976) ("The practice-in many areas of the law-has been to make *discovery* the 'sporting match' and an endurance contest.").

[167] Scott Dodson, New Pleading in the Twenty-First Century: Slamming the Federal Courthouse Doors? 75–78 (2013); Stephen Subrin & Thomas Main, *The Fourth Era of American Civil Procedure*, 162 U. Pa. L. Rev. 1839 (2014).

[168] Arthur. R. Miller, *Simplified Pleading, Meaningful Days in Court, and Trials on the Merits: Reflections on the Deformation of Federal Procedure*, 86 N.Y.U. L. Rev. 286, 288–90 (2013) [hereinafter Miller, *Simplified Pleading*]; Julian, *supra* note 72, at 1184–85.

[169] Julian, *supra* note 72, at 1186–87; Clark, *Practice and Procedure*, *supra* note 144, at 61.

Rules of 1938.[170] And now, the fourth era is that of the Federal Rules as reformulated since the Pound Conference.[171] Since then, responding to dissatisfaction with the administration of justice, through Rules amendment and extra-rules court precedent, procedures have moved and continue to move to limit discovery, hasten dispute resolution, and turn judges into "case managers."[172] In this fourth era, the Federal Rules are to control parties' access to courts ("plausibility pleading"), limit private investigations (numerical limits on depositions and interrogatories), restrict parties' access to trials (increased use of summary judgments) and leave more cases to judges and fewer to juries (more directed verdicts, special verdicts, judgments notwithstanding verdicts).[173] The changes focus on controlling private invocation of litigation and its tools of discovery. They show little concern for deciding cases according to law.[174]

Defenders of the Federal Rules of the third era, the proponents of private enforcement, challenge the changes that create the fourth. They argue that changes work against access to courts and, in the end, justice.[175] They claim that critics exaggerate expenses; they say most are proportionate.[176] Yet, when most litigating lawyers acknowledge cases with amounts in dispute under $100,000 are not viable, it is hard for defenders of the third era to seriously assert that the Federal Rules achieve their mission of securing the just, inexpensive, and expeditious resolution of every case. Indeed, already thirty years ago Professor Miller himself wondered whether "the adversary system as we know it has become too costly and inefficient a device for resolving civil disputes."[177]

Defenders have designed a different defense. It is an epic story of how the Federal Rules have taken on an alternative social role of private enforcement of public law.

5.4 Federal Rules—The Epic

> The aim of the movement served by these heroes has been to make judicial institutions more effective and more efficient in performing their assigned mission. In America, that mission has been not merely to resolve disputes, but also to give substance to the Constitution by enforcing the rights of citizens. Paul D. Carrington (1995)[178]

---

[170] *See* discussion *infra* Sect. 5.4.1.

[171] Dodson, *supra* note 167, at 30–46.

[172] *See id.* at 77.

[173] *Id.* at 75–81; Miller, *Federal Courthouse Doors*, *supra* note 36, at 59194, 597; Craig B. Shaffer & Ryan T. Shaffer, *Looking Past the Debate: Proposed Revisions to the Federal Rules of Civil Procedure*, 7 Fed. Cts. L. Rev. 178, 17879, 197 (2013).

[174] Dodson, *supra* note 167, at 77.

[175] Miller, *Federal Courthouse Doors*, *supra* note 36, at 59194, 597

[176] *See id.* at 598.

[177] Arthur R. Miller, *The Adversary System: Dinosaur or Phoenix*, 69 Minn. L. Rev. 1, 20 (1984).

[178] Carrington, *In Memoriam*, *supra* note 47, at 1901 ("Its father could be said to be Jeremy Bentham. Its seldom-sung American heroes include David Dudley Field, Roscoe Pound, Harry Wigmore, Charles Clark, and Maurice Rosenberg.").

Today, when American proceduralists celebrate, they fete the heroic years: the 1960s and the early 1970s. Those were years of civil rights lawmaking, of mass tort litigation, and of private enforcement of public norms.[179] It was an era when one could believe in "using the civil litigation system to deliver the promise of the law to those who were otherwise without much power in society."[180] Proceduralists lament later Supreme Court decisions that have turned those dynamic bright summer days of hope into desultory dark winter days of discontent. They ask, are the courthouse doors closing?[181]

Proceduralists tell an epic story of good versus evil that continues to this day. "[T]hose who oppose civil justice," former reporter Professor Paul D. Carrington writes, "are numerous, ubiquitous, and persistent.··· Every victory for the cause is therefore temporary, even evanescent, because each is predestined to evoke a response by the devils within us all. The forces of darkness return."[182]

Who can better tell that epic with more credibility and eloquence than Professor Carrington and his compatriots Professors Arthur R. Miller and Richard L. Marcus: three of only four living present and former reporters for the Advisory Committee of the Rules of Civil Procedure?[183] Their good will, decency, idealism, and ideals inspire us to achieve justice for all. They are the synoptic writers of the epic that is the Federal Rules: Miller, Marcus, and Paul Carrington.[184] Their epic is informed by important historical work of proceduralists of the last quarter century.

5.4.1 Founders' Era (1938–1959)

The epic begins a long time ago, a time out of mind, a time that none of us remembers: 1938. It was a time of great depression. Civil justice was debased by "debilitating technicalities and rigidity that characterized the prior English and American

---

[179] D. Michael Risinger, *Wolves and Sheep, Predators and Scavengers, or Why I Left Civil Procedure (Not With a Bang, but a Whimper)*, 60 UCLA L. Rev. 1620, 1631 (2013).

[180] *Id.* at 1622–23. *See generally* James Gordley, *The Meaning of Equal Access to Legal Services*, 10 Cornell Int'l L.J. 220 (1977).

[181] Dodson, *supra* note 167; Miller, *Federal Courthouse Doors*, *supra* note 36, at 587; Weinstein, *supra* note 6, at 1907 (speaking of an "anti-access movement").

[182] Carrington, *In Memoriam*, *supra* note 47, at 1901.

[183] *See* Advisory Comm. on Civil Rules, April 1011, 2014 Meeting 7 (2014), *available at* http://www.uscourts.gov/uscourts/RulesAndPolicies/rules/Agenda%20Books/Civil/CV2014-04.pdf (listing Richard L. Marcus and Edward H. Cooper as current reporters); *Federal Committee on Rules of Practice and Procedure Opens "Duke Rules Package" for Comment*, Duke Law School, (Aug. 22, 2013), http://law.duke.edu/news/federal-committee-rules-practice-and-procedure-opens-duke-rules-package-comment/ (describing Arthur R. Miller and Paul D. Carrington as former reporters).

[184] The fourth, Edward H. Cooper, so far as I know, does not disagree with the synoptic epic Miller, Marcus, and Carrington; but he has not told his views in publications known to the author.

procedural systems—that is, the common law forms of action and then the codes."[185] Disputes were resolved in sporting contests by "tricks or traps or obfuscation."[186]

A new world dawned September 16, 1938 when the Federal Rules of Civil Procedure took effect.[187] It was the "Golden Age of Rulemaking" when "giants trod the soil of rulemaking. Drawing from the legacy of Jeremy Bentham, David Dudley Field, and Roscoe Pound, a small band of drafters created the Federal Rules of Civil Procedure in the late 1930s and changed the American procedural landscape."[188] These giants, "the distinguished proceduralists who drafted the Federal Rules believed in citizen access to the courts and in the resolution of disputes on their merits."[189] They could do that. 1938 was a simpler time. It was easier to resolve cases on their merits. Litigation was about "relatively simple matters."[190]

The epic writers gloss over what Chief Justices Warren and Burger saw by the 1970s: the civil justice system was failing to meet the demands increased litigation was placing on it.[191] Instead, they prefer to remember from the first two decades of the Federal Rules how the Supreme Court supercharged the rules governing pleading and discovery. In *Conley v. Gibson*, the Court found almost any allegation might satisfy Rule 8's requirements for a complaint.[192] In *Hickman v. Taylor*, it approved use of discovery "to obtain the fullest possible knowledge of the issues."[193]

5.4.2 *Rights Revolution (the 1960s)*

How things have changed since 1959! "Today's worlds of civil rights, employment discrimination, environmental, consumer protection, pension, high-tech, and product safety litigation largely did not exist when the Federal Rules were formulated .... [T]here were not even law school courses on those subjects in the 1950s."[194] In the 1960s, there were notable increases in employment discrimination cases, and in

---

[185] Miller, *Simplified Pleading*, *supra* note 168, at 288–89.

[186] *Id.* at 288; Paul D. Carrington, *A New Confederacy? Disunionsim in the Federal Courts*, 45 Duke L.J. 929, 932 (1996) ("[N]ineteenth century civil procedure was a sport of chance in which the substantive merits of claims and defenses played a minor role.").

[187] Lately Professor Marcus has doubted whether it was quite so new. *See* Richard Marcus, *Bomb Throwing, Democratic Theory, and Basic Values—A New Path to Procedural Harmonization?*, 107 Nw. U. L. Rev. 475, 481 (2013).

[188] Marcus, *Modes*, *supra* note 18, at 157; *accord* Paul D. Carrington, *Politics and Civil Procedure Rulemaking: Reflections on Experience*, 60 Duke L.J. 597, 604 (2010) [hereinafter Carrington, *Politics*] (noting the "eminent lawyers" who were not quite giants).

[189] Miller, *Simplified Pleading*, *supra* note 168, at 288; *accord* Carrington, *supra* note 188, at 604.

[190] Miller, *Simplified Pleading*, *supra* note 168, at 290.

[191] *Id.* at 360–61.

[192] Conley v. Gibson, 355 U.S. 41, 47–48 (1957).

[193] Hickman v. Taylor, 329 U.S. 495, 501 (1947).

[194] Miller, *Simplified Pleading*, *supra* note 168, at 292.

assertions of new rights by consumers, and by those seeking to enforce complex environmental laws.[195]

"[L]awyers, fully armed in 1938 with the tools of discovery, could effectively uncover falsehood and wrongdoing in civil cases."[196] This was fortuitous drafting by the giants, for private enforcement had not been a guiding goal of their work in 1938. "In retrospect, it seems that the private enforcement orientation grew somewhat organically over the twentieth century."[197] It was a new development in American history that emerged largely only after World War II.

By the time the rights revolution rolled around, the Federal Rules as interpreted enabled parties to "conduct private investigations of business practices threatening harm to consumers, passengers, tenants, workers, patients, or franchisees."[198] 1970 saw, by Rules amendment, abolition of the Rule 34(a) requirement that parties needed good cause and a judicial order to obtain discovery of documents.[199] By then judges could "make law and policy to an extent not regarded as permissible in most other nations."[200]

5.4.3 Corporate Counterrevolution

Not everyone appreciated the super-charged Federal Rules. Against the private enforcement of public policies came, according to the epic, "a backlash that favors corporate and governmental interests against the claims of individual citizens."[201] The backlash has been hydra-headed—taking many forms—all promoted by a corporate interest-captured Supreme Court: rule reformations, new applications of previously little used rules, "retiring" of precedents that had super-charged rules for private enforcement, and new legislation through "interpretation."[202]

The epic writers tell how changes in the Federal Rules, both by amendment and by interpretation, threaten the private enforcement goal. "Not surprisingly,"

---

[195] Carrington, *Politics*, *supra* note 188, at 601–02.

[196] Paul D. Carrington, *Moths to the Light*: *The Dubious Attractions of American Law*, 46 U. Kan. L. Rev 673, 684 (1998) [hereinafter Carrington, *Moths to the Light*]; Carrington, *Politics*, *supra* note 188, at 605 ("To the extent that the Progressive reformers achieved their aims, private citizens gained the ability to enforce many diverse laws enacted or proclaimed to protect public interests as well as their own.").

[197] Marcus, *American Exceptionalism*, *supra* note 20, at 139.

[198] Carrington, *Politics*, *supra* note 188, at 610.

[199] Advisory Committee on Civil Rules, Preliminary Draft of the Proposed Amendments to the Discovery Rules app. B (1969), *available at* http://www.uscourts.gov/uscourts/RulesAndPolicies/rules/Reports/CV07-1969.pdf.

[200] Paul D. Carrington, *The American Tradition of Private Law Enforcement*, 5 German L.J. 1413, 1419 (2004) [hereinafter Carrington, *American*].

[201] Miller, *Simplified Pleading*, *supra* note 168, at 302.

[202] *See id.* at 302–06, 309.

Professor Marcus writes, "those who challenge the private enforcement goal in the U.S. also seem to want to dismantle the procedural apparatus that supports it."[203] Professor Miller writes of eight steps in "deformation" of procedure in federal courts: (a) reformulation of pretrial conferences; (b) summary judgment; (c) expert evidence; (d) class actions; (e) the Federal Arbitration Act; (f) pleading requirements; (g) personal jurisdiction; and (h) discovery.[204] Professor Carrington says that the Supreme Court "has evidenced a probusiness shift ··· to weaken private enforcement of public laws regulating business."[205] It has put its thumb on the scale in favor of business. The aspiration of "equal justice under law" has been supplanted, says Professor Miller, by intentions "to impede meaningful citizen access to our justice system or to impair the enforcement of our public policies and constitutional principles by constructing a procedural Great Wall of China or Maginot Line around the courtrooms in our courthouses."[206]

But the epic has not won over the public or the profession. Dispute resolution leads.

5.5 The Future on the Merits?

> It is sometimes assumed that the business of courts is merely dispute resolution, by whatever means may be effective to bring repose … I assume that this pre-Enlightenment purpose will not become the norm, and that we will continue to expect courts to decide cases by applying law to fact. Paul D. Carrington (1998)[207]

Professor Carrington has it right: courts exist to decide cases by applying law to facts. He quips: Mr. Legality points the way to the "Celestial City."[208] That's smart, but no surprise. The essential goal of every modern system of civil justice is the application of law to facts to determine rights and resolve disputes according to law and justice.[209] In this way, legal systems not only do right in individual cases, they make social life possible. They validate a nation's laws and facilitate its peoples' compliance with law.

---

[203] Marcus, *American Exceptionalism*, *supra* note 20, at 139.

[204] Miller, *Simplified Pleading*, *supra* note 168, at 287.

[205] Carrington, *Politics*, *supra* note 188, at 609.

[206] Miller, *Simplified Pleading*, *supra* note 168, at 372.

[207] Carrington, *supra* note 155, at 1522–23.

[208] *See id.* at 1517.

[209] Uzelac, *supra* note 1, at 3 ("It would be easy to state the obvious and repeat that in all justice systems of the world the role of civil justice is to apply the applicable substantive law to the established facts in an impartial manner, and pronounce fair and accurate judgments."). This collection includes twelve papers on the goals of civil justice in an approximately like number of countries. The paper from the United States is by Professor Marcus.

5.5.1 Learning from Foreign Systems

The Federal Rules fail because they do not apply law to fact. That is unfortunate, but it is no good reason to give up on the essential goal of civil justice systems. Other systems show it to be an attainable goal. Learn from others! There's nothing new in that. It is a mantra of our federal system, that every state is a laboratory for other states.[210] OK. Let's do it. There's no good reason to look at the work of only American laboratories. Sunderland himself called for us to see in civil law systems "the most valuable data upon which to base our own experiments in procedural reform."[211]

One system that we might learn well from is the German. It is among the finest and most admired in the world.[212] The German system takes seriously applying law to facts. In a nutshell,[213] here is why it works well:

Parties present facts to courts; courts find facts and determine rights under law. The idea is captured in the Latin maxim: *da mihi factum, dabo tibi jus*! (Give me the facts, I will give you your right).[214] Process does not exist for its own sake. It exists to facilitate determining rights under law.

German process parallels American process in outline, but differs in details that facilitate decisions on the merits.[215] Plaintiffs file complaints.[216] Courts determine sufficiency of complaints, help parties correct insufficient complaints, and direct parties that have gone to the wrong courts to the right ones.[217] Courts serve complaints and the defendants answer.[218] Pleadings identify key facts and point to evidence parties will rely on.[219]

Early on, courts meet with parties—not just lawyers—to discuss cases.[220] Together they identify applicable law and material facts in dispute.[221] If no material

---

[210] Gonzales v. Raich, 545 U.S. 1, 42 (2005) (O'Connor, J., dissenting).

[211] Edson R. Sunderland, *Current Legal Literature: Among Recent Books*, 15 A.B.A. J. 35, 36 (1929).

[212] It was the only foreign system that Pound named in his 1906 address: "the wonderful mechanism of modern German judicial administration." Pound, *supra* note 48, at 397. It may be better today. One-hundred six years later, the World Justice Project, partly funded and led by the American Bar Association, reviewed ninety-seven civil justice systems around the world. Of the civil justice systems in the twenty-nine wealthiest countries, the Project rated the German system third, behind only those of the Netherlands and Norway. The project scored the U.S. nearly twenty percent lower and ranked it nineteenth among the richest nations. Mark David Agrast et al., The World Justice Project: Rule of Law Index 2012–2013 2629 (2013).

[213] For an explanation of this system, see Maxeiner et al., *supra* note 50, along with three other books and dozens of articles authored by Maxeiner.

[214] Maxeiner, *supra* note 3, at 1283.

[215] *Id.* at 1280–88.

[216] *Id.* at 1285.

[217] *Id.* at 1285–86.

[218] *Id.*

[219] *Id.*

[220] Maxeiner, supra note 3, at 1286.

[221] *Id.*

facts are in dispute, courts may summarily decide.[222] If material facts are in dispute, courts invite parties to submit evidence.[223] Parties propose testimony and, if courts agree that the evidence proposed would contribute to resolving a material question in dispute, they order taking proof.[224] Parties have a fully developed right to be heard which is fully enforceable on appeal, so courts are reluctant to reject proffered proof.[225]

Courts decide nothing finally until they decide the entire case.[226] They may readdress issues that seemed settled.[227] They let parties know which issues they will be deciding and give parties the opportunity to respond.[228] Once courts have clarified all material issues in dispute, they proceed to making final decisions.[229] They explain their decisions in full: they give contentions of both sides and explain why they come to the conclusions they do.[230] If parties believe courts' decisions are wrong, they may appeal them.[231] On first appeal, other courts decide which party is right in law and not whether the first court failed to follow the rules of the game.[232]

German civil justice works because courts decide cases on the merits; they apply law to facts. German judges guide parties from the commencement of suits. Judges have freedom in structuring the order and content of proceedings. Because they control how proceedings go, they do not need to limit access to procedure. They are not gatekeepers, but facilitators. Courts do not decide issues conclusively until they decide the entire case at the end of proceedings.

Of course, the United States cannot simply adopt the German system. Process is not simple. It requires laws, processes, and institutions different from those we presently have. But those laws, processes, and institutions are of a piece with legal methods Americans have for two centuries aspired to as best practices. The United States can learn from the German and other foreign systems if only we would give them a look.

---

[222] *Id.*

[223] *Id.* at 1287.

[224] *Id.*

[225] *Id.*

[226] James R. Maxeiner, *Imagining Judges That Apply Law: How They Might Do It*, 114 Penn St. L. Rev. 469, 481 (2009).

[227] *See id.*

[228] *Id.* at 478.

[229] *Id.* at 476–81.

[230] James R. Maxeiner, *What America Can Learn from Germany's Justice System*, Atlantic (June 7,2012,11:00AM),http://www.theatlantic.com/national/archive/2012/06/what-america-can-learn-from-germanys-justice-system/258208/.

[231] Maxeiner, *supra* note 3, at 1282.

[232] *See* James R. Maxeiner, *Thinking Like A Lawyer Abroad: Putting Justice Into Legal Reasoning*, 11 Wash U. Glob. Stud. L Rev. 55, 85 (2012).

5.5.2 Sunderland to Miller, Marcus and Carrington: "Why Don't You Take Advantage of What Has Been Done by the Civil Law?"

Sunderland, in a book review that predated his work on the Federal Rules, raised the question: "Why don't you take advantage of what has been done by the civil law, that governs at least twice as many people as the common law, is two thousand years older, and embodies a much greater amount of human experience?"[233]

Professors Miller, Marcus, and Carrington, are internationally minded men. Yet for them, there are few lessons to be learned abroad. Where Sunderland sought out foreign solutions, his successors avert their eyes. Where Sunderland saw his work as experiments, independent of frontiers, in a universal search for better methods of dealing with fundamental problems of litigation, Miller and Carrington revere Sunderland's reforms as immovable and immutable building blocks peculiar to American culture.[234]

Not to look at foreign solutions is irresponsible. It is foolish. So said Sunderland.[235] So how do Miller, Marcus, and Carrington answer Sunderland?

5.5.2.1 American Exceptionalism

Americans have long known that through comparison of our institutions with those of foreigners, we learn "what is defective or excellent, and therefore of what is to be cherished and upheld, or to be disapproved and abolished in our institutions."[236] Those, however, who are unwilling to disapprove or even abolish institutions found wanting, maintain the failing institutions and assert that they serve unique American needs.[237] So it is with defenders of the failed Federal Rules.

American civil procedure is exceptional, they say, because its goals are exceptional.[238] Where foreign systems are concerned only with resolving disputes among

---

233 Sunderland, *supra* note 211, at 35.

234 Carrington, *Moths to the Light*, *supra* note 196, at 686 ("It would require deep cultural change … ."); *see* Stephen N. Subrin, *The Limitations of Transsubstantive Procedure: An Essay on Adjusting the "One Size Fits All" Assumption*, 87 Denv. U. L. Rev. 377, 397 (2010) (noting that some changes would be "too deep an assault on the historic role of civil litigation in our country"). *See generally* Oscar G. Chase, *American "Exceptionalism" and Comparative Procedure*, 50 Am J. Comp. L. 277 (2002) (examining the relationships between a society's culture and dispute resolution methods); Richard L. Marcus, *Putting American Procedural Exceptionalism into a Globalized Context*, 53 Am J. Comp. L. 709 (2005) (introducing works that examine the dispute resolution methods in other countries).

235 *See infra* note 269.

236 Caleb Cushing, *On the Study of the Civil Law*, 11 N. Am. Rev. 407, 408 (1820).

237 *See generally* Marcus, *American Exceptionalism*, *supra* note 20 (examining the unique goals of American civil litigation).

238 Marcus, *American Exceptionalism*, *supra* note 20, at 139 ("American procedure is exceptional because American procedural goals are exceptional… . The goal of public enforcement largely emerged after World War II, and there has recently been an effort in the U.S. to discredit the goal of private enforcement that seems now to explain so much about American procedure that baffles

private parties, the American system relies on private parties to enforce public law. This difference, they claim, defines the American system.[239] Professor Carrington explains:

> [D]iscovery is the American alternative to the administrative state. We have by means of Rules 26–37, and by their analogues in state law, privatized a great deal of our law enforcement, especially in such fields as antitrust and trade regulation, consumer protection, securities regulation, civil rights, and intellectual property. Private litigants do in America much of what is done in other industrial states by public officers working within an administrative bureaucracy.[240]

The story they tell is that because foreign systems do not do these things, they do not need American-style pleading and discovery and, therefore, there is not much to learn from their procedures in "dispute resolution."[241]

The story of American exceptionalism in civil procedure goals is fantasy. A recent multinational study, *Goals of Civil Justice and Civil Procedure in Contemporary Judicial Systems*, edited by Alan Uzelac, under the aegis of the International Association of Procedural Law, explodes the idea of American exceptionalism in goals for civil procedure.[242] Professor Uzelac, in summarizing the results of eleven studies of twelve systems of civil justice, finds in all twelve there to be two main goals of civil justice: dispute resolution and social policy.[243] The definitions and relative emphases given to each, especially the latter, varies.[244] But, there is no escaping the conclusion that the United States is not exceptional and that its use of private enforcement of social policy does not define our system.[245]

---

the rest of the world. Not surprisingly, those who challenge the private enforcement goal in the U.S. also seem to want to dismantle the procedural apparatus that supports it.").

[239] *See* Subrin & Woo, *supra* note 29, at 37("The role of civil litigation in America is somewhat different perhaps from its role in other countries, and it defines the character of our legal system. Rather than simply seeking courts to resolve private disputes (the conflict resolution model), Americans have relied on relatively open access to court and private civil litigation to be at the heart of a great deal of the enforcement of our public laws (the behavior modification or social control model). With a mistrust of big government and intrusive states, the American public has (probably more than most other countries) relied on private civil litigation rather than solely on state controlled litigation or state regulatory agencies to enforce our public values.").

[240] Paul D. Carrington, *Renovating Discovery*, 49 Ala. L. Rev. 51, 54 (1997); *accord* Carrington, *American*, *supra* note 200, at 1413; Paul D. Carrington, *Civil Procedure to Enforce Transnational Rights?*, (Mar. 3, 2007), *available at* http://scholarship.law.duke.edu/faculty_scholarship/1990; *see also* J. Maria Glover, *The Structural Role of Private Enforcement Mechanisms in Public Law*, 53 Wm. & Mary L. Rev. 1137 (2012); Marcus, *supra* note 234.

[241] Were these statements true, foreign experiences ought none the less lead Americans to ask: (1) should the United States abandon the "transsubstantive model," one size fits all, of forms of civil procedure and substitute a two-track approach, where one track is for dispute resolution and the other for social policy?; and (2) is the United States well served by private enforcement through civil justice or are there better ways to achieve policy goals?

[242] *See* Uzelac, *supra* note 1.

[243] *Id.* at 6.

[244] *Id.*

[245] Although the U.S. system is not exceptional in goals, it is exceptional in its methods: it hands over the power of the state to unchecked use by private parties. E. Donald Elliott, Twombly *in Context*: *Why Federal Rule of Civil Procedure 4(b) is Unconstitutional*, 64 Fla. L. Rev. 895, 898 (2012).

5.5.2.2 Foreign Fact Instead of Exceptionalism Fantasy

The proponents of American exceptionalism do not offer proof for their claims that other states orient civil justice exclusively on dispute resolution to the denigration of social policy. Professor Marcus alone obliquely states where he got the idea: "For most of the rest of the world, *we Americans are informed*, the administrative enforcement model is the favored method of achieving policy enforcement or behavior modification, and conflict resolution is the goal of private civil litigation."[246] When challenged, he cites his colleagues.[247] We can only speculate where he or they got the idea. My best guess: pre-conceptions about the defunct Soviet system.[248]

Foreign civil justice determines rights. In this way, it resolves conflicts. Foreign civil justice rests on private enforcement of rights.[249] In the case of the German system, it has done this for a century.[250] Private parties more than public officers enforce rights, both those found in traditional private law, and those based on newer public law.

The huge, centralized bureaucracy that American proceduralists imagine is not a feature of Germany. Its Federal Ministry of Labour and Social Affairs, which oversees the enforcement of employment law, social law, the labor courts and the social courts, has about eleven hundred employees.[251] Its Federal Ministry of Justice and Consumer Protection, which oversees enforcement of consumer protection laws and the ordinary civil courts, has about eight hundred employees.[252] To put those numbers in perspective, the Administrative Office of the United States Courts has more than thirty thousand employees.[253] Who, we should ask, has armies of public officials?

To dispel the notion of American exceptionalism it is sufficient to look at some of the areas where exceptionalism is supposedly evidenced[254]:

---

[246] Marcus, *American Exceptionalism*, *supra* note 20, at 129 (emphasis added).

[247] *Id.* at 129–34.

[248] Perhaps they read too robustly the words of Mirjan Damaska. Mirjan R. Damaska, The Faces of Justice and State Authority: A Comparative Approach to the Legal Process (1986).

[249] Uzelac, *supra* note 1, at 15–16.

[250] *See* Maxeiner et al., *supra* note 50, app. at 271.

[251] E-mail from Ralf Peters, Fed. Ministry of Labour and Soc. Affairs, to James R. Maxeiner (Feb. 12, 2014).

[252] *Aufbau und Organisation*, Bundesministerium der Justiz und für Verbraucherschutz, http://www.bmjv.de/DE/Ministerium/AufbauOrganisation/_node.html (last visited June 26, 2014).

[253] Office of Personnel Mgmt., Data, Analysis & Documentation Federal Employment Reports: Employment and Trends—September 2012 (2012), https://www.opm.gov/policy-data-oversight/data-analysis-documentation/federal-employment-reports/employment-trends-data/2012/September/table-3/.

[254] Different writers highlight different areas for mention. Employment law and consumer protection are two areas that have not only been mentioned but have received close attention. *See* Burbank, Farhang & Kritzer, *supra* note 28, at 667. This article was prepared as part of the fourteenth World Congress of the International Association of Procedural Law. *Id.* at 637 n.a1. It focuses on two areas of private enforcement: employment law and protecting consumers from unfair and deceptive acts and practices. *Id.* at 643.

1. **Employment law**. Americans boast that Federal courts handle yearly 20,000 cases of employment discrimination, mostly termination cases.[255] Most of these cases in Germany would fall in the jurisdiction of state labor courts. They handle 400,000 cases a year. [256] The great majority of these cases are private suits by employees against employers. The state labor courts are civil courts; their rules of procedure are those of ordinary civil courts.[257]
2. **Consumer protection**. Private litigation in the ordinary courts is the principal locus of enforcement of German laws of consumer protection, be they laws protecting consumers against unfair terms, product liability, misleading advertising, or deceptive sales practices.[258] Most of these laws now find counterparts throughout the EU thanks to EU Directives compelling their adoption. Under the German laws, private consumer organizations are authorized to send demand letters with the force of law and, if those do not cause corporate cessation of consumer damaging practices, to bring private suits.[259]
3. **Competition and antitrust law**. The former relies almost exclusively on private enforcement,[260] while the latter, modeled on American law, includes a significant private enforcement component.[261]

---

[255] David S. Schwartz, *Mandatory Arbitration and Fairness*, 84 NOTRE DAME L. REV. 1247, 1323 n.233 (2009).

[256] Until recently, Germany did not have a specific discrimination law. Joachim Wiemann, *Obligation to Contract and the German General Act on Equal Treatment (Allgemeines Gleichbehandlungsgesetz)*, 11 GERMAN L.J. 1131 (2010). Nevertheless German labor courts have long handled matters that in America would be raised as job discrimination. Since the U.S. has no general employment law, but instead applies a common law "employment at will" doctrine, plaintiffs who would bring unlawful discharge suits in Germany assert discrimination in employment. *See* Miller, *Simplified Pleading*, *supra* note 168, at 343 n.210.

[257] *See* MANFRED WEISS & MARLENE SCHMIDT, LABOUR LAW AND INDUSTRIAL RELATIONS IN GERMANY 149 (4th ed. 2008). For perspectives specifically on German labor courts and proceedings, see JÜRG ARNOLD, DIE ARBEITSGERICHTSBARKEIT: FESTSCHRIFT ZUM 100-JÄHRIGEN BESTEHEN DES DEUTSCHEN ARBEITSGERICHTSVERBANDES (1994); EBERHARD WIESER, ARBEITSGERICHTSVERFAHREN (1994); and still valuable and insightful, Ernst Fraenkel, *The Labor Courts in the German Judicial System*, *in* GERMAN LABOR COURTS 3–18 (1946).

[258] BARBARA GRUNEWALD & KARL-NIKOLAU PEIFER, VERBRAUCHERSCHUTZ IM ZIVILRECHT 7–10 (2010) (with an introduction and ten chapters each on a different form of consumer protection detailing its implementation); Stefan Lenze, *German Product Liability Law: Between European Directives, American Restatements and Common Sense*, *in* PRODUCT LIABILITY IN COMPARATIVE PERSPECTIVE 100–25 (Duncan Fairgrieve, ed. 2005).

[259] JAMES R. MAXEINER & PETER SCHOTTHÖFER, ADVERTISING LAW IN EUROPE AND NORTH AMERICA 228–32 (2d ed. 1999) (including a chapter on German law by George Jennes & Peter Schotthöfer); James R. Maxeiner, *Standard-Terms Contracting in the Global Electronic Age: European Alternatives*, 28 YALE J. INT'L L. 109, 157–59 (2003).

[260] *See generally* LAW AGAINST UNFAIR COMPETITION: TOWARDS A NEW PARADIGM IN EUROPE? (Reto M. Hilty & Frauke Henning-Bodewig eds., 2007) (examining the evolution of competition laws in Europe); THE ENFORCEMENT OF COMPETITION LAW IN EUROPE (Thomas M. J. Möllers & Andreas Heinemann eds., 2007) (analyzing the enforcement mechanisms of unfair competition law and antitrust law).

[261] DAVID ALEXANDER JÜNTGEN, DIE PROZESSUALE DURCHSETZUNG PRIVATER ANSPRÜCHE IM KARTELLRECHT *passim* (2007); JAMES MAXEINER, POLICY AND METHODS IN GERMAN AND AMERICAN ANTITRUST LAW: A COMPARATIVE STUDY 55 (1986).

4. **Private rights of action in civil courts under public law.** American proceduralists admire those oft-confusing and sometimes inconsistent precedents that permit private rights of action pursuant to New Deal (1930s) and subsequent legislation. The German Civil Code has anticipated such actions since its adoption in 1896. Section 828(2) provides that a person has a duty to pay damages is "held by a person who commits a breach of a statute that is intended to protect another person."[262]

By studying these and other areas where private parties enforce public law through civil justice, Americans would learn how the German system has minimized the difficulties encountered here.[263] The German approach is straight-forward. Civil justice is limited to enforcing rights that are already determined in law or determinable based on facts limited to the individuals concerned. Those rights may originate in private or public law. Where, however, law application requires policy decisions, i.e., political decisions for people beyond those immediately concerned, then administrative decision-making, with eventual political responsibility is appropriate and private enforcement through ordinary courts is not. Private challenges are still possible. They go first to the political authorities themselves, whose decisions are then are reviewable by administrative courts.[264]

5.6 Conclusion

Sunderland named two principal reasons why Americans do not learn from foreign civil justice: "ignorance, due to the fact that American lawyers are not usually good linguists," and "professional prejudice against new ideas, based on natural conservatism and the monopolistic nature of judicial agencies."[265]

Limited facility with foreign languages remains an impediment,[266] but one of ever declining importance as the English-speaking European Union harmonizes and reforms its laws. One consequence of that harmonizing is an explosion of English language materials by foreign experts.[267] That literature, some scholarly, some practical, offers American scholars a firm basis on which to write. If only one of ten new

[262] *See* Bénédicte Fauvarque-Cosson & Denis Mazeaud, European Contract Law: Materials for a Common Frame of Reference: Terminology, Guiding Principles, Model Rules 489 n.175 (2008).

[263] Professor Burbank and colleagues set out those difficulties in their recent article on private enforcement. Burbank, Farhang & Kritzer, *supra* note 28, at 667.

[264] Mahendra P. Singh, German Administrative Law in Common Law Perspective 219–22 (2nd ed. 2001).

[265] Sunderland, *supra* note 211, at 35. *See also* Colin Picker, *Comparative Law Methodology & American Legal Culture: Obstacles and Opportunities*, 16 Roger Williams U. L. Rev. 86 (2011).

[266] Ernst C. Stiefel & James R. Maxeiner, *Why are U.S. Lawyers not Learning from Comparative Law?*, *in* The International Practice of Law 213–36 (Nedim Peter Vogt et al. eds., 1997), available at http://ssrn.com/abstract=1250002.

[267] This offers a niche for U.S. law professors who do not know foreign languages. Since these foreign scholars do not know U.S. law, their work needs "translation" into American legal understanding.

scholars would put aside the U.S. judicial clerkships for serious foreign law studies abroad—preferably in the local language—we would soon have sufficient institutional knowledge to well utilize foreign law.[268]

Professional prejudice is another matter. It is simply stupid to ignore foreign successes because they are foreign. So thought Sunderland.[269] So said famously the German, Rudolf von Jhering:

The reception of foreign legal institutions is not a matter of nationality, but of usefulness and need. No one bothers to fetch a thing from afar when he has one as good or better at home, but only a fool would refuse quinine just because it didn't grow in his back yard.[270]

Let us follow Sunderland's invocation and "search[] for new and better methods, overcoming the barriers of language and forgetting the prejudices of nationality and race."[271] Then we may be able to avoid the tragedy that Chief Justice Burger warned of at the 1976 Pound Conference:

It is far easier to do what we lawyers often do—praise our system as the best ever devised and denounce anyone who dares to suggest that we consider, not only periodic adjustment, but major and systemic changes. The inertia of some lawyers, judges, and legislators is such that nothing less than a collapse of the system will bring them to consider change.[272]

---

[268] This would address Professor Clermont's claim that we cannot use foreign experiences because knowledge of foreign systems is too little diffused. *See* Kevin M. Clermont, *Three Myths About Twombly-Iqbal*, 45 WAKE FOREST L. REV. 1337, 1343 n. 36 (2010).

[269] *See, e.g.*, Edson R. Sunderland, *Joinder of Actions*, 18 MICH. L. REV. 571, 572 (1920) ("There is further striking failure which must be charged to the legal profession in America ··· and that is its ignorance of and indifference to improvements in procedural practice developed in other jurisdictions. It is safe to say that if a new method of treating cancer were discovered and successfully employed in England, every intelligent doctor in the world would almost immediately know about it and attempt to take advantage of it. But it is equally safe to say that if a new and successful method of treating some procedural problem were discovered in England, American lawyers as a class would remain in substantial ignorance of it for at least two generations, and would probably treat it with scornful indifference for a generation or two more. There are no state lines for progressive doctors, dentists, engineers, architects, manufacturers or business men. But not one lawyer in a hundred knows or cares what reforms are being employed by his profession on the other side of the political boundary. The American lawyer is satisfied with things as they are. As long as clients continue to come and the machinery of the law continues to move, he is ··· free from concern over the methods used elsewhere ··· .").

[270] Rudolf von Jhering, GEIST DES RÖMISCHEN RECHTS AUF DEN VERSCHIEDENEN STUFEN SEINER ENTWICKLUNG 8–9 (Basel: B. Schwabe, 1953).

[271] Sunderland, *supra* note 211, at 35.

[272] Warren E. Burger, *Agenda for 2000 A.D.—A Need for Systematic Anticipation*, 70 F.R.D. 79, 89 (1976).

Chapter 6
Dynamism in China's Civil Procedure Law: Civil Justice with Chinese Characteristics

Kristie Thomas

6.1 Introduction

It is clear that "the administration of civil justice plays a role of crucial importance in the life and culture of a civilised community".[1] Without effective procedural provisions, any substantive laws enacted are just empty pieces of paper. Civil procedure is also hugely significant due to the potential political implications involved, "affecting such issues as the enforcement of rights, the distribution of wealth, and the allocation of opportunity."[2] Such civic issues are of paramount concern in China as the central government is obsessed with containing any threats to social stability. Furthermore, it has even been argued that procedural systems are not only influenced by local conditions, but that they in turn also influence the society around them.[3] Therefore, the evolution of a comprehensive set of civil procedure rules marks an important step in the development of the post-1978 modern legal system in China.

In the majority of Western legal systems, there is a recognised preoccupation with securing procedural rights for litigants in the civil justice system and there is some consensus around the features that such a civil justice system should broadly include, regardless of whether the system falls into the category of civil or common

---

[1] Jacob, Sir Jack I. H. 1982. *The reform of civil procedural law and other essays in civil procedure.* London: Sweet & Maxwell.

[2] Chase, Oscar G. and Helen Hershkoff, eds. 2007. *Civil litigation in comparative context.* St. Paul, Minneapolis: Thomson-West, 2.

[3] Chase, Oscar G. 2007. *Law, culture and ritual: Disputing systems in cross-cultural context* New York: NYU Press.

K. Thomas (✉)
Nottingham University Business School,
Jubilee Campus, Wollaton Road, Nottingham NG8 1BB, UK
e-mail: kristie.thomas@nottingham.ac.uk

C.B. Picker, G.I. Seidman (eds.), *The Dynamism of Civil Procedure - Global Trends and Developments*, Ius Gentium: Comparative Perspectives on Law and Justice 48, DOI 10.1007/978-3-319-21981-3_6

law-based 'family'.[4] In contrast, such a preoccupation with procedural rights is alien to many domestic litigants in China, whose primary concern lies with the substantive outcome of any dispute. Many commentators maintain that "traditional Chinese cultural values that privilege substantive justice over procedural justice still dominate"[5] and as a result, procedural provisions have not necessarily been the foremost priority for legislators commencing the formidable task of reconstructing a functional legal system largely from scratch since reforms began in China in the late 1970s.

Nevertheless, civil procedure legislation has a rich history in reform-era China, from the provisional code passed in 1982[6] to the more detailed comprehensive law enacted in 1991.[7] The civil procedure law was further amended in October 2007[8] and August 2012.[9] The initial civil procedure laws, both the 1982 provisional law and the 1991 law, placed an increasing emphasis on dispute resolution via formal adjudication by the courts rather than informal mediation which had previously dominated from the founding of the People's Republic of China (PRC) in 1949 until the late 1970s.[10] This emphasis in the substantive laws on a more formal role for the courts led to a corresponding spread of legal professionalism and subsequently, the number of civil disputes brought before the courts rose dramatically throughout the 1980s and 1990s. The total number of civil disputes heard by a People's Court at first instance only amounted to around 300,000 in 1978, but had risen to around 2.5 million civil disputes by 1990 and had doubled again to nearly 5 million civil disputes by the end of the twentieth century.[11]

---

[4] Gerlis, Stephen M. and Paula Loughlin. 2001. *Civil procedure*. London: Cavendish Publishing Ltd.

[5] Woo, Margaret Y. K. and Mary E. Gallagher. 2011. Introduction. In *Chinese justice: Civil dispute resolution in contemporary China*, ed. Margaret Y. K. Woo and Mary E. Gallagher. Cambridge: Cambridge University Press, 13.

[6] PRC Civil Procedure Law (for Trial Implementation). 1982. http://old.chinacourt.org/flwk/show.php?file_id=2273 (in Chinese); http://www.novexcn.com/civil_procedure_law.html (in English).

[7] PRC Civil Procedure Law 1991. http://www.people.com.cn/zixun/flfgk/item/dwjjf/falv/9/9-1-1-01.html (in Chinese); http://www.china.org.cn/english/government/207339.htm (in English).

[8] Standing Committee of the National People's Congress' decision on amending the PRC civil procedure law. 2007. (*Quanguo renmin daibiao dahui changwu weiyuanhui guanyu xiugai < Zhonghua renmin gongheguo minshi susong fa > de jueding*) October 28 http://www.gov.cn/flfg/2007-10/28/content_788498.htm (in Chinese).

[9] The full text of the 2012 amendments and the amended Civil Procedure Law can be found at: Standing Committee of the National People's Congress' decision on amending the PRC civil procedure law. 2012. (*Quanguo renmin daibiao dahui changwu weiyuanhui guanyu xiugai < Zhonghua renmin gongheguo minshi susong fa > de jueding*) August 31 http://www.gov.cn/flfg/2012-09/01/content_2214662.htm (in Chinese).

[10] For a good introduction to dispute resolution in the Mao era, see: Lubman, Stanley. 1967. Mao and mediation: Politics and dispute resolution in Communist China. *California Law Review* 55(5).

[11] Annual statistics from PRC National Bureau of Statistics, data.stats.gov.cn. Note: prior to 2002, economic disputes and maritime disputes were categorised separately. As they have been counted together since 2002, the data for 1978–2002 also amalgamates these into the total civil disputes to allow for more consistent comparisons.

However, around the turn of the twenty-first century, the race towards formal judicial dominance of resolution processes began to slow and even reverse slightly, a move which has notoriously been dubbed by Carl Minzner, "China's turn against law."[12] Minzner argues that the Chinese authorities reconsidered the legal reforms enacted in the 1980s and 1990s due to political concerns that formal court-based dispute resolution was failing to quash citizen grievances against the state. He argues that China was seeking to revive traditional mediation as the main channel for civil dispute resolution in order to better maintain social stability. It is undeniable that the total number of civil suits filed stagnated in the early part of the twenty-first century, for example, from a peak of 5 million civil disputes heard at first instance in 1999, the total declined to an annual level of 4.3 to 4.4 million civil disputes in 2002–2006.[13]

Nevertheless, the latest statistics would suggest that civil litigation has again begun to grow in the past few years. The 2012 Supreme People's Court Work Report presented in March 2013[14] contained the relevant data for the 5 years 2008–2012 and stated that the number of civil cases concluded at first instance had increased by 37.8 % compared to the equivalent number of cases from 2003 to 2007. Although the number of civil disputes appears to have regained and even overtaken the previous peak reached in 1999, as this resurgence has only been apparent in the past few years, it is not clear whether these levels of formal disputes heard by the courts will be maintained or whether the recent increase is just a temporary blip.

Thus, it currently seems unclear exactly what role the courts play in resolving civil disputes in contemporary China compared to less formal channels and it is in this context that the latest amendments to the Civil Procedure Law (CPL) were passed in 2012. The latest amendments have led to improvements in the available enforcement mechanisms, but the status of civil procedural rules at the heart of the formal legal system is still uncertain, particularly when contrasted with the unerring popularity of the 'letters and visits' petitioning system known as *xinfang*.[15]*Xinfang* is a traditional method of seeking justice which encompasses a variety of practices that "parallel, overlap and in some cases replace formal legal channels,"[16] by offering citizens the opportunity to petition directly to higher-level bodies. Essentially, *xinfang* is based on the notion of appealing to an official to exercise their discretionary power and remains a popular option for Chinese citizens when faced with individual grievances. Indeed, some statistics suggest that the number of 'letters and visits' handled under this petitioning system outweigh the number of formal legal

[12] Minzner, Carl F. 2011. China's turn against law. *American Journal of Comparative Law* 59, no. 4.

[13] PRC National Bureau of Statistics (n 11).

[14] Supreme People's Court work report 2012. http://www.chinacourt.org/article/detail/2013/03/id/907830.shtml Accessed 11 March 2013.

[15] Minzner, Carl F. 2006. Xinfang: An alternative to formal Chinese legal institutions. *Stanford Journal of International Law* 42, no. 1.

[16] Ibid., 104.

cases filed with the courts.[17] In comparison, as will be discussed below, there is some uncertainty about the current status of civil litigation in China as opposed to mediation and alternative methods of petitioning such as *xinfang*.

From essentially starting at year zero as the 'opening-up and reform period' (*gaige kaifang*)[18] began in 1978, to a functional modern legal system in less than 30 years is quite an achievement. In order to achieve this outcome, China has demonstrated remarkable dynamism in moulding imported principles of civil procedure to its own local conditions. However, this dynamism could arguably be characterised as 'instrumental dynamism', as China has clearly forged a civil justice system with the primary aim of maintaining societal harmony, rather than aiming to promote any higher due process concerns out of respect for the rule of law.

In order to appreciate how this instrumental dynamism has manifested itself in the civil procedure laws in China, each key legislative change can be taken as a 'snap-shot' of the civil justice system at that time. As China's central government is in many ways strong enough to enforce its will on its citizens, so the changes to the civil procedure laws may be seen as not only a reflection of Chinese society at that time, but also a reflection of the directions in which the central government wishes to bend society. Thus, in part 2 of this chapter, a brief background of the civil procedure laws in China will be outlined, from imperial codes which focused on criminal liability to pre-reform era China which invoked socialist ideals that saw law as secondary to the resolution of disputes by citizens themselves. Next, for each of the main civil procedure laws passed since 1978 (the 1982 Provisional CPL, the 1991 revised CPL, and the 2007 and 2012 amendments), the key provisions will be outlined, as well as the broader context of the wider legal system and developing society at that time.

Then, the fourth section of the chapter will discuss some of the key issues in more detail to further illustrate China's instrumental dynamism in action; namely, the fluctuating status of mediation, the burgeoning use of summary procedures, and the overall status of the civil justice system within the wider political order in China. In each of these fundamental areas, China has demonstrated impressive levels of innovation in shaping the civil procedural rules to its unique domestic demands.

6.2 Historical Background to China's Civil Procedure Reforms

Prior to the start of the reform era from 1978 onwards, China lacked comprehensive rules of civil procedure, largely due to the traditional preference for substantive law over procedural law and for criminal measures over civil provisions which prevailed

---

[17] Ibid., 105–6 (suggesting that in 2002, *xinfang* bureaus handled 11.5 m cases, compared to 6 million cases dealt with by the judiciary).

[18] Henceforth, this period will be referred to as the 'reform era' in China.

in imperial China.[19] The traditional orthodoxy regarding the development of law in ancient China is that the theories of Confucianism and Legalism were fundamental in shaping the foundations of the entire Chinese legal system. The influence of these theories are said to have resulted in several distinctive characteristics in the legal system which continue to persist in the contemporary Chinese legal system, in particular the reluctance to litigate; the insignificance of individual rights compared to the collective good; the ingrained respect for authority and the secondary role of law in society overall.[20]

However, the precise role of formal court-based adjudication in the civil justice system in imperial China is subject to some debate amongst scholars, with little consensus on the matter emerging. Huang argues that there is actually a remarkable level of continuity in judicial theory from traditional China until the present day with the Qing judiciary rigorously following the legal codes in adjudicating between parties, whereas other scholars argue that judgments were based on a combination of applying the written legal codes, local customs and cultural norms.[21]

Regardless of the status of formal law in imperial China, after imperial rule came to an end following the 1911 Revolution, it is irrefutable that Chinese law began to look more to imported models and legal norms as sources of reform. Beginning soon after the Republican revolution in 1912, Nationalist (*kuomintang*) reformers drew upon Continental Europe via Japan as models for reform of the legal system. This led to reforms in the civil procedure arena during the 1920s and 1930s. For example, the Draft Code of Civil Procedure was enacted by Presidential Mandate on July 22nd 1921[22] and was largely modelled on the Japanese Civil Procedure Law 1890, which itself drew heavily upon the German Imperial Code of Civil Procedure from 1877. However, due to internal civil unrest, the Nationalist legal codes were not widely implemented.

Subsequently, following the establishment of the People's Republic of China in October 1949, the status of the legal system was significantly downgraded as ideology rose to prominence. Concurrently, Soviet instrumentalist ideals of law as a socialist tool became more influential. Consequently, civil disputes were largely seen as resulting from contradictions amongst the people and as such, were best resolved by People's Mediation Committees, rather than through the intervention of the courts.[23] For example, in 1950, Provisional Principles of Procedure were adopted

[19] Sang, Bin Xue. 1992. China's civil procedure law: A new guide for dispute resolution in China. *The International Lawyer* 26, no. 2.

[20] Ruskola,Teemu. 2012. The East Asian legal tradition. In *The Cambridge companion to comparative law*, ed. Mauro Bussani and Ugo Mattei. Cambridge: Cambridge University Press.

[21] Compare Huang, Phillip C. C. 1998. *Civil justice in China: Representation and practice in the Qing*. Stanford, Calif.: Stanford University Press and Allee, Mark A. 1994. Code, culture and custom: Foundations of civil case verdicts in a nineteenth-century county court. In *Civil law in Qing and Republican China*, ed. Phillip C. C. Huang and Kathryn Bernhardt. Stanford, Calif.: Stanford University Press.

[22] Commission on Extraterritoriality. 1923. *The regulations relating to civil procedure of the Republic of China*. Peking, China: Commission on Extraterritoriality.

[23] Lubman (n 10), 1307.

but never fully implemented as the court system was seen as secondary to the resolution of disputes through such committees. The only directive governing civil disputes was the simplistic ‘Sixteen Character Guideline’, namely “relying on the masses, based on investigation and research, resolving disputes on the spot, and using mediation as the primary method.”[24]

During the Cultural Revolution from the late 1960s to early 1970s, this trend of rejecting formal legal channels of dispute resolution accelerated with the virtual abandonment of law as a legitimate tool of government. At this time, the vast majority of law schools were closed and many legal scholars and professors were denounced and even sent to the countryside for re-education through labour. It was only in the late 1970s that China began to take tentative steps towards opening-up to the world and shifting away from a command economy and towards the greater use of market forces. However, the after-effects of the Cultural Revolution reverberated through the legal system for many years, largely due to the impact on legal education. In the initial years of the reform era which took place in the late 1970s and 1980s, the vast majority of legal professionals staffing and developing the legal system had no formal legal training and this clearly had a detrimental effect on the initial evolution of effective procedural codes discussed below.

6.3 Key Provisions of the Civil Procedure Law in Context

6.3.1 The 1982 Provisional Civil Procedure Law[25]

6.3.1.1 Context

The 3rd Plenum of the 11th Communist Party of China (CPC) Central Committee held in December 1978 is widely taken as the starting point for the ‘reform and opening-up’ period which followed. The Plenum drew consensus around the Four Modernisations (agriculture, industry, national defence, science and technology) as the path for future economic reform.[26] As a result, an obvious priority as the reform era began was the swift development of a rudimentary legal system in order to boost the confidence of potential foreign investors into China. Subsequently, China rushed to pass key legislation such as an updated Constitution; China’s first Criminal Law and Criminal Procedure Law since the founding of the People’s Republic in 1949; and basic Laws on the operation of courts and procuratorates.

---

[24] Fu, Yulin and Cao, Zhixun. 2012. The position of judges in civil litigation in transitional China. In *Towards a Chinese civil code: Comparative and historical perspectives*, ed. Lei Chen and C. H. van Rhee. Leiden: Martinus Nijhoff, 499.

[25] PRC Civil Procedure Law (for Trial Implementation), (n 6).

[26] For an overview of the reforms introduced from 1978 onwards, see: Perry, Elizabeth J. and Christine Wong. (eds.) 1985. *The political economy of reform in post-Mao China*. Cambridge: Harvard University Press.

It was in this context of reform efforts that the Civil Procedure Law of the People's Republic of China (for Trial Implementation) was promulgated on March 8th 1982 (1982 Provisional CPL). China was experiencing rapid changes at this time and a Civil Procedure Law was seen as a necessity, to not only ensure stability but also to maintain the path towards economic reform supported by a more formal legal system.[27] The 1982 Provisional CPL contained 23 chapters and 205 articles and thus represented a fairly detailed attempt to clarify civil procedural rules in China.

6.3.1.2 Key Provisions

Nevertheless, in 1981 Xinhua, the official news agency of China, emphasised that the law remained firmly focused on mediation as the primary method of dispute resolution: "The solution of civil disputes through mediation is a fine tradition of China's judicial work, and a good form for such mediations is through the People's Mediation Committee. The draft law specifies the legal status of the People's Mediation Committees and makes it clear that the courts should guide and supervise the work of such committees".[28] Therefore, there were various provisions in the 1982 Provisional CPL which underlined the importance of mediation.

A case in point would be Article 6, according to which "in conducting civil proceedings, the People's Courts *shall stress conciliation*; if conciliation efforts are ineffective, they shall render judgments without delay" (emphasis added). It has been argued that this focus on conciliation at all stages of the civil justice process actually played a part in undermining the development of the courts; "by steering parties toward mediation and arbitration, the Civil Procedure Law may have had the unintended side effect of further eroding the authority and stature of the courts".[29]

Other principles embodied in the 1982 Provisional CPL were drafted by blending together Continental Civil Codes, such as the German civil code (BGB), in combination with practical experience of civil disputes in China,[30] in order to offer a swift solution to the lack of formal procedural rules which it was feared would deter potential foreign investment. It is also notable that Article 56(2) empowered the court to collect and examine evidence independently. By restricting the parties' right to participate in the proceedings, the Provisional CPL formalised judicial dominance of the civil justice process overall. Although this level of judicial dominance is not unusual in other civil law systems, it was unprecedented in China for the judiciary to be afforded such powers and demonstrates that although mediation

[27] Potter, Pitman B. 2001. *The Chinese legal system: Globalization and local legal culture*. London: RoutledgeCurzon.

[28] Xinhua General News Service. 1981. China's civil procedural law (draft). December 7.

[29] Peerenboom, Randall. 2002. *China's long march toward rule of law*. Cambridge: Cambridge University Press, 318.

[30] Liu, Jiang. 1982. Legislative principles and conditions in the civil procedure law. (*Min su fa de lifa yuanze yu guoqing*). *Faxue* (Jurisprudence) 5, 30–2.

remained at the heart of the civil procedure system, the 1982 Provisional CPL did attempt to make sweeping changes to the civil system.

6.3.2 *The 1991 Civil Procedure Law*[31]

6.3.2.1 Context

After 9 years of civil procedure being guided by the 1982 Provisional CPL, the law was finally amended and formalised with the promulgation of the Civil Procedure Law of the People's Republic of China on April 9th 1991 (1991 CPL). The passing of the 1991 CPL represented a major expansion of the coverage of civil procedure rules in China, from 23 to 29 chapters and from 205 to a total of 270 articles. As the 1982 Provisional CPL was heavily influenced by European civil law models, particularly the German BGB, it is thought that the primary reasons for the 1991 changes were to adapt the CPL to the practical local conditions in China.[32] The 1991 CPL also needs to be seen in the broader context of reforms to the legal system taking place across the 1990s. Following the re-opening of the law schools post-1978, it took at least a decade for these newly qualified legal professionals to become a significant force in the legal system. For example, professionalization of the judiciary was only cemented by the passing of the Judges Law in 1995, which laid down educational requirements for membership in the judiciary for the first time. The moment was ripe for implementing such minimum educational thresholds as only 7 % of judges were college graduates in 1995.[33]

In addition, economic developments since 1982 had rendered the temporary CPL ineffective and amendments were required to "meet the needs of China's commodity economy".[34] In other words, as the pre-existing command economy began to be dismantled and the nature of Chinese industry began to diversify within a free market context, a noticeable increase in the volume of disputes emerged. From approximately 779,000 civil disputes at first instance heard in 1982 when the provisional CPL was passed, the total had already surged to around 2.5 million civil disputes by the time the 1991 CPL was passed.[35] There were also equally fundamental changes in Chinese society as individuals were freed from the hegemony of the *danwei* work-unit system and began to demonstrate stirrings of, if not 'rights conscious-

---

[31] PRC Civil Procedure Law 1991, (n 7).

[32] Potter, (n 27), 36.

[33] This proportion had risen to 52 % by 2004. Peerenboom, Randall. 2011. Economic development and development of legal profession in China. In *Chinese justice: Civil dispute resolution in contemporary China*, ed. Margaret Y. K. Woo and Mary E. Gallagher, 114–35. Cambridge: Cambridge University Press.

[34] Xinhua General News Service. 1991. China set to revise civil procedural law. April 2.

[35] PRC National Bureau of Statistics (n 11).

ness', then some awareness of legal rules and how they could be utilised for their own purposes.[36]

6.3.2.2 Key Provisions

One of the key provisions in the 1991 CPL was Article 10 which stipulated that trials should be conducted publicly, the first time that such a principle of openness and transparency had been formally included in the civil justice system. Despite the 1991 CPL introducing another radical but small change to the civil justice system in China, the 1991 CPL still faced a great deal of criticism, particularly relating to deficiencies in the definitions of key standards such as the burden of proof and of other evidentiary matters.[37] For example, Article 64 of the 1991 CPL stated that parties have to provide evidence in support of their claims, which would suggest that the parties themselves bear the burden of discovering and presenting the relevant evidence. However, the same article also goes on to dictate that if 'for objective reasons', a party is unable to collect the evidence for themselves, the People's Court shall investigate and collect the necessary evidence. This confusion presents a mixed picture of the role of the courts- should they act as a neutral arbiter or play more of an investigative role?[38] At that point in the evolution of a functioning legal system, China did not seem to have a coherent vision of the role of the formal court structures.

Nevertheless, the 1991 CPL did mark a shift from the 1982 provisional law which had stressed conciliation, as Article 9 now stated that conciliation should be conducted on a voluntary basis. This indication of growing support for formal adjudication by the courts, rather than dispute resolution through informal channels, led to significant increases in the number of disputes filed with the courts during the 1990s, from 2.5 million in 1989 to nearly 3 million in 1993, nearly 4 million in 1995 and over 5 million by 1999.[39] Correspondingly, from 1996 onwards, as reform momentum gathered pace, the proportion of cases resolved via mediation declined year-on-year from 70+% in the 1980s until it reached a nadir in the early 2000s of around 30 % of disputes resolved via mediation.[40]

---

[36] Fu, Hualing. 1992. Understanding people's mediation in post-Mao China. *Journal of Chinese Law*. 6, no. 2, 217.

[37] Sang, (n 19).

[38] For an overview of the changes in the role of judges in civil procedure, see: Fu and Cao, (n 24).

[39] PRC National Bureau of Statistics, (n 11).

[40] Fu, Hualing and Richard Cullen. 2011. From mediatory to adjudicatory justice: The limits of civil justice reform in China. In *Chinese justice: Civil dispute resolution in contemporary China*, ed. Margaret Y. K. Woo and Mary E. Gallagher. Cambridge: Cambridge University Press, 43.

6.3.3 *The 2007 Amendments*

6.3.3.1 Context

The CPL was further amended in 2007, as part of an overhaul of all of China's procedural laws (Criminal Procedure Law, Administrative Procedure Law and Civil Procedure Law). The stated rationale for the revision of the procedural laws was due to them lagging behind China's legal, social and economic development. An additional trigger was the constitutional amendment of 2004 which included the concept of human rights for the first time.[41] The constitutional amendment also increased recognition of private property rights, again showing the move towards greater recognition of individual rights. The specific changes made in the 2007 CPL amendment were proposed and debated extensively amongst legal scholars; in particular, a conference held by the China Law Society in October 2004 attracted more than 300 legal experts to debate the necessary changes to the three procedural laws.[42]

Furthermore, a specific trigger for the changes made to the CPL was due to the persistent difficulty in enforcing civil judgments in the local courts. As the professionalization of the judiciary and formalisation of legal procedures began to make significant changes in the civil system, the deep-rooted problem of enforcing the resulting formal court judgments became more pressing. From around 1988 onwards, the difficulty of enforcing judgments (*zhixing nan*) had been regularly reported, both in the legal press and in the SPC's annual work reports.[43] The reasons for this difficulty were various but some of the main issues were: local protectionism and the insolvency of the defendant, as well as internal factors such as the court's reluctance to use coercive measures in civil cases and the inadequacy of the available coercive measures.[44] By 2006, more than one million civil judgments had not been implemented and as a result, "the verdicts remain[ed] empty words on a piece of judicial paper".[45] This was an issue of grave concern, particularly as covered by the media.

---

[41] Article 33 was amended to read simply: 'The state respects and protects human rights.' Although this amendment did not relate directly to procedural rights, it is thought to have increased the notion of equality before the law. Chen, Jianfu. 2004. The revision of the constitution in the PRC: A great leap forward or a symbolic gesture? *China Perspectives*, no. 53, 6.

[42] China Rights Forum. 2005. Review of procedural laws raises hopes for justice. *China Rights Forum*, no. 2, 47.

[43] Clarke, Donald C. 1996. Power and politics in the Chinese court system: The enforcement of civil judgments. *Columbia Journal of Asian Law* Vol. 10, No. 1, 27.

[44] Ibid., 35–60.

[45] Ying, Gao. 2007. China to amend law to ensure civil rulings are carried out. *Xinhua*, June 24. However, such statistics are difficult to interpret as many cases are withdrawn or settled before being referred for execution, so it is impossible to accurately gauge the extent of the enforcement problem.

6.3.3.2 Key Provisions

In order to safeguard the administration of justice, the 2007 amendments aimed to introduce more robust sanctions for non-enforcement as well as increasing avenues of enforcement. Specifically, the limitation period for application for enforcement of civil judgments was extended from 6 months to 2 years, maximum fines for failure to comply with civil judgments were raised substantially from 1000 RMB to 10,000 RMB for individuals and from 30,000 RMB to 300,000 RMB for enterprises.[46] Also, if the court of first instance failed to carry out enforcement within 6 months, applicants were then permitted to apply to a higher-level court for enforcement. This measure in particular was designed to tackle local protectionism as higher-level courts were thought to have weaker links to the local government.

In addition to the primary goal of upgrading the enforcement process, the 2007 amendments also clarified retrial procedures, and streamlined the CPL by removing provisions which were dealt with by other legislation, such as the removal of chapter 19 on insolvent enterprises which had become irrelevant following the promulgation of the Enterprise Bankruptcy Law in June 2007. Although a provisional Bankruptcy Law had been passed in 1986, that law had only applied to state-owned enterprises and was thus of limited effect to the modern Chinese economy as reforms had led to a more market-centred economy. The comprehensive Enterprise Bankruptcy Law passed in 2007 modernised insolvency practices in China[47] and therefore rendered the inclusion of a chapter on insolvency in the Civil Procedure Law an unnecessary duplication.

6.3.4 The 2012 Amendments

6.3.4.1 Context

Despite providing a solid procedural framework, the 2007 amended CPL was not without its critics; in particular, the rules of evidence needed further formalisation / clarification, procedures for summary cases and small claims were needed to increase efficiency and rights for litigants required further simplification.[48] These areas were addressed in the most recent amendments to date, a draft of which was published for public comment in October 2011, before being approved on August 31 2012 and entering into force from January 1 2013. The 2012 amendments arguably

[46] These maximum fines roughly approximate to an increase from USD $150 to USD $1500 for individuals and from USD $5000 to USD $50000 for enterprises.

[47] For more details, see: Parry, Rebecca, Xu, Yongqian and Haizheng Zhang. eds. 2010. *China's new enterprise bankruptcy law: Context, interpretation and application*. Farnham: Ashgate Publishing.

[48] Clyde & Co. 2007. Civil procedure law of the People's Republic of China- Recent amendments. http://www.clydeco.com/attachments/published/2092/Civil%20Procedure%20Law%20of%20PRC%20(Nov07)v2.pdf.

constituted the most wide-ranging changes since the 1991 CPL was enacted and could be seen as the culmination of reform efforts led by the Supreme People's Court (SPC) which had been taking place since the late 1990s focusing on striking an appropriate balance between adjudication and mediation; and between judicial power and the rights of the parties.

6.3.4.2 Key Provisions

The first key change comprised improving and expanding the availability of summary procedures, now covered by Part 13 of the CPL. A summary procedure for minor civil claims was initially introduced by the 2007 amendments to the CPL, in order to offer claimants a simplified trial process for resolving civil disputes. However, this procedural avenue was sometimes abused by litigants maliciously appealing the outcome at first instance and thus unnecessarily delaying the final judgment.[49] The uncertainty regarding the finality of court judgments has also been linked to consequent delays in enforcement.[50] In order to combat this problem and deliver more certainty, Article 162 now provides that where a basic-level court tries a simple civil case under this procedure, if the amount subject to dispute is less than 30 % of the local average annual wage, then the first instance judgment shall be final. Local guidelines suggest that this 30 % threshold typically amounts to a maximum claim under the summary procedure of between 10,000 RMB and 15,000 RMB depending on the affluence of the area in question.[51] A case heard under this improved summary procedure is subject to a simplified procedure of summons, documentation and trial according to Article 159, as well as being subject to a three month deadline to conclude the case from the date when the case is accepted by the court (Article 161).

Such a simplified small claims procedure must be welcomed for striving to widen access to justice to a broader pool of litigants and by recognising that delaying justice can often deny justice. Indeed, the reforms and expansion of the summary and small claims procedure is arguably the element of the 2012 CPL amendments to receive the most attention within China itself, with each province, autonomous region or directly controlled municipality releasing local guidelines as

[49] Ye, Ariel and Yu Song. 2012. Justice, efficiency and the new civil procedure law. *China Law and Practice*.

[50] Liu, Nanping. 1999. Vulnerable justice: Finality of civil judgments in China. *Columbia Journal of Asian Law*. 13(1) 35–98.

[51] Roughly approximate to between USD $1500 and USD $2250. See, for example: Shanghai introduces the conditions for small claims trials. 2012. (*Shanghai chutai xiao e susong shenpan gongzuo xize*) 27 December http://www.civilprocedurelaw.cn/html/fldt_1171_2978.html accessed 2 March 2013, giving a threshold of 15,000 RMB in Shanghai; Jiangxi High Court issues guidance to standardise the small claims procedure. 2013. (*Jiangxi gao yuan chutai zhidao yijian guifan xiao e susong chengxu*) 7 February http://www.civilprocedurelaw.cn/html/fldt_1171_3085.html accessed 2 March 2013, giving a threshold of 10,000 RMB in Jiangxi.

to how the 30 % small claims limit applies in that area.[52] As cases can be decided swiftly and with a higher degree of certainty, this is an aspect of the reforms which has been implemented with some success since the amendments coming into force in January 2013. For example, the Nanfang Daily News reported in late January 2013 the conclusion of a labour dispute between an employee and employer which had been resolved in 15 days. Such a swift resolution was described by Jiang Heping, the President of the Dongguan City People's Court, as previously unimaginable[53] and represents a substantial advancement for the civil justice system overall as cases can now be resolved swiftly, improving access to justice and reducing associated legal fees.

A second key area of reform addressed by the 2012 amendments is improvements made to procedural rights of parties, including expanding the potential use of public interest litigation. Under the 2012 amendments, Article 55 provides that with respect to acts that prejudice the public interest such as the pollution of the environment and infringement of the lawful rights and interests of numerous consumers, the authorities and relevant organisations defined by law may institute legal action in the people's court.

Thirdly, the rules relating to evidence were subject to some much needed clarification. Evidence is undoubtedly a crucial aspect of civil procedure regardless of the jurisdiction concerned and the 2012 amendments have further clarified the rules relating to evidence which have been evolving in China since the 1980s. Article 65 now makes it clear that not only is it the parties' responsibility to provide evidence in support of their claims (Article 64), but also that this evidence should be presented promptly and what the consequences may be of failing to provide the evidence in a timely manner. In addition, Article 66 is also a new insertion and provides a fresh layer of formality to the evidence process, by establishing that the court must provide a stamped or signed and dated receipt to the party submitting the evidence indicating the nature of the evidence.

Other important provisions included improving transparency of court judgments and further adjusting the formal position of mediation within the dispute resolution system. Article 122 of the 2012 amendments is a newly inserted provision which states that if a civil dispute brought before the courts would be suitable for media tion, then mediation should be attempted first, unless the parties refuse mediation. This 'mediation first' policy is the culmination of an official fluctuation in policy back towards mediatory dispute resolution after emphasising formal court-based adjudication throughout the 1990s.

The 2012 Amendments also make significant improvements to the transparency of court judgments. In addition to the pre-existing stipulation that the court should

[52] See, for example, the News section at: http://www.civilprocedurelaw.cn/?list-1171.html which lists several areas as having already released local guidelines on implementing the 30 % small claims system, including: Chongqing, Shaanxi, Jiangxi, Shandong, Zhejiang and Jiangsu.

[53] 'Dongguan concludes first small claims case since the implementation of the new Civil Procedure Law' (*Dongguan shenjie xinminsufa shishi yilai shouzong xiao'e susongan*), January 29 2013, Nanfang Daily News, available at: http://news.timedg.com/2013-01/29/content_13571323.htm

give a public judgment regardless of whether the case was heard in public or in camera (now found in Article 148), the newly created Article 156 provides that the public can access legally effective judgments and rulings, except for those involving state secrets, trade secrets or personal privacy. This Article shows an unprecedented commitment to transparency in the formal legal system and links to the persistent debate surrounding the developing rule of law in China.

6.4 Dynamism in China's Civil Procedure Law

Now that the context and key provisions for each of the main legislative changes in China's civil procedure rules over the past 30 years have been outlined, several trends across these amendments will be teased out in order to illustrate the dynamism of China's modern civil procedure laws. The development path taken by China in the modernisation of its civil procedure rules has been impressive but could not accurately be described as linear. There have inevitably been twists and turns along the way, but the difficulties involved in shifting the entire foundations of the legal system should not be underestimated.

China has necessarily needed to be innovative in order to shift from relying on imported procedural norms and pre-existing informal mechanisms to effectively developing its own domestic civil procedure rules, ones more suited to modern China. The dynamic nature of China's civil procedure will be clearly shown through a consideration below of just a few of the current approaches within and the issues facing China's civil procedure system. Specifically, the oscillating official attitudes towards mediation as a key dispute resolution tool; the tension between efficiency and due process evident in the growing availability of summary procedures; and uncertainty about the role that the formal court structures should play in the wider political system.

6.4.1 The Status of Mediation

Mediation had been the primary method of dispute resolution since the founding of the People's Republic of China in 1949 and this dominance continued in the early years of the reform era post-1978. Indeed, mediation continued to function as the bedrock of the civil justice system throughout the 1980s as the judiciary relied on familiar principles and procedures, given few members of the judiciary at that time had received a formal legal education due to the devastating effects of the Cultural Revolution.[54]

[54] For an excellent overview of the legal system both pre-reform and in the early years of the reform era, see: Lubman, Stanley. 1999. Bird in a cage: Legal reform in China after Mao. Stanford, Calif.: Stanford University Press.

This dependence on mediation began to shift from the late 1980s onwards as not only did new graduates of the revitalised Law schools begin to reform the system from within, but there began a growing recognition that court mediation was not a panacea in dispute resolution. Indeed, as practised, mediated settlements were often not voluntarily entered into, or indeed concluded, as the judge would impose a settlement with little accountability or constraints placed upon them.[55] Perversely, mediated settlements were often more labour-intensive to achieve than adjudication, so some city courts, reflecting the system's dynamism, began to move toward quicker resolution of disputes through formal adjudication.

It was in this context that the 1991 CPL was passed. It emphasised that mediation must be voluntary and lawful and imposed a time limit for concluding cases. This marked an historic milestone in the shift towards more formal adjudication by the courts and was followed by a steady drop in the proportion of cases resolved via mediation versus those concluded via formal court judgment throughout the 1990s. In the early 2000s, the percentage of cases resolved through mediation reached a nadir of approximately 30 %.[56] This decline in mediation mirrored a general stagnation in the total number of civil disputes filed which plateaued at around 4.3 to 4.4 million between 2002 and 2006.[57]

However, from 2004 onwards, the leadership of the SPC began to advocate a 'mediate if possible, adjudicate if appropriate' (*neng tiao ze tiao, dang pan ze pan*) slogan.[58] At this stage, mediation was just encouraged rather than mandated; nevertheless the first increase in a decade in the number of cases resolved through the People's Mediation Committees was observed in 2005.[59] This focus on mediation was underlined by the adoption in 2007 of the SPC's Several Opinions on further enhancing the effect of court-based mediation to construct a harmonious society[60] and accelerated further by the appointment of Wang Shengjun as the SPC President. Wang's appointment led to a new wave of reform efforts directed at the court structure which could feasibly be characterised as instrumental as these measures reflected the key aim of increasing judicial power and authority, whilst accepting realignment back towards mediation as a necessary political compromise.

---

[55] Huang, Phillip C. C. 2006. Court mediation in China, Past and present. *Modern China* 32, no. 3.

[56] Fu and Cullen, (n 40), 43.

[57] PRC National Bureau of Statistics (n 11).

[58] See, for example: Provisions of the Supreme People's Court about several issues concerning the civil mediation work of the people's court (*Zuigao renmin fayuan guanyu renmin fayuan minshi tiaojie gongzuo ruogan wenti de guiding*). 2004. http://www.law-lib.com/law/law_view.asp?id=86820.

[59] Liebman, Benjamin L. 2008. China's courts: Restricted reform. In *China's legal system: New developments, new challenges*, ed. Donald C. Clarke. Cambridge: Cambridge University Press, 68.

[60] For full text, see: SPC several opinions on the role of mediation in building a socialist harmonious society (*Zuigao renmin fayuan guanyu jin yi bu fahui susong tiaojie zai goujian shehui zhuyi hexie shehui zhong jiji zuoyong de ruogan yijian*). 2007. http://www.lawinfochina.com/display.aspx?lib=law&id=5930&CGid=.

Consequently, the proportion of civil cases resolved by withdrawal or mediation rose from 55 % in 2006 to 65.3 % in 2010,[61] against a background of a rise in first instance civil disputes filed from 4.3 million to 6 million across the same time period.[62] This refocus on mediation as the preferred method of dispute resolution has been explained largely as a pragmatic response to growing social unrest and was thought to represent a push towards the official goal of constructing a 'harmonious society' which had been espoused by President Hu Jintao. In addition, the wider use of mediation was advocated in order to reduce the number of litigation-related petitions (*shesu xinfang*) received under the administrative 'letters and visits' system, essentially an alternative channel for complaints to be aired. As the number of petitioners to the central authorities in Beijing surged, the courts were increasingly seen as failing because they were not effectively containing disputes and promoting social stability / harmony.[63] This is because reaching a settlement through mediation is seen as more likely to be acceptable to both parties and thus, is less likely to result in one of those parties subsequently raising the same dispute via the *xinfang* system.[64] However, there is scepticism over whether the ideal of mediation as a more conciliatory mechanism of dispute resolution is realistically achievable in the long-term. It is not only unclear whether mediation rates correlate strongly with the number of litigation-related petitions, but also whether blindly coercing parties into mediation may actually increase dissatisfaction in the longer term.

The current position regarding the use of mediation in China is that mediation should be attempted first. This is reflected in Article 122 as amended in 2012. The various drafts and amendments of the CPL thus reflect these changing winds in relation to official attitudes towards mediation. Furthermore, it is not only the case that judges should encourage mediation where possible; more recent changes mean that judges' performance is evaluated partly according to the proportion of cases mediated. Thus, it is clear that the most recent changes to the CPL indicate an entrenchment of mediation as the primary and preferred option for civil dispute settlement. Accordingly, despite impressive and fundamental changes to the civil justice system in the reform era, the momentum of reform appears to be faltering, potentially calling into question the dynamic transformations that have taken place since 1978.

6.4.2 The Use of Summary Procedures

In parallel with shifting official attitudes towards mediation, China has also displayed a dynamic attitude to the use of summary procedures in civil dispute resolution. Although the CPL did recognise summary procedure in its 1991 incarnation,

---

[61] SPC Work Report 2011 (*Zuigao renmin fayuan baogao 2011*). http://www.china.com.cn/2011/2011-03/11/content_22112396.htm.

[62] PRC National Bureau of Statistics (n 11).

[63] Fu and Cullen, (n 40), 44.

[64] Minzner, (n 12).

the relevant provisions were vague and difficult to apply. Accordingly, a SPC judicial interpretation concerning the application of summary procedure to civil cases was issued in 2003. Although no remarkable increase in the frequency of summary procedures followed immediately, from 2008, statistical indicators used to evaluate judicial performance included the proportion of cases to which summary procedure was applied. Furthermore, this indicator was weighted disproportionately even compared to other priority areas such as the proportion of cases mediated.[65]

This intense promotion of summary procedures arises from a drive for greater 'judicial efficiency' (*sifa xiaolü*), a key theme within the agenda of the SPC since the first 5-year plan to develop the judicial system was released in 1999.[66] Thus, it is clear that summary procedures are being heavily promoted, but what is the reason for such procedures to be so prominent in official policy? The main reason usually given is the rising workload of the judiciary who must contend with surging levels of litigation.[67] To what extent is the judiciary truly overworked and can this justify the emphasis currently placed on summary procedures in the civil justice system?

It is undeniable that China initially experienced an unparalleled explosion in the sheer number of cases dealt with by the courts since the reform era began more than 30 years ago. In 1978, the total number of cases accepted by the courts was only 447,755, but by 1996 had reached over 5 million[68] and remained around the same figure across the early 2000s. However, what is arguably more remarkable is the proportion of civil cases within this total; from criminal cases accounting for up to 50 % of cases pre-reform, to only accounting for about 10–15% today. Therefore, civil cases have increased much more substantially since the reform era began in the late 1970s.

The most recent figures from the Supreme People's Court 2012 work report, as delivered to the National People's Congress in March 2013 reported that, over the past 5 years, civil cases concluded at first instance had grown by 37.8 %, whilst commercial cases had experienced an increase of 42.6 % year-on-year.[69] Such levels of proliferation clearly have implications for the stretched resources of the judicial system in China and indeed, although only 5 years elapsed between the amend-

[65] With the former accounting for 8 % of the total score and the latter only 5 %. Zhang,Taisu. 2012. The pragmatic court: Reinterpreting the Supreme People's Court of China. *Columbia Journal of Asian Law* 25, no. 1, 29.

[66] The People's Court 'first five-year reform program' and 'second five-year reform program'. (*Renmin fayuan* < *'yiwu' gaige gangyao* > *yu* < *'erwu' gaige gangyao*>). 30 April 2009. http://www.legaldaily.com.cn/zbzk/2009-04/30/content_1091822.htm. Accessed 3 March 2012.

[67] A phenomenon known as the 'litigation explosion' (*susong baozha*). See, for example: Strengthen mediation by the People's Courts to deal with the 'litigation explosion' (*Renmin fayuan jiaqiang tiaojie yingdui susong baozha*). 2010. http://www.china.com.cn/news/zhuanti/2010lianghui/2010-03/12/content_19590048.htm.

[68] Liang, Bin. 2008. *The changing Chinese legal system, 1978- present: Centralization of power and rationalization of the legal system*. Abingdon, Oxon: Routledge, 46.

[69] SPC 2012 Work Report (Summary) (*Zuigao renmin fayuan gongzuo baogao (Zhaiyao)*). 2013. http://www.chinacourt.org/article/detail/2013/03/id/907830.shtml.

ments of 2007 and 2012, these figures suggest that China's commercial sector and associated disputes grew strongly during this period.

On the other hand, overall figures do suggest that the huge increases in number of cases which took place across the 1980s and 1990s largely stagnated at the start of the twenty-first century, so there needs to be a note of caution in attributing recent changes in the use of summary procedures solely to pressure from an increasing number of cases coming before the courts. For example, Liebman carried out interviews with more than 200 judges, lawyers and academics in China between 2003 and 2007 which confirmed the levelling-out, if not even a slight decline, in the total number of court cases from 1999 onwards.[70] Nevertheless, since around 2007, there has been a steady rise in the overall number of civil cases heard by the courts nationwide, feasibly attributable to the improvements in enforcement after the 2007 amendments to the Civil Procedure Law, but also possibly linked to other factors in China's developing economy and society.

Accordingly, there appeared to be a clear need to increase the efficiency of formal litigation within the court system in order to prioritise the allocation of overstretched judicial resources. However, it has been noted that even if litigation volumes are beginning to increase after plateauing in the 2000s, judicial workload remains low relative to other jurisdictions.[71] Although direct comparisons of judicial workload can be a blunt instrument in a sense because such comparisons don't take into account systemic or structural differences which would account for such discrepancies, nevertheless judges in China do not appear to be significantly overworked compared to other jurisdictions. For example, a 2005 study of judges in Shanghai found an average of 82 civil claims handled each year,[72] compared to averages of 177 amongst judges in New South Wales, Australia and 183 amongst judges at a regional court in Stuttgart, Germany.[73] Thus, concerns about workload alone seem insufficient to fully explain the hefty emphasis placed on the application of summary procedures to cases regardless of the suitability of such cases. Zhang suggests rather that "the best explanation is simply the pragmatic pursuit of institutional self-interest, most notably financial health."[74] In other words, that the SPC is demonstrating instrumental dynamism by pursuing ever greater use of summary procedures largely to protect its own finances rather than because of easing workloads or any loftier ideals related to access to justice.

---

[70] Liebman, (n 60).

[71] Zhang, (n 65), 31–32.

[72] Liu, Juanjuan. 2005. Comparison and remodelling of judicial efficiency and judicial workload (*Sifa xiaolu yu faguan yuan'e zhidu zhi bijiao chongsu*) 18 April. http://www.hshfy.sh.cn/shfy/gweb/xxnr.jsp?pa=aaWQ9MjgONDEmeGg9MQPdcssPdcssz accessed 5 March 2013.

[73] Marfording, Annette and Ann Eyland. 2010. Civil litigation in New South Wales: Empirical and analytical comparisons with Germany. UNSW Law Research Paper No. 2010–28, 110.

[74] Zhang, (n 65), 34.

6.4.3 The Role of the Courts in the Wider Legal System

The wide-ranging reforms witnessed in China's civil procedure laws also reveal considerable dynamism in relation to the overall role of the courts. The expansion in the 2012 amendment of the availability of public interest litigation (PIL) to bodies which do not have a direct interest in a case is one aspect where China is striving to fulfil multiple policy goals such as offering an outlet for discontent whilst also maintaining a tight level of control over the operation of such mechanisms.

In many, particularly developing, countries, individual litigants can be intimidated not only by the costs of initiating a civil suit, but also by the formality of the justice system, so public interest litigation is seen as a useful tool, for example in India, to allow the rights and interests of ordinary citizens to be defended in court.[75] In addition, litigation in general is closely linked with the notion of empowering citizens and challenging the status quo in terms of power and this is particularly pertinent when considering group or class action litigation.[76] In a country such as China which is so large and diverse and still subject to rapid societal changes due to the developing economy, any reforms in litigation also need to consider not only efficiency but also access to the courts; particularly where legal representation is lacking which is frequently the case for impoverished or poorly educated litigants in China.[77] If the procedures become overly technical or formal, they may actually deter litigants from bringing cases to court. In other words, collective litigation as a democratic mechanism offers ordinary Chinese citizens the opportunity to participate in norm setting as well as expressing discontent. The use of public interest litigation is thus particularly interesting in China as it also demonstrates the rise of private rights in the consciousness of ordinary citizens.

Autonomous civil society organisations are seen as crucial in building a more responsive and democratic political system.[78] Given the tight control of the political system in China, the Chinese government is understandably worried about the rise of NGOs playing a larger and a more formal role in the legal system. The central government are seeking to strike a delicate balance between minimising citizens' discontent by providing outlets for complaints to be heard while not overly encouraging the growth of NGOs which might challenge the current power structures.[79]

---

[75] Desai, Ashok H. and S. Muralidhar. 2000. Public interest litigation: Potential and problems. In *Supreme but not infallible- Essays in honour of the Supreme Court of India*, ed. B. N. et al Kirpal. New Delhi: Oxford University Press, 3.

[76] Woo and Gallagher, (n 5), 19.

[77] Woo, Margaret Y. K. and Yaxin Wang. 2005. Civil justice in China: An empirical study of courts in three provinces. *American Journal of Comparative Law* 53(4), 913.

[78] Florini,Ann, Hairong Lai, and Yeling Tan. 2012. *China experiments: From local innovations to national reform*. Washington DC: Brookings Institution, 92.

[79] For an overview of NGOs in China, see: Ma, Qiusha. 2005. Non-governmental organizations in contemporary China: Paving the way to civil society? London: Routledge, particularly chapter 2, '"Small government, big society": The Chinese government's NGO policy and its dilemma'.

Thus, the expansion of the availability of PIL to litigants without a direct interest in the case seems to be primarily motivated by instrumental attempts to reduce the number of complaints emanating from ordinary citizens, similar to the motive supporting greater use of mediation discussed above, rather than encouraging the development of a wider civil rights movement.

The availability of public interest litigation can thus act as an important 'release' for wider civil discontent, but this release is also of concern to the government. This unease about the role of the legal system can be seen in the fluctuating attitudes to the courts and the status of litigation in the reform era overall. The central government is clearly uneasy with the notion of an independent judiciary challenging other institutions for power and thus the recent amendment allowing greater access to litigation for NGOs and 'relevant organisations' is an important shift.

PIL did exist in China prior to the CPL amendments of 2012 and a useful list of cases compiled by the China Labour Bulletin in Hong Kong in 2007[80] shows that in several previous cases, the claimant did not receive a favourable verdict from the court in question, but nevertheless received some kind of resolution to their complaint. Therefore, it is important to recognise that the impact of PIL can stretch beyond the formal litigation process and may actually have greater utility in simply raising public awareness of certain issues and rights. When public interest litigation does succeed in China, it is largely due to media attention and resultant public awareness, rather than due to the judgments passed by the courts.[81]

However, although the expansion of PIL to claimants without a direct interest in the case is noteworthy, it is important to recognise that infringement of consumer rights and environmental pollution are specified in the amendment as the only two causes of action which would allow for public interest litigation to be initiated (but further specified in press releases to be in response to food safety scandals specifically). This reflects China's dynamism in action by simultaneously opening up new channels for disputes to be aired, whilst also severely restricting access to such channels. Clearly, the causes of action specified in the CPL arose as a result of particular media outrages over food safety such as the Sanlu tainted milk scandal[82] and environmental pollution which is also of growing concern in the Chinese media. This suggests that the broader expansion of PIL to cover issues of public interest more generally, such as malfeasance by public bodies, is not contemplated by the legislation to date and thus the revised provision in the CPL may be of limited application to the overall expansion of such lawsuits.

[80] China Labour Bulletin. 2007. Public interest litigation in China: A new force for social justice. Hong Kong.

[81] Liebman, Benjamin L. 1998. Class action litigation in China. *Harvard Law Review* 111, no. 6.

[82] Liu, Chenglin. 2009. Profits above the law: China's melamine tainted milk incident. *Mississippi Law Journal* 79, no. 2.

6.5 Conclusion: Looking to the Future of Dynamic Civil Justice in China

The crucial question is whether the dynamic reforms witnessed since 1978 are primarily for the benefit of ordinary Chinese citizens or in the interests of maintaining the existing Party-state. It is undeniably correct to suggest that the amendments made to the CPL in 2012 and effective from January 2013 appear to largely follow the existing agenda of striving to minimise citizen discontent rather than espousing any higher ideals of the function of the civil justice system. This can be seen both in the emphasis on mediation and on the use of summary procedures to resolve disputes, and corroborates the notion that top-down efforts to reform the courts have focused primarily on a need to resolve disputes and grievances as they arise, rather than reflecting any concept that the formal role of the courts should be expanded vis-à-vis other dispute resolution mechanisms.[83]

Furthermore, this also represents bad news for the developing rule of law in China; it appears that attitudes towards the role of the legal system are reverting to an instrumentalist approach whereby the courts are only working if they maintain stability amongst the people. Thus, the remarkable dynamism that China has shown in its reform of civil procedure as outlined in this chapter could perhaps be more accurately described as instrumental dynamism because the reforms are primarily driven by political demands to maintain harmony in society. There is also a sense that the civil justice system in China is in a state of flux as the number of civil disputes initiated has risen sharply in the past few years, but the rate of cases mediated and resolved summarily has also increased. Thus, there is a great deal of uncertainty in the current system about whether the dynamic changes already witnessed will be maintained and even expanded further, or whether retrenchments to more traditional forms of dispute resolution will be undertaken.

Having said that, the future of the civil justice system is not without promise. Despite numerous imperfections remaining in China's procedural system, the majority of litigants report that courts formally comply with mandated trial procedures and the litigants are largely satisfied by the competency of the courts.[84] The civil justice system has also improved unrecognisably since the reform era began to embed in the 1980s. Nevertheless, improvements in the procedural code can only enhance the justice system overall, especially if the institutions are further strengthened. Ultimately, the proof of the pudding is in the eating, so it remains to be seen how the dynamic changes discussed in this chapter will alter the civil justice system as the latest amendments continue to be implemented nationwide and further clarified through actual court practice.

---

[83] Liebman, (n 59), 70.

[84] Pei, Minxin et al. 2010. A survey of commercial litigation in Shanghai courts. In *Judicial independence in China: Lessons for global rule of law promotion*, ed. Randall Peerenboom. Cambridge: Cambridge University Press.

Chapter 7
The Dynamism of China's Civil Litigation System

Margaret Woo

From China to the U.S., civil justice reform is the mantra of the day.[1] Globally, civil procedure is the locus of dynamic experiments often taking place under the radar screen of most political and social reformers. Viewed as technical answers to perceived increases in civil caseload and overburdened judges, civil procedure nevertheless contains within its rules clues about differing visions of civil justice and how that justice can be delivered. In China, civil procedure reforms take the form of the recent 2012 amendments to the Chinese civil procedure code. These reforms as a whole have focused on efficiency and economy using such tactics as greater case management by judges, encouragement of mediation, and greater pressure on parties to move the case along or face penalties.

Yet,while changes to the Chinese civil procedure code are said to be motivated by concerns of efficiency and economy, how these reforms take shape in China, as in elsewhere, are arguably part and parcel of a country's national identity. And China's civil dispute resolution reflects its identity of "order over freedom, duty over rights, collective over individual interests."[2] But perversely, in the effort to preserve "order over freedom, duty over rights, collective over individual interests," recent procedural reforms in China may undermine the raison d'etre of the procedure itself, with the potential to discourage rather than encourage the state's goal of a "harmonious society."

[1] Since 2002, there have been civil procedure reforms in the Netherlands, Germany, Austria, France, England, and China. See the essays in Rhee, C.H., Fu, Yulin, eds., *Civil Litigation in China and Europe* (Springer, 2014).

[2] Shao-Chuan Leng & Hungdah Chiu, *Criminal Justice in Post Mao China: Analysis and Documents* 171 (State University of New York Press, 1985).

M. Woo (✉)
School of Law, Northeastern University School of Law, Boston, MA, USA
e-mail: m.woo@neu.edu

C.B. Picker, G.I. Seidman (eds.), *The Dynamism of Civil Procedure - Global Trends and Developments*, Ius Gentium: Comparative Perspectives on Law and Justice 48, DOI 10.1007/978-3-319-21981-3_7

The Chinese Civil Procedure Code was first promulgated in 1982 for trial implementation, formally enacted in 1991, and amended in 2007. The 2007 amendments focused primarily on tightening the trial supervision provisions and enforcement of judgments. Since 2007, the ever increasing number of civil lawsuits and the overburdened workload of Chinese trial courts have led to yet another round of changes to the civil procedure code. In June, 10, 2011, the central committee legislative affairs bureau announced plans to revise both the civil and criminal procedure codes. The amendments were passed on August 31, 2012, effective January 1, 2013.

These changes to the civil procedure code came on the tail of growing social instability and public dissatisfaction with the work of the Chinese courts. With China's economic boom came also greater disparity in power and income resulting in growing social unrest and discontent. Chinese courts and government saw an increase in letters of complaint, as well as rising numbers of petitions (a method of seeking reviews of cases after final appeals).[3] Government officials attribute this rise in petitions to the courts' inability to resolve disputes as well as increased corruption and graft in the courts. Thus, a 2004 report on the official Chinacourt.org Website states that 40 % of all petitions to government letters and visit offices stem from complaints about courts, procuratorates, or the police.[4] Concerned that the courts are unable to constrain social discord, the Chinese government has equated improved legal work with greater consideration of the social and political context of cases.[5]

It is within the context of addressing problems of social instability and public dissatisfaction with the work of the courts that civil justice reforms in China must be understood. But these reforms also come at a time when China is striving to achieve international prominence and state building. Importantly, the reforms reflect the national identity of emphasizing "order over freedom, duty over rights, collective over individual interests." As a result, the 2012 amendments both empower and limit the courts. They empower the courts vis a vis the litigants but limit the court vis a vis the state. The amendments provide greater authority to courts to streamline cases but also greater oversight of them. A litigant's right to litigate is now measured by a requirement of good faith. New supervision provisions, in addition to the normal appeals process, are added to empower state actors such as procurators, not

[3] See Benjamin Liebman, A Populist Threat to China's Courts, in Margaret Woo & Mary Gallagher, ed., Chinese Justice: Civil Dispute Resolution in Contemporary China (Cambridge University Press 2011).

[4] Ye Wenbing, "Shixi fayuan dangqian xinfang cunzai wenti ji duice," (Analysis of the problems with and responses to letters and visits to courts at present), Zhongguo fayuan wang, January 7, 2004, http://www.chinacourt.org/public/detail.php?id=09316.

[5] *See China to Launch Education of "Socialist Concept of Rule of Law*," (stating socialist rule of law is the building of a socialist harmonious society, People's Daily, April 14, 2006 at http://english.peopledaily.com.cn/200604/14/eng20060414_258297.html; *See also* Guan yu jin yi bu fa hui su song tiao jie zai you jian she hui zhu yi he she shi hui zhong ji ji zuo yong de ruo gan yi jian, [Supreme People's Court, Regarding the Next Step Towards Litigation Development According to Socialist Principals and Harmonious Society Opinion, para. 2, available at http://rmfyb.chinacourt.org/public/detail.php?id=106477].

private litigants, to challenge and overturn court decisions under the rubric of supervision. Given the still emerging professionalism of Chinese courts, these numerous revisions keep a more careful check on judicial functions but at the same time, also limit access to the courthouse gates.

7.1 Structure of the Formal Chinese Court System

Before discussing the details of the new civil procedure amendments, it is important to understand the Chinese legal system in which these amendments operate. In its formal structure, the Chinese legal system resembles any other legal system. According to the Organic Law of the People's Court, amended in 1983, judicial power is exercised at four levels: the basic people's courts, intermediate people's courts, higher people's courts, and the Supreme People's Courts (plus specialized courts such Military, Railway Transportation and Maritime Courts). According to the latest figures, there are 400 Intermediate People's Courts, established in municipalities and prefectures, and over 3,000 Basic People's Courts, established in urban districts and rural counties. Not to be ignored are the some 17,000 People's Tribunals (renmin fating) that handle the majority of the disputes at the local level, which are established anywhere by the Basic People's Courts, with the tribunal's judgment having the same effect as a basic court judgment.[6]

Under the principle of "the four levels of courts and two trials to conclude a case" [one trial at first instance and one trial on appeal], most litigation is adjudicated in basic people's courts or intermediate people's courts while higher people's courts handle appeals. Finally, the Supreme People's Court (SPC) only hears appeals from the higher people's court, although occasionally itmay hear cases bearing on national issues – so far in the history of the SPC, the court has only once formed a special tribunal to try accusations against "the Gang of Four" in 1980.

The Chinese courts are staffed by some 190,000 judges (in 2009)[7] and nearly 300,000 judicial personnel (80 % work in the over 3,000 basic people's courts).[8] Increasingly, judges are asked to hold to a higher level of professionalism. While previously Chinese judges were appointed from the ranks of the military, today's Chinese judges are legally trained and must pass a national judges' exam. However, the disparity between provinces with reference to judicial resources and competence remains great and mirrors the economic disparity within the country. Thus, while Beijing can boasts a well-trained staff of 4,080 judges and judicial staff who

[6] *See* Regulations Concerning Several Issues with Respect to People's Tribunals (issued by the SPC on July 15, 1999).

[7] Wang Huazhong and Wang Jingqiong, *Courts hit by rising number of lawsuits*, China Daily, July 17, 2010, citing Annual Work Report of People's Courts in China, *available at* http://www.chinadaily.com.cn/china/2010-07/14/content_10102630.htm.

[8] Randall Peerenboom, *China's Law March Towards Rule of Law* (Cambridge: Cambridge University Press, 2002), at 281.

took the national judicial exam,[9] statistics from Sichuan Province indicates that judges make up 54.8 % of the court's staff, but only 2 % hold masters degree in law, and nearly half of them do not have a bachelor's degree.[10] Recent efforts to centralize court funding and amend the civil procedure are efforts to ameliorate this disparity caused by different provincial economic development.

Within the court, the judiciary operates under the principle of "democratic centralism." Each court has a president, one or more vice presidents, an Adjudication (or Judicial) Committee (*shenpan weiyuanhui*) composed of court leaders who review more difficult cases, judges who work in the divisions, and clerks.[11] While Chinese judges are better qualified than in the past, at least as measured by levels of education received, Chinese judges continue to be treated in their work as bureaucrats within a layered civil service system. While financial reform of the court system is under way,[12] local governments have in the past controlled the court budget, and judicial reward and promotion often depends on subservience to the local government's dictates and interests as well as to central policy dictates.[13] The Chinese Party state has successively charged judges with implementing policies that varied from "strike hard" campaigns to processing disputes efficiently, to most recently, promoting "harmony."[14]

Another important arm of the Chinese legal system is the people's procuracy, essentially the country's law enforcement arm. While the procuracy is predominately charged with prosecution of criminal cases, the Constitution empowers the people's procuracy to be the state organs for "legal supervision."[15] As the watchdog of China's bureaucracy and legal system, the procuracy is responsible for investigating cases involving official graft and corruption, and citizen complaints against state personnel. As part of this supervisory authority, if a people's procuracy discovers a mistake in a judgment or order of a people's court at the corresponding level in a case of first instance, it could protest the decision. Under the hierarchy of the

[9] Peerenboom, *supra* note, at 291.

[10] Advisor: China needs to axe number of judges but improve professionalism, Xinhua News Agency, March 9, 2008, *available at* http://english.peopledaily.com.cn/90001/90776/90785/6369338.html.

[11] Stanley B. Lubman, *Bird in a Cage: Legal Reforms in China After Mao* (Stanford: Stanford University Press, 1999) at 252.

[12] In 2008, the Political and Legislative Affairs committee of the Central Committee of the CCP issued an opinion urging a change from local to national financijng of the courts. See http://www.360doc.com/content/11/0421/11/1993767_111229089.shtml.

[13] *But see* Xin He, Debt Collection in the Less Developed Regions of China, China Quarterly, 206, June 2011, pp. 253–275, at 265 (concluded that "local protectionism" exists more as renqin (personal connections) and less as interference from local government because of a financial link between the local government and local enterprises.

[14] The socialist rule of law requires building a harmonious socialist society. *See China to Launch Education of "Socialist Concept of Rule of Law,"* Communist Party of China (Apr. 14, 2006), http://english.cpc.people.com.cn/66485/66498/66501/4501945.html; *see also Senior Chinese official calls for efforts to ensure stability*, People's Daily Online (Jan. 8, 2007), http://english.peopledaily.com.cn/200701/08/eng20070108_339031.html.

[15] Article 5 of the Organic Law of the People's Procuracies of the PRC (amended in 1983).

government, the Supreme People's Court and the Supreme People's Procuracy are in an equal position – both report to the National People's Congress.[16] As such, then, Chinese courts are subject to detailed supervision by the people's congress and the procuracy. And in a number of ways, the 2012 Chinese civil procedure amendments empowered the role of the courts, but limited the role of litigants and reaffirmed this role of supervision by the procuracy.

7.2 Reforms to China's Civil Dispute Procedure

First and foremost, the 2012 amendments to the Chinese Civil Procedure Code reemphasize mediation as an effective mechanism for resolving disputes, noting that "suitable cases should first be mediated."[17] While a brief period in the early 2000's saw the Chinese state encouraging the use of courts and litigation, recent concerns with instability and increased workloads on Chinese judges have led the government to promote "harmony" and mediation as the more harmonious way to resolve disputes. New subsections were added to strengthen the integrity of mediated agreements.[18] Litigants may apply for court enforcement of an extra-judicial mediated agreement so long as the agreement is filed in court within 30 days of the agreement.[19] Under the amended rules, a civil court may, after investigation, enforce the agreement or require the parties to mediate again, if it finds the agreement unlawful.[20]

Additionally, the dramatic caseload now facing the Chinese courts has also led to efforts to streamline and divert cases rather than to adjudicate them. According to the Supreme People's Court, the number of court cases rose by at least 25 % between 2005 and 2009 but the total number of 190,000 judges remained almost the same.[21] New provisions outline a multi-track civil litigation system in which the court must, in the early stages of a litigation, assess and track the case to one of the following: (1) an expedited procedure (du cu, translated loosely as "supervised procedure") if the case, such as a debt collection case, has little or no factual disputes; (2) mediation, if the litigants' dispute is more substantial, but believed to be capable of settlement; (3) simplified procedure or ordinary procedure, according to the needs of the case; and (4) procedure for litigants to exchange evidence to clarify the points of dispute for a case that will require a trial. (Newly added Art. 134). The goal is that such tracking will leave very few cases for full adjudication and trial. It is through a multi-track system that litigation will be narrowed.

[16] Articles 128 and 133 of the 1982 Constitution.

[17] 2012 Amendments, para. 25 (inserting a new Article 121).

[18] *Id.* para. 39 (amending Chapter 15 by inserting new Section 6 (Confirming Cases regarding Mediated Agreements) and Section 7 (Implementing Cases regarding Security Interests)).

[19] *Id.*

[20] *Id.*

[21] Huazhong Wang & Jingqiong Wang, *Courts Hit by Rising Number of Lawsuits*, China Daily, July 14, 2010, http://www.chinadaily.com.cn/china/2010-07/14/content_10102630.htm.

Along with this tracking system, the revisions also make clear that simplified procedures are to be used for many civil cases in which the facts are relatively undisputed and the amount in controversy is not large. A new article raised the jurisdictional amount for simplified procedure cases to 30 % of the average salaries in provinces, autonomous administrative zones and self-governing cities. Simple cases with a value below 5,000 RMB ($798 US) will be limited to one trial only.[22] A second amendment would expand the simplified procedures' parameters.[23] In addition to requiring some simple cases to use simplified procedures, parties themselves can agree to the use of simplified procedures.[24]

The new amendments also focus on giving courts more authority to manage the cases as in the U.S. through the use of a pretrial conference, at which the parties are called in to identify the major points in dispute and the nature of the evidence to be presented at trial.[25] Cases from the basic people's court and those sent out from the trial courts can also use more convenient methods to summon litigants, deliver documents and try cases, but in all cases protect the litigants' rights and opinions.[26]

At the same time, while a private party's right to litigation is recognized, it is now subject to the requirement of "good faith." (Amended Art. 13). New Arts. 112 and 113 now authorize the court to sanction with fines or custody any party involved in collusion and malicious prosecution in filing a new case and in execution cases. This "good faith" requirement is ambiguous and may have the effect of chilling litigation and can be used to discourage unwanted litigation. But responding to the problem of courts refusing to accept complaints, amended art. 123 (previously art. 112) now bears the added provision that "people's court must protect the parties' legal right in bringing litigation." A court must accept a case that "is filed and that meets the requirements of Art. 119" within 7 days and notify the litigants who will then have the right to appeal.

The state's authority to enter the case has also been bolstered, particularly for socially significant cases. In recent years, Chinese courts have discouraged group litigation and cases with a broader social impact; that is, generally cases that the government viewed as having the potential in leading to social unrest. Fears of instability have led courts to withdraw from accepting group litigation. Courts are urged to divide up group cases into individual lawsuits. In 2006, the All-China Lawyers Association even issued a "guiding opinion" instructing law firms to assign only "politically qualified" lawyers to cases involving ten or more litigants.

---

[22] *Id.* para. 35 (inserting a new Article 161). As of 1 June 2014, the highest monthly minimum wage was in Shanghai (1,820 yuan), closely followed by Shenzhen (1,808 yuan). The lowest minimum wage was in the south-western province of Guizhou (1,030 yuan). See China Labour Bulletin at http://www.clb.org.hk/en/content/wages-china.

[23] 2012 Amendments, para. 33 (changing Article 142 to new Article 156 and inserting a new subsection (2) in new Article 156).

[24] *Id.*

[25] *Id.* para. 25 (inserting a new Art. 121). *See* explanation 1.1 (Adding a Provision of Mediation after Register).

[26] *Id.* para. 34 (changing Article 144 to new Article 158 and modifying new Article 158).

The proposed procedural revisions recognize the social significance of some cases, and expand standing or in other words, the right to bring suit, beyond those who have sustained a direct injury to include relevant governmental organs and civil society organizations.[27] Substantively, as in the environmental and consumer area, this allows the state to designate a governmental agency or an appropriate representative civil society organization to have third party standing – that is, to stand as a party in the lawsuit even though it may not have been directly injured by defendant's conduct.[28] Expanding standing to government agencies will have the effect of bringing control of such cases back to the Chinese developmental state, this time as formal parties in litigation.[29]

Finally, the new provisions expand supervision over the courts by certain state actors. The procuracy (prosecutors) in China have the unique authority to supervise judicial work that is distinct from the role of appellate courts in reviewing cases. The Chinese civil procedure code provides for one prosecutorial supervision method – "*kansu*" – under which an upper level procurator can file a protest with a lower court seeking retrial (reopening) of a legally effective judgment or with an upper level court for review if the judgment is not yet legally effective. Under the new amendments, Chinese procurators can also propose another new supervision method – "*jianyi*" – under which a procurator would propose to a court *at the same level* the retrial of cases with legally effective judgments, mediated agreements or arbitration decisions, so long as there is a newly discovered error (or conditions under Art. 198) or if a mediated agreement harms the public good.[30] Alternatively, the procurator could also ask the procurator at an upper level to file a *kansu*.[31]

The 2012 amendments also increase the parameters of supervision. Said to avoid collusion between litigating parties and mediating organizations, a new provision would allow prosecutors to challenge any mediated outcome that may harm the public good.[32] Procurators may also protest (*kansu*) or petition for retrial in the executions of any judgments, The investigative authority of prosecutors is increased to allow a prosecutor to investigate whether to pursue a protest (*kansu*) to the court at the next level or a proposal for retrial (*jianyi*) to the court at the same level.[33] The prosecutor is also empowered to review court records, question the litigants and investigate beyond the case.[34] Through these various amendments, the Chinese state

---

[27] *Guiding Opinion of the All China Lawyers Association Regarding Lawyers Handling Cases of a Mass Nature*, Cong.-Exec. Comm'n on China (May 30, 2006), http://www.cecc.gov/pages/virtualAcad/index.phpd?showsingle=53258 (providing both the original Chinese and translated English versions).

[28] This third party standing is also inserted in a number of articles – e.g., Art. 56 to challenge legally effective judgments.

[29] *Id.*

[30] *Id.* para. 44 (changing Article 187 to new Article 206 and modifying new Article 206).

[31] *Id.*

[32] *Id.*

[33] 2012 Amendment, *supra* note 157, para. 45 (inserting two new articles as Articles 207 and 208).

[34] *Id.*

through its procuracy can be said to have given itself a formal role to challenge results it deems contrary to the public good.

Grievance petitions filed with the Chinese state have skyrocketed, with many of these petitions filed by litigants dissatisfied with court treatment.[35] Letters and petitions are informal complaints filed with governmental agencies frequently to protest improper government actions. Mass petitions to government authorities increased at double digit annual rates of growth throughout the 1990s and 2000's, while in 2009, the number of letters and visits filed with the Supreme People's Court rose to210,934 from 140,511 in 2006.[36] To avoid petitions by dissatisfied litigants, the amended article expand litigant's rightin cases involving private citizens to petition the original trial court for retrial under specified circumstances (amended Art. 204, previously Art. 181). Three circumstances then allow litigants to next petition the procurator for supervision: (1) when the people's court has declined the litigant's petition for retrial; (2) when the people's court failed to act on the retrial petition for a long time; and (3) if the case upon retrial contains clear error. (New Art. 209). Finally, to address the problem of repeated petitions for retrial, new Article 211 specifies that parties may not petition the procurator again to file a protest if the party has already filed one petition to the procurator and the case has been retried by people's court. (Amended Art. 211, previously Art. 188).

7.3 Harmony Over Justice

China's civil dispute resolution process reflects its identity of "order over freedom, duty over rights, collective over individual interests."[37] In giving more control to the courts over the litigation, it is placing order over the freedom of litigants. In urging acceptance of compromised outcomes, it emphasizes social duty over the assertion of individual rights. In the persistence of state presence, it emphasizes the collective over individual rights. While these goals are admirable, one must ask the more problematic question of who is defining the nature of this "order over freedom," the identity of which "duties" should prevail over which "rights", and what "group

[35] Carl Minzner, *Xinfang*: *Alternative to Formal Chinese Legal Institutions*, 42 Stan. J. Int'l. L. 103, 106 (2006) ("Many petitions . . . are extra-legal appeals for court decisions.").

[36] Zuigao Renmin Fayuan "Zuigao Renmin Fayuan 2009 nian gongzuo baogao" (2008 Supreme People's Court work report), xinhua she, March 22, 2008, https://news.xinhuanet.com/newscenter/2008-03/22/content_7837838.htm. (accessed August 25, 2008). Wang Shaonan, "Chuangxin shesu xinfang gongzuo fangfa, fangbian dangshiren yifa biaoda suqiu" (Create new methods to improve litigation related petition work, make it convenient for the parties to make their claims according to law), Zuigao renmin fayuan wang, Chinacourt Web, March 12, 2010, at http://www.court.gov.cn/lhzl/bgjd/201003/620100312.283.5.html.

[37] Shao-Chuan Leng & Hungdah Chiu, Criminal Justice in Post Mao China: Analysis and Documents CRIMINAL JUSTICE IN POST-MAO CHINA,171 (1985).

interests" override "individual ones." The answer for China is inevitably the Chinese Communist Party.[38]

To understand legal reform in China, one must take into account the role of the Chinese Communist Party as the driving force for the Chinese developmental state and how its involvement in legal reforms has resulted in its latest turn – one that establishes a multi-track litigation system, in which minor and relatively insignificant cases are mediated, commercial cases are adjudicated, and mass cases are carefully controlled and shaped by the Chinese state. Importantly, law in China has been a critical part of its nation-building. But equally important, absent a separation of law from this task, laws and justice will be subsumed under national goals.

Indeed, at each critical juncture of China's recent state building, law was very much a part of it. Speaking at the landmark national civil justice conference held between December 1978 and January 1979, Jiang Hua, the former President of the Supreme People's Court, spoke of the necessity and legitimacy of civil justice, positioned the SPC to take the lead in judicial administration, and started to assert the court's institutional autonomy.[39] After the conference, Chinese legal reformers enhanced their efforts at procedural and institutional change while the SPC decreed that Chinese courts should "further improve the work of trying civil cases, protect the civil rights and interests of citizens and legal persons according to the law, and promot[ing] the just, safe, civilized, and healthy development of society."[40]

Then, for a time in the mid-1990s, the Chinese state encouraged the use of the courts in the hopes that the courts could assist in stabilizing society and serve as a neutral forum for litigants trying to rein in local bureaucrats.[41] The Chinese Communist Party at its 15th National Congress in 1997 set the first ten year target for national economic and social development with a basic strategy of "governing the country according to law and building a socialist country ruled by law."[42] In the areas of court and legal procedures, Chinese legal reforms adopted some elements

[38] In December 2007, Chinese president Hu Jintao urged the judiciary to subordinate the written law to the interests of the Chinese Communist Party (CCP) and the maintenance of "social stability:" "In their work, the grand judges and grand procurators shall always regard as supreme the party's cause, the people's interest and the constitution and laws." *See* Jerome Cohen, Op-Ed., *Body Blows for the Judiciary*, S. China Morning Post, Oct.18, 2008, at 13.

[39] *See pinyin* (民事审判工作同等重要)[*Civil Justice is Equally Important*], Sina (Aug. 14, 2007), http://book.sina.com.cn/nzt/history/cha/jianghuaz/66.shtml, *cited in* Hualing Fu, *Access to Justice in China: Potential, Limits and Alternatives*, *in* Chinese Justice: Civil Dispute Resolution in Contemporary China, *supra* note 68, at 25.

[40] *Id.*

[41] Ren Jianxin (任建新), Supreme People's Court President, Address before the Fourth Session of the Eighth National People's Congress (Mar. 12, 1996), *in* BBC Summary of World Broadcasts, Apr. 9, 1996, at 26; Renmin Ribao (人民日报) [China Daily], Mar. 14, 1997.

[42] *Establishment of the Socialist System of Laws with Chinese Characteristics*, Info. Office of the State Council of the People's Republic of China (Oct. 27, 2011), http://www.china.org.cn/government/whitepaper/2011-10/27/content_23738846.htm.

of the adversary system including party autonomy and burdens of proof.[43] But while the language of rights may have been easy to import, the process of rights assertion was more difficult. Efforts to establish legal formality and legal markets in China led to the dominance of technocracy and great disparity in access to justice.[44]

In 2005, in the latest turn of nation-building, President Hu Jintao called for the construction of a "harmonious society" in an effort to stem the tide of social unrest.[45] With the great disparity in income and increasing stratification of society, China faces great unrest, with increased strikes, and collective incidents, and higher rates of petitions filed against the government asserting governmental misconduct. Law responded and the Supreme People's Court began a retreat from a decade long path of civil justice reform and adjudication with a return to mediation and an endorsement of enhanced mediation for cases of "great social concern."[46] The call is for preserving a "harmonious society," and the goal for courts is to stabilize society with the principle of "[u]sing mediation whenever possible, using adjudication whenever appropriate, combining mediation with adjudication, concluding the case and having the dispute resolved."[47] Despite the multiplicity of Chinese laws that have been enacted (by the end of August 2011, the Chinese legislature had enacted 240 effective laws including the current Constitution, 306 administrative regulations, and over 8,600 local regulations),[48] concerns for social stability have led the Chinese state to retreat from formal legal process and the assertion of rights in court if such assertion would result in social instability.

But perversely, recent reforms to civil dispute resolution procedures can undermine the raison d'etre of the procedures themselves, with the potential to discourage rather than encourage a "harmonious society." Injustice can breed disharmony. Rather than eliminating the problems underlying disputes, the recent Chinese strategy is to make the disputes go away. This may mean pacifying individual litigants momentarily but leaves the underlying structural or institutional injustices untouched. This can be seen in the labor equality area, where Chinese women workers challenging employment discrimination are often mediated or arbitrated out of the system with payment, but discouraged from bringing suit that could result in more systemic change. While settlements may give the individual litigant some

---

[43] *Features of the Socialist System of Laws with Chinese Characteristics*, Info. Office of the State Council of the People's Republic of China (Oct. 27, 2011), http://www.china.org.cn/government/whitepaper/2011-10/27/content_23738836.htm.

[44] See Fu Hualing, Access to Justice in China: Potential, Limits and Alternatives, (September 15, 2009), Available at SSRN http://dx.doi.org/10.2139/ssrn.1474073.

[45] *Building Harmonious Society CPC's Top Task*, China Daily (Feb. 20, 2005), *available at* http://www.ChinaDaily.com.cn/english/doc/2005-02/20/content_417718.htm.

[46] *Yang Xiao*, *supra* note 108; Si fa bu biao zhang min tiao gong zuo "shuang xian"(司法部表彰民调工作"双先") [Ministry of Justice Commends the 'Two Advances' in People's Mediation Work] (Mar. 1, 2005), http://www.legalinfo.gov.cn/moj/jcgzzds/2005-05/17/content_133971.htm (reemphasizing the importance of mediation in serving the interests of building a "harmonious society").

[47] *Id.*

[48] *Id.*

compensation, the underlying equality principle is left resolved. Similarly, inindividual arbitrations, while the individual dispute may be resolved,there is no pronouncement of equality principles by the courts that can reverberate throughout the community. Thus, as the Communist Party of China (CPC), in adopting the "Resolution on Major Issues Regarding the Building of a Harmonious Socialist Society" in 2006,[49] noted that "employment discrimination runs contrary to the building of a socialist harmonious society," the route to eliminating employment discrimination rests on the state taking action rather than private challenges as through litigation. Indeed, privatel group litigation is discouraged and is often viewed as attacks on the state and threats to social stability. Any disruptive collective demands – whether through protests or group litigation – are quickly stifled.

It is within such a complex backdrop that China's multi-track civil dispute resolution system as established by the 2012 amendments can best be understood. Simplified procedures make sense for rural and poor litigants lacking legal assistance, and litigant autonomy holds sway in the "run of the mill" commercial litigation. But in socially significant cases, the Chinese state is heavily involved – both through greater control of the litigation by the court and through greater supervision of the courts. Collective cases are disaggregated into smaller individual suits and discouraged or diffused through settlement. Collective suits, and if brought, are directed to be brought only by "public interest" representatives, who are often determined by the Chinese state.

Indeed, the recent amendments anticipate the participation less of private lawyers and civil society, but more of GONGO's, that is, government organized nongovernmental organizations that have been set up by a government to look like an NGO in order to qualify for outside aid or mitigate specific issues. GONGO's in China include such groups such as the All China's Women's Federation or the All China Federation of Trade Unions. Thus, Art. 6 of the Women's Protection Law provides that "government committees for work of women and children at the county and higher levels shall organize, co-ordinate, guide and urge the relevant government departments to do a good job of protecting women's rights and interest," and Art. 54 requires organizations such as All China Women's Federation to lend assistance to any female victim seeking litigation. The environmental area is one area that appears to be an exception.[50] Recent amended environmental laws now allow environmental NGOs registered with city-level or higher governments in China, with five years of experience in environmental matters and in good standing, the right to bring public interest litigation against polluting enterprises. According to the U.S. based National Resource Defense Council's Beijing office, this will apply to about 300 NGOs in China. This is a major improvement over earlier drafts of the amendment, which would have limited NGO standing to only one government-sponsored NGO, the All-China Environment Federation.[51]

---

[49] See "Resolution on Major Issues Regarding the Building of a Harmonious Socialist Society," translated in http://www.china.org.cn/english/report/189591.htm.

[50] See Fazhi Ribao, at http://epaper.legaldaily.com.cn/fzrb/content/20140704/Page05TB.htm.

[51] For more see http://switchboard.nrdc.org/blogs/dpettit/a_step_forward_for_public_inte.html.

China's multi-track system, while born of necessity, may serve to defuse the potential of courts to serve democratic reforms. Under this view, China's legal system will focus more on efficiency and dispute resolution than on participation by ordinary citizens seeking more systemic change, giving more weight to the state's view of justice than to the interests of the ordinary litigant. Indeed, just as China embarked on "socialism with Chinese characteristics," we are also witnessing "rule of law with Chinese characteristics." And the "rule of law with Chinese characteristics" means a multi-track approach to rendering justice – one that focuses on preserving harmony rather than adjudicating right from wrong, dispute resolution rather than enunciation of public norms.

The presence of the Chinese state and "rule of law with Chinese characteristics" may be inevitable. Indeed, the Chinese term *fazhi* may be more accurately translated as "rule by law" or "govern according to law" than as "rule of law." The challenge for future legal reformers is then to recognize the reality of a dominant state but also to look for ways to incorporate citizens' voices into Chinese law and governance, even within the structure of the dominant state. But while a State Council (the chief administrative arm of the Chinese government) 2010 Opinion Regarding Strengthening Construction of a Government that is Rule by Law "calls fordeeper reforms, stronger institutions, enhanced government supervision, restriction of administrative powers", and a "government ruled by law," the Opinion contains little encouragement of private enforcement of public norms. Similarly, while there are promising signs, such as in the area of increasing judicial transparency. For example, the new amendments of the Civil Procedure Code would require that all judgments and judicial orders be made public and that the basis for the decision be explained in writing (New Arts. 151, 153, 155).[52] Nevertheless, civil litigants must be given the freedom and opportunity to shape and formulate their own civil litigation before civil litigation can truly serve the democratic role of preserving citizen voices.

7.4 Conclusion: Rule of Law with Chinese Characteristics

The dynamism of Chinese civil procedure continues unabated but it is a dynamism dominated by the Chinese state. On October 23, 2014, the 4th Plenum of the 18th Central Committee of the Chinese Communist Party (CCP) promulgated the CCP Central Committee Decision concerning Some Major Questions in Comprehensively Promoting Governing the Country According to Law (the Plenum Decision).[53] This is the first time a CCP central committee plenary session devoted an entire decision on the topic of law. Faced with a rising number of disputes of growing complexity,

[52] *See* 2012 Amendments, para. 32 (inserting a new article as new Article 155).

[53] An English translation of the Decision is available at http://chinacopyrightandmedia.wordpress.com/2014/28/ccp-central-committee-decision-concerning-some-major-questions-in-comprehensively-moving-governing-the-country-according-to-the-law-forward/.

the CCP recognizes that political interference, low compensation and corruption have undermined public trust in the legal system. In focusing attention on law, the Plenum Decision represents the Party's attempt to recapture law as a "socialist rule of law with Chinese characteristics." Containing both symbolic messages and concrete proposals, the Decision is an unapologetic position outlining the dominance of the Chinese Communist Party in the legal system and by extension, in the civil litigation process.

For one, as a nod towards greater transparency but more so, as an assertion of unchallenged authority, the Plenum Decision reaffirmed the role of the CCP in delivering and guiding the development of law. For the first time, the Plenum Decision clearly acknowledged that "in all cases where legislation involves adjustment to major structures or major policies, it must be reported to the Party Centre Committee for discussion and decision." To ensure that leaders in all sectors take law seriously, the Plenum also ordered that law indicators be written into annual cadre performance evaluations, and that government officials and judges be held permanently accountable for their decisions. While this may be viewed as a move to a more law focused Party, the Plenum Decision also reemphasizes that Party discipline is to be asserted according to internal Party regulations, which according to the Decision, is more stringent than the law. This certainly diverges from western hopes and notions of rule of law in which politics is subsumed by majoritarian enactments of law, and the idea that government and political parties are subject to the rule of law.

But the Plenum Decision is also to be commended on being unrelenting in its criticism that laws remain unenforced or selectively enforced, that there exists problems of "judicial unfairness and corruption," and that state personnel and leading cadres' consciousness about handling affairs according to law is not strong and their abilities insufficient. And so, concrete reforms include establishing a circuit court system to alleviate local protectionalism, a form of local government interference with judicial decisions, a new system for case filing to ensure that cases are accept, perfecting the appeals system so that disgruntled litigants are assured of sufficient review of judicial decisions.

In sum, the Plenum Decision represents some tangible steps in increased transparency of the entire judicial process which will certainly improve the civil litigation process. It promisesmore open trials and the reform that that judicial decisions nationwide be posted online. It also emphasizes the need to increase legal education including adding legal studies in the comprehensive education as well as in the Party's own political education. But whether these efforts to inject more legality into the Party or the metamorphsis of a more legalistic Partyis unclear. More likely, this will continue the trajectory of the Chinese development of "governing according to law with Chinese characteristics."

Part III
Dynamism of Civil Procedure Devices & Instruments

Chapter 8
Responding to Cost and Delay Through Overriding Objectives – Successful Innovation?

Michael Legg and Andrew Higgins

8.1 Introduction

Arguably the primary objectives of civil procedure are to assist courts to resolve legal disputes justly within a reasonable time and at proportionate cost.[1] Procedures such as the use of witnesses, discovery and appeals exist to assist in the right decision being reached. However those objectives should be pursued subject to minimising costs, as cost may hamper access to the legal system to enforce substantive rights, and as the resources available to the legal system are not limitless. Further, justice must be rendered in a timely manner so as to avoid delay which increases the possibility of error, may reduce or eliminate a decision's utility, create uncertainty

[1] Jeremy Bentham, *Scotch Reform* (1808 reprinted 2007) p 5, Richard Posner, "An Economic Approach to Legal Procedure and Judicial Administration" (1973) 2 *Journal of Legal Studies* 399, Adrian Zuckerman, "Justice In Crisis: Comparative Dimensions of Civil Procedure" in Adrian Zuckerman (ed), *Civil Justice In Crisis: Comparative Perspectives of CivilProcedure* (1999) pp 3–5.

M. Legg (✉)
University of New South Wales Law, Sydney, NSW, Australia
e-mail: m.legg@unsw.edu.au

A. Higgins
Faculty of Law and Mansfield College, University of Oxford, Oxford, UK
e-mail: andrew.higgins@law.ox.ac.uk

C.B. Picker, G.I. Seidman (eds.), *The Dynamism of Civil Procedure - Global Trends and Developments*, Ius Gentium: Comparative Perspectives on Law and Justice 48, DOI 10.1007/978-3-319-21981-3_8

and cause emotional and financial stress to the parties.[2] Despite these truisms, cost and delay have remained major problems for civil justice.[3]

To emphasise the importance of minimising cost and delay, courts and legislatures in common law countries devised the innovative approach of adopting the concept of an overriding or overarching objective or purpose for their civil justice systems[4] that requires attention to justice, cost and delay ("Purpose Requirement").[5] The Purpose Requirement applies to all of the court rules and procedures in the civil jurisdiction, but is of particular relevance to pre-trial preparations such as compliance with timetables for pleadings, discovery/disclosure and the filing of evidence.[6] The concept's innovation stems from it setting an express objective for a civil justice system of not only 'doing justice' but achieving that aim without undue cost or delay, acting as guide to the interpretation of rules of civil procedure and as a consequence being the fulcrum upon which case management pivots. As the terminology 'overriding' or 'overarching' expresses, a Purpose Requirement is meant to be at the centre of civil justice. A Purpose Requirement now exists in England & Wales' Civil Procedure Rules,[7] the United States Federal Rules of Civil Procedure (FRCP)[8] and in almost all Australian jurisdictions.[9]

---

[2] *Aon Risk Services Australia Ltd v Australian National University* (2009) 239 CLR 175 ('*Aon Risk*'), 213 [98], 214 [101]; Adrian Zuckerman, "Justice In Crisis: Comparative Dimensions of Civil Procedure" in Adrian Zuckerman (ed), *Civil Justice In Crisis: Comparative Perspectives of Civil Procedure* (1999) 6–10 and Michael Legg, *Case Management and Complex Civil Litigation* (2011) 23.

[3] See eg James Kakalik, Terence Dunworth, Laural Hill, Daniel McCaffrey, Marian Oshiro, Nicholas Pace and Mary Vaiana, *Just, Speedy and Inexpensive? An Evaluation of Judicial Case Management Under the Civil Justice Reform Act*, RAND Institute for Civil Justice (1996); Lord Justice Jackson, *Civil Litigation Costs Review – Final report* (December 2009); Australian Government Productivity Commission, *Access to Justice Arrangements – Draft Report* (April 2014) 118–120.

[4] The Purpose Requirements do not apply to the criminal justice system. The civil justice system, generally speaking, incorporates all other disputes regardless of the substantive law in issue. There may be occasional exceptions. For example in Australia the Purpose Requirement does not apply to the Family Court of Australia.

[5] Hong Kong is a notable exception having rejected an overriding objective on the grounds that it might permit specific procedural provisions to be ignored or given insufficient weigh given insufficient weight: Hong Kong Special Administrative Region Government, *Civil Justice Reform: Final Report* (2004) [95]-[100].

[6] For an overview of pre-trial steps in England & Wales and the United States see Oscar Chase, Helen Hershkoff, Linda Silberman, Yasuhei Taniguchi, Vincenzo Varano and Adrian Zuckerman, *Civil Litigation in Comparative Context* (Thomson 2007) 15–35.

[7] Civil Procedure Rules (England & Wales) r 1.1.

[8] Federal Rules of Civil Procedure (US) r 1.

[9] See *Federal Court of Australia Act1976* (Cth) s 37 M, *Court Procedure Rules 2006* (ACT) Ch 2 Pt 2.1 r 21, *Civil Procedure Act 2005* (NSW) s 56, *General Rules of Procedure in Civil Proceedings 1987* (NT) Pt 3 r 1.10, *Uniform Civil Procedure Rules 1999* (Qld), r 5, *Supreme Court Civil Rules 2006* (SA) r 3, *Civil Procedure Act 2010* (Vic) s7 and *Rules of the Supreme Court 1971* (WA) r 4B. The only jurisdiction without an overriding/overarching purpose is Tasmania.

This chapter explains the operation of the Purpose Requirement in each of the aforementioned jurisdictions with a view to highlighting similarities and differences, as well as successes and problems, with this innovation.

8.2 The Role of the Overriding Objective in English Civil Procedure

In his 1996 report on Access to Justice Lord Woolf, then Master of the Rolls and Head of Civil Justice in England & Wales,[10] recommended a new procedural code to replace the old Supreme Court and County Court rules of procedure. Lord Woolf recommended that at the beginning of this procedural code, there should be a statement of the purpose of the rules or 'overriding objective.' The overriding objective, in summary, is that the role of the court was not just to deliver correct judgments, but to do so at proportionate cost and in a timely manner. Quite apart from its content, the very idea of an overriding objective was a bold recommendation based on a belief that achieving the objectives of the civil justice system, properly understood, depends on more than just the content of procedural rules. Lord Woolf stated:

> Every word in the rules should have a purpose, but every word cannot sensibly be given a minutely exact meaning. Civil procedure involves more judgement and knowledge than the rules can directly express. In this respect, rules of court are not like an instruction manual for operating a piece of machinery. Ultimately their purpose is to guide the court and the litigants towards the just resolution of the case. Although the rules can offer detailed directions for the technical steps to be taken, the effectiveness of those steps depends upon the spirit in which they are carried out. That in turn depends on an understanding of the fundamental purpose of the rules and of the underlying system of procedure.
>
> In order to identify that purpose at the outset, I have placed at the very beginning of the rules a statement of their overriding objective.[11]

The content of the overriding objective was principally inspired by a recognition that English judges had been preoccupied with delivering justice on the merits, without due regard to the deleterious effects of costs and delay on individual cases and the civil justice system as a whole. Civil Procedure Rule 1.1 now states:

> (1) These Rules are a new procedural code with the overriding objective of enabling the court to deal with cases justly *and at proportionate cost*.
> (2) Dealing with a case justly *and at proportionate cost* includes, so far as is practicable –
>
> (a) ensuring that the parties are on an equal footing;
> (b) saving expense;
> (c) dealing with the case in ways which are proportionate –
>
> (i) to the amount of money involved;
> (ii) to the importance of the case;

---

[10] The Master of the Rolls is one of the most senior judges in the English judiciary. He is a judge of the Court of Appeal and is the President of its Civil Division.

[11] Lord Woolf, *Access to Justice, Final Report* (London, HMSO, 1996), ch 20 [10]–[11].

(iii) to the complexity of the issues; and
(iv) to the financial position of each party;

(d) ensuring that it is dealt with expeditiously and fairly;
(e) allotting to it an appropriate share of the court's resources, while taking into account the need to allot resources to other cases; and
(f) *enforcing compliance with rules, practice directions and orders.*[12]

CPR 1.2(b) also states the court must seek to give effect to the overriding objective when it interprets any rule, while CPR 1.3 imposes a duty on the parties to help the court further the overriding objective.

The concept of an overriding objective has been enthusiastically embraced. It became the first rule of the new civil procedure rules, it is routinely invoked by judges when interpreting the rules, and other common law jurisdictions have moved to incorporate their own overriding objective within their rules or relevant enabling legislation. Despite its acceptance at an institutional level, the overriding objective has been less successful in remedying the ills it was designed to overcome. The costs of civil justice continued to rise to the point where just 10 years after the new CPR came into force, one of Lord Woolf's successors as Master of the Rolls, Lord Clarke, felt it necessary to conduct another major review of the system specifically on costs.[13] Lord Justice Jackson, a judge of the Court of Appeal for England & Wales, carried out the review and published his final report in December 2010. The majority of his recommendations were adopted by the Government and came into effect in April 2013.[14] Those changes included an amendment to the overriding objective to put greater emphasis on the need to keep costs proportionate.

---

[12] The words in italics were added in 2013 by virtue of The Civil Procedure (Amendment) Rules 2013.

[13] B Prentice MP, Statement of November 5, 2012 reproduced at http://www.judiciary.gov.uk/publications-and-reports/review-of-civil-litigation-costs/civil-litigation-costs-review-press-notices [Accessed 21 December 2013] The Review's objective was 'to carry out an independent review of the rules and principles governing the costs of civil litigation and to make recommendations in order to promote access to justice at proportionate cost': See Lord Justice Jackson, *Civil Litigation Costs Review – Final report* (December 2009) p 1–2. By way of example, the recoverable costs of civil litigation, i.e. court ordered costs that the unsuccessful party must pay to the successful party, often exceeded the amount in dispute and varied considerably depending upon the way cases were funded and the identity of the successful party. Based on data collected as part of the Jackson review, in cases funded by conditional fee agreements (CFAs) which were won by claimants, claimant costs amounted to approximately 158 % of damages. In non-CFA cases, claimant costs amounted to approximately 51 % of damages. In cases won by defendants, defendant costs amounted to approximately 15 % of the sums in issue: Lord Justice Jackson, *Final report* (December 2009) p 16.

[14] Recoverable conditional fee agreements have been scrapped for all but very limited categories of cases, and replaced by a package of reforms which includes the introduction of damages based agreements (contingency fees), qualified one way cost shifting in personal injury claims, fixed costs or costs management/budgeting for most courts, and an increase in general damages of 10 % in personal injury cases: see Legal Aid, Sentencing and Punishment of Offenders Act 2012, The Civil Procedure (Amendment) Rules 2013, Damages Based Agreements Regulations 2013,

While the CPR has been more successful in reducing delay than cost, delays still remain a problem for the justice system.[15] According to Sir Rupert Jackson's report, a major cause of delay was a lax approach to case management and non-compliance with process requirements. Jackson stated:

> [C]ourts at all levels have become too tolerant of delays and non-compliance with orders. In so doing they have lost sight of the damage which the culture of delay and non-compliance is inflicting upon the civil justice system.[16]

English law's approach to non-compliance with procedural rules and court orders provides an illuminating case study on the challenges faced by courts in giving effect to the overriding objective, and the inter-relationship between specific procedural rules and the overriding objective. Historically, the courts have taken a lax attitude to non-compliance with procedural rules and court orders based on the philosophy that procedural rules were not trip wires to access to justice, and that except in cases of intentional non-compliance or inordinate delay which prejudiced the rights of the other party, the court should decide the case on the merits if it was still able to do so.[17]

The overriding objective and the CPR was designed to tackle this culture of non-compliance, and the delay and cost associated with it. CPR 3.8 introduced an automatic sanctions regime in which any sanctions identified in a rule, or specified in a court order, took effect automatically in the event of non-compliance with the relevant rule or court order, but the defaulting party could then apply to the court for relief under CPR 3.9.[18] The court had a discretionary power to grant relief taking into account all the circumstances of the case, including a list of nine non-exhaustive factors:

(a) the interests of the administration of justice;
(b) whether the application for relief has been made promptly;
(c) whether the failure to comply was intentional;
(d) whether there is a good explanation for the failure;
(e) the extent to which the party in default has complied with other rules, practice directions and court orders and any relevant pre-action protocol;
(f) whether the failure to comply was caused by the party or his legal representative;
(g) whether the trial date or the likely date can still be met if relief is granted;
(h) the effect which the failure to comply had on each party; and
(i) the effect which the granting of relief would have on each party.

Simmons v Castle [2012] EWCA Civ 1039, Stuart Sime and Derek French, *Blackstone's Guide to the Civil Justice Reforms 2013* (Oxford University Press, 2013).

[15] Lord Justice Jackson, 'Civil Justice in an Uncivil World' in Michael Legg (ed), *The Future of Dispute Resolution* (2013) 26–27.

[16] Sir Rupert Jackson, *Review of Civil Litigation Costs: Final Report*, 21 December 2009, Chapter 39 'Case Management' [6.5].

[17] See for example *Birkett v James* [1978] AC 297.

[18] In keeping with the principles of proportionality sanctions in the rules were linked to the purpose of the process requirement and the impact that non-compliance would have on the litigation or litigation generally: for example, the failure to serve a witness statement on time meant the witness could not be called to give evidence without the court's permission (CPR 32.10), while the failure to pay court fees (CPR 3.7) meant the claim would be struck out.

This check list of factors has been described as a menu or laundry list, containing a variety of items which bore little relationship to each other and which contained no particular normative message. Furthermore, the nine factors represented a 'cognitive overload', as Levy put it, which tended to burden the decision maker with the need to examine, sometime in considerable detail, each factor even if the exercise led in no particular direction.[19] However hard a judge analysed each factor, the judge was left to give particular weight to the factors that she thought were most appropriate, to arrive at the outcome she considered most appropriate.[20] Since the court was not guided by any overarching principle the outcome of the exercise was difficult to predict, which meant that satellite litigation was bound to increase and that a whole jurisprudence developed explaining the meaning of the different factors.[21] Of course the courts were always required to have regard to the overriding objective in interpreting CPR 3.9, but reconciling the nine non-exhaustive factors with the overriding objective was not a straightforward task. Even if courts could work out the full significance of the overriding objective for CPR 3.9, many were unwilling to apply in practice what the overriding objective implied in theory.[22]

In his final report on civil litigation costs Sir Rupert Jackson recommended that the list of factors in CPR r.3.9 be repealed and replaced by just two criteria:

- the requirement that litigation should be conducted efficiently and at proportionate cost; and
- the interests of justice in the particular case.

This recommendation was criticized by several commentators on the grounds that while it recognized that an appropriate balance must be struck between routine enforcement of process requirements and the flexibility needed to avoid injustice in particular cases, it gave the court no practical guidance as to how to strike this balance. Thus the problem of unpredictability created by courts taking either a robust or lax approach to enforcing process requirements under CPR 3.9 was likely to remain.[23] The phrase 'the interests of justice in the particular case' would enable judges to continue taking a lax attitude to non-compliance, notwithstanding Sir Rupert Jackson's desire to see a greater emphasis on enforcement. Although Lord Justice Jackson did not accept all these criticisms, following consultation he did

[19] I Levy, 'Lightening the Overload of CPR rule 3.9' (2013) 32 *Civil Justice Quarterly* 139.

[20] A Higgins, 'The Costs of Case Management: What Should be done Post Jackson?' (2010) 29 *Civil Justice Quarterly* 317, 319.

[21] See, for example, the lengthy discussion in *Hansom v E Rex Makin & Co* [2003] EWCA Civ 1801.

[22] A Zuckerman, 'The Revised CPR 3.9: A Coded Message Demanding Articulation' (2013) 32 *Civil Justice Quarterly* 123.

[23] A Higgins, 'The costs of case management: what should be done post Jackson?' (2010) 29 *Civil Justice Quarterly* 317, 323.

acknowledge there may be value in providing more concrete guidance, and thus recommended the two non-exhaustive criteria be revised to provide as follows:

> (a) the primary need to enforce compliance with rules, practice directions and orders save where there has been good reason for the default or in exceptional circumstances; and
> (b) the interests of justice in the particular case.[24]

These revised criteria were a welcome improvement in that they identified the circumstances in which it was appropriate to depart from the 'primary' need to enforce compliance, but the Civil Procedure Rule Committee still felt the formulation did not give sufficient steer in favour of enforcement. Instead it promulgated a new rule which is an odd amalgamation[25] of the previous proposals. CPR 3.9 now provides that:

> (1) On an application for relief from any sanction imposed for a failure to comply with any rule, practice direction or court order, the court will consider all the circumstances of the case, so as to enable it to deal justly with the application, including the need–
>
> (a) for litigation to be conducted efficiently and at proportionate cost; and
> (b) to enforce compliance with rules, practice directions and orders.[26]

The difficulty with the new rule, however, is that it merely restates key aspects of the overriding objective.[27] CPR 3.9 has moved from a menu option of 9 non-exhaustive factors with no real normative message, to a rule that contains a clear normative message with no specific criteria or guidance for courts as to how to exercise their discretion as to whether to grant relief from sanctions. Zuckerman has lamented that the revised CPR 3.9 uses 'grotesquely anodyne language' in a 'seemingly content free rule' that adds 'nothing whatever of significance' to what was already in the overriding objective.[28]

---

[24] *Rupert Jackson, Amendment of CPR 3.9—Rupert Jackson's note to the Rule Committee re Rule 3.9 (second draft) (Civil Procedure Rule Committee—Ministry of Justice, June 6, 2011).*

[25] I Levy, 'Lightening the Overload of CPR rule 3.9' (2013) 32 *Civil Justice Quarterly* 139, 151.

[26] CPR 3.9. *Civil Procedure Rule Committee, Amendment of CPR 3.9 (Ministry of Justice, CPR 11(23), July 8, 2011).* According to the drafting notes 'the amendment is made following the recommendation to amend rule 3.9 made at *paragraph 8.1(vi) of Chapter 39 of the Review of Civil Litigation Costs: Final Report, 21 December 2009 (the Costs Review).* At the June 2011 CPRC meeting, the Committee discussed two alternative forms of amendment proposed by Lord Justice Jackson: the version set out at *paragraph 6.7 of the Costs Review* and the version set at paragraph 7 of paper CPR (11)11. The Committee preferred an amalgamation of the two and invited Lord Justice Jackson and MOJ lawyers to produce a revised draft on this basis.'

[27] Factor (a) is in substance included in the definition of the overriding objective in rule 1.1(2) of enabling the court to deal with cases justly; and factor (b) is included in the definition of the overriding objective in identical language at rule 1.1(2)(f).

[28] A Zuckerman, 'The Revised CPR 3.9: A Coded Message Demanding Articulation' (2013) 32 *Civil Justice Quarterly* 123, 125.

8.2.1 The Mitchell Guidance

The Court of Appeal articulated the message behind the new CPR 3.9, and provided some much needed content to the rule, in November 2013 in *Mitchell v News Group Newspapers Ltd.*[29] The claimant brought an action for defamation, but failed to discuss costs with the defendant and failed to file a costs budget seven days before the first case management conference (CMC), in breach of PD 51D [4.1] and [4.2]. Master McCloud ordered that although the claimant's budget was filed shortly before the CMC, it was to be treated as comprising only of court fees, by analogy to CPR 3.14 which deals with failure to file a budget altogether. The Master refused the claimant's application under CPR 3.8–3.9 for relief from sanction. The claimant excused the default by saying that he was represented by a small firm of solicitors with limited resources, which was especially stretched at the time due to the absence of some staff. The Master did not consider the explanation satisfactory:

> The explanations put forward by the Claimant's solicitors are not unusual ones. Pressure of work, a small firm, unexpected delays with counsel and so on. These things happen, and I have no doubt they happened here. However even before the advent of the new rules the failure of solicitors was generally not treated as in itself a good excuse and I am afraid that however much I sympathise with the Claimant's solicitors, such explanations carry even less weight in the post *Jackson* environment.[30]

Highlighting the systemic effects of delay, the Master drew attention to the fact that, in order to find time in her diary to list the application for relief within a reasonable time, she needed to vacate a half day appointment which had been allocated to deal with claims by persons affected by asbestos-related diseases.[31] The Master rested her judgment in large part on the new overriding objective and the Jackson reforms to CPR 3.9. She stated:

> The new overriding objective is in marked contrast to the old one in form and, in my judgment, in substance. The court must now, as a part of dealing with cases justly, ensure that cases are dealt with at proportionate cost and so as to ensure compliance with rules, orders and practice directions. In that sense what we now mean by '*dealing with cases justly*' has changed, or if it has not changed then at the very least there is a significant shift of emphasis towards treating the wider effectiveness of court management and resources as a part of justice itself.[32]

The Court of Appeal upheld Master McCloud's decision.[33] While acknowledging that the decision could be described as robust, it held that the Master did not err

[29] *Mitchell v News Group Newspapers Ltd* [2013] EWCA Civ 1537. The decision followed importance guidance provided by the Master of the Rolls extra curially in the 18th Implementation Lecture on the Jackson Reforms: Lord Dyson MR, '*The Application of the Amendments to the Civil Procedure Rules*: *18th Lecture in the Implementation Programme*' (speech delivered at the District Judges' Annual Seminar, Judicial College, 22 March 2013).

[30] *Mitchell v News Group Newspapers Ltd* [2013] EWHC 2355 (QB) [53].

[31] Ibid [28].

[32] Ibid [65].

[33] *Mitchell v News Group Newspapers Limited* (2013) EWCA Civ 1537.

in exercising her discretion under CPR 3.9. The Court of Appeal also provided crucial guidance as to how lower courts should exercise their discretion under the revised CPR 3.9. Delivering the judgment on behalf of the Court of the Appeal, the Master of the Rolls, Lord Dyson, said that it was significant that the need (i) for litigation to be conducted efficiently and at proportionate cost and (ii) to enforce compliance with rules, practice directions and court orders are the only considerations which have been singled out for specific mention in the rule. This represents a deliberate 'shift in emphasis' and the factors listed in CPR 3.9 should be given greater weight than other relevant factors.[34] Moreover, the Court of Appeal indicated the types of non-compliance that might justify relief from sanctions and those that would not. The first task is to consider the nature of the non-compliance. If the non-compliance can be properly regarded as trivial the court will usually grant relief provided that an application is made promptly. The principle *de minimis non curat lex* (the law is not concerned with trivial things) applies here as it applies in most areas of the law. Narrowly missing a deadline or a failure of form rather than substance could be considered trivial.[35] If the non-compliance is not trivial, a court should only grant compliance if there was a good reason for it. Merely overlooking a deadline, whether on account of overwork or otherwise, is unlikely to be a good reason. On the other hand, if more work is required to meet the deadline than was anticipated at the time the order was initially made, this may constitute a good reason.[36]

All of these factors make a good deal of sense, which raises the question why they were not included in the revised CPR 3.9 rather than simply repeating the overriding objective and emphasizing the importance of enforcing rules, which is to state the obvious. The Court of Appeal's decision gives proper weight to the interests of the administration of justice by recognising that litigants who take more than their fair share of court resources do so at the expense of others, and that solicitors cannot externalise the cost of their inefficiency and impose it on others.[37] It ought to remembered that professional negligence insurance providers already put a price on the cost of missing procedural deadlines through increased 'excess charges' in the event of a claim against the lawyer. The insurance costs for missed time limits may well increase if procedural time limits are enforced more robustly, but the market is capable of ensuring the costs of non-compliance are allocated efficiently (which in turn will improve compliance rates). A lax approach to non-compliance distorts this allocation process, undermining the normative force of procedural rules and inevitably the courts' capacity to further the overriding objective of dealing with cases justly, at proportionate cost and within a reasonable time.

[34] *Mitchell* [36].

[35] *Mitchell* [40].

[36] Mitchell [41].

[37] A Zuckerman, 'Implementation of Mark II Overriding Objective and CPR 3.9' (2014) 33 C.J.Q 1.

8.2.2 The Reaction to Mitchell

The Mitchell decision received a hostile reaction from many English lawyers, with warnings of a return to tactical, satellite litigation and a knock-on effect on firms' professional indemnity insurance. The phrase 'to Mitchell' a defaulting party soon became part of the vernacular of legal practice. Some lawyers, however, were supportive of the decision and thought that it would lead to more efficient litigation and the implementation of better internal file management systems by law firms (many successful firms already used such systems).[38] The application of the *Mitchell* guidance by the courts was also mixed. Some courts were arguably overly enthusiastic, and too technical, in applying the new robust approach to case management, while some courts gave decisions which appeared to disregard the guidance altogether, or distinguished *Mitchell* in a way that suggested a deliberate attempt to avoid its application.[39] Some critics of the Mitchell decision also argued that there was a lack of clarity over how the principles enunciated by the Court of Appeal fit together. In particular what was the relationship between the trivial breach and good reason principles and the requirement in the chapeau of CPR 3.9(1) that the court must consider all the circumstances of the case so as to deal with the application justly?[40]

8.2.3 Revising Mitchell – The Denton Guidance

Subsequently in *Denton v TH White & Or*[41] the Court of Appeal heard three combined appeals from lower courts purporting to apply the *Mitchell* guidance. A powerful bench, comprising the Master of the Rolls, Lord Dyson, Vos LJ and Jackson LJ, the judge who had authored the civil litigation costs review, unanimously upheld all of the appeals. One of the aims of hearing the appeals was to clarify the *Mitchell* guidance,[42] but regrettably the Court of Appeal split over the proper approach to CPR 3.9. While all three judges agreed that the *Mitchell* guidance should be revised, Jackson LJ gave a separate judgment that provided different guidance on the correct approach to CPR3.9 to that set out in the joint judgement of Lord Dyson MR and Vos LJ.

In *Denton* the Court of Appeal held that the judge should not have granted relief from sanctions to a litigant who served six witness statements in December 2013, five months late and only one month before the case was fixed for a 10 day trial. The

---

[38] N Rose (n 6).

[39] For a useful discussion of some of the cases see S Sime 'Sanctions After Mitchell' (2014) 33 *Civil Justice Quarterly* 133.

[40] Sime (n 28) at 146.

[41] *Denton v TH White & Or, Decadent Vapours Limited v Bevan & Ors, Utilise TDS Limited v Davies & Ors* [2014] EWCA Civ 906.

[42] *Denton* [33].

statements were said to be in response to a change of circumstances which had occurred four months earlier in August 2013. The Judge gave permission to rely on the statements under CPR 32.10 which prevents witnesses from being called to give evidence if their witness statements are not served within time without the courts permission. Permission was granted even though it meant the trial had to be adjourned. The Court of Appeal ruled that 'the judge's order was plainly wrong and was an impermissible exercise of his case management powers'[43]

However in the other two cases, the Court of Appeal held that relief from sanctions ought to have been granted. In *Decadent Vapours Ltd v Bevan & Ors*, a case had been struck out for late payment of fees, while in *Utilise TDS Ltd v Davies*, the lower court decided that two trivial breaches could be aggregated to become one significant breach. In *Decadent*, the claimant failed to comply with an unless order for payment of court fees, breach of which would result in the claim being struck out. The claimant had posted a cheque to the court on the due date but it went astray. The non-payment only came to the attention of the parties when the judge mentioned it at a pre-trial review. The fees were paid two days later. However the judge refused relief from the automatic strike out sanction. In *Utilise* the claimant's first breach was to file a costs budget some 45 min late, triggering the sanction in CPR 3.14 which limited the recoverable costs to the applicable court fees. The claimant then committed a second breach when they were 13 days late in notifying the court of the outcome of negotiations between the parties. The district judge declined to grant relief from the sanctions in CPR 3.14, holding that the second breach rendered the first breach, which would otherwise have been trivial, a non-trivial one. The judge on the first appeal dismissed the appeal holding that, while there had been no default in the late filing of the cost budget, there was no good reason to interfere with the district judge's case management discretion.

In the Court of Appeal's view, not only should relief have been granted in both *Decadent* and *Utilise*, the defendants in both cases ought to have consented to relief being granted.[44] Such co-operation is consistent with the parties' duty to co-operate with the court in achieving the overriding objective as set out in CPR 1.3.[45] In explaining the results Lord Dyson MR and Vos LJ stated that while some judges appear to have taken a technical approach to the *Mitchell* guidance, others have wrongly continued to give pre-eminence to deciding cases on the merits disregarding *Mitchell* altogether.[46] According to Lord Dyson MR and Vos LJ the guidance in *Mitchell* had been 'misunderstood and is being misapplied by some courts.'[47] Lower courts had mistakenly interpreted *Mitchell* to mean that relief from sanctions could only be granted if the default was trivial or there was there a good reason for it. Even if neither criterion was satisfied, a court could still grant relief if it was just to do so taking into account all the circumstances.

---

[43] *Denton* [53].

[44] *Denton* [65], [80].

[45] *Denton* [40].

[46] *Denton* [81]. See also Jackson LJ at [89].

[47] *Denton* [3].

Because of the apparent confusion regarding *Mitchell*, in *Denton* the Court of Appeal effectively replaced the *Mitchell* guidance with a three stage inquiry. At the first stage of the inquiry, the court should identify and assess 'the seriousness or significance of the 'failure to comply with any rule, practice direction or court order which engages rule 3.9(1). This seriousness or significance inquiry should stand instead of the triviality of criteria applied in Mitchell. In considering this factor the court could look at whether the breach imperils future hearing dates or otherwise disrupts the conduct of the instant litigation or other litigation.[48] At the second stage the court should consider why the failure or default occurred and, by implication, whether these are 'good' or 'bad' reasons. The Court of Appeal said it would be inappropriate to produce an encyclopaedia of good and bad reasons and stressed that the examples given in *Mitchell* were no more than examples.[49] At the third stage the court should evaluate all the circumstances of the case, so as to enable it to deal justly with the application including the factors listed in CPR 3.9(1)(a) and (b). As already mentioned, these factors are incorporated in the overriding objective. They are the need: (a) for litigation to be conducted efficiently and at proportionate cost, and (b) to enforce compliance with rules, practice directions and orders. Issues that could be taken into account at this third stage could include the promptness of the application and other past or current breaches.[50]

The *Mitchell* guidance and the *Denton* guidance only need to be stated to appreciate they differ significantly from each-other, and neither can be said to be more or less compatible with CPR 3.9 given the vagueness of the rule. However, the most worrying aspect of the decision in *Denton* is that Jackson LJ, who had authored the review of civil litigation costs recommending that CPR 3.9 be amended, issued his own separate guidance which differed in one critical respect from the majority. While endorsing the new three stage inquiry, Jackson LJ dissented on the weight to be given to the two criteria set out in CPR 3.9(1)(a) and (b). Whereas the majority stated that the factors should be given particular importance (downgrading them from the 'paramount importance' they were accorded in *Mitchell*),[51] Jackson LJ stated that they should be given the same weight, no more and no more less, as all the other relevant circumstances of the case. Ultimately what CPR 3.9 requires is that the court should 'deal justly with the application' taking into account all the circumstances of the case. Endorsing the submission of the Bar Council, Jackson LJ stated that 'factors (a) and (b) should "have a seat at the table, not the top seats at the table"'.[52] This analysis is unconvincing. Given these factors are already incorporated in the overriding objective, and judges are required to give effect to the overriding objective when applying the rules, there would be no point in listing the factors in CPR3.9 if they were not meant to be given greater weight. According to Jackson LJ the reason why the rule requires courts to give specific consideration to

---

[48] *Denton* [25]–[27].

[49] *Denton* [30].

[50] *Denton* [36].

[51] *Denton* [32].

[52] *Denton* [85].

factors (a) and (b) is that previously courts were not doing so.[53] This is a serious charge as the need to comply with court orders and conduct litigation at proportionate cost is always a relevant consideration. It is more likely that judges were failing to give proper weight to these factors than forgetting them altogether, which suggests, in turn, that they ought to be given greater weight when judges exercise their discretion under CPR 3.9.

Jackson LJ's approach also has the potential to undermine the overriding objective. If the factors listed in CPR 3.9 are to given equal weight with any other circumstances, the effect of incorporating parts of the overriding objective into CPR 3.9 is that it denuded the overriding objective of its overriding function when it comes to CPR 3.9. This would be ironic given that the overriding objective was itself amended to specifically include a reference to the need to enforce compliance with rules, practice directions and court orders.[54] The result is not a promising recipe for sound case management. The majority were surely right to observe that unless greater weight is attached to the criteria expressly set out in CPR 3.9 the courts will inevitably slip back to the old culture of non-compliance which the Jackson reforms were designed to eliminate.[55]

According to Zuckerman the fact that the CPR failed to deliver the hoped for benefits of court control of litigation was, by and large, the responsibility of the Court of Appeal.[56] The *Denton* revision to the *Mitchell* guidance is unlikely to bring greater clarity or consistency to case management decisions. Moreover, courts will rarely be able to reason by analogy from the results in the combined cases in *Denton*. As Jackson himself noted, all the cases before the court were extreme examples, and in more difficult cases, the difference between the reasoning of the majority and Jackson may well matter.[57] This is virtually a judicial invitation to engage in further satellite litigation.

Yet the ultimate failure for this episode lies not with the Court of Appeal in either the *Mitchell* or *Denton* cases, but with the drafters of the new CPR 3.9 and their almost exclusive reliance on the overriding objective in defining its content. The experience with the old CPR 3.9 and the *Mitchell* and *Denton* guidance to the new CPR 3.9 is that while the overriding objective provides a clear normative message to assist the courts interpret the rules and exercise their case management powers, the overriding objective cannot stand in place of clear rules, nor render complex, open ended rules, more predictable or 'just'. It is most unfortunate that a disagreement has emerged within the Court of Appeal as to the correct approach of CPR 3.9 which does little more than repeat the overriding objective. There is, however, unanimous agreement amongst the judges in *Denton*, and indeed everyone involved in administering the civil justice system in England & Wales, that delivering correct outcomes at proportionate cost and within a reasonable time is the overriding

[53] *Denton* [86].

[54] See text to footnote 10.

[55] *Denton* [38].

[56] A Zuckerman (n 26) 10.

[57] *Denton* [97].

objective that courts will strive to deliver in as many cases as possible. That such a consensus exists owes much to Lord Woolf's recommendation that courts be guided by an overriding objective which should be stated at the outset of the rules. Any effective system of management, whether it be managing civil justice or managing health services, requires a clear objective. What is remarkable about case management in England is the length of time the system went without a mission statement.

8.3 Australia

Australia is a federal system comprised of six states and two territories. This chapter focusses on two of those jurisdictions: New South Wales, who's Court of Appeal has given repeated attention to its Purpose Requirement, and the Federal Court of Australia. Each of the Australia state court systems and the Federal Court are separate judicial hierarchies, but they all culminate in the High Court of Australia which is the peak appellate court for both state and federal systems. The state courts are courts of general jurisdiction enabling them to hear all matters except those which are in the exclusive jurisdiction of a federal court, while the Federal Court is a court of limited jurisdiction which is specified by the Federal Parliament.[58]

8.3.1 New South Wales

The *Civil Procedure Act 2005* (NSW) s 56(1) provides that the overriding purpose of the Act and the court rules, in their application to a civil dispute or civil proceedings, is 'to facilitate the just, quick and cheap resolution of the real issues in the proceedings'.[59] The overriding purpose is given practical effect by s 56(2) requiring that the court must seek to give effect to the overriding purpose when it exercises any power or interprets any provision of the Act or court rules. Further s 56(3) imposes a duty on parties to assist the court to further overriding purpose, and s 56(4) requires that lawyers or other persons with an interest in the proceedings to

[58] See eg *Supreme Court Act 1970* (NSW) s 23 ('The Court shall have all jurisdiction which may be necessary for the administration of justice in New South Wales.'); *Federal Court of Australia Act 1976* (Cth) s 19(1) (the Court 'has such original jurisdiction as is vested in it by laws made by the Parliament'). The Federal Court only has such jurisdiction as is conferred on it by the Commonwealth Parliament, together with accrued jurisdiction over non-federal claims as arise out of transactions and facts common to the federal claims: *Fencott v Muller* (1983) 152 CLR 570.

[59] An overriding purpose was incorporated into pt 1 r 3 of the *Supreme Court Rules 1970* (NSW) in 2000. Prior to that it existed in the directions making power in pt 26 r 1. See Chief Justice JJ Spigelman, 'Opening of Law Term: Just, Quick and Cheap – A Standard for Civil Justice' (Speech delivered at NSW Parliament House, Sydney, 31 January 2000); *Giorgi v European Asian Bank Aktiengesellschaft* (Unreported, Supreme Court of NSW, McLelland J, 3 March 1986).

not cause a party to breach that duty.[60] Section 56(4) was amended and s 56(6) added in 2010 to extend the overriding purpose to any person with a relevant interest in the proceedings, including litigation funders and insurers.[61] Section 57(1) provides that proceedings in any court are to be managed having regard to:

(a) the just determination of the proceedings,
(b) the efficient disposal of the business of the court,
(c) the efficient use of available judicial and administrative resources,
(d) the timely disposal of the proceedings, and all other proceedings in the court, at a cost affordable by the respective parties.

The *Civil Procedure Act* s 58 then provides guidance as to the considerations relevant to the making of an order or direction through mandating regard to the provisions of ss 56 and 57, and setting out a number of discretionary considerations.

The statutory duty imposed upon NSW Courts by s 56(2) of the *Civil Procedure Act 2005* (NSW) requires the Court, in mandatory terms, to give effect to the overriding purpose to facilitate the just, quick and cheap resolution of the real issues in the proceedings.[62] The operation of the overriding purpose has been usefully explicated through recourse to administrative law. In *Halpin v Lumley General Insurance Ltd*, Basten J explained that a court will act erroneously in law if it fails to take [ss 56 and 57] into account. His Honour observed that the statutory requirement to 'have regard to' a specific matter had been considered by the High Court and NSW Court of Appeal previously, where they explained that to 'have regard to' a specific matter, requires the Court to give the matter weight as a fundamental element in the decision-making process. An equivalent formulation is that the matter so identified must be the focal point of the decision-making process.[63]

Justice Basten found that the above principles had a clear operation in relation to section 57(1) which identifies four specific objects to which regard shall be had. The judge must take those factors into account and give weight to them as a fundamental element in making his/her determination. However, the operation of the principles in relation to section 56 was less clear because the requirements of just, quick and cheap would frequently be in conflict such that that in most cases there will need to be a 'resolution of a tension between speed (including avoidance of delay), reduction of costs and the proper consideration of the issues raised by the parties,

[60] *The Age Company Ltd v Liu* [2013] NSWCA 26, [103]–[104].

[61] *Courts and Crimes and Legislation Further Amendment Act 2010* (NSW) schedule 6.

[62] *Dennis v Australian Broadcasting Corporation* [2008] NSWCA 37, [28]–[29]. See also *Richards v Cornford (No 3)* [2010] NSWCA 134, [100]–[101]; *McMahon v John Fairfax Publications Pty Ltd* [2010] NSWCA 308, [30], [45].

[63] *Halpin v Lumley General Insurance Ltd* (2009) 78 NSWLR 265, 271–2 [24]–[26] citing *R v Hunt; Ex parte Sean Investments Pty Ltd* (1979) 180 CLR 322, 329; *R v Toohey; Ex parte Meneling Station Pty Ltd* (1982) 158 CLR 327, 333, 337–8; *Evans v Marmont* (1997) 42 NSWLR 70, 79–80; *Zhang v Canterbury City Council* (2001) 51 NSWLR 589, 602; *Commissioner of Police (NSW) v Industrial Relations Commission (NSW)* [2009] NSWCA 198, [73]. See also *Hans Pet Constructions Pty Ltd v Cassar* [2009] NSWCA 230, [41].

especially in cases of complexity'.[64] Justice Sackville (concurring) illustrated the point by observing that providing a party with a reasonable opportunity to lead evidence, cross-examine witnesses and present a case may be difficult to achieve quickly and cheaply, as required by the overriding purpose in New South Wales.[65] Justice Basten addressed the issue by determining that the overriding purpose requires the judge to rule in a way that involves an appropriate resolution of the conflicting tensions inherent in the attributes of being just, quick and cheap. Further section 57 helped guide the resolution of any conflict.[66] These principles then link directly to case management through s 58 which sets out the matters to be considered in making case management decisions in a particular case, including having regard to ss 56 and 57.[67]

The necessity in undertaking the balancing exercise is illustrated by *Hans Pet Constructions Pty Ltd v Cassar*, where Allsop ACJ found that the discretion of a magistrate at first instance had miscarried. The magistrate, relying on s 56, struck out the defence and ordered the proceedings to proceed to a damages hearing due to non-compliance with directions. Acting Chief Justice Allsop found that the power to strike out a defence was subject to s 58, which in turn mandated consideration of ss 56 and 57, including s 57(1)(a) 'the just determination of the proceedings'. As the magistrate's reasons did not demonstrate a consideration of what justice required in his decision-making process the magistrate erred.[68]

The operation and goals of the overriding purpose may be summarised as follows[69]:

> Section 56 CPA with its statement of overriding purpose expresses an obligation and confers a discretion. The overall intention of ss 56–58 is to permit courts to exercise their powers so as to reduce delay and costs, both public and private, in the conduct of proceedings. In order to achieve that, Courts are directed to "have regard" to particular matters.

8.3.2 High Court of Australia

In *Aon Risk* the High Court, was asked to determine whether a late amendment to a pleading which would occasion an adjournment of the trial should be granted. The High Court's decision ultimately turned on the construction of the terms of the

[64] *Halpin v Lumley General Insurance Ltd* (2009) 78 NSWLR 265, 272 [28].

[65] *Halpin v Lumley General Insurance Ltd* (2009) 78 NSWLR 265, 287 [93]. See also Justice Ronald Sackville, 'Access to Justice: Assumptions and Reality Checks' (Speech delivered at Law & Justice Foundation of New South Wales Access to Justice Workshop, NSW Parliament House, Sydney, 10 July 2002) 5–6.

[66] Ibid 272 [29]–[30].

[67] *Hans Pet Constructions Pty Ltd v Cassar* [2009] NSWCA 230, [38].

[68] Ibid [36]–[48]. See also *McMahon v John Fairfax Publications Pty Ltd* [2010] NSWCA 308, [30]; *Cicek v The Estate of the Late Mark Solomon* [2014] NSWCA 278, [82]–[84], [133].

[69] *Wilkinson v Perisher Blue Pty Ltd* [2012] NSWCA 250, [58].

particular court rules at issue, the *Court Procedures Rules 2006* (ACT),[70] which included r 21: 'to facilitate the just resolution of the real issues in civil proceedings with minimum delay and expense'.[71] The plurality (Gummow, Hayne, Crennan, Kiefel and Bell JJ) explained the role of r 21 as follows[72]:

> ... a just resolution of proceedings remains the paramount purpose of r 21; but what is a 'just resolution' is to be understood in light of the purposes and objectives stated. Speed and efficiency, in the sense of minimum delay and expense, are seen as essential to a just resolution of proceedings.

The plurality went on to explain that the objectives stated in r 21 did not require that every application for amendment should be refused because it involves the waste of some costs and some degree of delay. Rather, what was called for was an explanation from the party seeking the exercise of the discretion in their favour. This was to allow for the consideration of such factors as the circumstances giving rise to the need for an amendment, the nature and importance of the amendment to the party, the extent of the delay and the costs, the prejudice which might follow, and the point the litigation has reached relative to a trial. There may be cases where it may properly be concluded that a party has had sufficient opportunity to plead their case and that it is too late for a further amendment, having regard to the other party and other litigants awaiting trial dates.[73]

The High Court was afforded an opportunity to apply its reasoning in *Aon Risk* to the NSW overriding purpose in *Expense Reduction Analysts Group Pty Ltd v Armstrong Strategic Management and Marketing Pty Limited*. In *Expense Reduction* documents subject to legal professional privilege were inadvertently disclosed to a party, who when asked to return them, refused on the basis that privilege had been waived.[74] The High Court reiterated its holding in *Aon Risk*: stating that '[s]peed and efficiency, in the sense of minimum delay and expense, are essential to a just resolution of proceedings' and further indicated that the principles in *Aon Risk* applied to all interlocutory proceedings.[75] The High Court took the view that discovery was a court process which the court should control so as to avoid satellite litigation. If a party mistakenly disclosed privileged documents then the mistake should be corrected to allow for the real issues in the dispute to be the subject of the parties' and court's resources. This meant ordering the return of the privileged documents and amending the List of Documents.[76] The High Court also emphasised that the

[70] The court rules at issue were those for the Australian Capital Territory.

[71] *Aon Risk*, 191–2 [31]–[32] (French CJ); 205 [71]–[72], 209–210 [85]–[88] (Gummow, Hayne, Crennan, Kiefel and Bell JJ); 219 [120], 221 [131] (Heydon J).

[72] *Aon Risk*, 213 [98].

[73] *Aon Risk*, 214–215 [102]–[103].

[74] [2013] HCA 46 (6 November 2013).

[75] Id at [51].

[76] Id at [58]–[60].

parties and their lawyers are required to assist in the achievement of the overriding purpose and should not unnecessarily pursue interlocutory disputes.[77]

The High Court's observations in *Aon Risk* demonstrate that concerns about cost and delay are legitimate considerations for courts seeking to achieve a just resolution of proceedings. However, while cost and delay must now factor into the exercise of a court's discretion they do not displace justice, but rather are to be weighed together.

8.3.3 Federal Court of Australia

An overarching purpose was introduced into *Federal Court of Australia Act 1976* (Cth) by the *Access to Justice (Civil Litigation Reforms) Amendment Act 2009* (Cth). Section 37 M provides:

> (1) The overarching purpose of the civil practice and procedure provisions is to facilitate the just resolution of disputes:
>
> (a) according to law; and
> (b) as quickly, inexpensively and efficiently as possible.

The purpose of the amendment was to introduce case management and procedural reforms, in particular, an overarching obligation upon the Court, the parties to litigation and legal practitioners to facilitate the just resolution of disputes according to law and as quickly, inexpensively and efficiently as possible. The amendments in s 37P also clarified the kinds of directions the Court can make to control the progress and conduct of proceedings.[78]

The Federal Court considered both *Aon Risk* and the above amendments in *Cement Australia Pty Ltd v Australian Competition and Consumer Commission* (ACCC). A unanimous Full Federal Court refused leave to appeal a trial judge's ruling allowing the ACCC to amend its pleadings on the first day of the trial when taken by surprise by the Respondents' position on market definition in the Respondents' opening. The Full Federal Court observed that giving weight to the achievement of justice, as the trial judge had done, was not contrary to the decision in *Aon Risk* or 37 M or 37 N of the *Federal Court Act*. Rather, achieving justice was not allowed to trump other considerations, such as cost and delay.[79] There needed to be a weighing of factors with the weight given varying with the facts in the individual case.[80] The Full Federal Court sees the operation of the overarching purpose as requiring a balancing of justice, cost and delay. The Full Federal Court also

[77] Id at [56], [64].

[78] Explanatory Memorandum, Access to Justice (Civil Litigation Reforms) Amendment Bill 2009 (Cth) 3.

[79] *Cement Australia Pty Ltd v Australian Competition and Consumer Commission* (2010) 187 FCR 261, 274 [45].

[80] Ibid 279 [67]–[68].

seemed to place weight on the fact that an explanation for the amendment was proffered, namely Counsel for the ACCC had not appreciated the way in which the respondents intended to run their case and Counsel's error may have been avoided if the respondents' pleadings had been less opaque.[81] Further, the amendment whilst going to the important issue of market definition, did not result in an entirely new case.[82] As a result *Aon Risk* could be distinguished on the basis that there no explanation for the late amendment was given and the amendment raised new issues.

The Full Federal Court in *Samsung Electronics Co. Limited v Apple Inc.* also provided helpful guidance when it declined an application for leave to appeal from an interlocutory judgment in which Samsung's application to file two witness statements nearly 12 months after the specified time for filing of such evidence was denied.[83] Samsung argued that leave to appeal should be granted because the docket judge had failed to take account of the prejudice Samsung was likely to suffer if unable to rely on the statements, ignored the reasons for delay and failed to consider the absence of any real prejudice to Apple.[84] Leave to appeal was denied as the docket judge's discretion had not been shown to have miscarried as she had weighed all matters relevant to the discretion.[85] The matters included the necessity to resolve civil litigation as '*quickly, inexpensively and efficiently as possible*' and a recognition of the fact that the '*achievement of a just but timely and cost-effective resolution of a dispute has effects not only upon the parties to the dispute but upon the court and other litigants*'.[86] The fact that a different judge may have reached a different conclusion was irrelevant.[87] The docket judge was faced with a discretionary decision on a matter of practice and procedure, even though the decision went directly to the ability of a party to put its case before the Court.[88] The 'yardstick' is whether there has been an error in the exercise of the discretion: acting upon a wrong principle, mistaking facts, taking account of irrelevant matters or failing to take account of relevant matters.[89] No such errors existed.

The Purpose Requirement in Australia has largely been a successful innovation through a consistent approach to the need to balance justice, cost and delay in the circumstances of individual cases. Judges are required to consider all of the elements. Unlike England & Wales there is no system of automatic sanctions and provision for relief from those sanctions. Rather, a party who disagrees with the way in which a judge has applied the Purpose Requirement must seek to bring an

[81] Ibid 277–78 [55]–[60].

[82] Ibid 278 [62].

[83] [2013] FCAFC 138.

[84] Ibid [6].

[85] Ibid [8], [32].

[86] Ibid [48] citing *Federal Court of Australia Act 1976* (Cth) s 37 M and *Expense Reduction Analysts Group Pty Ltd v Armstrong Strategic Management and Marketing Pty Limited* [2013] HCA 46, [51].

[87] Ibid [49].

[88] Ibid [43], [50].

[89] Ibid [17] citing *House v R* (1936) 55 CLR 499, 505.

interlocutory appeal and show that the judge's discretion miscarried. The matters to be considered by the primary judge are those contained in the Purpose Requirement. Appellate courts take the view that they should be slow to interfere and ought not reverse the primary judge's decision on a matter of practice and procedure unless convinced it is plainly erroneous.[90] Sanctions are not automatic but instead subject to the considered judgement of the primary judge who must weigh and resolve the competing goals of a just, timely and efficient outcome. It is not the case that every missed deadline or application for an indulgence should be sanctioned or refused if it involves delay and the incurring of costs. Equally the impact on costs and delay are not to be disregarded. The decision making process is nuanced and fact specific. However, the framework established by the Purpose Requirement must be followed. Guidance from the High Court and intermediate courts of appeal is necessary to reduce uncertainty and promote consistency in the balancing of justice, cost and delay.

8.4 United States of America

The *Federal Rules of Civil Procedure* (US) Rule 1 states[91]:

> These rules govern the procedure in all civil actions and proceedings in the United States district courts, except as stated in Rule 81. They should be construed and administered to secure the just, speedy, and inexpensive determination of every action and proceeding.

Rule 1 predates the Purpose Requirements discussed above by many years having been included when the rules were originally adopted in 1938. Rule 1 was amended in 1993 to add 'and administered'. The purpose of the amendment was 'to recognize the affirmative duty of the court to exercise the authority conferred by

[90] See *Adam P Brown Male Fashions Pty Ltd v Philip Morris Inc* (1981) 148 CLR 170, [9]; *Cicek v The Estate of the Late Mark Solomon* [2014] NSWCA 278, [69]–[70].

[91] The majority of American state jurisdictions have adopted a version of Rule 1. See Ala. R. Civ. P. 1; Alaska R. Civ. P. 1; Ariz. R. Civ. P. 1; Ark. R. Civ. P. 1; Del. Super. Ct. R. Civ. P. 1; D.C. R. Civ. P. 1; Fla. R. Civ. P. 1.010; Haw. R. Civ. P. 1; Ind. R. Trial Proc. R. 1; Minn. R. Civ. P. 1; Miss. R. Civ. P. 1; Mont. R. Civ. P. 1; Nev. R. Civ. P. 1; N.M. R. Civ. P. 1–001; N.D. R. Civ. P. 1; R.I. Super. Ct. R. Civ. P. 1; S.C. R. Civ. P. 1; S.D. Codified Laws 15-6-1; Tenn. R. Civ. P. 1; Vt. R. Civ. P. 1; Wash. Civ. R. 1; W.V. R. Civ. P. 1; Wyo. R. Civ. P. 1. States with a Purpose Requirement that varies from FRCP include Cal. Rules of Court R. 1.5 (construing rules "liberally ··· to ensure the just and speedy determination of the proceedings that they govern"); Colo. R. Civ. P. 1 (construing rules "liberally ··· to secure the just, speedy, and inexpensive determination of every action"); Idaho R. Civ. P. 1 (construing rules "liberally ··· to secure the just, speedy and inexpensive determination of every action and proceeding"); Kan. Stat. Ann. § 60–102 (West 2010) (construing rules "liberally ··· to secure the just, speedy and inexpensive determination of every action and proceeding"); Ohio R. Civ. P. 1 (construing rules to "eliminat[e] delay, unnecessary expense and all other impediments to ··· justice"); Tex. R. Civ. P. 1 (calling for rules "to obtain a just, fair, equitable and impartial adjudication ··· . [w]ith as great expedition and dispatch and at the least expense"); Utah R. Civ. P. 1 (construing rules "liberally ··· to achieve the just, speedy, and inexpensive determination of every action").

these rules to ensure that civil litigation is resolved not only fairly, but also without undue cost or delay'.[92]

The US Supreme Court has stated that '[t]he Federal Rules of Civil Procedure are to be construed to secure the just, speedy, and inexpensive determination of every action'[93] and rule 1 reflects a 'national policy ··· to minimize the costs of litigation'.[94] Other Federal Courts have reiterated the centrality and importance of rule 1.[95] This has included acknowledgements that 'delay in reaching the merits ... is costly in money, memory, manageability, and confidence in the process'[96] and that the effective administration of justice turns to a significant extent on 'a reasoned cost/benefit vigil by the judiciary'.[97] Rule 1 has been cited in relation to amendment of pleadings,[98] summary judgment,[99] discovery[100] and adherence to court timetables.[101] However, rarely has it been the touchstone for the outcome with greater reliance placed on individual rules.

Despite FRCP 1 being frequently cited, and a recognition that Rule 1 places the objectives of 'speedy' and 'inexpensive' on a plane of equality with 'just',[102] it has largely been unsuccessful at providing the impetus for reducing cost and delay.[103] One explanation for FRCP 1 failing to play the central role that is seen in the UK

---

[92] See Steven Gensler, 'Judicial Case Management: Caught in the Crossfire' (2010) 60 *Duke Law Journal* 669 at 679–680 citing Advisory Committee's note to 1993 amendment.

[93] *Bankers Trust Co v Mallis* 435 US 381, 386–87 (1978), *Nelson v Adams USA, Inc*, 529 US 460, 465 (2000).

[94] *Farmer v Arabian Am. Oil Co* 379 US 227, 234 (1964).

[95] For a summary of relevant cases see The Late Charles Alan Wright, Arthur Miller, Mary Kay Kane, Richard Marcus and Adam Steinman, 4 *Federal Practice & Procedure – Civil* § 1029 (3d ed.) and Elizabeth Cabraser, Uncovering Discovery available at http://www.uscourts.gov/uscourts/RulesAndPolicies/rules/Duke%20Materials/Library/Elizabeth%20Cabraser,%20Uncovering%20Discovery.pdf.

[96] *Finazzo v Hawaiian Airlines* 2007 WL 1876072 (D Haw 2007).

[97] *Anthony v Abbott Laboratories* 106 FRD 461, 465 (D RI 1985); *Foxley Cattle Co v Grain Dealers Mutual Insurance Co* 142 FRD 677, 682 (SD Iowa 1992).

[98] See eg *Berg v Popham* 2001 WL 36161391 (D Ala 2001); *Powell v Henry* 2006 WL 2160896 (ED Mich 2006); *Commerce Benefits Group Inc v McKesson Corp* 2008 WL 239550 (ND Ohio 2008).

[99] *Celotex Corp v Catrett* 477 US 317, 327 (1986) ("[s]ummary judgment procedure is properly regarded not as a disfavored procedural shortcut, but rather as an integral part of the Federal Rules as a whole, which are designed to 'secure the just, speedy and inexpensive determination of every action'".).

[100] See eg *Da Silva Moore v Publicis Groupe* 287 FRD 182, 191 (SDNY 2012) ("Courts and litigants should be cognizant of the aim of Rule 1, to 'secure the just, speedy and inexpensive determination' of lawsuits".)

[101] See eg *Marmo v Tyson Fresh Meats Inc* 457 F3d 748, 760 (8th Cir 2006); *Al-Misehal Commercial Group Ltd v Armored Group LLC*, 2011 WL 2147599, *2 (D. Ariz. 2011).

[102] See The Late Charles Alan Wright, Arthur Miller, Mary Kay Kane, Richard Marcus and Adam Steinman, 4 *Federal Practice & Procedure – Civil* § 1029 (3d ed.).

[103] James Maxeiner, 'The Federal Rules at 75: Dispute Resolution, Private Enforcement or Decisions According to Law?' (2014) 30 *Georgia State University Law Review* 983, 990–991; Harold Koh, 'The Just, Speedy, and Inexpensive Determination of Every Action?' (2014) 162 *University of Pennsylvania Law Review* 1525; E. Donald Elliott, 'Managerial Judging and the Evolution of Procedure' (1986) 53 *University of Chicago Law Review* 306, 310.

and Australia is that the objectives are seen as vague, conflicting and failing to provide guidance to the parties, lawyers or judge.[104] Indeed, the supporting rules or legislative provisions that provide guidance in the UK and Australia, as well as imposing obligation on legal practitioners and parties, are absent from the FRCP. Further the detailed decisions seen in the UK and Australian appeal courts where the conflicting requirements are analysed appears to be missing in the US. Moreover academic analysis of the provision is scant. Another issue is that views about the role of procedure have changed since the inception of FRCP 1. Originally procedure was seen as being about efficient institutional design which simply required the application of expertise by judges granted wide discretion. Consequently FRCP 1 operated as an exhortation to avoid technicalities and facilitate substantively correct decisions. Rules of procedure were liberally construed, including in relation to pleadings and discovery.[105] The 1960–70s saw procedure become viewed as political. Choices about procedure were seen as involving value choices that harmed or helped particular parties, and in an era of civil rights, environmental protection and consumer protection, choices that facilitated or restricted political objectives. Tradeoffs between 'justice', speed and expense were no longer instrumental choices but politically charged choices[106] – choices that largely turn on 'the judge's values, beliefs about procedure, and perceptions of the nature and severity of litigation problems'.[107] The concern about FRCP 1 is consistent with a more general concern among American academics about judicial discretion lacking accountability and being open to abuse.[108] Moreover, FRCP 1 runs counter to a culture that is highly legalistic and adversarial where zealous advocacy can mean taking every point and leaving no stone unturned which are causes of cost and delay.[109]

The political nature of civil procedure in the US is clearly seen in the ferocious debate over pleading after the Supreme Court of the United States decisions in *Bell*

---

[104] Robert Bone, 'Improving Rule 1: A Master Rule for the Federal Rules' (2010) 87 *Denver University Law Review* 287, 288–289. See also The Late Charles Alan Wright, Arthur Miller, Mary Kay Kane, Richard Marcus and Adam Steinman, 4 *Federal Practice & Procedure – Civil* § 1029 (3d ed.) ("Rule 1 does not pronounce a single canon of construction but rather delineates the inherent tension throughout the rules. … Rule 1 is Janus-faced, simultaneously supporting and betraying a particular construction of the rules. In short, Rule 1 is an introduction to analysis and thought, rather than a conclusion, as to the judge's choice of procedure.).

[105] Ibid 290–294.

[106] Ibid 294–297. James Maxeiner, 'The Federal Rules at 75: Dispute Resolution, Private Enforcement or Decisions According to Law?' (2014) 30 *Georgia State University Law Review* 983, 989.

[107] Ibid 300.

[108] See eg Judith Resnick, 'Managerial Judges' (1982) 96 *Harvard Law Review* 374, 425–428, 430–431; Jonathan Molot, 'An Old Judicial Role for a New Litigation Era' (2003) 113 *Yale Law Journal* 27, 93 and Jay Tidmarsh, 'Pound's Century, and Ours' (2006) 81 *Notre Dame Law Review* 513, 559 ("Customizing rules for each case also raises a concern of great significance in a democratic society: the fear that judges will use their discretionary power, consciously or subconsciously, to tailor rules in a way that influences the outcome of individual litigation.").

[109] See Robert Kagan, *Adversarial Legalism – The American Way of Law* (2001) Harvard University Press.

Atlantic Corp. v Twombly, 550 US 544 (2007) and *Ashcroft v Iqbal*, 556 US 662 (2009) replaced notice pleading with a plausibility requirement.[110] The Supreme Court was concerned that to allow a case to go forward based on a pleading with conclusory allegations rather than plausible facts would impose considerable costs, especially through discovery, in what may be an unmeritorious case.[111] The new plausibility requirement is argued to make access to the courts more difficult, uncertain and expensive as plaintiffs must obtain more facts before commencing proceedings otherwise those proceedings are likely to be struck out through a motion to dismiss.[112] The debate in the US proceeds on the basis that political or social objectives, such as ensuring citizens access to the courts or preventing the pursuit of unmeritorious litigation, are contestable choices which are given effect through civil procedure.[113]

To be added to the above explanations is also a more simple observation that the federal judiciary adopts a greater focus on specific rules rather than FRCP 1 because of the approach to interpretation of the rules. The FRCP is treated similarly to a statute and courts apply the plain meaning of the rules.[114] Although FRCP 1 refers

---

[110] The plausibility standard is explained in *Ashcroft v Iqbal*, 556 US 662, 677–678 (2009) as follows (citations omitted):

> Under Federal Rule of Civil Procedure 8(a)(2), a pleading must contain a "short and plain statement of the claim showing that the pleader is entitled to relief." The pleading standard Rule 8 announces does not require "detailed factual allegations," but it demands more than an unadorned, the-defendant-unlawfully-harmed-me accusation. A pleading that offers "labels and conclusions" or "a formulaic recitation of the elements of a cause of action will not do." Nor does a complaint suffice if it tenders "naked assertion[s]" devoid of "further factual enhancement."
>
> To survive a motion to dismiss, a complaint must contain sufficient factual matter, accepted as true, to "state a claim to relief that is plausible on its face." A claim has facial plausibility when the plaintiff pleads factual content that allows the court to draw the reasonable inference that the defendant is liable for the misconduct alleged. The plausibility standard is not akin to a "probability requirement," but it asks for more than a sheer possibility that a defendant has acted unlawfully. Where a complaint pleads facts that are "merely consistent with" a defendant's liability, it "stops short of the line between possibility and plausibility of 'entitlement to relief.'

[111] *Bell Atlantic Corp. v Twombly*, 550 US 544, 559–560 (2007)

[112] Testimony of Professor Arthur Miller, before the Sub-committee on the Constitution, Civil Rights and Civil Liberties of the House Committee on the Judiciary, 111th Congress, 27 October 2009; Adam Steinman, 'The Pleading Problem' (2010) 62 *Stanford Law Review* 1293, 1347–1356; Kevin Clermont and Stephen Yeazell, 'Inventing Tests, Destabilizing Systems' (2010) 95 *Iowa Law Review* 821; Robert Bone, 'Plausibility Pleading Revisited and Revised: A Comment on Ashcroft v Iqbal' (2010) 85 *Notre Dame Law Review* 849, 879; Erwin Chemerinsky, 'Closing the Courthouse Doors' (2012) 90 *Denver University Law Review* 317, 328.

[113] Michael Legg and James Metzger, 'US Supreme Court Revolutionises Pleading Requirements' (2011) 85(2) *Australian Law Journal* 81.

[114] See eg *Business Guides Inc v Chromatic Communications Enterprises Inc* 498 US 533, 540–541 (1991) ("We give the Federal Rules of Civil Procedure their plain meaning." ... As with a statute, our inquiry is complete if we find the text of the Rule to be clear and unambiguous."); *Pavelic & LeFlore v Marvel Entertainment Group*, 493 US 120, 126 (1989) ("Our task is to apply the text, not to improve upon it."). See also Karen Nelson Moore, 'The Supreme Court's Role in Interpreting the Federal Rules of Civil Procedure' (1993) 44 *Hastings Law Journal* 1039 (discussing Supreme

to construing and administering the rules, the need to give effect to specific rules reduces the field of operation for FRCP 1.

The restrictive operation of FRCP 1 is borne out by a proposed amendment to the rule that the FRCP should be construed, administered and 'employed by the court and the parties' to secure the just, speedy, and inexpensive determination of every action and proceeding.[115] The revision is in response to requests to discourage 'overuse, misuse, and abuse of procedural tools that increase cost and result in delay' and aims to emphasise that parties share responsibility with the court to employ the rules in a manner consistent with the just, speedy, and inexpensive determination of litigation.[116]

8.5 Conclusion

Cost and delay are major problems for an effective civil justice system. Indeed, cost and delay can undermine the function of the civil justice system by preventing the achievement of justice.

The reference to cost and delay in a Purpose Requirement raises awareness and signals the need to be conscious of the corrosive effects of cost and delay on civil justice. Consequently a Purpose Requirement may operate as a way to facilitate change to the traditional reference point where 'doing justice' was a goal to be pursued without regard to delay and expense. However for a Purpose Requirement to be successful it must be more than a ritualised incantation that precedes a judge granting indulgences to parties in the name of justice.

The above discussion demonstrates that judges and legal practitioners require guidance as to how to apply, or comply with, a Purpose Requirement. Guidance can come from legislation, court rules or appellate court decisions but it must be provided. However, there is no escape from the reality that a Purpose Requirement which embodies justice, cost and delay is promoting conflicting requirements. Reducing cost and delay can facilitate justice, but equally too great an emphasis on these concerns may undermine justice if real issues are excluded, evidence cannot be gathered or argument is truncated. A Purpose Requirement provides a framework or guide for decision making. It does not specify an outcome. This is what allows it to apply to all procedural steps. Guidance must necessarily focus on the application of the Purpose Requirement to the process requirements imposed on parties and the court's role in enforcing them ··· England & Wales and Australia having recognised the need for guidance have gone to great lengths to seek to provide it. However,

---

Court's use of the plain meaning approach in interpreting the FRCP and arguing for a more activist role in interpretation consistent with the spirit of the Federal Rules, as enunciated in FRCP 1.)

[115] Judicial Conference Committee on Rules of Practice and Procedure, *Preliminary Draft of Proposed Amendments to the Federal Rules of Bankruptcy and Civil Procedure* (June 2013) 281 http://www.uscourts.gov/uscourts/rules/preliminary-draft-proposed-amendments.pdf.

[116] Ibid.

their experiences with that guidance have varied. The English Court of Appeal has now had two attempts at providing guidance on its rule for relief of sanctions – *Mitchell* and *Denton*– but disagreements still exist. In Australia a much more uniform approach has prevailed with the same message emanating from the High Court of Australia and the intermediate courts of appeal.

The US on the other hand has recognised the conflicting requirements and decried the prospect of abuse. The US concerns demonstrate that inserting a Purpose Requirement at the beginning of rules of civil procedure is not a straightforward solution to controlling cost and delay. A generally expressed Purpose Requirement allows for guidance to courts on the numerous factual matrices that they may encounter. Consistency of application is unlikely to be readily ascertainable, and simply may not exist as judicial minds differ on close calls. Equally, one may see the political preferences of judicial officers given full rein. Much depends on whether judicial discretion is seen as a positive method for achieving effective case management guided by a Purpose Requirement, or an evil to be avoided.

The US experience also demonstrates that the mere adoption of a Purpose Requirement is insufficient. The courts, legal practitioners and parties need to embrace the Purpose Requirement and ensure its effective application. The Purpose Requirement at its most effective changes the approach to civil litigation by becoming engrained in the culture of the courts and of its legal practitioners.[117] The US demonstrates that the simple effluxion of time will not achieve this transformation. FRCP 1 has a far longer history than the English or Australian Purpose Requirements but because courts and legal practitioners have not embraced its guidance it has not achieved the desired cultural change. Appellate courts in particular play an important role in ensuring that the framework created by a Purpose Requirement is correctly applied. Depending on the circumstances this may mean directing inferior courts about the need to give weight to cost and delay considerations, or to ensuring that justice is not left out of the equation. To ensure the judge's refrains are taken seriously obligations need to be imposed on legal practitioners and parties, for which there are consequences for non-compliance.

The Purpose Requirement innovation appears to have been successful in raising awareness and changing attitudes to costs and delay in England and Australia. Although empirical support is difficult to find it appears that reducing delay has been achieved more readily than reductions in cost.[118] More remains to be done. The amendment of the English Purpose Requirement to add 'at proportionate cost' signals the need for greater focus on cost reduction. It should also be remembered that the Purpose Requirement works with case management, judicial discretion and continued attempts to formulate and disseminate best practice in relation to procedural steps such as pleading, discovery and expert witnesses.

[117] Anthony Clarke, 'The Woolf Reforms: A Singular Event or an Ongoing Process?' in Deirdre Dwyer (ed), *The Civil Procedure Rules Ten Years On* (2009) 41–46.

[118] See eg Lord Justice Jackson, 'Civil Justice in an Uncivil World' in Michael Legg (ed), *The Future of Dispute Resolution* (2013) 26–27; James Spigelman, 'Access to Justice and Access to Lawyers' (2007) 29 *Australian Bar Review* 136, 143.

Chapter 9
Towards Proportionality – The "Quick, Cheap and Just" Balance in Civil Litigation

Brenda Tronson

> On such an afternoon the various solicitors in the cause, some two or three of whom have inherited it from their fathers, who made a fortune by it, ought to be--as are they not?--ranged in a line, in a long matted well (but you might look in vain for truth at the bottom of it) between the registrar's red table and the silk gowns, with bills, cross-bills, answers, rejoinders, injunctions, affidavits, issues, references to masters, masters' reports, mountains of costly nonsense, piled before them.
>
> For the question at issue is only a question of costs, a mere bud on the forest tree of the parent suit, and really will come to a settlement one of these days. –*Bleak House*, Charles Dickens (1853)

The fictional case of *Jarndyce v Jarndyce*, central to the plot of *Bleak House* by Charles Dickens, is better known than many real civil proceedings. Like many of Dickens' caricatures, it is said that it is not far from the truth.

A modern-day reader of *Bleak House* with knowledge of certain twenty-first century litigation might wonder what has changed. In Australia alone, cases such as the *C7* litigation, *Bell*, *Westport Insurance Corporation v Gordian Runoff Ltd* and *Rinehart v Hancock*[1] spring to mind. At times, it can seem that those with a grievance and deep pockets might let no cost deter them from pursuing the justice they seek.

Further, judicial determination following a lengthy trial provides justice in one sense but, in many instances, might result in damage to both the winner and the loser,

---

Barrister, Level 22 Chambers, Sydney Australia.

[1] *Seven Network Ltd v News Ltd* [2007] FCA 1062; *The Bell Group Ltd (in liq) v Westpac Banking Corporation* [2008] WASC 239; (2008) 39 WAR 1; *Westport Insurance Corporation v Gordian Runoff Ltd* [2011] HCA 37; (2011) 244 CLR 239; finally, litigation between Gina Rinehart and three of her children took up a considerable amount of time in the NSW Supreme Court and Court of Appeal during 2011 to 2014.

B. Tronson (✉)
Level 22 Chambers, 52 Martin Place, Sydney, NSW 2000, Australia
e-mail: btronson@level22.com.au

C.B. Picker, G.I. Seidman (eds.), *The Dynamism of Civil Procedure - Global Trends and Developments*, Ius Gentium: Comparative Perspectives on Law and Justice 48, DOI 10.1007/978-3-319-21981-3_9

including through further loss or damage of the kind that led to the dispute in the first instance, lack of certainty for an extended period of time, futility in the result due to changes of circumstances or destruction of the subject matter of the proceedings, breakdown of relationships (whether personal or commercial), reputational loss and the exposure of matters otherwise private or confidential. To add insult to injury, the legal result might not give any party what they really want.

The result is that litigation can seem to be a sledgehammer used to crack the nut of a legal problem.

In many jurisdictions, positive steps have been taken (by legislatures, courts, lawyers and parties) to reduce the costs of litigation, particularly where the quantum in issue is not large. Many jurisdictions also give strong encouragement to parties to use alternative dispute resolution (ADR) at an early stage. If successful, ADR can reduce costs and permit parties to reach a settlement that might be a more appropriate resolution of a particular dispute than the purely legal answer a judge might give.

A keyword in these discussions is often "proportionality". It is now a common requirement for courts, litigants and legal representatives to work to ensure costs are proportionate. Examples of this include s 60 of the *Civil Procedure Act 2005* (NSW) and r 1.1(2) of the *Civil Procedure Rules 1998* (UK).

This is perhaps unsurprising, as there is a real question as to the utility of the concept of "proportionality" in achieving the relevant goals.

One significant barrier in this regard is the courts' inability to impose requirements on parties not to incur disproportionate expenditure as a matter of fact. Legislative requirements may be expressed in terms which seem to be compulsory but, as a matter of practicality, such provisions tend to be aspirational rather than enforceable.

The courts' main power is to order one party to pay another's costs, or to refuse to do so in circumstances where such an order might otherwise be expected, may be exercised by reference to the conduct of the parties. The potential for the exercise of such powers may have little impact on a party with deep pockets and which believes it can exhaust the resources of its opponent, or on a party which knows that *any* costs order against it will cause insolvency. Given this, the courts' control of parties' expenditure is not only indirect but can be weak.

Nevertheless, potential costs orders can be powerful motivating factors for some parties, and the courts powers are strengthened to some extent by the range of other orders that may be made. For example, courts may make interim costs orders in relation to particularly egregious conduct, especially if it appears to be directed to driving up the costs of the litigation or producing delay. Orders for security for costs in appropriate cases can protect against continued litigation by a litigant who would not be able to afford an adverse costs order, particularly if the litigant's case is weak.

In addition, courts often have the power to order that legal practitioners pay costs which ought not have been incurred.[2] The concept of proportionality has a role to play in respect of each of these kinds of orders. Further, a client can seek to have the fees chargedby their lawyer assessed through a process overseen by the court,

[2] See, for example, *Civil Procedure Act 2005* (NSW), s 99. This has recently been considered: *Re Felicity* [2015] NSWCA 19.

although proportionality is less likely to be relevant here, particularly if the client was fully advised of the likely costs in advance.

It is a combination of orders such as these, used appropriately, which has the potential to achieve the cultural change required to move towards a general proportionality of litigation.

There then arises the question of what is meant by "proportionality". Reference is often made to a comparison of costs with the quantum in dispute, although the legislative statements tend to refer also to the importance or complexity of the issues. It must be borne in mind that discussion about proportionality by reference to quantum alone can overlook important factors.

As Davies has observed, proportionality can also mean "maintaining a balance between cost and the amount or value in dispute [and] also a balance between these, on the one hand, and the risk of unfairness, on the other."[3] This balance is recognisable in the various statements of an "overriding purpose", or equivalent, now used as a touchstone in many jurisdictions, with examples including s 56 of the *Civil Procedure Act 2005* (NSW) and r 1.1 of the *Civil Procedure Rules 1998* (UK).

It is in this way that proportionality can be distinguished from reasonableness in relation to costs. Proportionality has a holistic element, whereas the concept of reasonableness in relation to costs is generally considered on a case by case basis, that is, whether a particular item of expenditure was reasonably incurred. The assessment of reasonableness generally requires a consideration of the circumstances at the time, including the knowledge of the parties and their legal representatives, without any need to give consideration to an overall balance.

Proportionality can also be distinguished from reasonableness in relation to conduct in a similar way, in that reasonable conduct is to be assessed by reference to the circumstances at the time, and whether or not a particular manner of conducting litigation is proportionate is more holistic.

Despite the distinctions that can be drawn, whether considered by reference to costs or conduct, proportionality and reasonableness often go together.

For reasons referred to above, the third aspect of the overriding purpose, speed or efficiency (including both the time taken by parties and their lawyers to do the work, the impact on court resources and the duration of the litigation as a whole), must also be added to the balance between costs, quantum and fairness or justice.

In other words, the use of an overriding purpose recognises the multiple calculations inherent in the concept of proportionality, even if those subtleties are sometimes overlooked in discussion of particular cases.

In both Australia and the United Kingdom, proportionality and the overriding purpose (albeit given slightly differently names in different jurisdictions) have been accorded increasing importance over the past few decades. In both jurisdictions, this can be seen in both legislative reform and approaches developed through judicial comment. However, there are differences in the practical application in the two countries. This chapter will explore the developments in both jurisdictions and what

---

[3] Davies, Geoffrey. 2006. Civil justice reform: Some common problems, some possible solutions. *Journal of Judicial Administration* 16: 5–17, at 6.

might be expected for each in the future, as well as the utility of proportionality as a concept in reducing litigation costs, compared to proportionality as an aspiration to be achieved.

9.1 History of Civil Procedure Reforms – United Kingdom

The observations made by Dickens demonstrate that there has been concern about the proportionality of the approach to civil litigation since at the least the 1800s. Reforms in that century included the *Common Law Procedure Amendment Act* and the establishment of the County Court, both with at least the partial aim of serving the needs of business litigants more efficiently. However, in the 1930s and 1940s, it was becoming clear that litigation in the UK was highly expensive.[4] This trend has continued, and by the 1980s and 1990s, the need for further reform was becoming increasingly clear.

A significant driver of the modern reforms is generally seen to be Lord Woolf's reports on the civil justice system in the United Kingdom. In his summary of his findings, he said[5]:

> The system should:
>
> (a) be *just* in the results it delivers;
> (b) be *fair* in the way it treats litigants;
> (c) offer appropriate procedures at a reasonable *cost*;
> (d) deal with cases with reasonable *speed*;
> (e) be *understandable* to those who use it;
> (f) be *responsive* to the needs of those who use it;
> (g) provide as much *certainty* as the nature of particular cases allows; and
> (h) be *effective*: adequately resourced and organised.

The reforms outlined in the balance of the report were designed to promote a system which could achieve these aims through a combination of factors, including requiring changes to court structures and procedural rules. Relevantly, Lord Woolf recommended fixed costs in certain matters, early costs estimates which would have an impact upon ultimate costs orders and amendments to the test for assessing the amount to be paid once one party was ordered to pay another's costs to incorporate a reasonableness test.

The drive for reform and the recommendations made did not exist in a vacuum. Discussion about the need for case management to better marshal court resources and resolve disputes more efficiently had been growing in both academic circles and amongst judges.[6]

---

[4] Genn, Hazel. 1997. Understanding civil justice. *Current Legal Problems* 50: 155–187, at 165–166.

[5] Lord Woolf. 1996. *Access to Justice – Final Report*. Section I [1].

[6] See, for example, Sourdin, Tania. 1996. Judicial management and alternative dispute resolution process trends. *Australian Bar Review* 14: 185–213; Wolski, Bobette. 2009. Reform of the civil justice system two decades past – implications for the legal profession and for law teachers. *Bond Law Review* 21: 192-232.

Lord Woolf's report resulted in the enactment of the *Civil Procedure Act 1997* (UK) and the *Civil Procedure Rules 1998* (UK), which were largely true to the recommendations in the report. The Rules included the "overriding objective" in r 1.1, which provided:

The overriding objective

1. These Rules are a new procedural code with the overriding objective of enabling the court to deal with cases justly.
2. Dealing with a case justly includes, so far as is practicable—

(a) ensuring that the parties are on an equal footing;
(b) saving expense;
(c) dealing with the case in ways which are proportionate—

   (i) to the amount of money involved;
   (ii) to the importance of the case;
   (iii) to the complexity of the issues; and
   (iv) to the financial position of each party;

(d) ensuring that it is dealt with expeditiously and fairly; and
(e) allotting to it an appropriate share of the court's resources, while taking into account the need to allot resources to other cases.

Amendments which came into effect on 1 April 2013 added the words "and at proportionate cost" after the word "justly" in each of r 1.1(1) and 1.1(2), and adding a further paragraph (r 1.1(2)(f)): "enforcing compliance with rules, practice directions and orders."

The application of the overriding objective and other relevant rules in the *Civil Procedure Rules 1998* (UK) was never easy or straightforward.

One example of this can be seen with *Lownds v Home Office* [2002] EWCA Civ 365; [2002] 1 WLR 2450, an appeal relating to an assessment of costs, some of which had been incurred prior to the commencement of the *Civil Procedure Rules 1998* (UK) and some of which had been incurred after that commencement. Lord Woolf CJ gave the judgment of the Court of Appeal and held that a two stage approach was required, "a global approach and an item by item approach"[7]:

> If … the costs as a whole appear disproportionate then the court will want to be satisfied that the work in relation to each item was necessary and, if necessary, that the cost of the item is reasonable.

In the *Jackson Report*, Sir Rupert Jackson observed that the decision in *Lownds*, while appearing at the time to be "a neat way of applying the proportionality test, which would bring costs under proper control", did not in fact provide satisfactory guidance and that it "insert[ed] the Victorian test of necessity into the modern concept of proportionality."[8]

---

[7] *Lownds* at [31].

[8] Sir Rupert Jackson, 2009, *Review of Civil Litigation Costs: Final Report*, 37.

Given the indirect and, perhaps, weak power of the courts to control expenditure, perhaps the difficulties in "bring[ing] costs under proper control" should not have been surprising.

In addition, within a few years after the commencement of the *Civil Procedure Rules 1998* (UK), there was widespread criticism about the reforms.[9] Zuckerman has observed[10]:

> Although the [Court of Appeal] was quick to articulate the demands of the overriding objective, it was less successful in implementing them in the day-to-day management of litigation. In particular, it tended to lose sight of the demands of expedition and of proportionate use of resources when it came to dealing with litigant failure to comply with rules and court orders, or when it had to deal with litigant attempts to escape the strictures of case management directions.

Zuckerman has also commented that there was a "lingering judicial attachment … to the justice on the merits approach and a commensurate tendency to disregard the resource and time dimensions of justice."[11]

Further, in relation to r 3.9 of the *Civil Procedure Rules 1998* (UK), which governs relief from sanctions, as Zuckerman says[12]:

> the multiplicity of the factors and the fact that they stood in no particular relative order of importance meant that the court had almost unfettered discretion. The outcome of applications for relief from sanctions was therefore unpredictable.

Zuckerman also considers the failure of the Court of Appeal to provide clear guidance on r 3.9 resulted in a significant volume of satellite litigation, resulting in further expenditure and increased time. The enumerated factors were also applied to applications for extensions of time, causing further confusion.[13]

It was in this context that the Jackson review was commissioned.

9.2 History of Civil Procedure Reforms – Australia

In Australia, the *Supreme Court Rules 1987* (NT) have, since commencement, included r 1.10, which provides that "the Court … shall endeavour to ensure that all questions in the proceeding are effectively, completely, promptly and economically determined" (sub-r (1)(a)).

---

[9] See, for example, Zander, Michael. 2003. Where are we heading with the funding of civil litigation. *Civil Justice Quarterly* 22: 23–40, see generally, and particularly at 25 where there is a description of practitioners' views about inconsistency, uncertainty and lack of predictability.

[10] Zuckerman, Adrian. 2013. The revised CPR 3.9: a coded message demanding articulation. *Civil Justice Quarterly* 32: 123–138, 130.

[11] Zuckerman, Adrian. 2013. The revised CPR 3.9: a coded message demanding articulation. *Civil Justice Quarterly* 32: 123–138, 134.

[12] Zuckerman, Adrian. 2013. The revised CPR 3.9: a coded message demanding articulation. *Civil Justice Quarterly* 32: 123–138, 132.

[13] Zuckerman, Adrian. 2013. The revised CPR 3.9: a coded message demanding articulation. *Civil Justice Quarterly* 32: 123–138, 132–133.

In 1993, O 1 rr 4A and 4B were inserted into the *Rules of the Supreme Court 1971* (WA), the stated goal of these being to eliminate delay and introduce a system of case management to promote justice and efficiency.

A comparison between the Northern Territory and Western Australian and the approach adopted more recently in other jurisdictions (beginning in the late 1990s) suggests the concept of the "overriding purpose" has developed from the idea that this obligation is an obligation of *the Court*, a notion which is also reflected to a significant extent in the Western Australian rules, to obligations of parties and their legal representatives.

In 1998, Spigelman CJ was appointed to the NSW Supreme Court and commenced a process of reducing the backlogs in NSW courts.[14] This process can also be seen as an important part of case management, and a demonstration of the changing attitudes of the time.

In 1999, Queensland introduced its *Uniform Civil Procedure Rules 1998*. Chapter 1, r 5(1) provides:

> The purpose of these rules is to facilitate the just and expeditious resolution of the real issues in civil proceedings at a minimum of expense.

Also in 1999, the Australian Law Reform Commission recognised the increasing importance of case management in ALRC Report 89, published in 2000, entitled "Managing Justice: A review of the federal civil justice system".

In 2000, the *Supreme Court Rules 1970* (NSW) were amended to include a new Pt 1 r 3, which provided in part:

> (1) The overriding purpose of these rules, in their application to civil proceedings, is to facilitate the just, quick and cheap resolution of the real issues in such proceedings.

In 2005, the *Civil Procedure Act 2005* (NSW) introduced an essentially uniform civil procedure across all NSW courts. It included the "overriding purpose" in s 56(1):

> The overriding purpose of this Act and of rules of court, in their application to civil proceedings, is to facilitate the just, quick and cheap resolution of the real issues in the proceedings.

Rule 2.1 of the *Uniform Civil Procedure Rules 2005* (NSW) supports this overriding purpose.

The other Australian jurisdictions have followed suit with equivalent provisions enacted between 2006 and 2011.

Hand in hand with legislative reform came a change in judicial approach. In 2009, the High Court of Australia delivered the landmark judgment in *Aon Risk Services Australia Ltd v Australian National University* [2009] HCA 27; (2009) 239 CLR 175 (*Aon v ANU*). In that case, the High Court held that case management principles permit courts to take into account the impact of litigation on public

[14] Spigelman, J. J. 2009. Case management in New South Wales. *Paper prepared for the judicial delegation from India, Sydney 21 September 2009*, at 26-30. Spigelman has also observed that the NSW reforms might be better described as a "need to change … driven by new pressures that have emerged": Spigelman, J. J. 2007. Access to justice and access to lawyers. *Australian Bar Review* 29: 136–149, 143.

resources and "the potential for loss of public confidence in the legal system which arises where a court is seen to accede to applications made without adequate explanation or justification".[15]

Aon v ANU is generally seen to demonstrate a departure from the principles outlined in the earlier case of *Queensland v JL Holdings Pty Ltd* (1997) 189 CLR 146, a case in which the Court had said that, "except perhaps in extreme circumstances", justice would generally require a court to grant a party leave to amend pleadings in order to "litigat[e] an issue which is fairly arguable", particularly where costs were available to cure any prejudice.[16]

It is arguable that the factual situation in *Aon v ANU* was such that a direct application of the principles in *Queensland v JL Holdings* would have resulted in the same conclusion.[17] However, the plurality in *Aon v ANU* made it clear that the approach to case management needed to change, and the relevance of the history of reforms to civil procedure to the reasoning in *Aon v ANU* was patent in each of the judgments delivered by the Court.[18]

In light of *Aon v ANU* and the various procedural rules which operate in all jurisdictions, the position in Australia now is that courts are expected to take into account all facets of the overriding purpose (however expressed) when engaging in case management.

This is a very important factor in increasing the proportionality of civil litigation. If all parties involved in particular proceedings are so inclined, case management under the current regime should allow the matter to be moved towards hearing with considerable expedition. For example, the Local Court of NSW aims "to finalise 90 % of civil proceedings within 6 months of commencement and 100 % within 12 months".[19] In the Supreme Court of NSW, proceedings in directions lists which were commenced 2 or more years previously are sufficiently rare as to be notable.

On the other hand, the powers of the courts, exercised in light of the overriding purpose and the principles in *Aon v ANU*, give them considerable latitude in ensuring any recalcitrant parties are required to at least account for any laxity. This appears to have affected the attitudes of the legal profession as a whole in relation to complying with timetables and directions.

In the *C7* litigation, in comments about the limitations faced by a presiding judge in attempting to manage a case, Sackville J observed: "parties to mega-litigation are often able effectively to ignore (albeit politely) directions made by the court, if they consider that their forensic interests will be advanced by doing so."[20] It is also worth

[15] *Aon v ANU* at 192 [30] (French CJ).

[16] *Queensland v JL Holdings* at 154–155 (Dawson, Gaudron and McHugh JJ); see also 167 (Kirby J).

[17] See, for example, *Aon v ANU* at 191 [28] (French CJ); see also 205 [72] (Gummow, Hayne, Crennan, Kiefel and Bell JJ).

[18] *Aon v ANU* at 183 ff [9] ff (French CJ); 210-215 [90]-[103], 217-218 [111]-[114] (see in particular 213 [97]) (Gummow, Hayne, Crennan, Kiefel and Bell JJ); see also 222-223 [133] (Heydon J).

[19] Local Court of NSW Practice Note Civ 1 [3.4].

[20] *Seven Network Ltd v News Ltd* [2007] FCA 1062 [20].

noting that the *C7* litigation took place before the High Court's decision in *Aon v ANU*, and before s 37 M of the *Federal Court of Australia Act 1976* (Cth) was inserted. If the same set of circumstances were present in the Federal Court now, parties, even to mega-litigation, might find it more difficult "effectively to ignore [politely or otherwise] directions made by the court".[21]

That said, where there is more at stake (or apparently at stake), it is still likely to be the case that that a party will press with more force towards a situation which benefits them in relation to the determination of the case on the merits, regardless of case management principles. This makes intuitive sense, at least as far as the parties are concerned. Justice Sackville's comments suggest it is a position which leaves something to be desired in terms of the use of public resources.

9.3 Proportionality of Costs

The question of costs under strict case management regimes has remained a significant issue. As Chief Justice Spigelman, as he then was, observed, "[c]ase management may impose disproportionate, indeed even unnecessary, costs on the parties", for example, by frontloading costs "in many matters that would in the normal course have settled without incurring any such costs at all."[22] Nevertheless, case management which permits parties to identify at the earliest possible stage issues which are agreed and issues which are truly in dispute, a process which is likely to involve some frontloading of costs, may facilitate either settlement or a more expeditious (and cheaper) hearing.

In the *Jackson Report*, it was observed that the decision in *Lownds v Home Office* [2002] EWCA Civ 365; [2002] 1 WLR 2450, while appearing at the time to be "a neat way of applying the proportionality test, which would bring costs under proper control", did not in fact provide satisfactory guidance. Jackson recommended that "proportionality should prevail over reasonableness and the proportionality test should be applied on a global basis."[23] The recommendation was that an assessment of reasonableness by reference to individual items be carried out first, and that the court should then consider whether the total was proportionate to the quantum in issue and the complexity and importance of the case. This more holistic approach is intended to restrict costs orders in appropriate cases. Where parties know that

[21] Although that plainly still takes place, and the only practical consequence for defaulting parties and lawyers can be comments made in reasons for judgment: see, for example, *Superior IP International Pty Ltd v Ahearn Fox Patent and Trade Mark Attorneys* [2012] FCA 282; see also *Superior IP International Pty Ltd v Ahearn Fox Patent and Trade Mark Attorneys (No 2)* [2012] FCA 977.

[22] Spigelman AC, The Hon J. J. 2007. Access to justice and access to lawyers. *Australian Bar Review* 29: 136–149, 145.

[23] Sir Rupert Jackson. 2009. *Review of Civil Litigation Costs: Final Report*, 37.

approach will be taken, it will potentially provide some control over expenditure, albeit indirect and weak, as outlined above.

This recommendation was adopted, with effect from 1 April 2013.[24]

9.4 Proportionality and Parties' Forensic Decisions

Quite apart from any question of frontloading, increased costs (and decreased proportionality and achievement of the overriding purpose) can result from forensic decisions made by parties. For example, where a party files a significant amount of evidence which is not relevant, or which is inadmissible for other reasons, parties are likely to incur costs as follows:

- the party responding to the evidence will incur costs in reviewing and analysing the evidence which it would not otherwise have incurred;
- there is likely to be an extended (and, thus, costly) argument about admissibility, which would not otherwise have been necessary, and if the inadmissible evidence is integrated with admissible evidence, this will not be a straightforward task; and
- if submissions on admissibility will not be heard until after any evidence in response or reply must be filed, the responding party might need to expend costs in collecting evidence to respond to the inadmissible evidence (in case it is not found to be inadmissible).

As it is not reasonable that parties ought to be required to respond to a significant amount of irrelevant or otherwise inadmissible evidence, such costs would be beyond what might be regarded as reasonable.

In *Thomas v SMP (International) Pty Ltd* [2010] NSWSC 822, Pembroke J described an affidavit filed by one of the parties as "inappropriate, confusing and unhelpful" and "a gallimaufry" which was "oppressive" due to its length alone: "6,657 paragraphs spread over nearly 500 pages".[25] He observed[26]:

> It is common for some litigants to want to use their evidence as an opportunity to unburden themselves in unmanageable detail of the many facts which have preoccupied them in the years preceding the hearing of their case. But a fair hearing of their case can be seriously hindered by such unfiltered outpourings. That is why, among other things, counsel have a duty to the court which is additional to their duty to the party whom they represent. This duty is a legal duty, not merely a rule of practice or etiquette.
>
> The efficient hearing of a large or complex case requires recognition of that duty and sensible co-operation and sound judgment on the part of the Bar. …

---

[24] For a discussion of the philosophy underlying the amendments, see Lord Dyson MR. 2014. The application of the amendments to the Civil Procedure Rules. *Civil Justice Quarterly* 33: 124–132.

[25] *Thomas* at [9]–[10].

[26] *Thomas* at [19]-[20] (references omitted).

The concept of the overriding purpose plainly underlies this discussion, with the "fairness" of a hearing being about more than a party simply having the opportunity to tell their story is part of this, as is the duty of lawyers to ensure the focus of evidence and to co-operate with one another. These observations that the "co-operation and collaboration" inherent in a "tempered" adversarial approach is more "efficient", and "is more likely to ensure that a just result is reached – sooner and with less expense"[27] is essentially a definition of proportionality.

In that case, Pembroke J dealt with the problematic affidavit by rejecting it as evidence and permitting evidence in chief to be given orally.

In the same matter, oral evidence led to further problems. It appears that all defendants sought an opportunity to cross-examine one of the plaintiffs. He was unwell. Justice Pembroke limited cross-examination of the witness by counsel for one defendant. In doing so, he observed: "[u]nduly lengthy, ineffective or unnecessary cross-examination can be a significant factor contributing to delay and unwarranted cost".[28]

In considering the appropriate exercise of the discretion to limit cross-examination, Pembroke J also took the following factors into account[29]:

> ... This case was listed for a six week hearing. The parties assured me that the estimate was generous. On that basis they requested an adjournment for one week, which I granted. At the time of my decision to limit further cross-examination, there were less than four weeks remaining and I was still hearing the evidence of the first witness. There were at least 20 further witnesses. I was concerned that if this case did not conclude in the time allotted, it may have deprived other litigants, with hearings pending, of the opportunity to have their claims determined on the dates allocated by the court.

Once again, the concept behind the overriding purpose appeared to inform the reasoning.

Justice Pembroke is not the only judge to have engaged in such criticism of parties' forensic decisions, and the Supreme Court of NSW is not the only court in which such criticism has been made. In *Superior IP International Pty Ltd v Ahearn Fox Patent and Trade Mark Attorneys* [2012] FCA 28, Reeves J was scathing of the parties' conduct of the case before him, describing the hearing as "the absolute antithesis of the overarching purpose".[30] The dispute involved a statutory demand which had been issued for a "relatively small amount". The judge "attempted to introduce some proportionality into the matter by directing the two lawyers ... to notify his respective client how much he intended to charge it in legal fees." He observed: "The fact that the total legal and filing fees involved approached twice the amount of the statutory demand still did not deter the clients from their headlong pursuit of this dispute."[31]

---

[27] *Thomas* at [22].

[28] *Thomas* at [13] (reference omitted).

[29] *Thomas* at [22].

[30] *Superior IP International* at [9].

[31] *Superior IP International* at [5].

Other circumstances attracted further criticism by Reeves J. There were "more than 400 pages of affidavit material", which he described as "voluminous" and "replete with allegations of falsity and untruthfulness", all of which was irrelevant. He considered the focus (or lack thereof) of the evidence "reflected a complete lack of appreciation by the two lawyers concerned as to what it was they had to direct their minds to at the hearing of this application."[32] Objections to evidence took up "a large part" of the full day hearing and what the judge described as "[t]he final travesty" was the attempt by the lawyer for one party "to rely upon a large amount of additional material that he had not put forward earlier" – at the end of the hearing.[33]

Justice Reeves was explicit in the importance he ascribed to the overarching purpose, and his criticism of the parties for what he appeared to consider an absolute disregard for that purpose.

The Victorian Court of Appeal has also confirmed the importance of the overarching purpose in interpreting obligations pursuant to the *Civil Procedure Act 2010* (Vic). The issue before the Court of Appeal in *Yara Australia Pty Ltd v Oswal* [2012] VSCA 337 concerned an application for leave to appeal from a decision in respect of security for costs. A number of parties were involved in the matter. The court observed that, at the one day hearing, there were "five senior counsel, six junior counsel and five firms of solicitors representing the parties" and the application books consisted of "six lever arch folders of material".[34] The amount sought by way of security for costs was less than $150,000 in total.

The court, in a unanimous judgment, engaged in a detailed discussion of the importance of proportionality and the overarching purpose. The particular aspects of proportionality the court considered relevant to the matter at hand were unnecessary representation and the volume of material filed. Submissions were made concerning the relevance of the context of the broader proceedings to the particular application for security for costs and associated application for leave to appeal.

Ultimately, the court considered the level of representation at the hearing had been sufficiently explained and did not constitute a breach of the overarching purpose.[35] However, the context of the broader litigation was less persuasive in relation to the volume of material filed. In this respect, the court held expenditure incurred on an interlocutory application must be proportionate to interlocutory application itself, and that there had been a breach of the overarching obligation in relation to the volume of material,[36] although this did not support an order for indemnity costs (rather than costs on the ordinary basis).[37]

[32] *Superior IP International* at [2]–[3].

[33] *Superior IP International* at [7]–[8].

[34] *Yara Australia v Oswal* at [2].

[35] *Yara Australia v Oswal* at [39].

[36] *Yara Australia v Oswal* at [51]–[52].

[37] *Yara Australia v Oswal* at [57].

Proportionality has also recently been taken into account as follows:

- in considering an application for a further adjournment of proceedings[38] – the application was unsuccessful as it would have been disproportionate to allow such further adjournment;
- in relation to an application to discharge a jury – Warren CJ would have dismissed an appeal on the grounds that the primary judge ought to have discharged the jury, in part due to the application of the overarching purpose in the *Civil Procedure Act 2010* (Vic)[39];
- an application to dismiss proceedings based on a plaintiff's "failure to comply with the court's directions and for want of due prosecution" – the application was successful, and it was relevant that "there [was] a substantial risk that, even assuming the plaintiff [was] successful, the costs of the action [had] already become disproportionate to any award of damages"[40]; and
- in relation to an application for costs by the respondent to NSW Civil and Administrative Tribunal proceedings which had been withdrawn at an early stage, the respondent's conduct in making the application (which was unsuccessful) and the manner in which it was run led to a finding that it had acted disproportionately – for that reason, among others, the applicant was granted her costs of the respondent's costs application.[41] This is particularly noteworthy as the Tribunal is a jurisdiction in which the general rule is not to make costs orders between parties.

It can also be seen as a motivating factor behind changing judicial attitudes towards discovery.[42]

[38] *Karam v Clark Toop and Taylor* [2014] VSC 104 [26].

[39] *Hudspeth v Scholastic Cleaning & Consultancy Services Pty Ltd* [2014] VSCA 3 [35]–[36], noting that Warren CJ was in dissent in relation to the appeal.

[40] *Al-Shennag v Woodcock* [2013] NSWSC 696 [6], [111].

[41] *Boscolo v Axciom Australia Pty Ltd* [2015] NSWCATAD 28.

[42] See, for example, the NSW Supreme Court Practice Note SC Eq 11 "Disclosure in the Equity Division", which continued a general limitation on discovery "unless it is necessary for the resolution of the real issues in dispute" (at [5]) and imposed a strict bar on discovery before service of evidence (at [4]). There has been a significant amount written on discovery, cost and proportionality: see, for example, Black AC, Hon Michael. 2009. The role of the judge in attacking endemic delays: Some lessons from Fast Track. *Journal of Judicial Administration* 19: 88–99; Davies, Geoffrey. 2006. Civil justice reform: Some common problems, some possible solutions. *Journal of Judicial Administration* 16: 5–17; Legg, Michael and Turner, Nicholas. 2011. When discovery and technology meet: The pre-discovery conference. *Journal of Judicial Administration* 21: 54–70; Ryan, Adrian. 2008. Discovery: The law's need to adapt to changing times. *Journal of Judicial Administration* 18: 116–135; Vickery, Hon Justice Peter. 2012. Managing the paper: Taming the Leviathan. *Journal of Judicial Administration* 22: 51–75. Given the existing literature, this chapter does not deal with discovery and its implications.

9.5 Current Australian Approach

Clear and detailed statements, such as the examples above, about the proportionality or otherwise of proceedings, particularly with reference to parties' forensic decisions, are not particularly common in published judgments. Where they are made, they are generally motivated by what a court considers an extreme example or egregious breach of the parties' or lawyers' obligations to the court, as seen in the cases outlined above.

It is the author's experience that judges and registrars frequently comment on proportionality, the overriding purpose and parties' obligations during the course of hearings, including directions hearings, and that such concerns often motivate orders made in the course of case management. Courts' concerns are often related to factors of costs, delay and impact on third parties, which were material to the reasons in *Aon v ANU*.

Of particular interest is the growing acceptance that justice and fairness, taken in their totality, affects the right of a party to their "day in court". Traditionally, that concept included a significant tolerance for the manner in which a party chose to present their case. Now, as the High Court has observed, there is an assumption that the overriding purpose in case management legislation "will coincide with the dictates of justice."[43] In other words, justice and fairness no longer necessarily mean providing a party with every opportunity to present their case, but now require a court to take into account the impacts of litigation (including costs and delays) on the parties, on third parties and on the administration of justice in general.

In Australia, these developments have occurred organically, on the basis of legislative reform taking place over a lengthy period of time combined with changes in judicial attitudes, sometimes represented by strong statements in published reasons for decision or extra-judicial comments.

The approach across a range of Australian jurisdictions and courts is consistent, with *Aon v ANU* representing agreement by the High Court with the developments that had been taking place since *Queensland v JL Holdings* as opposed to an indication that lower courts had been travelling in the wrong direction.

9.6 Current UK Approach

An important part of the recent reforms in the United Kingdom included the amendments to r 3.9 of the *Civil Procedure Rules 1998* (UK). Prior to 1 April 2013, that rule took the form of a checklist of factors to be taken into account in relation to an application for relief from sanctions. It now provides:

---

[43] *Expense Reduction Analysts Group Pty Ltd v Armstrong Strategic Management and Marketing Pty Limited* [2013] HCA 46; (2013) 303 ALR 199, 212 [57].

1. On an application for relief from any sanction imposed for a failure to comply with any rule, practice direction or court order, the court will consider all the circumstances of the case, so as to enable it to deal justly with the application, including the need –
   (a) for litigation to be conducted efficiently and at proportionate cost; and
   (b) to enforce compliance with rules, practice directions and orders.
2. An application for relief must be supported by evidence.

The rule now "explicitly refers back to the overriding objective, stressing the need in dealing with a case justly to take account of proportionate cost and the need to enforce rule compliance."[44]

In *Mitchell v News Group Newspapers Ltd* [2013] EWCA Civ 1537; [2014] 2 All ER 430, the Court of Appeal of England and Wales has delivered a judgment "intended to send out a clear message that the civil justice reforms have brought in a new robust approach to rule compliance."[45] The matter was a high-profile defamation case. The relevant practice direction required exchange and lodgment of costs budgets within a certain period. The claimant failed to file his costs budget until the day before the relevant hearing, and it was necessary to vacate that date. The reason given was the pressure of other litigation within the firm. A mandatory sanction applied, which deemed the claimant to have filed a costs budget limited to court fees. The claimant applied for relief from the sanction. Relief was refused. The claimant appealed to the Court of Appeal. The appeal was dismissed.

Lord Dyson MR held in the course of delivering the judgment of the Court that considerations of efficiency, proportionality of costs and compliance with rules "should now be regarded as of paramount importance and be given great weight." While it is still necessary to have regard to "all the circumstances of the case", since this is expressly required by r 3.9, circumstances other than those enumerated are less important.[46]

Lord Dyson MR went on to note "[t]he importance of the court having regard to the needs and interests of *all* court users", commenting on the fact that the adjourned hearing had been relisted by vacation of a time "which had been allocated to deal with claims by persons who had been affected by asbestos-related diseases."[47] In making this reference, giving specificity and life to the normally generalised statement that excess use of court time by one matter could have been applied to the resolution of other disputes, he further emphasised the importance of the proportionality factors which are now the only enumerated factors in r 3.9.

While it is likely the courts will still grant relief where there are "circumstances outside the control of the party in default",[48] the Court of Appeal has nevertheless confirmed that strict application of r 3.9 is appropriate.

[44] For a discussion of the philosophy underlying the amendments, see Lord Dyson MR. 2014. The application of the amendments to the Civil Procedure Rules. *Civil Justice Quarterly* 33: 124–132, 129.

[45] Sime, Stuart. 2014. Sanctions after Mitchell. *Civil Justice Quarterly* 33: 133–156, 142.

[46] *Mitchell* at 441 [36]–[37].

[47] *Mitchell* at 442 [39] (emphasis added).

[48] *Mitchell* at 443 [43].

More recently, the Court of Appeal has given further explanation of the correct interpretation of r 3.9. In *Denton v TH White Limited* [2014] EWCA Civ 906, Lord Dyson MR and Vos LJ observed there had been some "criticism" of *Mitchell*, but ultimately considered this was because "the judgment in *Mitchell* [had] been misunderstood and [was] being misapplied by some courts." Accordingly, it required certain clarification and amplification.[49]

Lord Dyson MR and Vos LJ went on to give specific guidance on the application of r 3.9, holding that an application for relief from sanctions should be addressed in three stages, with consideration of proportionality takes place at the third stage. They confirmed that factors other than the enumerated factors are not of "little weight", simply of "less weight". The use of the words "paramount importance" "may have given rise to some confusion", and "particular weight" might be more appropriate wording.[50]

Their Lordships also criticised the "opportunism" they considered to have been displayed by some parties in terms of attempts "to take advantage of [] minor inadvertent error[s]",[51] which in their view had given rise to satellite litigation.

However, Jackson LJ held that the enumeration of the two specific factors "does not require that [those factors] be given greater weight than other considerations", simply that "the two factors be specifically considered in every case."[52] This does suggest some difference of emphasis within the Court of Appeal, even where the same result is reached (as was the case in *Denton*). There may still be room for confusion in the application of r 3.9.

Accordingly, while the language used by the Court of Appeal of England and Wales and in the amended *Civil Procedure Rules 1998* (UK) reflects the approach that can be seen in practice in Australia, there remains confusion as to the application of the rules in the United Kingdom which has resulted, and which may continue to result, in satellite litigation. This is somewhat ironic in the context of the overriding objective.

9.7 The Problem of Satellite Litigation

In the *Preliminary Jackson Report*, it was observed[53]:

> There is no doubt that litigation over costs has increased dramatically in recent years, and that this growth is one of the driving factors behind the present review. Whilst many such disputes concerned issues which would need to be resolved under any system which involves costs-shifting, the disputes over the enforceability of conditional fee agreements ('CFAs') have generated more litigation, arguably to less useful purpose, than any other.

---

[49] *Denton* at [3].

[50] *Denton* at [31]–[32].

[51] *Denton* at [43].

[52] *Denton* at [85].

[53] Sir Rupert Jackson. 2009. *Review of Civil Litigation Costs: Preliminary Report*, 27.

Secondary litigation generated in this way – that is, litigation about costs and other issues not directly related to the substance or merits of the case – is referred to as satellite litigation.

As noted above, satellite litigation in the United Kingdom has been generated not only by costs arguments but also by arguments about relief against sanctions.

Zuckerman has observed that it is likely satellite litigation has been rife in the United Kingdom because "the [Court of Appeal] did not develop a coherent approach to late performance, [so] the outcome of applications was uncertain". Further, Zuckerman considers the "self-imposed constraint on appellate interference with case management decisions" exercised by the Court of Appeal is to some extent contributory to the uncertainty (and so to satellite litigation).[54] This makes intuitive sense. However, Australian appellate courts are also very hesitant to interfere with case management decisions, so it seems unlikely this provides the whole of the answer.

Satellite litigation does not appear to be as widespread a problem in Australia. It is difficult to be certain of the reasons for this, although some potential factors can be identified.

First, it is important to note there can also be uncertainty in the Australian approach. Looking at the legislation and rules alone, it might almost be expected that there would be more uncertainty, as rules of court in Australian jurisdictions tend to be less prescriptive than the *Civil Procedure Rules 1998* (UK) in relation to the considerations that must be taken into account by a judge or other judicial decision-maker in relation to costs, sanctions and so on. In that way, there is more apparent latitude.

In fact, that lack of prescription often results in the judge or registrar focusing on one or two considerations which have particular importance to the specific case. From a practitioner's point of view, it is usually possible to predict those limited factors and so to predict the outcome. This is consistent with Zuckerman's own earlier observation that a larger number of factors which were mandatory considerations made it difficult to predict the weight each would be accorded by a court.[55]

On the other hand, in relation to costs, in Australia, the courts are reluctant to depart from the general rule that costs follow the event (or to award costs on an indemnity basis rather than the ordinary basis – the considerations tend to be similar) unless there has been a very severe departure by the successful party from the standards expected. Thus, as outlined above, even where the Victorian Court of Appeal held there had been a lack of proportionality in the approach the parties took to the relevant application, the usual order was made and on an ordinary basis.[56]

Again, this contributes to a high degree of predictability, and so there is less reason for satellite litigation.

---

[54] Zuckerman, Adrian. 2014. Implementation of mark II overriding objective and CPR 3.9. *Civil Justice Quarterly* 33: 1–12, 9–10.

[55] Zuckerman, Adrian. 2013. The revised CPR 3.9: a coded message demanding articulation. *Civil Justice Quarterly* 32: 123–138, 132.

[56] *Yara Australia v Oswal* at [57].

There are several additional factors which may contribute to the lower level of satellite litigation in this area in Australia. It is the author's understanding that Australian litigation is conducted in a less formalised manner than litigation in the United Kingdom. While courts in Australia have practice notes or practice directions, and compliance with these is *prima facie* expected, they are often intended to provide guidance rather than as strict protocol with which parties *must* comply. It is not uncommon for a judge or registrar to direct parties to take a course of action which differs from a practice note if it is appropriate to do so in the case at hand. This is often directed at ensuring the relevant directions and timetable are "realistic and achievable" and not "unattainable". This exercise tends to take place on a case-by-case basis rather than in accordance with guidance from intermediate courts of appeal.

On the basis of this understanding, the fact that directions and timetables are more likely to be tailored in Australian litigation may be a significant contributing factor to the lower level of satellite litigation for the simple reason parties are less likely to be unhappy with case management orders.

Whether the apparently less formalised approach to litigation is a matter of legal culture or due to external factors is a matter for debate. For that matter, a longstanding culture of satellite litigation in the United Kingdom may be a significant part of the problem.[57]

Further, and perhaps for related reasons, there are far fewer appeals of case management decisions in Australia than there appear to be in the United Kingdom. This is to be expected in a smaller jurisdiction, but the *rate* of appeals also seems to be lower. That appellate courts are reluctant to interfere with case management decisions is also likely to contribute to a lower appeal rate.

In addition, the size of the courts in Australia may have an impact. Each Australian jurisdiction is significantly smaller than the jurisdiction of England and Wales. The judicial body for each jurisdiction is also significantly smaller than the judicial body for England and Wales. It is, perhaps, easier for each court in Australia to develop and maintain a more uniform approach within that court. Where appropriate, the courts also draw from each other so that the approach between jurisdictions is also fairly uniform. Where it is not uniform, it is likely the issue will come before the High Court of Australia in due course.

Finally, as a practical matter, costs of litigation tend to remain lower in Australia than in the United Kingdom. Where there is less at stake, it is unsurprising that parties are less inclined to engage in the additional expense of satellite litigation.

9.8 Proportionality as a Tool or Aim?

Proportionality as a concept is often used as a touchstone. This can be seen in the *Jackson Report* in the United Kingdom, in the relevant legislative provisions and in comments made by courts, both in published reasons for decision and during hearings and directions hearings.

[57] Zuckerman, Adrian. 2013. The revised CPR 3.9: a coded message demanding articulation. *Civil Justice Quarterly* 32: 123–138, 125.

However, there is real difficulty in giving concrete definition to the concept, and it may be better comprehended as an aim rather than as a tool in itself.

As illustrated by the foregoing, as a general rule, there has been real success in Australia in relation to the achievement of the overriding purpose and proportionality. Although there remain cases in which significant departures occur, the author's experience is that parties and their legal representatives take a pragmatic approach in most cases, often with significant encouragement from the courts (including the greater general predictability in relation to procedural matters), which results in less dispute about side matters which have little or no bearing on the merits of the case. The significantly lower rate of satellite litigation would appear to be a symptom of this. The fact that the costs of litigation are not as extreme in Australia as they are in the United Kingdom is no doubt in large part due to this.

Costs and proportionality do remain live issues in Australia, particularly in low value claims.[58] There is no easy answer.

Similarly, the apparent increase in cultural tolerance for an emphasis on proportionality does not mean every individual agrees, or will act accordingly. It is always likely to be difficult to convince an individual who considers some injustice has been done that they should not take avenues open to them to seek redress and, as noted above, proportionality alone does not address the problem of a litigant with deep pockets, or a litigant who has nothing to lose.

While it is possible to say that the general movement in Australia is towards a system in which litigation is more likely to be conducted proportionately, it is not possible to say that this has been done by application of the principle of proportionality. Rather, proportionality has been aspirational, and some cultural change has occurred that results in a better achievement of that aim.

The differences between Australia and the United Kingdom appear to result from a combination of legal culture and fortuitous legislative choices over time. This means the Australian experience may be difficult to replicate, particularly in the circumstances presently seen in the United Kingdom.

In the United Kingdom, the Court of Appeal itself, in *Denton*, noted that proportionality is more likely to be achieved when there is a culture of both compliance and co-operation between parties.[59] However, it remains to be seen whether the Court of Appeal's clarification in that case in relation to relief against sanctions will have the desired effect. Zuckerman appears to consider this unlikely, and has called for a broader system of accountability.[60]

---

[58] See, for example, *Condensing Vaporisers Aust Pty Ltd v FDC Construction & Fitout Pty Ltd (No 2)* [2014] NSWCA 89; (2014) 307 ALR 370, 375 [24]-[26], where the NSW Court of Appeal confirmed that the interpretation of s 101(2)(r)(i) of the *Supreme Court Act 1970* (NSW), which provides that leave to appeal is required in respect of matters where less than $100,000 is in dispute, is informed by questions of proportionality.

[59] *Denton* at [40].

[60] Zuckerman, Adrian. 2015. The continuing management deficit in the administration of civil justice. *Civil Justice Quarterly* 34: 1–10, 10.

In any event, there does not seem to be any clear path to either cultural change or a broader system of accountability, and with them, the broader goal that litigation generally be conducted in a proportionate manner. Indeed, a recent illustration of the difficulties faced can be found in *Summit Navigation Ltd v Generali Romania Asigurare Reasigurare SA* [2014] EWHC 398 (Comm); [2014] 1 WLR 3472. The claimants had been ordered to give security for costs. They were one day late in doing so, resulting in an automatic stay being imposed. The defendants sought a permanent stay due to that default. The hearing of that application resulted in general default from the timetable which had been imposed by the Court in the substantive matter. Justice Leggatt held it was the defendants' response to the claimants' default, not the default itself, which was unreasonable and which resulted in the derailment.[61] He refused the stay and ordered that the defendants pay the claimants' costs of the application, as well as the claimants' costs of their own application to lift the automatic stay.

The overall result in *Summit Navigation* is precisely what might be thought necessary to contribute to control of costs at an earlier stage: first, the imposition of security for costs, to provide some protection for the defendants against being required incurring unreasonable or disproportionate costs by reason of the conduct of the claimants; secondly, an interim costs order in response to unreasonable conduct by the defendants, to motivate them not to engage in similar conduct in the future.

But the facts of *Summit Navigation* reveal a continuing cultural approach to litigation which results in disproportionate expenditure – precisely what the Court of Appeal observed needed to change. Indeed, the requirement for a new timetable and the time taken up by the hearing meant there was also disproportionate use of public resources.

In other words, the attempts to give the concept of proportionality content as a tool to provide guidance do not appear to be meeting with success. As such, while proportionality remains an aspiration in the United Kingdom, it does not appear to be a concept which can be employed, in itself, to achieve the necessary cultural change.

Even the broad accountability called for by Zuckerman is likely to result in similar problems, in the sense that accountability is another high level concept.

It may be necessary to identify concrete steps which may be taken. As with the general reference to the concept of proportionality, this is also something which is easier said than done, and many obvious suggestions have already been attempted at earlier times. However, one lesson that can be learnt from the Australian experience is that the achievement of overall proportionality is highly unlikely to occur in one leap. Perhaps the identification of individual steps, rather than an overall reform program, might assist in a gradual movement in the right direction in the United Kingdom as well.

[61] *Summit Navigation* at [53]–[54].

Chapter 10
Group Actions À *La Mode Européenne*: A Kinder, Gentler Class Action for Europe?

Elisabetta Silvestri

In June 2013, the European Commission issued several important documents concerning group actions. These documents are conceived as a package of measures including a Communication (hereinafter, the Communication)[1] that expands on the European debate revolving around the topic of mass claims and elucidates the policy underlying a new Recommendation (hereinafter, the Recommendation)[2] on the common principles that should guide Member States in regulating collective redress. Along with the Communication and the Recommendation, the Commission adopted a proposal for a Directive on actions for damages arising out of the infringement of antitrust law, both European and domestic.[3] As explained later below, the documents

[1] Communication from the Commission to the European Parliament, the Council, the European Economic and Social Committee and the Committee of the Regions, 'Towards a European Horizontal Framework for Collective Redress', COM(2013) 401/2. http://ec.europa.eu/justice/civil/files/com_2013_401_en.pdf. Accessed 11 January 2015.

[2] Commission Recommendation on common principles for injunctive and compensatory collective redress mechanisms in the Member States concerning violations of rights granted under Union Law, C(2013) 3539/3. http://ec.europa.eu/justice/civil/files/c_2013_3539_en.pdf. Accessed 11 January 2015. For some general comments on the Commission's Communication and Recommendation, see Voet, Stefaan. 2014. European Collective Redress: A *Status Quaestionis*, *International Journal of Procedural Law* 4: 97–128; Jones, Graham. 2014. Collective Redress in the European Union: Reflections from a National Judge, *Legal Issues of Economic Integration* 41: 289–304.

[3] Proposal for a Directive of the European Parliament and of the Council on certain rules governing actions for damages under national law for infringements of the competition law provisions of the Member States and of the European Union, COM(2013) 404 final, 2013/0185 (COD). http://eur-lex.europa.eu/LexUriServ/LexUriServ.do? uri = COM:2013:0404:FIN:EN:PDF. On 26 November 2014 a Directive of the European Parliament and of the Council on certain rules governing actions for damages under national law for infringements of the competition law provisions of the Member

E. Silvestri (✉)
Dipartimento di Giurisprudenza, University of Pavia, Strada Nuova 65, Pavia 27100, Italy
e-mail: elisabetta.silvestri@unipv.it

C.B. Picker, G.I. Seidman (eds.), *The Dynamism of Civil Procedure - Global Trends and Developments*, Ius Gentium: Comparative Perspectives on Law and Justice 48, DOI 10.1007/978-3-319-21981-3_10

issued by the Commission discuss 'collective redress'. This author has decided to alternate the use of the expression 'collective redress' and another one, namely, 'group actions', which seems functionally equivalent to the former: both portray (at least in a no-frills way) 'a procedural mechanism that allows, for reasons of procedural economy and/or efficiency of enforcement, many similar legal claims to be bundled into a single court action'.[4]

The landscape of group actions in the Member States of the European Union is a kaleidoscope of different procedures, each one having its own distinctive features. To analyze them all is beyond the scope of this chapter, and it is an endeavor requiring much more than the many pages that would be necessary just to provide the reader with a perfunctory description of every single national procedure, taking into account also the fact that things are changing at a fast pace. As an example, in March 2014 France adopted a brand-new form of group action for damages in the field of consumer protection and competition law.[5] In France, as in the majority of Member States in which statutes providing for collective redress have been passed, an 'opt-in' system is the rule[6]; at the same time, one could not venture safely to say

States and of the European Union was signed into law: the text is available at http://ec.europa.eu/competition/antitrust/actionsdamages/damages_directive_final_en.pdf. Accessed 11 January 2015.

For clarity's sake, it is worth mentioning that directives are one type of 'legal acts' that European Union institutions can adopt. According to Article 288 of the Treaty on the Functioning of the European Union: 'A directive shall be binding, as to the result to be achieved, upon each Member State to which it is addressed, but shall leave to the national authorities the choice of form and methods.' Put simply, directives must be implemented by national legislators. The implementation of directives, that is, their 'transposition' into the laws of Member States, must take place within a deadline. In case of untimely or defective transposition, the European Commission can initiate an infringement procedure against the defaulting Member State in the European Court of Justice: see Sprungk, Carina. 2013. Legislative Transposition of Directives: Exploring the Other Role of National Parliaments in the European Union, *JCMS: Journal of Common Market Studies* 51: 298–315. Craig, Paul- de Búrca, Gráinne. 2011. *EU Law: Text, Cases and Materials* (5th edn.). Oxford: Oxford University Press, 191–216.

[4] See Section 1.2. of the Communication, at p. 4.

[5] Reference is made to the so-called 'Loi Hamon' (Statute no. 2014–344) concerning consumer law and adopted in March 2014. See Amrani-Mekki, Soraya. 2014. Décret sur l'action de groupe. La procedure… enfin!, *La Semaine Juridique*, no. 42: 1822–25; Haeri, Kami-Javaux, Benoît. 2014. L'action de groupe à la française, une curiosité, *La Semaine Juridique*, no. 13: 586–89; Rebeyrol, Vincent. 2014. La nouvelle action de groupe. *Recueil Dalloz*, no. 16: 940–46; Piedelièvre, Stéphane. 2014. La loi du 17 mars 2014 et l'action de groupe, *La Gazette du Palais*, no. 2: 829–31.

[6] It seems appropriate to emphasize that the 'opt-in' system adopted by the French legislators is quite peculiar, since class members must join the action (meaning, they must opt-in) at a late stage of the judicial proceeding, that is, after the judgment finding against the defendant has been issued: group members who choose to 'accept' the judgment by a formal act by which they express their will to join the *action de group* shall receive compensation for the loss suffered, and shall be bound by the *res judicata* effect of the judgment. It has been argued that the French model of group action is 'a *de facto* opt-out system', since class members are not required to do anything during the development of the proceeding, and are expected to 'show up' (so to say) only if they are inclined to accept the judgment and receive their share of damages: for this interesting thesis, see Nagy,

that 'opt-in' is a common trait of aggregate litigation within the European Union, since procedures based on an 'opt-out' mechanism do exist in a few Member States.[7]

Reading the Communication and the Recommendation (which are the sole object of this chapter), one is inclined to think that the Commission has resolved to address the issue of devising a pan-European model of group actions that would supersede the multitude of different class procedures existing in Member States and advance the cause of cross-border mass claims. On the contrary, a closer analysis of the measures suggested shows that the approach taken by the Commission is still tentative, and that the prospect of a coherent European approach to collective redress, envisioned by the European Parliament,[8] is not likely to bring about a harmonized and uniform model of European group actions any time soon.

A recount of the most significant steps taken by the Commission in the field of group litigation is in order. From the very beginning the Commission has identified two main areas of interest, namely, competition law and consumer protection, insomuch as both the so-called private enforcement of competition law and an effective redress of consumer claims are deemed to be of paramount importance with the view to allowing the European Union 'to remain competitive at the global level and to have an open and functioning single market'.[9]

As far as competition law is concerned, in 2005 and 2008 the Commission issued two important documents[10] in which the problems touching upon the so-called private enforcement of European antitrust regulations were analyzed with the view to establishing collective actions for damages, since 'there is a clear need for mechanisms allowing aggregation of the individual claims of victims of antitrust infringements',[11] most of all when those who have been harmed are not encouraged to embark on judicial proceedings due to the costs, the delays, and the uncertainties of adjudication.

With reference to consumer protection, the European initiatives aimed at providing for collective actions date back in time and find their source in several Directives, among which of paramount importance is Directive 98/27/CE on injunctions for the

---

Csongor István. 2014. The European Collective Redress Debate after the European Commission's Recommendation: One Step Forward, Two Steps Back? (unpublished manuscript on file with the author), at 8.

[7] See n. 37 below.

[8] See European Parliament resolution of 2 February 2012 on 'Towards a Coherent European Approach to Collective Redress' (2011/2089(INI)). http://www.europarl.europa.eu/sides/getDoc.do?pubRef=-//EP//NONSGML+TA+P7-TA-2012-0021+0+DOC+PDF+V0//EN. Accessed 11 January 2015.

[9] See Section 1.1. of the Communication, at p. 2.

[10] Reference in the text is made to the Green Paper – Damages actions for breach of the EC antitrust rules, Brussels, 19.12.2005, COM(2005) 672 final (http://eur-lex.europa.eu/LexUriServ/site/en/com/2005/com2005_0672en01.pdf. Accessed 11 January 2015), and to the White Paper on Damages actions for breach of the EC antitrust rules, Brussels, 2.4.2008, COM(2008) 165 final. http://eur-lex.europa.eu/LexUriServ/LexUriServ.do?uri = COM:2008:0165:FIN:EN :PDF. Accessed 11 January 2015.

[11] See White Paper on Damages actions for breach of the EC antitrust rules, n. 5 above, at 2.1., p. 4.

protection of consumers' interests.[12] According to the Directive, certain 'qualified entities' identified by Member States as the official representative of the collective interests of consumers can petition a court (or an administrative authority) and seek injunctive relief, that is, 'an order with all due expediency, where appropriate by way of summary procedure, requiring the cessation or prohibition of any infringement'.[13] In principle, the importance of injunctive relief for the enforcement of the collective rights of consumers cannot be underestimated: the implementation of the Directive, though, has not been uniform throughout Member States, and has produced successful outcomes only in a few Member States. In a report on the implementation of the Directive, the Commission, while acknowledging the importance of injunctive actions for the protection of consumers' collective interests, emphasized the following:

> However, important disparities exist among Member States in its level of use and effectiveness. In any event, even in those Member States where injunctions are considered quite effective and are widely used, their potential is not fully exploited due to a number of shortcomings identified in this report. The most important are: the **high costs** linked to the proceedings, the **length** of the proceedings, the **complexity** of the procedures, the relatively **limited effects** of the rulings on injunctions and the difficulty of enforcing them. These difficulties are even more present in injunctions with a cross-border dimension.[14] (Bold text in original.)

Furthermore, injunctive procedures did not address another problem, namely, the problem of the damages suffered by consumers, as underlined by the Commission:

> In most Member States, there is no link between an injunctive action and the granting of compensation to consumers for the harm suffered due to an illegal practice. Thus, consumers whose rights have been infringed have to enforce their rights by bringing an action before an ordinary Court, either individually or collectively, in those Member States where collective redress mechanisms exist. Moreover, in many Member States, Courts dealing with such proceedings initiated by consumers to obtain compensation are not bound by the earlier ruling on the injunctive action. Consumers seeking damages will have to prove the infringement, the damage and the causal link between the two.[15]

---

[12] Directive 98/27/CE has been repealed and replaced by Directive 2009/22/EC of the European Parliament and of the Council of 23 April 2009 on injunctions for the protection of consumers' interests (Codified version). http://eur-lex.europa.eu/LexUriServ/LexUriServ.do?uri = OJ:L:2009:110:0030:0036:EN:PDF. Accessed 11 January 2015. The literature on the so-called Injunction Directive is extensive: see, among others, Hodges, Christopher. 2008. *The Reform of Class and Representative Actions in European Legal Systems. A New Framework for Collective Redress in Europe*. Oxford: Hart Publishing. 93–115; Cafaggi, Fabrizio and Micklitz, Hans-Wolfang (eds.). 2009. *New Frontiers of Consumer Protection – The Interplay between Private and Public Enforcement*. Cambridge-Antwerp-Portland: Intersentia; Cafaggi, Fabrizio, Micklitz, Hans-Wolfang. 2008. Collective Enforcement of Consumer Law: A Framework for a Comparative Assessment, *European Review of Private Law* 16: 391–425.

[13] See Arts. 2–3 of Directive 2009/22/EC, n. 12 above.

[14] See Report from the Commission to the European Parliament and the Council concerning the application of Directive 2009/22/EC of the European Parliament and of the Council on injunctions for the protection of consumers' interest, Brussels, 6.11.2012, COM(2012) 635 final. http://ec.europa.eu/consumers/enforcement/docs/report_inj_2012_en.pdf, at para. 6, p. 16. Accessed 11 January 2015.

[15] See ibid., at para. 3.3.a), p. 9.

The problem of how to provide effective procedural instruments suitable to make it easier for consumers (both as a class and as individuals grouped under the label 'consumers') to claim compensation for the harm suffered is certainly a problem having a bearing on any policies aimed at advancing the cause of consumer protection. On this matter, in 2008 the Commission remarked:

> As a consequence of the weaknesses of the current redress and enforcement framework in the EU, a significant proportion of consumers who have suffered damage do not obtain redress. In mass claim cases that affect a very large number of consumers, although sometimes the harm may be low for the individual consumer, it can be high for the size of the market. As these markets become more cross-border in nature, effective cross-border access to the mechanisms of redress become necessary.[16]

In short, having found that, 'The overall performance of the existing consumer redress and enforcement tools designed at [the] EU level is not satisfactory',[17] the Commission appeared determined to get involved in the difficult task of devising for the entire European Union a harmonized pattern for group actions, flexible enough to suit the judicial enforcement of the collective rights arising out of areas of substantive law other than consumer protection and antitrust law. Less clear were the Commission's ideas on the features that such a harmonized pattern was supposed to have: in this regard, the only certainty was the intent to look for an alternative to the American-style class actions, which in the eyes of the Commission were not only at odds with European legal traditions, but also a 'toxic cocktail'[18] that could open the door to abusive litigation, replicating the problems that have given a bad name to class actions even in their native country.[19]

Against this background, the Communication and the Recommendation sketch (or better yet, attempt to sketch) some basic features of a prospective European model of group actions that – at least in the Commission's expectations – would improve access to justice for the victims of infringements of rights granted by Union law and, at the same time, provide for adequate procedural safeguards against the risk of abusive litigation.

Both the Communication and the Recommendation make reference to 'collective redress'. Such an expression, already recurring in previous documents issued

---

[16] See Green Paper on Consumer Collective Redress, Brussels, 27.11.2008, COM(2008) 794 final. http://ec.europa.eu/consumers/redress_cons/greenpaper_en.pdf, at para. 15, p. 5. Accessed 11 January 2015.

[17] Report from the Commission, n. 14 above, para. 3.17, p. 6.

[18] The definition of class actions as 'toxic cocktails', that is, a deadly combination of dangerous elements, such as punitive damages, contingency fees, pretrial discovery and the like, comes from a press release accompanying the Green Paper on Consumer Collective Redress: see Green Paper on Consumer Collective Redress – Questions and Answers, memo/08/741, Brussels, 27 November 2008. http://europa.eu/rapid/press-release_MEMO-08-741_en.htm, at § 9. Accessed 11 January 2015.

[19] See extensively the essays prepared for the session on Cultural Dimensions of Group Litigation of the IAPL World Conference on Civil Procedure, 18–21 September 2012, Moscow, Russian Federation, and published in Maleshin, Dmitry (ed.). 2012. *Civil Procedure in Cross-Cultural Dialogue: Eurasia Context*. Moscow: Statut, 413–548.

by the Commission, seems to receive a sort of official 'blessing' in the texts at issue. One may infer that, from now on, in the language of the European Union the official denomination of group actions, whether aimed at obtaining injunctive relief or commenced with the view to claiming damages, will be 'collective redress mechanisms'. As a matter of fact, the Recommendation itself offers a definition of these mechanisms:

> For the purpose of this Recommendation:
> (a) "collective redress" means (i) a legal mechanism that ensures a possibility to claim cessation of illegal behaviour collectively by two or more natural or legal persons or by an entity entitled to bring a representative action (injunctive collective redress); (ii) a legal mechanism that ensures a possibility to claim compensation collectively by two or more natural or legal persons claiming to have been harmed in a mass harm situation or by an entity entitled to bring a representative action (compensatory collective redress).[20]

As mentioned before, the Commission has always been adamant in its rejection of class actions. The choice of 'collective redress' as the expression that defines the legal actions available when 'mass harm situations'[21] occur seems to emphasize the resolve of the Commission even more.

The Recommendation lays down a set of principles common to injunctive and compensatory collective actions, followed by more principles applicable only to the former or to the latter. All in all, these principles are supposed to represent the 'minimum standards' that Member States are encouraged to apply in the domestic regulation of collective redress, since compliance with these standards – according to the Commission – would improve the judicial protection offered to group rights by means of procedures that are 'fair, equitable, timely, and not prohibitively expensive'.[22]

The principles common to injunctive and compensatory collective redress deal with issues such as standing, admissibility of actions, adequate information to potential claimants, funding of collective actions, and application of the 'loser pays' principle to the costs of lawsuits.

The prospective European collective action is conceived as a representative action, since standing to sue is granted only to 'representative entities' identified in advance by Member States or to public authorities: both shall act on behalf of a group of individuals (or legal persons) equally affected by unlawful acts performed by the same defendant. Group members shall not become parties to the lawsuit.[23] Member States are advised to pay special attention to the criteria according to which 'representative entities' are chosen. The Recommendation itself lists some requirements, such as the non-profit character of the entity, a direct connection between the

---

[20] See sec. II, Definitions and scope, of the Recommendation, para. 3.

[21] See ibid., para. 3 '(b): "mass harm situation" means a situation where two or more natural or legal persons claim to have suffered harm[-]causing damage resulting from the same illegal activity of one or more natural or legal persons'.

[22] See sec. I, Purpose and subject matter, of the Recommendation, para. 2.

[23] See ibid., para. 3 (d); also sec. III, Principles common to injunctive and compensatory collective redress, of the Recommendation, para. 4–7 'Standing to bring a representative action'.

goals pursued by the entity and the rights that the collective action is supposed to protect, and evidence of the fact that the entity has the financial and human resources as well as the legal expertise necessary to conduct the lawsuit in the best interest of group members.

The admissibility of a collective action must be tested at the very outset of the lawsuit: to this end the courts of Member States shall conduct a thorough examination of the elements that, according to domestic law, are the requirements to be met in order to 'certify' the action as a collective one.[24] Needless to say, the purpose of this scrutiny (which courts are expected to perform *ex officio*) is to prevent groundless cases from crowding the dockets of courts.

The Commission ascribes high value to adequate information about prospective collective actions: Member States shall ensure that the 'representative entities' are allowed to advertise their intention to seek redress on behalf of a class and that the stakeholders are kept abreast of the developments of the lawsuit, once it has commenced.[25] All that makes sense most of all in the context of compensatory collective actions, since – as explained below – potential claimants must join the lawsuit, that is, they must opt in order to receive compensation for the harm suffered. In any event, the right of potential or actual stakeholders to be fully informed about collective actions brought on their behalf should always be balanced against the risk of damaging the reputation of the defendant when he has not yet been found responsible for the alleged violations.

As far as the costs of collective litigation are concerned, it is recommended to Member States that in the regulation of this matter the so-called 'loser pays principle' be followed, that is, that the costs incurred by the winning party are reimbursed by the losing party.[26] In this regard, too, the Commission shows its rejection of American-style class actions, whose success depends to a great extent on the fact that they are made financially affordable by contingency fee agreements between representative plaintiffs and the attorneys for the class. For the Commission, contingency fee agreements are essential components of the above-mentioned 'toxic cocktail' that could poison European collective redress by stimulating frivolous lawsuits. By the same token, the Recommendation seems particularly cautious in allowing another financial feature of contemporary litigation that seems to encourage abusive cases, namely, third-party litigation funding. In fact, the Recommendation provides for a series of safeguards that Member States are expected to implement with the view to maintaining that third-party funding is 'designed in a way that serves in a proportionate manner the objective of ensuring access to justice'.[27]

[24] See sec. III, Principles common to injunctive and compensatory collective redress, of the Recommendation, para. 8–9 'Admissibility'.

[25] See ibid., para. 10–12 'Information on a collective redress action'.

[26] See ibid., para. 13 'Reimbursement of legal costs of the winning party'.

[27] See ibid., para. 14–16 'Funding'. Third-party litigation funding (often referred to as TPLF) is one of the 'new frontiers' of financing litigation: quite popular in common law jurisdictions, TPLF does not seem to have conquered the civil law world yet. TPLF in practice may take different forms that share a common feature: at their basis there is always a contract by which the plaintiff commits

For injunctive collective redress the Recommendation lays down two specific principles.[28] With the first the Commission urges Member States to set up procedures that 'with all due expediency' can grant cease and desist orders against the defendant. Time is of the essence when it is necessary to prevent the unlawful conduct of the defendant from continuing, causing further harm to the victims of such conduct: therefore, it is suggested that injunctive collective redress be conceived as a summary procedure, based on the assumption that summary proceedings can be the optimal choice when the inescapable delay of full-fledged ordinary proceedings would be detrimental to the rights at stake.

If the time-factor is essential for the effectiveness of injunctions, the same holds true as regards compliance with injunctive orders. That is why the Recommendation advises Member States to provide for 'appropriate sanctions'[29] to be applied if the defendant fails to comply with the court order. National laws shall identify the sanctions that are most suitable for acting as a threat powerful enough to persuade the defendant to comply spontaneously, but the Recommendation makes express reference to a type of sanction closely resembling the French *astreinte*, that is, a penalty amounting to a fine for each day (or another unit of time) of delay in the enforcement of the injunctive order.[30]

All in all, there is nothing really new in the principles devoted to injunctive collective redress. To the contrary, it seems that the model originally devised by Directive 98/27/CE on the procedure for injunctive relief in the interest of consumers is confirmed in its (disputable, one might say) efficiency to the point of being presented as the general model for the collective protection of other rights. This is in spite of the warning given by the European Parliament according to which

himself to grant the third party a percentage of the amount of money he will recover in case of victory in the lawsuit; in exchange, the third party relieves the plaintiff of the financial risk of litigation, since the third party will not be entitled to claim any money if the outcome of the case is against the plaintiff. For an accurate analysis of TPLF, see De Morpurgo, Marco. 2011. A Comparative Legal and Economic Approach to Third-Party Litigation Funding. *Cardozo Journal of International and Comparative Law* 19: 343–412.

[28] See sec. IV, Specific principles relating to injunctive collective redress, of the Recommendation, para. 19 'Expedient procedures for claims for injunctive orders' and para. 20 'Efficient enforcement of injunctive orders'.

[29] See ibid., para. 20 'Efficient enforcement of injunctive orders'.

[30] The French *astreinte* was originally devised by courts in order to overcome the rule laid down by the Civil Code (Art. 1142) according to which failure to comply with legal duties to do something or to refrain from doing something has no consequences other than the right for the creditor to claim damages, since the debtor's will cannot be forced. The penalty amounting to a fine for each day of delay courts can impose works as an effective threat that is likely to persuade the debtor to comply with his duties. At present, courts are allowed to resort to the 'persuasive' force of *astreintes* in a wide variety of situations, well beyond the specific circumstances of their initial use. See Perrot, Roger. L'astreinte à la française. 2004. In *Mélanges Jacques van Compernolle*. 487–510. Brussels: Bruylant; Desdevises, Yves. 2004. Astreintes – Introduction, *JurisClasseur Procédure Civile*, 2120.

the framework of collective injunctive relief 'can be significantly improved',[31] considering the important role it might play in the protection of the rights granted to individual and legal entities under EU law.

More significant are the principles laid down for collective actions for damages, or, in the language of the Recommendation, compensatory collective redress mechanisms. Again the Commission seems inclined to mark the distance between these mechanisms and American-style class actions by stating that 'the claimant party should be formed on the basis of express consent of the natural or legal persons claiming to have been harmed ("opt-in" principle)'.[32]

It is well known that the debate over the advantages and disadvantages of 'opt-in' in contrast to 'opt-out' as the methods of choice to determine the subjects that will be bound by the outcome of a group action is very much alive.[33] The Commission takes a stand in this debate and expands on the reasons that should (at least in principle) make 'opt-in' a basic feature of future European collective actions for damages. According to the Communication, it is essential that the represented group be identified before the court issues the final judgment on the collective action: that becomes possible only insofar as the members of the 'class' willingly take the necessary steps to participate in the proceeding. In the view of the Commission:

> The "opt-in" system respects the right of a person to decide whether to participate or not. It therefore better preserves the autonomy of parties to choose whether to take part in the litigation or not. In this system the value of the collective dispute is more easily determined, since it would consist of the sum of all individual claims. The court is in a better position to assess both the merits of the case and the admissibility of the collective action. The "opt-in" system also guarantees that the judgment will not bind other potentially qualified claimants who did not join.[34]

But the 'philosophy' of the Commission on the superiority of an opt-in system is condensed in the following passage:

> The right to an effective remedy cannot be interpreted in a way that prevents people from making (informed) decisions on whether they wish to claim damages or not. In addition, an "opt-out" system may not be consistent with the central aim of collective redress, which is to obtain compensation for harm suffered, since such persons are not identified, and so the award will not be distributed to them.[35]

---

[31] See European Parliament resolution of 2 February 2012 on 'Towards a Coherent European Approach to Collective Redress', n. 8 above, at § 11.

[32] See sec. V, Specific principles relating to compensatory collective redress, of the Recommendation, para. 21–24, at 21 'Constitution of the claimant party by "opt-in" principle'.

[33] On the debate at the European level, see, e.g., Benör, Iris. 2013. Consumer Dispute Resolution after the Lisbon Treaty: Collective Actions and Alternative Procedures, *Journal of Consumer Policy* 36: 87–110; Tzakas, Dimitrios-Panagiotis. 2011. Effective Collective Redress in Antitrust and Consumer Protection Matters: A Panacea or A Chimera?, *Common Market Law Review* 48: 1125–1174; Hodges, Christopher. 2010. Collective Redress in Europe: The New Model, *Civil Justice Quarterly* 29: 370–387; Stuyck, Jules. 2009. Class Actions in Europe? To Opt-In or To Opt-Out, That is the Question, *European Business Law Review* 20; 483–505; Fairgrieve, Duncan & Howells, Geraint. 2009 Collective Redress Procedures – European Debates, *International and Comparative Law Quarterly* 58: 379–409.

[34] See § 3.4 of the Communication, at p. 12.

[35] See ibid.

It must be emphasized, though, that the principle encouraging the adoption of an opt-in system is a principle that Member States may disregard: in relation to this issue, the wording of the Recommendation is quite fuzzy, since it makes reference to exceptions to the principle 'duly justified by reasons of sound administration of justice',[36] a vague expression whose meaning is left open to many possible interpretations, due to the fact that neither the Recommendation itself nor the Communication offers any clues. Maybe, in order to understand the attitude of the Commission, one must recall that even though most Member States have group actions geared to 'opt-in' systems, there are a few examples of very successful collective procedures for damages that work on an 'opt-out' basis,[37] and which certainly national legislators would not be inclined to change just for the sake of accommodating the Commission's wishes.

It is commonly accepted that the Commission has great expectations for alternative dispute resolution (ADR) to offer individuals swift and affordable processes by which to seek justice without resorting to traditional litigation. The same attitude is displayed towards collective actions for damages. In fact, the Recommendation encourages Member States to foster the settlement of collective disputes,[38] not only by way of out-of-court procedures, but also when the litigation is in progress, that is, entrusting the court with the power to invite the parties to attempt mediation or other procedures with the view to bringing their dispute to an end by reaching a mutually acceptable agreement.[39]

---

[36] See sec. V, Specific principles relating to compensatory collective redress, of the Recommendation, para. 21–24, at 21 'Constitution of the claimant party by "opt-in" principle'.

[37] On the different models of group actions adopted in Member States, see, in general, Werlauff, Eric. 2013. Class Actions and Class Settlement in a European Perspective, *European Business Law Review*, 24: 173–186; Mulheron, Rachael. 2009. The Case for an Opt-Out Class Action for European Member States: A Legal and Empirical Analysis, *Columbia Journal of European Law* 15: 409–451. One of the most interesting and successful opt-out collective procedures existing in the European Union is the one provided for by the Dutch Act on the Collective Settlement of Mass Damage Claims (known as WCAM) that dates back to 2005. In short, according to the Act a collective settlement agreement can be negotiated between one or more entities – representing a class of individuals who were identically harmed by the defendant – and the defendant. Once a settlement agreement is reached, the parties may jointly request the Amsterdam Court of Appeal to declare the collective settlement binding on the class, except for those class members who have expressed their wish not to be bound by the agreement, that is, those who have decided to opt out within the time-limit set by the court; on this procedure, see van Boom, Willem H. 2009. Collective Settlement of Mass Claims in The Netherlands. In *Auf dem Weg zu einer europäischen Sammelklage?*, eds. Casper, Matthias, Janssen, André, Pahlmann, Petra, Schulze, Reiner, 171–192. Munich: Sellier.

[38] See sec. V, Specific principles relating to compensatory collective redress, of the Recommendation, para. 25–28 'Collective alternative dispute resolution and settlements'.

[39] The Recommendation makes reference to Directive 2008/52/EC on certain aspects of mediation in civil and commercial cases, whose Art. 5, sec. 1 provides: 'A court before which an action is brought may, when appropriate and having regard to all the circumstances of the case, invite the parties to use mediation in order to settle the dispute.' More generally, Member States are advised to take into account all the requirements laid down by the Directive.

With reference to ADR and collective redress, two principles are worth mentioning: the first one emphasizes the voluntary character of ADR procedures, even when their use is suggested by the court handling a collective case. According to the Commission:

> The Member States should ensure that judicial collective redress mechanisms are accompanied by appropriate means of collective alternative dispute resolution available to the parties before and throughout the litigation. Use of such means should depend on the consent of the parties involved in the case.[40]

The rejection of mandatory ADR procedures has a special value for the author of this essay, since in her native country (Italy) there is an ongoing debate on whether out-of-court mediation should be mandatory or strictly voluntary. As a matter of fact, in Italy mediation in civil and commercial cases was made mandatory in 2010; the relevant rules were repealed by the Constitutional Court in 2012, but the legislators reinstated mandatory mediation in 2013[41]: the perfect scenario for yet another time-consuming institutional round of 'arm-wrestling'.

The second principle recommends that the collective settlement reached by the parties be subject to judicial control:

> The legality of the binding outcome of a collective settlement should be verified by the courts taking into consideration the appropriate protection of interests and rights of all parties involved.[42]

From the wording of the Recommendation it seems possible to conclude that the court should not only verify the legality of the settlement, but also evaluate its merits, at least as far as the fairness of the agreement is concerned, since due consideration must be paid to 'the appropriate protection of interests and rights of all parties involved'.

As regards the costs of compensatory collective redress,[43] the concern of the Commission is to prevent the regulation of attorneys' fees and other financial aspects of group actions from turning into a source of abusive litigation. Therefore, Member States – at least in principle – should not allow contingency fee agreements, nor should they provide for third-party litigation funding insofar as the amount of the damages awarded to the class is the basis on which the remuneration of the third party is calculated. Again the Recommendation reveals that, while the ends it is aimed to achieve are stated clearly, the means by which these very ends should be attained are not put forth in a straightforward way. Neither contingency

---

[40] See sec. V, Specific principles relating to compensatory collective redress, of the Recommendation, at para. 26 'Collective alternative dispute resolution and settlements'.

[41] On the vicissitudes of mediation in Italy, see Silvestri, Elisabetta & Jagtenberg, Rob. 2013. Tweeluik – Diptych: Juggling a Red Hot Potato: Italy, the EU, and Mandatory Mediation, *Nederlands-Vlaams tijdschrift voor Mediation en conflictmanagement* 17: 29–45.

[42] See sec. V, Specific principles relating to compensatory collective redress, of the Recommendation, at para. 28 'Collective alternative dispute resolution and settlements'.

[43] See ibid., para. 29–30 'Legal representation and lawyers' fees' and para. 32 'Funding of compensatory collective redress'.

fee agreements nor third-party litigation funding is welcome, but they are not completely banned, since

> [t]he Member States that exceptionally allow for contingency fees should provide for appropriate national regulation of those fees in collective redress cases, taking into account in particular the right to full compensation of the members of the claimant party.[44]

On the contrary, the attitude of the Commission towards punitive damages is clear-cut: the damages awarded in compensatory collective actions 'should not exceed the compensation that would have been awarded, if the claim had been pursued by means of individual actions',[45] and therefore punitive damages should not be allowed by Member States. Even stronger is the approach taken by the Communication: 'punitive damages should not be part of a European collective redress system',[46] in which damages are expected to be solely compensatory. Nothing new under the sun here, one might say, since most Member States are averse to punitive damages and refuse the recognition and enforcement of foreign judgments imposing punitive damages on the losing party.[47]

The purpose of this chapter was to describe the plans of the European Commission for a uniform and harmonized model of collective redress mechanisms. The question remains whether they truly represent a step forward along the path to a coherent approach to group actions or are a bit of a 'damp squibb', an exercise in wishful thinking if not a dangerous *faux pas* that will not advance the cause of collective redress.[48] It has been emphasized already that the approach taken by the Commission in regard to some important aspects of group actions covered by the Recommendation seems tentative and inconclusive: principles are laid down, but ample room is left for Member States to deviate from them, which is likely to leave the 'patchwork' of national group actions as it is right now. Whether or not one is inclined to subscribe to this judgment, no one can deny that to devise a common framework for European collective redress implies delicate policy choices, choices that the European institutions, faced with the problems of an unprecedented economic crisis threatening the very stability of the Union, perhaps cannot afford to make at the moment.

---

[44] See ibid., para. 30.

[45] See ibid., para. 31 'Prohibition of punitive damages'.

[46] See Communication from the Commission to the European Parliament, the Council, the European Economic and Social Committee and the Committee of the Regions, 'Towards a European Horizontal Framework for Collective Redress', n. 1 above, at 3.1., p. 10.

[47] On this issue, see, e.g., Koziol, Helmut. 2008. Punitive Damages. A European Perspective. *Louisiana Law Review* 68: 741–764; Pinna, Andrea. 2008. Recognition and *Res Judicata* of US Class Action Judgments in European Legal Systems. *Erasmus Law Review* 1: 31–61, in particular 49–56.

[48] These comments on the documents issued by the Commission derive from Hodges, Christopher. 2014. Collective Redress: A Breakthrough or a *Damp Squibb*? *Journal of Consumer Policy* 37: 67–89.

Chapter 11
Class Action Procedure in Australia – Issues and Challenges

Lang Thai

11.1 Introduction

Shareholder class action is still relatively new in Australia. Part IVA of the *Federal Court of Australia Act* 1974 (C'th) ("FCAA") governs the procedure for a class action. It has been available in Australia since March 1992. Prior to 1992, Australia did not have any form of statutory class action; there was no common law equivalent.

Part IVA provides a *general* procedure for a class action in the sense that the procedure can be used in any situation. The only requirement is that a representative is required to show that seven or more persons all have the same, similar or related circumstances in respect to their claims against the same defendant. For example, a passive smoker of tobacco could launch a class action on behalf of all other passive smokers against a tobacco company for injuries sustained due to the inhalation of the toxic by-products. Another example is that a shareholder who has suffered financial loss in the investment because of the company's failure to provide full and frank disclosure of the company's financial position to the shareholders at the relevant time could launch a class action on behalf of all affected shareholders against the company and its directors.

BSc, LLB (Monash), GradDipEd (Melb), LLM (Monash), Lecturer in the Law School, Deakin University, Australia; Barrister and Solicitor of the Supreme Court of Victoria and High Court of Australia.

L. Thai (✉)
School of Law, Deakin University, Melbourne Burwood Campus, Victoria, Australia
e-mail: lang.thai@deakin.edu.au

C.B. Picker, G.I. Seidman (eds.), *The Dynamism of Civil Procedure - Global Trends and Developments*, Ius Gentium: Comparative Perspectives on Law and Justice 48, DOI 10.1007/978-3-319-21981-3_11

The Part IVA procedure was not utilised by shareholders until 1999,[1] and since then, at least thirty shareholder class actions have been commenced in court, but only four of those proceeded to trial,[2] and, as of publication of this book, none has proceeded to final judgment. Most of those cases settled prior to a court hearing and there is no clear explanation for this. One possible explanation could be because of the uncertainty in the procedure in Part IVA, in particular the ambiguity in the interpretation of the "opt out" provision in section 33J.

It should be noted that although the *Corporations Act* 2001 (C'th) is the main piece of legislation for dealing with corporate law matters, and for regulating directors' and officers' duties and for the provision of shareholders' rights and remedies, it does not have any provision relating to class action or representative action. Instead and as noted above, Part IVA of the FCAA provides a useful general class action procedure, which has become an important weapon for shareholders of large companies to seek compensation and damages since 1999.

In shareholder class actions, common grounds of complaint by shareholders are often about "misleading or deceptive conduct" by the company and its directors and officers under the Australian *Corporations Act* 2001 (C'th).[3] When facts revealed later that they had purchased shares in the company at an inflated price or had sold them at less than the true market value, they alleged that the directors and officers of the company had failed to provide full disclosure of the company's financial position at the relevant time. In the alternative, they alleged that the company had failed to comply with the "continuous disclosure obligations" under the relevant legislation and under the Australian stock exchange Listing Rules.[4]

This chapter will consider shareholder class action as an example to illustrate why there are problems in the Australian class action procedure, and why the "opt out" provision is in need of clarification. The example as illustrated will be applicable to other forms of class action in Australia. The chapter divides into the following parts. Part 2 briefly explains the nature of an Australian class action and its special features. Part 3 then examines some of the difficulties in the Australian class action procedure; in particular, it will look at how an "opt out" class action under section 33J of the FCAA has often been turned into an "opt in" class action, contrary

[1]The first reported Australian shareholder class action case was in *King v AG Australia Holdings Ltd (formerly GIO Australia Holdings Ltd)* [2003] FCA 980

[2]These are *Dorajay Pty Ltd v. Aristocrat Leisure Ltd* [2005] FCA 1483; (2005) 147 FCR 394; *Watson v. AWB Limited (No.7)* [2010] FCA 41; *Kirby v. Centro Properties Limited (No.6)* [2012] FCA 650; and *Modtech Engineering Pty Limited v GPT Management Holdings Limited* [2013] FCA 626; [2013] FCA 1163

[3]The misleading or deceptive conduct provisions relied upon by shareholders in class action cases are generally in ss.670A, 953A, 1022A, 1041E, 1041 F, 1041H, 1308 and 1309 of the *Corporations Act* 2001 (C'th), and in s.12DA of the *Australian Securities and Investments Commission Act* 2001 (C'th)

[4]The "continuous disclosure obligations" provisions are contained in Ch 6-6D of the *Corporations Act* 2001 (C'th). The Australian Securities Exchange also has mandatory Listing Rules to be complied with by all public companies that are listed on the stock exchange, including rules relating to compliance with continuous disclosures.

to the intention of the provision. It will also explain the difficulty in proving the necessary causation in a case where there is uncertainty in the class size under the FCAA. The recent developments in the law relating to third party litigation funding will also be considered briefly within this Part. Part 4 provides a review of some important shareholder class actions in Australia to illustrate how these cases have shifted from being an "opt out" class action to an "opt in" class action. Part 5 concludes with a note that until the volatile state of the litigation funding industry is sorted out, amendments to the class action procedure are unlikely to be effective in the long term.

11.2 What Is an Australian Class Action?

Australia has what is known as an "opt out" class action. Part IVA (sections 33A-33ZJ) of the FCAA regulates the class action procedure in Australia and it has been available since 1992. Four years prior to the enactment of Part IVA of the FCAA, the Australian Law Reform Commission made a recommendation in its 1988 Report for an "opt in" class action.[5] However, the Australian Federal Parliament rejected that recommendation and introduced a class action with an "opt out" mechanism as now seen in section 33J. There was no clear explanation as to why an "opt out" class action was preferred for Australia, but the theory was that the Parliament cautioned against a floodgate effect as seen in the examples in the United States class actions.

To commence a class action in Australia, section 33C requires a class member or a representative in that class to prove that seven or more persons have the same, similar or related circumstances in respect to their claims against the same defendant. The representative is also required to prove that the claims of those persons give rise to a substantial common issue of law or fact.

There are two points to note about the Australian class action. First, when one member decides to be the plaintiff and represents six other members in the class, there is a very high chance that the plaintiff will also be representing numerous other eligible class members whom he may have no idea who they are until perhaps when litigants from both sides are about to settle the case, either in court or by way of an out-of-court settlement (which the latter is subject to the court's approval). The numerous other eligible class members, who have not been formally identified in the court documents, may decide not to come forward at the early stage of the court proceedings. They can choose to remain anonymous until they hear about a successful outcome or until they hear about an out of court settlement, at which time they will come forward to make a claim for a share of the compensation. Sections 33X and 33Y empower the court to make an order requiring the representative plaintiff to inform the potentially eligible members about the existing class action,

[5] Australian Law Reform Commission, *Grouped Proceedings in the Federal Court*, Report No 46, 1988, Australian Government Publishing Service, Canberra

either in the form of newspaper advertisement or through radio or television broadcast. It is then within the right of the eligible members to decide whether to remain anonymous or to come forward to make a claim under the current class action framework. The delay in coming forward could be as late as when they hear of a successful outcome in the class action.

Section 33E(1) states that "consent of a person to be a group member in a representative proceeding is not required unless subsection (2) applies" and subsection (2) refers to a list of government officials who must give consent to join as group member. This means that any person other than a government official who has an interest in the matter arising from the same similar or related circumstances will *automatically* become a class member. There is no need for an eligible member to obtain consent from the representative plaintiff to become a member of that class action. If the class action is successful and compensation has been awarded by the court or the class action has reached an out of court settlement sum, an eligible member will need to prove that he or she has a claim or claims arising from the same, similar or related circumstances as those seven other class members. In practice, the pool of eligible members may be large and there is no requirement for all of these members to come forward at the start of the class action. Some members may not be aware of the existing class action, or they simply do not want to be involved and would rather sit back and wait to see what would happen next. These other members may decide to appear later, even during the trial or when settlement is about to occur. Section 33E therefore creates much uncertainty for both the representative plaintiff and the defendant. It creates a "free-rider" problem, and it creates uncertainty in the class size that puts an enormous pressure on the defendant to settle the court action quickly. In essence, section 33E does not mandate members to disclose their identity until they are ready to come forward to make a claim under the existing class action case.

The second point to note about the class action in Australia is the "opt out" mechanism referred to in section 33J. This provision provides a way for a class member to "opt out" of the class action. It reads:

> (1) The Court must fix a date before which a group member may opt out of a representative proceeding.
> (2) A group member may opt out of the representative proceeding by written notice given under the Rules of Court before the date so fixed.

Essentially, section 33J means that if a class member does not wish to have any of the decision binding on him in a class action, then the class member is required to file a written notice informing the court of his or her intention to opt out of the class action by the date fixed by the court. Section 33ZB states that the decision of the court will be automatically binding on all eligible members except those who choose to opt out of the class action.

The phrasing of section 33J appears simple and unassuming. However, the provision is conceptually difficult to apply in practice, as will be examined further in the next two parts of this chapter.

11.3 Some Difficulties in the Australian Class Action Procedure

11.3.1 Problems with the "Opt Out" Provision Under Section 33J

The term "opt out" referred to in section 33J has not been defined anywhere in Part IVA of the FCAA, which is a key feature in the Australian class action procedure. It may be accurate to say that the purpose of section 33J is to allow a person who is classed as an eligible member of a particular class action to opt out if he so desires, so that the outcome of that class action would not be binding upon him and he could choose to pursue a separate court action either on his own or with others. Besides this purpose, there is a general lack of clarification about the "opt out" mechanism in section 33J which could give rise to a number of problems.

First, there is an assumption that an eligible member of the class would be able to opt out of the class action under section 33J. However, the reality is that some people in the general population may have no idea whether they are in fact an eligible member of the class action in the first place. Not everyone can financially afford to engage a lawyer to ask "Am I an eligible member in respect to that class action?" Those who decide to engage a lawyer for an answer and if the answer turns out that they are not an eligible member of the particular class action, then they are still liable to pay their lawyer's professional fees. For some people, this is not a fruitful process for them to decide on whether or not to opt out of the class action. For those who are financially constraint and cannot afford to engage a lawyer to answer that preliminary question, whether an eligible member or not an eligible member, their best and cheaper approach in this instance would be to do nothing under section 33J but to sit back and watch the class proceedings unfold, and in the event that the outcome is successful, they could then come forward and make a claim and hope to receive some compensation, if their claim is assessed as being within the class.

The second problem flows on from the first. In the case where some people may have some idea that they may be a member of the class, but they have no idea what to do or where to go or who to turn to for more information or advice on matters relating to whether or not to opt out under section 33J, and who are also financially constraint from engaging a lawyer for advice because the expenses may outweigh the amount they may be entitled to claim in the recovery process, these eligible members, due to their lack of information, advice and finance, may decide to ignore the "opt out" provision under section 33J and watch the class proceedings unfold and make a claim later if the outcome is successful.

It would not be surprising to hear that a great majority of people in the community would be slow to learn about the precise nature of any court actions. Even if members are aware of the existing class action, perhaps through the media or through other forms of public announcement, not everyone has the ability to react quickly and to know what to do or where to go from there.

Another problem stemming from section 33J is that some class members who may be dissatisfied with the outcome of the class action and who have not opted out in time under section 33J may try to have a second chance at suing the same defendant, perhaps on a different ground. One plausible argument could be that they had no knowledge at all of the previous class action, they were unaware of being a member of that class and so they did not know about the need to opt out under section 33J. A shareholder may try to make a claim on an "oppression/unfair prejudice" ground as a second attempt in suing the same defendant. Under section 232 of the Australian *Corporations Act* 2001 (C'th), the court could grant an "oppression" order in favour of the minority shareholder if the conduct of the company's affairs or the act of the directors is:

> contrary to the interests of the members as a whole; or
> oppressive to, unfairly prejudicial to, or unfairly discriminatory against a member or members whether in that capacity or in any other capacity.

The oppression/unfair prejudice ground is commonly relied upon by shareholders of a small proprietary company or a family-owned company where the remedy awarded by the court is *personal* to the shareholder applicant, and given the company being small in size, the court can in fact tailor-make the remedy to suit the shareholder applicant.[6] The only exception under an oppression/unfair prejudice ground is that the court cannot award damages.[7] For example, the court can order the company to buy back shares currently held by the oppressed shareholder, but cannot award damages.

In essence, section 33J assumes that all class members are familiar with the class action law and the procedure and it assumes that the class members know how to go about opting out of the class action proceedings when in fact they are unlikely to know any of these. Further and without any proper legal advice, a class member would have no idea whether it would be good or bad to opt out of the class action and thus would be indecisive on whether to file a written notice in court to opt out or to stay within the group and participate in the proceedings. Some class members may not even know whether they are *in* the group proceedings or *not* in the group proceedings. Elderly and fragile people and migrants with limited English are the ones who may be most at risk of not knowing what to do and are less likely to make inquiries. Under sections 33X and 33Y, the court may exercise its discretion and order the representative plaintiff to make an announcement in the media as a way of informing the group members of the commencement of the class action, either in the form of press advertisement, radio or television broadcast. However, under the current class action framework, provided there are already seven members being identified as in the group, the representative plaintiff is not required to do more than what has been ordered by the court, that is, there is no need for a representative

[6] Section 233 of the Australian Corporations Act 2001 (C'th) provides a list of 10 different orders that the Court can make in a successful oppression claim, and the list does not include damages.

[7] There is no mention of damages or monetary compensation as a form of remedy for an oppression claim.

plaintiff to make personal contact with any of the other eligible members. The class size may be very large, but there is no obligation on the representative plaintiff to provide additional information to the unidentified eligible members other than the information noted in the media as ordered by the court. Lehane J of the Federal Court of Australia[8] in *Bright v. Femcare* has made an important observation that[9]:

> It is an inevitable aspect of proceeding under Part IVA, I should think, that in many cases a substantial number of members of the represented group will be unknown.

Further, Peter Cashman, who is a practising lawyer, has noted in his published work that[10]:

> It will often be the case that there will be a lack of clarity about a number of people affected and the nature and extent of the losses allegedly suffered. The identity of all of the affected individuals will also be difficult, if not possible, to ascertain, at least at the outset of the litigation.

Overall, the "opt out" mechanism under section 33J is not a user-friendly procedure. Some eligible class members who are entitled to compensation may be less fortunate, and may well miss out a chance to receive any under the current Australian class action procedure.

A further problem with section 33J relates to its interaction with the third party funding concept. Since 2006 when the High Court of Australia[11] permitted a class action to be commercially funded by a third party,[12] the class action in Australia now appears to look more like an "opt in" class action rather than an "opt out" class action as intended under section 33J. This is examined further under the next heading below.

11.3.2 Problems with Commercially Funded Class Action

When a commercial litigation funder is involved in the class action, the Australian "opt out" class action appears to have become an "opt in" class action, which is contrary to the legislative intention.

---

[8] The Federal Court of Australia sit immediately below the High Court of Australia in the hierarchy of Courts. The High Court of Australia is the highest Court in Australia. While both the Federal Court of Australia and the High Court of Australia can consider matters relating to federal legislation, the Federal Court of Australia is concerned more with the interpretation and application of the federal legislation.

[9] *Bright v. Femcare* [2000] FCA 1179 at [19] (per Lehane J)

[10] P. Cashman, "Class actions on behalf of clients: Is this permissible?" (2006) 80 *Australian Law Journal* 738 at 738

[11] The High Court of Australia is the highest Court in Australia. It can consider matters relating to constitutional issues and has the jurisdiction in laying down precedents.

[12] See *Campbells Cash and Carry v. Fostif* [2006] HCA 41; (2006) 229 CLR 386

In 2006 in the case of *Campbells Cash and Carry v. Fostif* ("*Fostif*"), the High Court of Australia[13] by a majority of 5:2 gave its approval to the idea of commercial litigation funding in a retailer class action case.[14] The same Court reiterated its support in 2009 in another case, *Jeffrey and Katauskas Pty Ltd v. Rickard Constructions Pty Ltd*.[15] The High Court in both cases found that litigation funding by a third party was not contrary to public policy nor was it an abuse of process. Kirby J has stated that third party litigation funding has made it possible for some individual plaintiffs to bring their case to Court and "secure access to justice". Kirby J has this to say[16]:

> ... The individual claim may (as in the case of many tobacco retailers in these proceedings) be comparatively small and hardly worth the expense and trouble of suing. But the aggregate of the claims of those willing to proceed together, as proposed by a funder and organiser such as Firmstones, might be very large indeed. What is a theoretical possibility, as an individual action or series of actions, needs therefore to be converted into a practical case by the intervention of someone willing to undertake a test case (258), followed by others willing to organise litigants in a similar position, and under appropriate conditions, to recover their legal rights by helping them to act together.

In a shareholder class action case, Finkelstein J of the Federal Court of Australia[17] has made a similar remark about third party litigation funding. In *Dawson Nominees Pty Ltd v. Multiplex Limited*, which will be considered further in this chapter, Finkelstein J has said[18]:

> The advantage of the retainer and the funding agreements to each group member is obvious. If it were not for those agreements and the class action procedure, the action would probably not have gotten off the ground. Individually, most group members would not have the financial strength to bring their opponents to court. For those that do the potential benefits of bringing an action would be outweighed by the quantum of the costs.

The overall effect of the High Court rulings is that individual class members can now rely upon a third party commercial litigation funder to assist with the financing of their court case. The rulings also mean that since 2006, new litigation funders can now easily enter the Australian market, as commercial litigation funders are exempt

---

[13] The High Court of Australia is the highest Court in Australia. It can consider matters relating to constitutional issues and has the jurisdiction in laying down precedents.

[14] *Campbells Cash and Carry v. Fostif* [2006] HCA 41; (2006) 229 CLR 386 (Gleeson CJ, Gummow, Kirby, Hayne and Crennan JJ; with Callinan and Heydon JJ dissenting)

[15] See *Jeffrey and Katauskas Pty Ltd v. Rickard Constructions Pty Ltd* (2009) 83 ALJR 1180 (French CJ, Gummow, Hayne and Crennan JJ; with Heydon J dissenting). See also discussion from Baxt R, "Litigation funding: crossing the cross roads" (2010) 28 *Company and Securities Law Journal* 54

[16] *Campbells Cash and Carry v. Fostif* [2006] HCA 41; (2006) 229 CLR 386, at 449 (per Kirby J); Gleeson CJ, Gummow, Hayne and Crennan JJ expressed similar sentiment in the same case

[17] The Federal Court of Australia ranks just beneath the High Court of Australia in the hierarchy. While both the Federal Court of Australia and the High Court of Australia can consider matters relating to federal legislation, the Federal Court of Australia is concerned more with the interpretation and application of the federal legislation.

[18] See, *Dawson Nominees Pty Ltd v. Multiplex Limited* [2007] FCA 1061, at para 34 (Finkelstein J).

from the need to have an Australian Financial Services Licence.[19] The outcome is that there is now a rapid rise in the number of shareholder class actions in Australia. Currently commercial litigation funders are not subject to any specific law or regulation, apart from the minimal requirement provided in the *Corporations Regulations* 2001 (C'th) which came into operation on 12 July 2013, that third party litigation funders must now have adequate processes in place to manage any conflicts of interests with their clients or with the clients' solicitors.

It is important to note that apart from the minimal requirement of having adequate procedures in place for managing conflicts of interests, commercial litigation funders are still largely unregulated. Unlike solicitors whose fees are regulated under various state legislation, third party commercial litigation funders are *not* subject to any fees restriction. Commercial litigation funders can impose any fees on the plaintiffs for financing their court proceedings, and the financing agreement between them does not need to be approved by the court.

It is important to be aware too that there is increasing pressure on the Australian Government to introduce a stricter control and regulation of commercial litigation funders. The Productivity Commission, which is a branch of the law reform body in Australia, has released its final Inquiry Report called *Access to Justice Arrangements* on 3 December 2014, with volume 2 being the relevant part in respect to the call for regulation of the litigation funding industry.[20] In its recommendation to the Australian Government that all commercial litigation funding companies must be regulated and must hold a financial services licence, the Inquiry Report in volume 2 states[21]:

> The Australian Government should establish a licence for third party litigation funding companies designed to ensure they hold adequate capital relative to their financial obligations and properly inform clients of relevant obligations and systems for managing risks and conflicts of interest.
>
> - Regulation of the ethical conduct of litigation funders should remain a function of the courts.
> - The licence should require litigation funders to be members of the Financial Ombudsman Scheme.
> - Where there are any remaining concerns relating to categories of funded actions, such as securities class actions, these should be addressed directly, through amendments to underlying laws, rather than through any further restrictions on litigation funding.

The Inquiry Report is currently being considered in Parliament.

---

[19] This exemption was announced by the High Court of Australia in *International Litigation Partners Pte Ltd v. Chameleon Mining NL (receivers and Managers Appointed)* [2012] HCA 45 when examining the width of the "credit facility" exemption provision under the *Corporations Act* 2001 (C'th). Soon after, the Parliament passed the *Corporations Amendment Regulations* 2012 (No.6), to confirm that commercial litigation funders are exempt from the need to have an AFSL.

[20] Productivity Commission, *Inquiry Report on Access to Justice Arrangements*, Volume 2, Final Report No 72, 5 September 2014, Canberra. The Report submitted to the Australian Government was available to the public on 3 December 2014

[21] Productivity Commission, *Inquiry Report on Access to Justice Arrangements*, Volume 2, Final Report No 72, 5 September 2014, Canberra, Recommendation 18.2 at page 633

11.3.2.1 How Does Commercial Litigation Funding Work?

Commercial litigation funding works on the basis that a third party is funding a class action; it involves the persons receiving the funds (ie members in the class action) to sign a funding agreement with the litigation funder. Class members who agree to sign into the funding agreement will effectively be *opting into* the funding arrangement, and so the class action will be run as an "opt in" class action. Common practice is that a litigation funder agrees to fund all legal costs and expenses incurred in a court case such as a shareholder class action, and this includes providing any security for costs required by the court.[22] In exchange for litigation funding, class members must agree to two conditions:

1. They must pay all costs and expenses to the litigation funder when there is a successful outcome in the class action or when a class member withdraws from the case before it is settled; and
2. They must pay the litigation funder an agreed percentage of the compensation received from the successful class action, irrespective of how the compensation comes about, whether by way of settlement before the trial or when final judgment is handed down.

As noted earlier, commercial litigation funding is largely unregulated. The problem with this is that a litigation funder can impose any fees on the class members who have chosen to opt in. A litigation funder can demand an agreed percentage to be as high as two-thirds of the total compensation amount.[23] A further problem could be that a litigation funder would be suggesting a law firm to take on the class action, which then enables the funder to request for a regular update directly from the law firm. In essence, a commercial litigation funder is arguably the key driver in the class action and the representative plaintiff would just be a nominal figure named in the court documents as required under the class action procedure in Part IVA of the FCAA. The involvement of the representative plaintiff and members in that class is only to provide facts and evidence to "assist" in securing a substantial settlement figure.

The main objective of the litigation funder is to generate income from as many successful court actions as possible. The funding agreement is prepared in a way that ensures maximum benefit for the litigation funder. When a class member decides to opt out of the funding arrangement with the litigation funder or decides to inform the court under section 33J to opt out of the class action, the funding agreement is set up to ensure that the funder will get back all of its costs plus inter-

---

[22] See, Morabito V, "Corporate Accountability, Third Parties and Class Actions" from Corporate Law and Accountability Research Group, Working Paper No. 3, October 2006, at pp. 17–18.

[23] See Standing Committee of Attorneys-General, *Litigation Funding in Australia* (Discussion Paper, May 2006) p.4, at http://www.scag.gov.au/lawlink/SCAG/ll_scag.nsf/pages/scag_pastconsultations. See also, Morabito V, "Corporate Accountability, Third Parties and Class Actions" from Corporate Law and Accountability Research Group, Working Paper No. 3, October 2006, at p.18; see also, Clark S and Harris C, "The push to reform class action procedure in Australia: Evolution or revolution?" (2008) 32 *Melbourne University Law Review* 775

ests and penalties from the member who has opted out. The litigation funder may take full control over the proceedings to the extent possible by law. One could argue that "behind the curtain", the client of the law firm is in fact the commercial litigation funder, and not the class members or the representative plaintiff named in the court documents.

To avoid any confusion, the term "commercial litigation funding agreement" is not the same as "contingency fees agreement", the latter of which is commonly used in the United States.[24] The Australian law prohibits the use of "contingency fees agreement" or "contingency fees arrangement".[25] Instead, "commercial litigation funding agreement" is the alternative as approved by the High Court of Australia in 2006. The key difference between the two is that in a contingency fees arrangement, as used in the United States, the plaintiff's law firm or solicitor is the one entering into an agreement with the client to deduct a portion of the recovery from a successful court case. By contrast, in a commercial litigation funding arrangement, which is now available in Australia, an external third party is financing the court action, so as to avoid any potential conflict of interest between the solicitor or law firm and the client. An external litigation funder is not constrained by the same prohibition as a law firm or a solicitor, and given the lack of legislative regulation in commercial litigation funding, there is no limit on how much a commercial litigation funder can demand from the class members in the event of a successful outcome in the class action.[26]

It should be noted that not all class members would want to agree to sign into the litigation funding agreement, which means that they will not be bound by that agreement. However, whether these non-funded class members will still be entitled to some compensation from a successful outcome in the class action is entirely dependent on how judges in different courts have interpreted section 33J and this, as will be discussed later through examples of shareholder class action cases, is problematic. There is no clear precedent for which the courts can regulate litigation funders in Australia. In short, there is no consistency in the judicial interpretation and application of the provision under section 33J. There is also the problem of free riders.

If one were to put aside the differences in the "opt in" and "opt out", one would indeed accept the argument that commercial litigation funding is doing good for the

[24] For reading on the United States contingency fees arrangement, see Macey JR and Miller GP, "The Plaintiffs' Attorney's Role in Class Action and Derivative Litigation: Economic Analysis and Recommendations for Reform (1991) 58 *University of Chicago Law Review* 1. See also, Lambert KA, "Class Action Settlements in Louisiana", (2000) 61 *Louisiana Law Review* 89; and Mulheron R, *The Class Action in Common Law Legal System: A Comparative Perspective* (Oxford, Hart Publishing, 2004)

[25] See, for example, *Legal Profession Act 2004* (Vic) s 3.4.29(1)(b); *Legal Profession Act 2006* (ACT) s 285; *Legal Profession Act 2004* (NSW) s 325(1)(b); *Legal Profession Act 2006* (NT) s 320(1); *Legal Profession Act 2007* (Qld) s 325; *Rules of Professional Conduct and Practice 2003* (SA) r 42; *Legal Profession Act 2007* (Tas) s 309(1); *Legal Profession Act 2008* (WA) s 285(1).

[26] For further reading relating to "contingency fees arrangement" and other fees structures, see Damian Grave and Ken Adam, *Class Actions in Australia* (2012).

community, that the financially less fortunate plaintiffs can depend on third party litigation funding to pursue a court action and see justice served. However, the difficulty is not so much on the litigation funding itself, but on whether by getting people to *sign into* the litigation funding agreement, that is, by getting people to opt in to the litigation funding agreement that this would make it inconsistent with the opt out procedure contained in Part IVA of the FCAA, particularly under section 33J. In other words, the assistance of commercial litigation funding has the effect of *excluding* some eligible class members from the class action, and this is contrary to the opt out procedure contained in Part IVA of the FCAA of which focus is on *including* all class members. There is no provision in Part IVA of the FCAA that requires the winning plaintiff to find all the members of the eligible class and share the winnings with them other than the provision that requires the plaintiff to make a public announcement through the media.[27]

11.3.3 Causation Is Difficult to Prove When There Is Uncertainty in the Class Size

Another difficulty in the Australian class action procedure is in relation to the proof of causation, whether all members in the class action must individually prove causation, or whether it is sufficient for the representative plaintiff to prove, on behalf of all class members, a more general causation.

Ordinarily, there is less complication in proving causation when a case involves only a small number of parties, for example, when a case has only a plaintiff and a defendant to deal with. However, proving causation can become difficult when multiple parties are involved. It is difficult to prove causation not only because there are numerous class members involved, but also because there is uncertainty in the class size which makes it even more difficult to establish consistency in the evidence. It is difficult to obtain evidence from non-participating class members. Under section 33E, a member does not need to give consent to be in a class action, which means that the class member, provided he has a claim or claims arising from the same similar or related circumstances, is entitled to compensation in the same way as all the other class members. The legislative framework in Australia for a class action has not made it clear on how causation is to be established. It is not clear:

(a) whether there is a need for all shareholders to appear in court and individually prove actual reliance on the misleading or deceptive statements contained in the company's disclosure document, in which case this can be an extremely slow and a difficult task when there is uncertainty in the class size; or
(b) whether it is sufficient for the representative plaintiff to prove *general* reliance on the misleading or deceptive statements provided by the company and its directors and officers that had caused investment loss to the shareholders.

---

[27] Sections 33X and 33Y of the *Federal Court of Australia Act* 1974 (C'th)

By comparison with the United States' position, shareholder class actions in the United States use the "fraud on the market" theory to prove causation.[28] The United States shareholder class action is governed under section 10(b) of the federal *Securities Exchange Act* 1934 (US). The "fraud on the market" theory was first articulated by the Supreme Court of the United States which is the highest court in the United States, in *Basic Inc. v. Levinson* (1988).[29] The Supreme Court in that case, quoting from an earlier case in *Peil v. Speiser* (1986),[30] stated[31]:

> … in an open and developed securities market, the price of a company's stock is determined by the available material information regarding the company and its business … Misleading statements will therefore defraud purchasers of stock even if the purchasers do not directly rely on the misstatements.

Essentially, this theory is based on a hypothesis that, in an open market transaction, the price of the exchange of traded shares will reflect the financial information that is generally available. Where there is a fraud on the market, the shares will trade at an artificially inflated price. The amount of the inflation, determined by economists and experts, becomes the amount of the loss sustained by the shareholder in relation to the shares purchased. The advantage of relying on the "fraud on the market" theory by the representative plaintiff in proving causation is that a shareholder is said to have suffered a loss by the fact of his purchase, without the need to prove that he was "in fact" misled or deceived by the inaccurate information provided by the company or misled or deceived by non-disclosure.

It is important to note that in the recent United States shareholder class action case in *Halliburton Co v. Erica P John Fund* (2014),[32] the United States Court of Appeal for the Fifth Circuit was requested in November 2013 by the defendant to reconsider the validity of the "fraud on the market" theory. The argument related to an out of date economic theory. However, the United States Court of Appeal declined to entertain the matter further, as it considered that the 1988 decision in *Basic Inc. v. Levinson* is still good law.

Coming back to Australia, the courts have not made any ruling on whether this "fraud on the market" theory or a similar theory applies to proof of causation in shareholder class claims. The legislative framework in Australia has not referred to any model to be used in proving causation in a class action case. If there is general reluctance from Australian courts to adopt the "fraud on the market" theory, the alternative would be for every shareholder to individually prove that their loss was due to the misleading or deceptive statements contained in the company's disclosure documents or due to the non-disclosure, which can be extremely time consuming

[28] See *Basic Inc. v. Levinson* 485 US 224 (1988) (US Supreme Court); *Peil v. Speiser* 806 F 2d 1154 (1986); *Re LTV Securities Litigation* 88 FRD 134 (1980). Shareholder class actions in the United States are usually brought under s.10(b) of the federal *Securities Exchange Act* 1934 (US).

[29] *Basic Inc. v. Levinson* 485 US 224 (1988)

[30] *Peil v. Speiser* 806 F 2d 1154 (1986)

[31] *Basic Inc. v. Levinson* 485 US 224 (1988), at 241–242. See also *Re LTV Securities Litigation* 88 FRD 134 (1980) where the Court referred to the share valuation process in an open market.

[32] *Halliburton Co v. Erica P John Fund Inc.* 134 Sup Ct 2398 (2014)

and a costly exercise.[33] The uncertainty in this area could be another reason why many of the class actions have settled before the trial or soon after the trial has begun.

11.4 Review of Some Shareholder Class Actions in Australia

As noted in the above discussion, since 2006, it is now possible and common for a class action to be funded by a third party commercial litigation funder. The High Court of Australia has decided that this would provide class members a chance to get access to justice. However, as seen in the examples that follow, the idea of commercial litigation funding appears to have turned the legislative prescriptive opt out class action into what appears to be an "opt in" class action. This part of the chapter illustrates the general trend of shareholder class actions.

It should be noted at the onset that in all shareholder class actions, the claims typically made by shareholders are that their investment loss is due to the reliance on inaccurate financial information provided by the company's directors and officers, or due to the company's failure to disclose such information. They rely on the misleading or deceptive conduct provision or the breach of continuous disclosure obligations required by the company. Both the Australian *Corporations Act* 2001 (C'th) and the Australian *Securities and Investments Commission Act* 2001 (C'th) have provisions that prohibit misleading or deceptive statements in the disclosure documents produced by companies, directors, officers, financial service providers and financial product issuers.[34] Shareholders have conveniently relied on these provisions to bring a class action.

11.4.1 Dorajay Pty Ltd v. Aristocrat Leisure Ltd (2005)[35]

Dorajay Pty Ltd v. Aristocrat Leisure Ltd ("*Dorajay*")[36] was the first landmark case on shareholder class action in Australia involving a third party commercial litigation funder. The case commenced in 2003 with the help of "IMF Limited"[37] as the provider of litigation funding, with 556 shareholders having signed the funding

[33] For further reading on the "fraud on the market" theory, see Grave D, Watterson L, and Mould H, "Causation, loss and damage: Challenges for the new shareholder class action" (2009) 27 *Company and Securities Law Journal* 483, at 491–495; see also Drinnan R, and Campbell J, "Causation in securities class actions" (2009) 32 *University of New South Wales Law Journal* 928

[34] For example, *Corporations Act* 2001 (C'th) under ss.670A, 728, 953A, 1022A, 1041E, 1041 F, 1041H, 1308 and 1309; and *Securities and Investments Commission Act* 2001 (C'th) under s.12DA

[35] *Dorajay Pty Ltd v. Aristocrat Leisure Ltd* [2005] FCA 1483; (2005) 147 FCR 394

[36] *Dorajay Pty Ltd v. Aristocrat Leisure Ltd* [2005] FCA 1483; (2005) 147 FCR 394

[37] IMF Limited was a company with no relationship to the International Monetary Fund.

agreement. About 2,300 shareholders had not signed the funding agreement. Instead, many of them chose not to participate in the proceedings but to sit back and watch the case unfold.

In this case, Aristocrat Leisure Ltd ("Aristocrat") was in the business of design, manufacture and sale of electronic gaming machines and gaming software. Aristocrat was a listed public company on the Australian Stock Exchange ("ASX") and operated in Australia, North America, South America and some parts of Asia. As a listed company, it was bound by the Listing Rules of the ASX, including the obligation to immediately disclose to the ASX any information about the company that a reasonable person would expect to have a material effect on its share price or value.

At various times during the reporting period, Aristocrat announced that it was confident that the company would achieve a market forecast of approximately $109 million net profit after tax. Aristocrats stated in its annual report that all the company's businesses were profitable and were expected to remain so. However, Aristocrats later announced that the company would anticipate a breakeven result for the half year. It then announced later again that the company anticipated a loss of $32 million after tax for the half year.

The 556 shareholders alleged that the company's financial accounts were incorrect due to the inclusion of certain revenues on the balance sheets in circumstances not permitted by the accounting standards, and alleged that the company had overstated its profits. They alleged that, at various times during that period, Aristocrat was aware or ought to have been aware of the material information concerning the company's true financial position which it was obliged to immediately disclose to the ASX but had failed to do so. The shareholders further alleged that due to late or incomplete disclosure of material information, the shareholders had suffered loss and damage.

As the class action was commercially funded, the case quickly turned to the legality of the funded action, whether the shareholders were legally permitted to engage a commercial litigation funder to fund their class action. It was argued by the defendant Aristocrat that the involvement of a commercial litigation funder in a class action would contravene the purpose of the "opt out" provision in section 33J as intended by the legislature. Aristocrat argued that by allowing a commercial litigation funder to be involved in the class action, it created a scenario that these 556 shareholders had opted in to the class action funded by the litigation funder and this was contrary to section 33J of the FCAA. In other words, the defendant argued that the commercial litigation funding arrangement had only permitted the 556 funded shareholders to be in the class action, while leaving out the approximately 2,300 non-funded shareholders from the class action. It was not to the benefit of the defendant to make a point regarding the contravention of the "opt out" provision in section 33J, as this would potentially mean a larger liability against the defendant if all shareholders were included as a "class" in the class action. The defendant raised this point merely as an attempt to persuade the Court to dismiss the class action in the entirety.

In October 2005 after a full hearing, Stone J of the Federal Court of Australia decided against the idea of a commercially funded class action. Her Honour stated that the legislature had "made a clear choice" for an "opt out" class action.[38] She added[39]:

> I find that the requirement that group members opt in to the proceeding to be inconsistent with the terms and policy of Part IVA. It is inappropriate that the proceeding continue under Part IVA while the MBC[40] criterion is part of the description of the representative group. I also find that, in the way in which the [law firm] criterion subverts the opt out process, it is an abuse of the Court's processes as established by Part IVA.

It should be noted that the above statement was delivered well before the High Court of Australia handed down its commercial litigation funding decision in 2006, which permitted a retailer class action to be commercially funded by a third party. Not surprisingly and after hearing of the High Court's approval of commercial litigation funding in a retailer class action in *Campbells Cash and Carry v. Fostif*, the defendant Aristocrat decided to settle the case in August 2008 by agreeing to pay $144.5 million in compensation inclusive of all costs and charges, which was approved by the Court.[41] In her approval, Stone J imposed two conditions, one of which was that after deducting all relevant costs and charges the remaining amount to be distributed would be the same for *all* shareholders irrespective of whether they were in the funded or non-funded group, and the second condition was that any amount unclaimed by the non-funded shareholders would need to be returned to the defendant.[42]

11.4.2 *Dawson Nominees Pty Ltd v. Multiplex Ltd (2007)*[43]

The second shareholder class action case worth considering is *Dawson Nominees Pty Ltd v. Multiplex Ltd*. The case commenced in 2007. The case is important because it goes to show how both the original court and the appellate court have taken a different and more generous approach in dealing with the "opt out" provision contained in the legislative framework, after the High Court's approval of the litigation funding concept in 2006.

Multiplex Ltd entered into a construction contract to build a stadium. Unfortunately, it was unable to complete the project on time and so the final costs of the construction exceeded the original estimate. This meant that the delay in the

---

[38] *Dorajay Pty Ltd v. Aristocrat Leisure Ltd* [2005] FCA 1483; (2005) 147 FCR 394, at 429 (Stone J)

[39] *Dorajay Pty Ltd v. Aristocrat Leisure Ltd* [2005] FCA 1483; (2005) 147 FCR 394, at 431 (Stone J)

[40] MBC stands for Maurice Blackburn Cashman, the name of a law firm.

[41] *Dorajay Pty Ltd v Aristocrat Leisure Limited* (2008) 67 ACSR 569

[42] *Dorajay Pty Ltd v Aristocrat Leisure Limited* [2009] FCA 19

[43] *Dawson Nominees Pty Ltd v. Multiplex Ltd* [2007] FCA 1061

construction had caused a massive drop in the company's profit and share value. The shareholders alleged that the company had failed to disclose the full extent of the significant cost increases and failed to inform of the delay in the construction.[44]

Maurice Blackburn, a law firm, did some investigation and subsequently announced on the radio for shareholders of Multiplex to come forward and engage the law firm to commence a class action on their behalf. At the time, there were approximately 40 claimants interested in taking part in the class action with sixteen of those being institutional shareholders who made up 90 % of the potential claims in the class action. Dawson Nominees, one of the institutional shareholders, agreed to be the representative plaintiff. These shareholders signed a retainer agreement with the law firm, and a litigation funding agreement with "ILF", a Singapore-based litigation funding company. There were common clauses in both agreements that the arrangement would be terminated if any of the group members: (a) terminated any of the two agreements; or (b) settled the claim individually and personally with the defendant; or (c) notified the court under section 33J to "opt out" of the class proceedings. There was also a clause requiring a group member who terminated the arrangement to reimburse all legal costs and expenses and pay the agreed percentage of the sum received in settlement. The defendant, in citing *Dorajay's case* for support, argued that such arrangement was against the "opt out" class action procedure contained in Part IVA of the FCAA.

Finkelstein J rejected the defendant's argument and allowed the commercially funded class action to proceed. His Honour declined to view the funding agreement as an opt in mechanism. His view was that there was nothing in the two agreements that would prevent any of the funded group members from opting out of the class action under section 33J at the appropriate time if they so desired.[45] His Honour stated that the group members had chosen to "purchase the funding", and in the same way, they could choose to opt out of that arrangement anytime. In citing authority from *Campbells cash and Carry v. Fostif*, his Honour made a point that "the action would probably not have gotten off the ground" had it not been for the assistance of the law firm and the litigation funding arrangement with a third party.[46]

On appeal, the Full Federal Court sided with Finkelstein J. Jacobson J, with whom French and Lindgren JJ agreed, stated that "the plain fact … is that group members are entitled to opt out" any time, without elaborating on why this was so.[47] The Court unanimously allowed the class action to proceed. However, 3 months

[44] Breaches of the misleading or deceptive conduct were raised under s.674 and s.1041H(1) of the *Corporations Act* 2001 (C'th), under s.12DA(1) of the *Australian Securities and Investments Commission Act* 2001 (C'th) and under the old s.52 of the then *Trade Practices Act* 1974 (C'th). The latter has now been brought forward to s.18 of the *Consumer and Competition Act* 2010 (C'th) with substantially identical terms.

[45] *Dawson Nominees Pty Ltd v. Multiplex Ltd* [2007] FCA 1061, at para 38

[46] *Dawson Nominees Pty Ltd v. Multiplex Ltd* [2007] FCA 1061, at para 34 and 38

[47] *Multiplex Funds Management Limited v. P Dawson Nominees Pty Ltd* [2007] FCAFC 200 (21 December 2007), French, Lindgren and Jacobson JJ , at para 150

prior to the trial, the defendant agreed to settled the action in July 2010, and with the approval of the Court, it agreed to pay a total of $110 million to all eligible group members in the class action, inclusive of all legal costs and expenses. The amount were distributed to all group members in proportion to the shares they held in Multiplex Ltd.

11.4.3 *Kirby v. Centro Properties Limited (No.6) (2012)*[48]

The third important case is *Kirby v. Centro Properties Limited (No.6)*. This case involved two separate class actions run by two different law firms. One law firm, Slater and Gordon, represented 5000 individual shareholders, while a second law firm, Maurice Blackburn, represented 1000 other retailer shareholders. IMF Limited was the provider of litigation funding for the class action run by the second law firm.[49] In total, there were about 6000 shareholders in the two class actions.

Centro Properties Limited ("Centro Properties") was an Australian property investment company specialising in ownership and management of shopping centres around Australia. In both of the class actions run by the two separate law firms, the shareholders claimed that the accounts of Centro Properties for the period of 2006-2007 had significant errors. On the accounts, more than $3 billion of short term debt was wrongly classified as long-term debt, and furthermore, a number of guarantees that Centro Properties made in favour of a US-based company after the balance date were not disclosed. When difficulties arose for Centro Properties to refinance the short term debts, this triggered an internal review into all its debts, which amongst other things, revealed that a long-time auditing firm, Price Waterhouse Cooper, had made serious errors in its audit, which resulted in misleading or deceiving the shareholders.

Both class actions commenced around the same time in 2008. Given the commonality in the claims between these two class actions, the Federal Court decided to bring the two class actions into a single case, and this was largely funded by IMF Limited. Half way through the trial, the defendant, Centro Properties, agreed to settled in May 2012 with the agreed payout figure of $200 million in compensation, of which $133 million to be paid by Centro properties and its related companies and the balance of $67 million to be paid by the auditing firm Price Waterhouse Cooper. This is still the largest settlement figure in Australia in a shareholder class action. Middleton J of the Federal Court approved the settlement figure, saying that the sum was "fair and reasonable".[50] He noted that if the case were to be continued, the final decision would hinge "on difficult and controversial points of law and appeals would be inevitable", and added that, "[s]uch a process brings greater uncertainty

[48] *Kirby v. Centro Properties Limited (No.6)* [2012] FCA 650

[49] IMF Limited was an Australian company that had no relationship to the International Monetary Fund. The company has recently changed its name to Bentham IMF Limited.

[50] *Kirby v. Centro Properties Limited (No.6)* [2012] FCA 650, para 14

to recovery, and would involve substantial delay even if liability were to be established."[51]

By the time the case went to a court hearing in 2008, there was no dispute over the nature of the litigation funder and no dispute over whether the class action was an opt out or opt in. Both parties and the Federal Court had accepted that it is now common practice for a class action to be commercially funded.

11.4.4 *Modtech Engineering Pty Limited v GPT Management Holdings Limited (2013)*[52]

Modtech Engineering Pty Limited v GPT Management Holdings Limited is the latest shareholder class action case in Australia involving a commercial litigation funder. The case commenced in 2011 with about 92 % of the shareholders executing both the litigation funding agreement with a commercial funder and the solicitors' retainer agreement with a law firm. The other 8 % of the shareholders were not on the class action list, nor did they choose to opt out of the action – they were simply in the background assessing the progress of the proceedings. The funded shareholders alleged that the defendant, GPT Management Holdings, had engaged in misleading or deceptive conduct and had breached its continuous disclosure obligations.

In May 2013, at the conclusion of the trial but before the final judgment, the defendant agreed to settle and the settlement proposal was presented to court for approval. On 21 June 2013, the Federal Court approved the settlement sum of $75 million to be paid proportionately to all shareholders, but refused to approve the sum of $9.3 million claimed in respect of the law firm's legal fees and the sum of $53,530 in respect of the class plaintiff's out of pocket expenses.[53] A Registrar of the Court was requested to assess the costs and report back to the Court. The law firm independently engaged a costs consultant to provide an opinion that the legal fees charged were reasonable.

11.4.4.1 Law Firm's Legal Fees and the Class Plaintiff's Out of Pocket Expenses

The Registrar's finding was that $8.5 million would be right for the law firm's legal fees and disbursements and $10,000 would be right for the class plaintiff's out of pocket expenses, both of which Gordon J approved in a subsequent judgment

---

[51] *Kirby v. Centro Properties Limited (No.6)* [2012] FCA 650, para 4

[52] *Modtech Engineering Pty Limited v GPT Management Holdings Limited* [2013] FCA 626; and *Modtech Engineering Pty Limited v GPT Management Holdings Limited* [2013] FCA 1163

[53] *Modtech Engineering Pty Limited v GPT Management Holdings Limited* [2013] FCA 626

on 7 November 2013.[54] Gordon J was highly critical of the costs consultant's report, noting that the amount claimed by the law firm was almost three times the original estimate of $3.5 million, which the report failed to explain, and that the hourly charge rate seemed to have increased by 5 % with no notice of the increase provided to the clients.

11.4.4.2 Commercial Litigation Funder's Fees

As for the fees of the litigation funder, the funding agreement provided that the commercial funder would receive a commission of between 25 and 30 % of the net recoveries after reimbursement of all litigation costs.

The settlement proposal proposed that the funding commission be deducted from the entitlements of all shareholders, including the 8 % of the shareholders who did not execute the litigation funding agreement and the solicitor's retainer agreement. Gordon J rejected this proposal saying that the commercial funder had made a commercial decision to fund the class action with just 92 % of the shareholders. The funding agreement could not be imposed on the other 8 % of the shareholders because they had not entered into an agreement with the commercial funder.[55]

In order to ensure that the 8 % of the unfunded shareholders would not receive more compensation than the 92 % of the funded shareholders, Gordon J decided that the commission, which would have been deducted and paid to the commercial funder under the settlement proposal, would be pooled and distributed pro rata to all class shareholders.[56]

11.4.5 Main Points in the Review of Shareholder Class Actions

In all of the shareholder class action cases, the consensus of the courts is that shareholders can now engage a litigation funder to assist with the settlement of their claims against the defendant company. The involvement of an external litigation funder enables shareholders a chance to bring a class action in a collective organised manner as a way of getting access to justice, in a way that would not have been financially possible for individual shareholders. Part IVA of the FCAA is now the main pathway for shareholders to commence a class action. They are armed with the knowledge that the defendant will most likely agree to settle and pay compensation, as seen in the above cases and in many other shareholder class actions. The selection

---

[54] *Modtech Engineering Pty Limited v GPT Management Holdings Limited* [2013] FCA 1163

[55] *Modtech Engineering Pty Limited v GPT Management Holdings Limited* [2013] FCA 626, at para 57

[56] *Modtech Engineering Pty Limited v GPT Management Holdings Limited* [2013] FCA 626, at para 58. This method, known as the "equalisation factor", has been used in a number of class action settlements.

of cases examined above illustrates how the Courts have gone from being critical of a funded class action, as seen in *Dorajay Pty Ltd v. Aristocrat Leisure Ltd*, to saying that a commercially funded class action has delivered what Finkelstein J in *Dawson Nominees Pty Ltd v. Multiplex Ltd* has called a "fair and reasonable" outcome for shareholders.

Although section 33J of the FCAA refers to the "opt out" mechanism as being the *standard* approach in the class action, the courts in Australia appear not to be too concerned with that provision in cases where third party commercial litigation funding is involved. The High Court of Australia has permitted a litigation funder to assist some plaintiffs and group members in various class action cases. The courts have been flexible in the handling of the class action procedure under Part IVA of the FCAA. The benefits of a class action being funded by a commercial litigation funder appear to outweigh the concerns that Part IVA has not been followed through.

11.5 Concluding Remarks

This chapter has highlighted some difficulties in the Australian class action procedure, in particular, it has examined how an "opt out" provision in section 33J can easily be confused and turned into an "opt in" class action. In the current form and given the fact that commercial litigation funding has become widely accepted in the legal community, it is now harder to see whether a class action is run as an opt in class action or whether it is still run as an opt out version as originally intended by the legislature. The chapter has also considered how proof of causation can be problematic for the representative plaintiff. If a defendant decides to challenge the misleading or deceptive conduct allegation or the allegation of a breach of the company's continuous disclosure obligations, then this may well result in the need for all shareholders to prove their claims in court. So far, the courts have not had any opportunity to make a ruling as to what method would be most appropriate for proving causation. If direct causation is expected from every shareholder in the case, it would be an extremely time consuming and a costly exercise for all parties concerned, particularly when the pool of members who are eligible to take part in the class action is not known at the early stage of the proceeding. When the pool is very large, the defendant could potentially expect a very large liability.

The class action problem is exacerbated when a litigation funder is involved. There is an enormous pressure on the defendant to settle the class action sooner than later. The main objective of the litigation funder is to make money from a court action and for this reason, it would do anything to secure a win. It would conduct some preliminary investigation into the case before agreeing to fund the class action, and once a class action has started, the litigation funder would then try to force a settlement as seen in the high-profile shareholder class action cases examined earlier. Putting pressure on the defendant to settle does not prove in any way that the defendant has in fact breached its disclosure obligations.

A further problem with the current class action procedure is the complexity in the allocation of the settlement sum, as seen in *Modtech Engineering Pty Limited v. GPT Management Holdings Limited*. The parties who have an interest in the settlement are the litigation funder, lawyers acting for the shareholders, the class plaintiff, and shareholders from both the funded group and non-funded group. However, both the litigation funder and lawyers are the ones who pocket most of the money in a successful class action, not in the form of "compensation" as such but in the form of an "earning" for the services they provide. As for the shareholders and depending on the pool of shareholders, they are generally entitled only to a pro rata amount which is dependent on the number of shares they held in the company. If the pool is very large, such as in the case of *Kirby v. Centro Properties Limited* where 6,000 shareholders were involved, then this could mean that shareholders will each receive only a nominal amount in compensation. As noted in *Kirby v. Centro Properties Limited*, the earnings received by the commercial litigation funder and by lawyers in the successful class action were far greater than the total sum received by shareholders. In real term, this is not really a satisfactory outcome for shareholders; there is no real financial gain for shareholders in pursuing a class action other than acquiring a sense of victory at the end of the case.

Clearly, the procedure under Part IVA of the FCAA will need to be clarified, particularly in relation to section 33J regarding the opt out mechanism, and in relation to sections 33C and 33E regarding proof of claim. There is a need to clarify whether individual members would be required to prove their claims individually in court or whether it would suffice for the representative plaintiff to prove the claims that are common amongst all members. The author is of the clear view that until a stricter control is placed on regulating the litigation funding industry, it would not be feasible to clarify or amend the class action procedure under Part IVA of the FCAA.

Chapter 12
Australian Statutory Derivative Action – Defects, Alternative Approaches and Potential For Law Reform

Lang Thai

12.1 Introduction

A derivative action is a corporate action brought on behalf of and in the name of the company against a person, such as a director or an officer of the company, who has allegedly committed a wrong to the company. In Australia, this action is regulated under the *Corporations Act* 2001 (C'th) ("CA"),[1] and under s.237 of the CA, leave of the court is required to commence a statutory derivative action. Generally, a shareholder or former shareholder, or an officer or former officer of the company is entitled to apply to the court for leave to commence a derivative action. The provisions however have not been user-friendly and have been underutilised. There are several reasons for this.

The first problem relates to a need to apply for leave of the court to commence a derivative action and yet the criteria for leave under s.237 are overly restrictive and burdensome on the applicants. For example, an applicant is required to prove that he or she is acting in "good faith" when applying for leave to commence a derivative action. Another example is that an applicant is also required to demonstrate that the derivative action applied for is "in the best interests of the company". The second problem relates to the uncertainty in the recovery of legal and court costs incurred by the applicant. Under s.242, the court has a general broad discretion to decide when to issue a costs order and against whom, and this seems to be the case

BSc, LLB (Monash), GradDipEd (Melb), LLM (Monash), Lecturer in the Law School, Deakin University, Australia; Barrister and Solicitor of the Supreme Court of Victoria and High Court of Australia.

[1] *Corporations Act* 2001 (C'th) is the main statute that applies to corporate law in Australia.

L. Thai (✉)
School of Law, Deakin University, Melbourne Burwood Campus, Victoria, Australia
e-mail: lang.thai@deakin.edu.au

C.B. Picker, G.I. Seidman (eds.), *The Dynamism of Civil Procedure - Global Trends and Developments*, Ius Gentium: Comparative Perspectives on Law and Justice 48, DOI 10.1007/978-3-319-21981-3_12

regardless of the outcome of the leave application. The third problem is the inability of the applicant to get access to company documents in order to assess the strength of the case and to assess whether there is a derivative action case to be brought to the court. Under s.247A, if a person intends to make an application to the court for a derivative action, he or she could also apply to the court for inspection of company documents, however, for a shareholder who is not an officer or director of the company, application for inspection of documents would be challenging. An applicant would be required to identify with precision the documents to be inspected.

The purpose of this chapter is to review the Australian statutory derivative action and examine the areas of defect in the legislative provisions, placing those defects in the context of the need for innovation and modern approaches. In addition to showing how the system can work around the dated cumbersome and opaque procedures, this chapter will also make some suggestions for reform in order to improve the use of the derivative action and to make it a more effective tool for shareholders. The chapter's structure is as follows: Sec. 12.2 provides a brief history of the common law derivative action. Section 12.3 examines the areas of defect in the Australian statutory derivative action, followed by a discussion in Sec. 12.4 of how shareholders have attempted to avoid the use of the statutory derivative action and how they have turned towards a shareholder class action or an oppression action as an alternative means of seeking remedies. Section 12.5 provides some suggestions for amending the statutory derivative action procedure. Section 12.6 is the conclusion.

12.2 A Brief History of the Common Law Derivative Action

Historically, the rule in *Foss v. Harbottle* was that the company was a proper plaintiff and only the company could sue for any wrong done to the company.[2] However, in practice, a company was unable to bring a derivative action because the wrongdoers were often directors who control the company. These director/wrongdoers could easily prevent the company from pursuing any legal action against themselves.

As a way of overcoming this obstacle, the common law derivative action became an exception to the rule in *Foss v. Harbottle*, which allowed a shareholder to act on behalf of the company in bringing a lawsuit against the wrongdoer, including against the board of directors, provided that the matter was serious enough that warranted a derivative action.[3] Frauds and illegal activities were examples of a serious matter.[4] However, it was not easy to prove either of these, and the success of a court action was heavily dependent on other prior cases with similar fact scenarios. Experience has shown that the common law derivative action was too narrow and too restrictive in its scope for it to have any effective use. Research has shown that minority

[2] *Foss v. Harbottle* (1843) 2 Hare 461; (1843) ER 189.

[3] *Cope v. Butcher* (1996) 20 ACSR 37.

[4] *Prudential Assurance Co Ltd v. Newman Industries Ltd (No.2)* [1981] Ch 257 at 323; *Daniels v. Daniels* [1978] Ch 406 at 414.

shareholders had avoided common law derivative action and opted for other forms of litigation such as an oppression action.[5] This was a key reason for the Australian legislature to abolish the common law derivative action and introduce the statutory version that came into effect on 13th March 2000, which is now located in Part 2 F.1A (ss.236–242) of the CA.

12.3 Defects in the Current Australian Statutory Derivative Action Provisions

There are four main areas of defect in the current Australian statutory derivative action provisions.

12.3.1 The Leave Requirement Under s.237(2) is Unclear

Under s.237, an applicant must apply for leave of the court to bring a derivative action, and if leave is granted, the applicant can then proceed to commence a derivative action on behalf of and in the name of the company. For ease of discussion, s.237(2) is reproduced as follows:

> The Court must grant the application if it is satisfied that:
>
> (a) It is probable that the company will not itself bring the proceedings, or properly take responsibility for them, or for the steps in them; and
> (b) The applicant is acting in good faith; and
> (c) It is in the best interests of the company that the applicant be granted leave; and
> (d) If the applicant is applying for leave to bring proceedings – there is a serious question to be tried; and
> (e) Either:
>
> (i) At least 14 days before making the application, the applicant gave written notice to the company of the intention to apply for leave and of the reasons for applying; or
> (ii) It is appropriate to grant leave even though subparagraph (i) is not satisfied.

Paragraphs (a), (d) and (e) of s.237(2) do not appear to create any problem for a shareholder applying for a derivative action. However, paragraphs (b) and (c) are most difficult to prove to the satisfaction of the court and these warrant further explanation below.

[5] Ian M Ramsay, "An Empirical Study of the Use of the Oppression Remedy" (1999) 27 *Australian Business Law Review* 23–37. Unlike a derivative action which is an action belonging to the company and any award of remedies would go back to the company, a successful plaintiff in an oppression action would expect to pocket all of the remedies awarded by the court.

12.3.1.1 Lack of Clarity in the "Good Faith" Requirement Under s.237(2) (b)

The first defect in the Australian provisions is the lack of clarity in the "good faith" requirement under s.237(2)(b). Although this requirement has been pointed out as necessary in order to prevent an applicant from taking out any personal vengeance or vexatious action,[6] there is, however, no definition of "good faith" in the CA, nor does it provide examples of "bad faith" to show that the applicant has not been acting in good faith. The term "good faith" under s 237(2)(b) is broad and vague, creating uncertainty, in the sense that the term could mean anything to anybody and multiple interpretations are possible. In Canada where the "good faith" provision is also found in its statutory derivative action,[7] one commentator has noted, "I have no idea what this means, and I get the sense that no one else does either".[8] This sentiment is a true reflection of what we now see in Australia in the three cases that follows.

Swansson v RA Pratt Properties Pty Ltd of 2002 is the first significant case on a leave application for a derivative action.[9] In refusing to grant leave, Palmer J provided two signposts for determining whether the shareholder applicant was acting in good faith[10]:

> [I]n my opinion, there are at least two interrelated factors to which the Courts will always have regard in determining whether the good faith requirement of s 237(2)(b) is satisfied. The first is whether the applicant honestly believes that a good cause of action exists and has a reasonable prospect of success. Clearly, whether the applicant honestly holds such a belief would not simply be a matter of bald assertion; the applicant may be disbelieved if no reasonable person in the circumstances could hold that belief. The second factor is whether the applicant is seeking to bring the derivative suit for such a collateral purpose as would amount to an abuse of process.

In other words, the first signpost was whether the applicant had honestly believed that the company had a good cause of action and that the company would have a reasonable prospect of success. The second point was whether the shareholder applicant had any collateral purpose in the proposed derivative action that would amount to an abuse of process. Palmer J then provided a cautionary note that the issue of good faith should not be restricted to those two factors:

> At this early stage in the development of the law on the statutory derivative action created by Pt 2 F.1A it would be unwise to endeavour to state compendiously the considerations to which the courts will have regard in determining whether applicants in all categories … are acting in good faith. *The law will develop incrementally as different factual circumstances come before the courts.*[11]

[6] See Explanatory Memorandum to the CLERP Bill 1998 at [6.36] and [6.37].

[7] See *Ontario Business Corporations Act* 1982, s.245.

[8] Bruce Welling, *Corporate Law in Canada* (2nd ed, Butterworths, 1991) at 528.

[9] *Swansson v RA Pratt Properties Pty Ltd* (2002) 42 ACSR 313.

[10] *Swansson v RA Pratt Properties Pty Ltd* (2002) 42 ACSR 313, at [36].

[11] *Swansson v RA Pratt Properties Pty Ltd* (2002) 42 ACSR 313, at [35], emphasis added. This approach has been followed in a number of subsequent first instance decisions, for example,

The implication of Palmer J's remark is that the term "good faith" has no definitive meaning. The court is required to look beyond the fact and decide from the surrounding circumstances.[12]

The second significant case is the 2010 case, *Vinciguerra v MG Corrosion Consultants Pty Ltd*,[13] where a shareholder applicant was successful in the leave application for a derivative action. A shareholder applicant alleged breaches of directors' duties as a ground for pleading with the court for leave to commence proceedings on behalf of and in the name of the company against the alleged wrong-doers.[14] The defendants on the other hand provided the court with a list of factors to show that the applicant had not acted in good faith when making that leave application, including factors such as[15]:

- the applicant had unreasonably rejected an offer to buy back his shares;
- the applicant had declined to engage in discussion in order to settle the matter; and
- the applicant who owned 30 % of the shares in the company had threatened to wind up the company.

Gilmour J of the Federal Court rejected the defendant's claim, and in granting leave to commence a derivative action, held that the shareholder applicant had satisfied the court with all five criteria under s.237(2), including the good faith requirement.[16] Gilmour J examined the good faith criterion in a different light, not by applying the two tests provided in *Swansson v. R A Pratt Properties Pty Ltd*, but by examining the conduct of both parties, and by "assessing the nature of the allegations and the circumstances out of which [those allegations] arose".[17] He formed the view that both parties were "less than mutually co-operative"[18] and that those allegations were substantiated, and on these bases, the shareholder applicant be granted leave to bring a derivative action in order to resolve these issues. Gilmour J appeared to have played down the good faith requirement and focused on the conduct of both parties and the alleged breaches of the duties in determining whether there was a case for a derivative action.

The third significant and most recent case on the issue of good faith is *Vicad Pty Ltd – Pottie v. Dunkley & Others*,[19] decided in 2011. A shareholder applied to the court for a range of remedies, including an oppression remedy, a winding up order,

---

Carpenter v Pioneer Park Pty Ltd [2004] NSWSC 1007, *Charlton v Baber* (2003) 47ACSR 31 and *Fiduciary Ltd v Morningstar Research Pty Ltd* (2005) 53 ACSR 732.

[12] The NSW Court of Appeal in *Chahwan v Euphoric Pty Ltd* (2008) 65 ACSR 661 (per Tobias JA, with whom Beazley and Bell JJA agreed, at para 69–84) has unanimously supported Palmer J's reasoning.

[13] *Vinciguerra v MG Corrosion Consultants Pty Ltd* [2010] FCA 763.

[14] *Vinciguerra v. MG Corrosion Consultants Pty Ltd* [2010] FCA 763, [para 75, 128, 152, and 153].

[15] *Vinciguerra v. MG Corrosion Consultants Pty Ltd* [2010] FCA 763, [para 30, 47, 70, 76, and 98].

[16] Gilmour J's approach was perhaps consistent with the approach in *Chahwan v. Euphoric Pty Ltd* (2008) 65 ACSR 661where the NSW Court of Appeal [at para 83 per Tobias JA] noted that the onus was on "the applicant to satisfy the court that ... he or she is acting in good faith".

[17] *Vinciguerra v. MG Corrosion Consultants Pty Ltd* [2010] FCA 763, [para 54, 56].

[18] *Vinciguerra v. MG Corrosion Consultants Pty Ltd* [2010] FCA 763, [para 64].

[19] *Vicad Pty Ltd – Pottie v. Dunkley & Ors* [2011] NSWSC 166.

and in the alternative a derivative action to restore the value of the shares in the company. In granting leave to commence a derivative action, Wade J of the NSW Supreme Court made a powerful statement which could be translated as a *turning point* from the "collateral purpose" test handed down in *Swansson v. R A Pratt Properties Pty Ltd*. Wade J said[20]:

> … a derivative action sought to be instituted by a current shareholder for the purpose of restoring value to his or her shares in the company would not be an abuse of process even if the applicant is spurred on by intense animosity, even malice, against the defendant.

The applicant in this case was a current shareholder of the company. Other shareholders were her brother and his son, her sister and her mother who was the surviving spouse of the founder of the company. The court found that the relationship amongst the siblings was beyond repairs, and given the shareholder applicant had the support of her sister to commence legal proceedings[21]; Wade J had no difficulty in concluding that the shareholder applicant, who sought leave to bring a derivative action against her brother and his son for breach of fiduciary and statutory duties, was:

> …acting in good faith (even though she may bear some personal animosity towards her brother and even though she may have commenced these proceedings due to dissatisfaction with the succession arrangements within the family…[22]

In summary, the above discussion has shown at least three different approaches to the "good faith" requirement under s.237(2)(b). The approach taken by the court in *Vicad Pty Ltd – Pottie v. Dunkley & Others* (decided in 2011) was a clear departure from the approach of Palmer J in *Swansson v. R A Pratt Properties Pty Ltd* (decided in 2002). Palmer J held that the court would refuse to grant leave to commence a derivative action where an applicant was found to have a collateral purpose in the leave application. The divergent view from Wade J in the 2011 case was that the shareholder applicant could still be successful for leave for a derivative action *even if* her motive was malice and fuelled with intense animosity. The third approach was from *Vinciguerra v. MC Corrosion Consultants Pty Ltd* (a 2010 case). In that case, the court ignored the good faith issue and focused on examining the conduct of *both* the shareholder applicant and the defendant. The court assessed the weight of the allegations made and the evidence presented to the court to decide whether the conduct of the shareholder in applying for leave to bring a derivative action had been reasonable in all circumstances.

---

[20] *Vicad Pty Ltd – Pottie v. Dunkley & Ors* [2011] NSWSC 166, at para 43.

[21] The mother who was the other shareholder and director of the corporation was shown to have suffered from dementia and there was no evidence that she attended the board meeting to approve certain matters arranged by the defendants. However, the court found no difficulty in allowing the shareholder applicant to bring a derivative action, as the other shareholder had agreed to such action.

[22] *Vicad Pty Ltd – Pottie v. Dunkley & Ors* [2011] NSWSC 166, at para 58.

12.3.1.2 The Term "In the Best Interests of the Company" Under s.237(2)(c) is Unclear

The second area of defect in the Australian statutory derivative action is about the need of an applicant to convince the court that the proposed derivative action applied for is "in the best interests of the company" under s.237(2)(c). Similar to the good faith requirement, the CA has not attempted to define the expression "in the best interests of the company". This lack of clarity under s.237(2)(c) could be explained in the following ways.

First, the question to ask is, what is a "company"? The traditional view is that a company is defined to mean "shareholders as a whole", meaning that ownership of the company belongs to the shareholders collectively.[23] In modern day corporate law, in addition to the shareholders' interests in the company, the company may also feel compelled to have other corporate social responsibilities towards other stakeholders, such as employees, customers, suppliers, and even the general community, the environment and other socio-economic and political forces. The difficulty for a shareholder applicant is that he or she may also need to satisfy the court that the proposed derivative action is in the best interests of not only the shareholders but also all other stakeholders. This point has not been raised in court, but the society is gradually putting pressure on all companies, large and small, to accept some form of corporate social responsibilities for their stakeholders.[24]

The second difficulty relates to the combined reading of s. 237(2)(c) *and* s. 237(3) because subsection (3) also refers to "in the best interests of the company". Under the current formulation of the statutory derivative action, s. 237(3) provides a presumption that directors have acted properly in discharging their duties and that the decisions they have made for the company were the correct and proper decisions. Under s. 237(3), the onus is on the shareholder applicants to rebut that presumption when proving that the leave application for a derivative action is "in the best interests of the company". Section 237(3) reads as follows:

> A rebuttable presumption that granting leave is not in the best interests of the company arises if it is established that:
>
> (a) ...
> (b) ...
> (c) All of the directors who participated in that decision:
>
> (i) Acted in good faith for a proper purpose; and
> (ii) Did not have a material personal interest in the decision; and
> (iii) informed themselves of the subject matter of the decision to the extent they reasonably believed to be appropriate; and
> (iv) Rationally believed that the decision was in the best interests of the company.

---

[23] *Percival v. Wright* [1902] 2 Ch 421.

[24] See, for example, the reports from: Parliamentary Joint Committee on Corporations and Financial Services, *Report on Corporate Social Responsibility: Managing Risk and Creating Value* (June 2006, Canberra); and Corporations and Market Advisory Committee (CAMAC), *Report on the Social Responsibility of Corporations* (December 2006, Canberra).

> The director's belief that the decision was in the best interests of the company is a rational one unless the belief is one that no reasonable person in their position would hold.

Section 237(3) is worded similar to the business judgment rule in s.180(2) which provides a defence mechanism for directors and officers of the company who are alleged to be in breach of their duty of care and diligence under s.180(1). The existence of s.237(3) means that directors are presumed innocent of any wrongdoing in the company and the onus is on the applicant applying for leave to bring a derivative action to rebut that presumption. In other words, s.237(3) is adding a further obstacle on the applicant for leave to bring a derivative action. For example, when a company is in a state of good health, with all its financial records in place, it is unlikely that an applicant applying for leave to commence a derivative action would be able to rebut the presumption under s.237(3). Rebutting the presumption may be easier when the company is in financial distress or the share price of the company has dropped, in which case a derivative action applied for could be in the best interests of the company. *Vicad Pty Ltd – Pottie v. Dunkley & Others* is an example where the shareholder applicant attempted to restore the share price that had dropped considerably because of the alleged misconduct and breach of fiduciary duties on the part of the directors. For an event so drastic to occur before the leave application can be approved by the court for a derivative action may prove to be futile if the aim is to rescue the company and claim back any damages the company may have suffered as a result of the wrongdoing by the directors or officers of the company.

The third difficulty with s.237(2)(c) is the uncertainty in the amount of evidence required to demonstrate that a derivative action applied for is "in the best interests of the company". There is no fixed rule for establishing "best interests". What is "best" for one person may not be good enough for another person. Proof of "best interests" is a hit and miss case and much is dependent on the attitude of the court on the standard accepted by it. In *Talisman Technologies Inc v. Old Electronic Switching Pty Ltd*, the court has stated that the best interests of the company must be "from the perspective of the company" and not from the applicant.[25]

In *Swannson v. RA Pratt Properties Pty Ltd*, Palmer J provided some examples to assist with the definition of the term "in the best interests of the company":

(i) It may be "relevant to take into account the effect of the proposed litigation" if the company involved as a plaintiff is a "closely held family company" but not if the company is publicly listed.[26]
(ii) If there are other means in compensating the shareholder applicant, "… if the applicant can achieve the desire result in proceedings in his or her own name, [then] it is not in the best interests of the company to be involved in litigation at all".[27]

---

[25] *Talisman Technologies Inc v. Old Electronic Switching Pty Ltd* [2001] QSC 324 at para 31, where Mullins J refers to the term "best interests" as requiring an objective test.

[26] *Swansson v. R A Pratt Properties Pty Ltd* (2002) 42 ACSR 313, para 57.

[27] *Swansson v. R A Pratt Properties Pty Ltd* (2002) 42 ACSR 313, para 59.

(iii) "... the ability of the defendant to meet at least a substantial part of any judgment in favour of the company in the proposed derivative action [is important to] ascertain whether the action would be of any practical benefit to the company."[28]

The court in *Vicad Pty Ltd – Pottie v. Dunkley & Others* was mindful of the costs being blown out of proportion and noted that some consideration must be given on "whether the company would be prejudiced by being exposed to the costs and expenses of litigation and the risks of an adverse costs order".[29] In *Vicad Pty Ltd – Pottie v. Dunkley & Others*, the Court granted leave to the applicant to bring a derivative action on the proviso that the applicant would give an undertaking that she would indemnify the company against all costs, charges and expenses incidental to the bringing and continuation of the derivative action. The Court also noted that the applicant should not be denied of the right to seek reimbursement through the company in the event that the proceedings against the defendants were successful.

In summary, one could argue that the inconsistencies in the approaches of the courts stem from both the unknown magnitude of the "good faith" requirement in s. 237(2)(b) and the lack of clarity in the need to prove that the derivative action applied for is "in the best interests of the company" in s.237(2)(c). There is no guideline in the CA to assist the judiciary in clarifying the "good faith" and the "best interests" requirements. Currently, there is no appeal case to the High Court of Australia on s.237. These factors weigh heavily on the minds of the shareholders in making a decision on whether to apply for leave to commence a derivative action. It is not surprising to say that the Australian statutory derivative action provisions have been under-utilised. When statutory derivative action was introduced into Australia in March 2000, Thai argued that the derivative action procedure under Part 2 F.1A of the CA was merely "a reformulation of the common law position" and projected that it could never be popular in its current form.[30] That projection has proved accurate when examining the survey results carried out by Ramsay and Saunders, who noted that of the 31 leave applications for a statutory derivative action in the period of March 2000 to August 2005, only 19 of those leave applications had been successful in getting leave from the court.[31] This figure is relatively low when comparing with for example the number of oppression action cases.[32]

---

[28] *Swansson v. R A Pratt Properties Pty Ltd* (2002) 42 ACSR 313, para 60.

[29] *Vicad Pty Ltd – Pottie v. Dunkley & Ors* [2011] NSWSC 166, at para 59.

[30] Lang Thai, "How popular are statutory derivative actions in Australia? Comparisons with USA, Canada, and New Zealand", (2002) 30 *Australian Business Law Review* 118–137, at 136 and 137.

[31] Ian Ramsay and Benjamin Saunders, "Litigation by Shareholders and Directors: An Empirical Study of the Australian Statutory Derivative Action" (2006) 6 *Journal of Corporate Law Studies* 397–446.

[32] Ian Ramsay, "An empirical study of the use of the oppression remedy" (1999) 27 *Australian Business Law Review* 23–37. The term "oppression remedy" or "oppression action" is explained in Sect. 12.4 of this chapter.

12.3.2 Uncertainty in the Recovery of Costs Under s.242

The third area of defect in the Australian statutory derivative action is the uncertainty in the recovery of costs and this is a major concern for all shareholders. Section 242 is the only provision in the CA that deals with the costs of the leave application for a derivative action. Section 242 reads as follows:

> The Court may at any time make any orders it considers appropriate about the costs of [the applicant, the company or any other party] … in relation to proceedings brought or intervened in with leave under section 237 …

The discussion below highlights the conflicting views of the judges on s.242.

The first controversial case to consider is *Roach v. Winnote Pty Ltd.*[33] In this case, the shareholder was successful in the leave application to bring a derivative action under Part 2 F.1A of the CA, but was unsuccessful in the request for costs to be paid by the company. Barrett J of the NSW Supreme Court gave his reason as follows[34]:

> It is thus clear that courts are concerned in some cases to ensure that the person granted leave under s.237 should bear, either wholly or in part, the burden of the company's costs in relation to the proceedings which that person is to represent the company. Measures of that kind are intended to protect the company's financial resources and are merely part of the domestic arrangements within the company as to the basis on which the person concerned will be permitted to act for it.

In another derivative action case, *Sub Rosa Holding Pty Ltd v. Salsa Sudada Production Pty Ltd.*,[35] Barrett J attempted to insist that his approach on the interpretation of s.242 was the right approach. He noted[36]:

> It is common place for a person given permission to pursue a claim on behalf of a company to be required, in the first instance, to bear the burden of costs.

An opposing view comes from *Woods v. Link Golf Tasmania Pty Ltd.*[37] In this case, Finkelstein J of the Federal Court expressed a strong opposition to Barrett J's approach in the earlier decisions. Finkelstein J stated that "to be quite frank, it is by no means clear why this general approach … has been adopted.[38] In making a costs order against the company, requiring the company to pay for the "fair and reasonable costs" of running the derivative action, Finkelstein J further stated[39]:

> The purpose of permitting a person to bring an action in the name of the company is to prevent conduct which involves some element of harm. In most cases the wrongdoer will be in control of the company. That will be the reason the company itself is not bringing the action. … In those circumstances, I can think of no reason why the company should not

---

[33] *Roach v. Winnote Pty Ltd* [2006] NSWSC 231; (2006) 57 ACSR 138.

[34] *Roach v. Winnote Pty Ltd* [2006] NSWSC 231; (2006) 57 ACSR 138, [at para 29].

[35] *Sub Rosa Holding Pty Ltd v. Salsa Sudada Production Pty Ltd* [2006] NSWSC 916.

[36] *Sub Rosa Holding Pty Ltd v. Salsa Sudada Production Pty Ltd* [2006] NSWSC 916 [at para 49].

[37] *Woods v. Links Golf Tasmania Pty Ltd* [2010] FCA 570.

[38] *Woods v. Links Golf Tasmania Pty Ltd* [2010] FCA 570, [at para 8].

[39] *Woods v. Links Golf Tasmania Pty Ltd* [2010] FCA 570, [at paras 9–12].

bear the costs. ... [but] this is not to suggest that a costs order will be made in all cases ... If a costs order is made and at any later time it turns out the claim is unmeritorious, the costs order can be recalled.

Finkelstein J's decision to order the company to pay for the initial costs of the derivative action is not inconsistent with old common law practices in derivative action cases. In *Wallersteiner v. Moir (No.2)*, the court allowed a derivative action and ordered the company to pay for the shareholder's costs of the derivative proceedings.[40] In *Farrow v. Registrar of Building Societies*, an order was made initially requiring the company to pay for the costs of the derivative action at common law. However, that action was later found to have no merits after a discovery was made at trial, and thus the court ordered the plaintiff to discontinue the derivative action and issued an order to recall the original costs order, making the plaintiff ultimately liable for reimbursement of all costs.[41]

The decisions on costs from Barrett J and Finkelstein J were both first instance cases, and thus both are non-binding on other future cases. However, this is a concern for shareholder applicants planning to have a derivative action as there is no certainty on who will be liable for costs and expenses in the bringing of a statutory derivative action and the continuation thereof. What is certain is that shareholder applicants are liable to bear all costs and expenses if the leave application is unsuccessful, or if the leave application is successful, the actual derivative action may have to be terminated to save from further losses. There is no provision in the CA that permits a shareholder applicant to claim for reimbursement from fellow shareholders.

12.3.3 Application for Inspection of Company Documents Under s.247A is Problematic

The fourth area of defeat in the Australian statutory derivative action is the uncertainty in getting an order from the court for inspection of company documents under s.247A. Section 247A permits a shareholder to apply to the court for inspection of company documents, however under s.247A(5), the applicant is required to prove "good faith" in making that application and is required to prove that the inspection is "for a purpose connected with ... s.237 [ie, statutory derivative action] and that it is for a "proper purpose". There is no definition of "good faith" or "proper purpose" in the CA.

In Theory, s.247A may be useful if a shareholder applicant is not already an officer or director of the company and is in need of certain tangible documents or information from the company to determine whether to proceed with the leave application for a derivative action. However, in practice, request for inspection of

---

[40] *Wallersteiner v. Moir (No.2)* [1975] QB 373.

[41] *Farrow v. Registrar of Building Societies* [1991] 2 VR 589, 595.

company documents can be challenging for a shareholder applicant. While s.247A(5) expressly states that applying for leave to commence a derivative action could be a "proper purpose", there is no certainty that the court will grant leave to inspect company documents. Even if the court grants leave to inspect certain documents, directors who are in control of the company could still find ways to prevent or delay the release of highly sensitive information or information that would be damaging to their position.[42]

There are numerous cases on s.247A and judicial decisions on whether to grant leave to inspect company documents are diverse. Discussion of these cases is beyond the scope of this chapter. However, as a summary, in some cases, the courts have limited the scope of inspection of documents under s.247A.[43] In other cases, the courts have denied the shareholders' applications for inspection under s.247A on the ground that the applicant lacked "special interest" in the subject matter,[44] and on the ground that the type of inspection applied for was too broad or too general and that such application was made not for a proper purpose for a derivative action.[45] The courts have also rejected the shareholders' applications for inspection on the ground that those applicants had not provided sufficient evidence to demonstrate the need for inspection and had not fully identified the reasons for inspection.[46]

Overall, it is extremely difficult for shareholders to utilise the inspection provision under s.247A.

12.4 Ways in Avoiding the Use of Statutory Derivative Action in Australia

12.4.1 Availability of Funded Shareholder Class Action in Australia

As noted in the above discussion, statutory derivative action has not been popular as a source of remedy for shareholders. The strict leave requirement under s.237,[47] the uncertainty in the recovery of costs under s.242, and the difficulty in getting leave

[42] Arad Reisberg, *Derivative Actins and Corporate Governance: Theory and Operation* (Oxford University Press, 2007), Chapter 3, pp. 85–86.

[43] See, for example, *Majestic Resources NL v Caveat Pty Ltd* [2004] WASCA 201, and *London City Equities Ltd v Penrice Soda Holdings Ltd* [2011] FCA 674.

[44] See, for example, *Hanks v Admiralty Resources NL (No.2)* [2011] FCA 1464 at [24].

[45] See, *Smartec Capital Pty Ltd v Centro Properties Ltd* [2011] NSWSC 495 at [66]-[67].

[46] See, for example, in *Keenfern Pty Ltd v Thorlock International Ltd* (2002) 20 ACLC 1,322 at 1,323, the court refused to allow inspection of documents because it found that the information to be acquired was for the applicant to decide whether to file for winding up of the company and this was noted by the court as an improper purpose. For further reading on s.247A, see: C Mantziaris, "The member's right to inspect the company books: *Corporations Act*, s.247A" (2009) 83 *Australian Law Journal* 621–640.

[47] In particular, in relation to the requirement of proof of "good faith" under s.237(2)(b) and the requirement of proof of "in the best interests of the company" under s.237(2)(c).

from the court to inspect company books and documents under s.247A have made it all too difficult for shareholders to apply for a statutory derivative action. Instead, many shareholders from large and major companies have turned to class actions to seek compensation.

Class action in Australia is governed under Part IVA of the *Federal Court of Australia Act* 1974 (C'th) ("FCAA"). In Australia, a class action is a lawsuit that enables seven or more persons who have a claim or claims from the same similar or related circumstances to come together as a representative of the class to sue a defendant or defendants.[48] The class action procedure in Australia is non-specific and can be used by any person in any context, including shareholders of the company. Shareholder class actions have become increasingly popular in Australia for two good reasons.

First, there is the relative ease in the use of the class action procedure under Part IVA of the FCAA, in particular leave of the court is not required to commence a class action.[49] Under s.33 J of the FCAA, the class action procedure in Australia has an "opt out" mechanism,[50] which means that a representative who has agreed to initiate a class action is in fact representing not only his or her or its own interests but also the interests of all other members, both known and unknown to him or her or it. These other members must also have a common claim or claims and their circumstances must be the same, similar or related. Members who become aware of being in that class action, whether through media or through other means, may "opt out" of that class by filing in court a notice to "opt out" if they do not wish to be a part of that class proceeding.[51]

Second, there is the relative ease in getting finance from a commercial litigation funder for a class action. Currently, as far as known, there is no court case where shareholders have been successful in getting funding support from a commercial litigation funder purely for a statutory derivative action. This is not to assume that shareholders have not attempted to approach a litigation funder for this purpose. It is more likely that a commercial litigation funder has been *unwilling* to fund a statutory derivative action owing to the difficulty with the leave requirement and the uncertainty in the costs provision.

---

[48] Federal Court of Australia Act 1974 (C'th), s.33C.

[49] The first notable case on shareholder class action was in *Dorajay Pty Ltd v. Aristocrat Leisure Ltd* (2005) 147 FCR 394 and in [2009] FCA 19, where the proceedings commenced in 2003 and the court handed down its decision and reasons, followed by an out of court settlement with the approval of the court in 2009 in the sum of $144.5 million. Analysis of this case and other subsequent cases may be found in Lang Thai, "Is there a need to reform the corporate class action procedure in Australia?" (2011) 8 *Macquarie Journal of Business Law* 134–160.

[50] This is very different from the American opt in class action, where members generally need to consent to being represented in the class action.

[51] For a further discussion of the "opt out" mechanism and the ineffectiveness and the problem in controlling the class size and the whereabouts of the members, see Lang Thai, "Is there a need to reform the corporate class action procedure in Australia?" (2011) 8 *Macquarie Journal of Business Law* 134–160.

An interesting point to note is that although the High Court of Australia has approved the use of commercial litigation funding in 2006[52] and again in 2009,[53] the litigation funding industry and commercial litigation funders are still largely unregulated in Australia. On 12 July 2013, the Parliament in Australia has put into effect some legislative provisions to deal with issues relating to the potential conflicts of interests that may arise when a litigation funder is involved with a plaintiff and the plaintiff's lawyers.[54] However, the legislation does not address issues relating to the earnings of the litigation funders or the percentage of compensation or settlement sum for which litigation funders may be entitled to retain. This means that a commercial litigation funder is free to impose any fees and conditions it likes on a plaintiff. A commercial litigation funder is generally a corporate entity that agrees to assist a plaintiff by providing finance for a court action, and in return, the litigation funder insists on retaining an agreed percentage of compensation awarded by the court or any earnings received from an out of court settlement. If a plaintiff decides to withdraw a court action, the litigation funder can insist on the return of the fund with interests.[55]

A commercial litigation funder is more willing to fund a class action than a statutory derivative action possibly because of these four main reasons:

(a) Where there is a large pool of shareholders in the company, in the range of hundreds or thousands of shareholders, a litigation funder could expect to receive from individual shareholders a large percentage of profits at the end of a successful class action[56];
(b) Unlike a statutory derivative action, there is no hurdle for commencing a class action;
(c) In a successful shareholder class action, and similar to many other civil litigation, the lead plaintiff is expected to seek recovery of costs from the unsuccessful defendant, and the recovery of these costs will ultimately go back to the litigation funder who initially funded the class action; and
(d) In a shareholder class action, the defendant is the "company", which means that the litigation funder is very well aware that the company can "afford" to pay for

[52] *Campbells Cash and Carry v. Fostif Pty Ltd* (2006) 229 CLR 386.

[53] *Jeffrey & Katauskas Pty Ltd v. SST Consulting Pty Ltd* (2009) 239 CLR 75.

[54] The Conflicts Rules applicable to litigation funding arrangements are imposed by the Federal Parliament through the enactment of the *Corporations Amendment Regulation* 2012 (No.6), which came into force on 12 July 2013 and is now located in Part 7.6 of the *Corporations Regulations* 2001 (C'th).

[55] For further discussion on commercial litigation funding and why government intervention and regulation are necessary, see L. Thai, "Commercial litigation funding: The need to impose regulations to improve the outcome of the shareholder class actions" (2011) 4 *Journal of the Australian Law Teachers Association* 1–16.

[56] Litigation funders are only willing to provide funding where there is a large pool of shareholders from a large public company; this is how a litigation funder makes profits from individual shareholders in the one class action. A litigation funder is reluctant to fund a case when there is only a handful of shareholders in a small company, the only alternative for these shareholders other than the statutory derivative action is to proceed with an oppression action.

the compensation. Thus after a period of protracted litigation and with some pressure placed on the defendant, the directors (including those wrongdoers in the company) will tend to agree to an out of court settlement, as seen in many of the shareholder class action cases.[57]

12.4.2 Availability of Oppression Action

If shareholders are unable to obtain funding support from a commercial litigation funder for a shareholder class action because the pool of shareholders in a company is not large enough, then an alternative for shareholders would be to rely on Part 2 F.1 of the CA, commonly known amongst corporate lawyers as an "oppression action" or an "unfair prejudice action".

Under s.232, which is located within Part 2 F.1 of the CA, the grounds for commencing an oppression action are when a shareholder can show that the conduct of a company's affairs is contrary to the interests of the company as a whole, or is oppressive, unfairly prejudicial or unfairly discriminatory. The conduct may affect shareholders in their capacity as shareholders or in any other capacity. The conduct of the company's affairs may comprise an actual act or proposed act or an omission by or on behalf of a company.

An oppression action has been very popular among shareholders of small and medium sized companies.[58] This is because leave of the court is not required in an oppression action, and if there is a successful outcome, any remedy awarded by the court will be awarded to the shareholder plaintiff personally and not to the company.

When a shareholder plaintiff seeks relief through an oppression action, the court has a broad general power to decide on the most appropriate remedy. The list of remedies available to a successful shareholder plaintiff includes regulating the conduct of the company's affairs in the future, compelling the company to purchase the shares held by the plaintiff, ordering the company to amend its constitution, winding up the company, or restraining an offending director from engaging in certain conduct.[59] The flexibility in the oppression action, that is, no statutory leave requirement and the remedy awarded by the court is personal to the plaintiff, is a further reason for shareholders to avoid a statutory derivative action. In short, there are no procedural obstacles in an oppression action.

---

[57] See, for example, *Kirby v Centro Properties Limited (No 6)* [2012] FCA 650 (19 June 2012) which was the latest shareholder class action case with about 6000 shareholders involved where the Federal Court of Australia (Middleton J) on 19 June 2012 had approved $200 million out of court settlement, the largest settlement figure in history in shareholder class action; see also *Dorajay Pty Ltd v. Aristocrat Leisure Ltd* (2005) 147 FCR 394 and in [2009] FCA 19; and *Dawson Nominees Pty Ltd v. Multiplex Ltd* [2007] FCA 1061.

[58] Ian Ramsay, "An empirical study of the use of the oppression remedy" (1999) 27 *Australian Business Law Review* 23–37; see also Richard Brockett, "The valuation of minority shareholdings in an oppression context – a contemporary review" (2012) 24 *Bond Law Review* 101–124.

[59] Section 233 of the *Corporations Act* 2001 (C'th).

12.5 Suggestions for Reform

For statutory derivative action to become an effective tool for shareholders to seek remedy, reform to Part 2 F.1A of the CA is necessary. This part of the chapter provides some suggestions for reform.

12.5.1 Clarifying the Terms "Good Faith" and "In the Best Interests of the Company"

The terms "good faith" and "in the best interests of the company" in ss.237(2)(b) and (c) are arguably the two most difficult criteria for shareholder applicants to establish in court for leave to commence a derivative action. Both of these criteria are subjective and vague and multiple interpretations are possible. If it is not possible to remove these two criteria because of the need to ensure that the derivative action applied for by the applicant is meritorious and not vexatious or malicious, then there must be examples contained in Part 2 F.1A of the CA to assist the court and the parties in understanding the scope and magnitude of these criteria. Examples of "good faith" and "best interests" could be in the form of a list placed *within* Part 2 F.1A to avoid any confusion with other provisions outside Part 2 F.1A.

Currently, in a leave application for a derivative action, the onus is on the applicant to prove why he or she deserves leave of the court to commence a court action on behalf of and in the name of the company. The focus is not on the offending director because there is a presumption under s.237(3) that the alleged offender has made a good business judgment. In one sense, the presumption of good business judgment in s.237(3) operates as a defence mechanism for the alleged offenders. In order to improve the use of the statutory derivative action in Australia, the presumption in s.237(3) needs to be removed. Instead, if an offending director is being sued for misconduct or for mismanagement of the company, the alleged offender should be compelled to play an *active* role in defending within a given timeframe and at the early stage of the leave application proceeding. There needs to be a provision to allow the offending director to file a notice in court to set aside the leave application on the ground that the derivative action applied for is either frivolous, vexatious or without merit. This is equivalent to the general civil procedure rules where a defendant has an opportunity to file what is known as a notice of "defence".

12.5.2 Amending the Costs Provision

The costs provision under s.242 of the CA should be removed and be reserved till the end of the case and be determined in the ordinary manner like all other civil cases depending on the outcome of the derivative action (if granted by the court). In the alternative, there should be a default option requiring the company to meet the costs of the derivative proceedings subject to a successful outcome in the leave application. If the statutory criteria for leave are met, indicating that the court believes that there is a strong prospect of success in the derivative action, s.242 should be modified to enable the court to make an order requiring the company to indemnify the applicant in every case. If the prospective costs, relative to the benefits of the action, are considered too high, this could be considered as part of the substantive test for the granting of leave rather than as a reason to deny a costs order on just and equitable grounds. Further if a derivative action that has been granted leave later turns out to have no merits, then in fairness to the company, the original costs order made against the company could be recalled and the applicant of that leave application be made liable for reimbursement of all costs and expenses.[60]

In the author's view, there is no prospect of the Australian statutory derivative action becoming a significant remedy in the hands of those who apply for leave for these derivative actions to be instituted, unless the risk of costs are reduced considerably for the initiating applicants. There are enough other safeguards to prevent frivolous and vexatious actions, in particular the discretion of the court in granting leave under s.237 that such proceedings could be instituted. There is no need to impose additional burden on the applicants with a costs provision that contains so much uncertainty in the wording.

12.5.3 Amending the Inspection of Document Provision

As noted in the above discussion, a shareholder who applies to the court to bring a statutory derivative action under Part 2 F.1A of the CA may also be permitted to apply for inspection of company books and documents under s.247A, on the proviso that the request for inspection is made in "good faith" and for a "proper purpose". Section 247A(5) provides that making an application to the court for a derivative action could be considered as a "proper purpose". However, there are inconsistencies in the judicial reasoning on s.247A, with many applicants being unable to obtain a full inspection order because of their inability to specify precisely the documents for inspection.

It should be noted that shareholders who are an outsider of the company, that is who are not an officer or director of the company, would find it extremely difficult to pin point the exact title of the documents to be inspected. The court in one recent case has also insisted that the applicant must prove "special interest" for inspecting company documents, an interest that is above the interests of all other shareholders.[61] One way of easing this burden on the shareholder applicant could be to remove

[60] See *Woods v. Links Golf Tasmania Pty Ltd* [2010] FCA 570, (at para 9–12, per Finkelstein J); *Farrow v. Registrar of Building Societies* [1991] 2 VR 589, 595; and *Wallersteiner v. Moir (No.2)* [1975] QB 373.

[61] *Hanks v Admiralty Resources NL (No.2)* [2011] FCA 1464 at [24].

the need to prove "good faith" under s.247A and replace it for a list of generic documents that the applicant may be able to inspect if the applicant simultaneously applies for leave to bring a statutory derivative action. A presumption should be made that if an applicant is willing to spend money on applying for leave of the court to bring a statutory derivative action and the applicant has proven to the satisfaction of the court for leave, then that should be sufficient proof that the applicant is acting in good faith when requesting for inspection of documents.

12.6 Conclusion

The statutory derivative action was a major development in Australia in March 2000. However, the provisions have been of limited use. The main cause of this is the lack of clarity in the leave requirement and the uncertainty in the costs provision coupled with the difficulty in getting access to company documents. Instead, many shareholders have turned to funded class actions as these class actions do not require leave of the court to commence and there is the relative ease in getting funding support from an external commercial litigation funder. If shareholders are unable to get funding from a litigation funder because the pool of shareholders is small in a small proprietary company, then an oppression action appears to have been an alternative popular choice. In an oppression action, leave of the court is not required, and if successful, any remedy awarded by the court is personal to the shareholder plaintiff and is not shared with other shareholders.

This chapter has highlighted some suggestions for law reform. It is hoped that these suggestions will improve the use of the statutory derivative action and provide a more meaningful remedy for both minority shareholders and other officers of the company who have a genuine best interest in the company. Without such reform, the recent history of these statutory derivative actions in Australia has shown that the applicants, such as minority shareholders, are in no better position than the previous shareholders under the old common law rule on derivative action. Shareholders will continue to avoid the use of the statutory derivative action and will continue to lean towards either a shareholder class action if the pool of shareholders is large enough to attract litigation funding support or an oppression action if the company has only a small pool of shareholders and if shareholders are not able to obtain external funding.

Chapter 13
Dynamism in U.S. Pleading Standards: Rules, Interpretation, and Implementation

Jeffrey E. Thomas

13.1 Introduction

In the United States, a common law jurisdiction with a long-standing and robust doctrine of judicial review, the courts are powerful and have significant independence. Notwithstanding the proliferation of legal codes adopted by Federal and State legislatures, the power of the courts to interpret (or construct or construe) statutes and rules gives the courts a major role. This role is substantial even when rules are clear and adopted through legitimate means. The power and independence of U.S. court creates dynamism in U.S. law. By "dynamism" I mean rapid, and sometimes unpredictable, changes. My focus here is on the courts, which can create rapid and radical changes to what otherwise appears to be a static and established rule. Somewhat ironically, however, the very same judicial power and independence that creates change operates to moderate it. Courts at different levels use their own power and independence in response to judicial changes and thereby may moderate radical changes. Some of this moderation comes through adherence to stare decisis, but U.S. courts may aggressively interpret judicial decisions so as to avoid or modify precedential effects.

This chapter explores the dynamic nature of U.S. law in the context of the rule for pleading a complaint in Federal court. The rule was adopted through legitimate means and was construed consistently for many years, but in a last few years the Supreme Court adopted a radical interpretation of the rule to substantially alter pleading requirements. It did so in a pair of cases through a common law technique

J.E. Thomas (✉)
UMKC School of Law, 5100 Rockhill Road, Kansas City, MO 64110, USA
e-mail: thomasje@umkc.edu

C.B. Picker, G.I. Seidman (eds.), *The Dynamism of Civil Procedure - Global Trends and Developments*, Ius Gentium: Comparative Perspectives on Law and Justice 48, DOI 10.1007/978-3-319-21981-3_13

rather than through the rule-making process it overseas for modification of the rules of civil procedure.

Rule 8 (a) of the Federal Rules of Civil Procedure (FRCP) provides:

CLAIM FOR RELIEF. A pleading that states a claim for relief must contain:

(1) a short and plain statement of the grounds for the court's jurisdiction, unless the court already has jurisdiction and the claim needs no new jurisdictional support;
(2) a short and plain statement of the claim showing that the pleader is entitled to relief; and
(3) a demand for the relief sought, which may include relief in the alternative or different types of relief.

This rule represents "notice pleading," whereby the defendant is put on notice of the general nature of the claim with the understanding that a defendant can learn the particulars of the claim through pre-trial discovery.[1] For well over 50 years, this requirement has been liberally construed. The classic statement of the standard for what constituted enough for notice was from the case of *Conley v. Gibson*[2]: "a complaint should not be dismissed for failure to state a claim unless it appears beyond doubt that the plaintiff can prove no set of facts in support of his claim which would entitle him to relief."[3]

In 2009, the U.S. Supreme Court adopted a much stricter standard for pleading. In the case of *Ashcroft v. Iqbal*,[4] the court explicitly adopted the standard of "plausibility" for pleadings. To survive a motion to dismiss, the complaint "must contain sufficient factual matter, accepted as true, to 'state a claim to relief that is **plausible** on its face.'"[5] (emphasis added) To be "plausible" the complaint must include "factual content that allows the court to draw the reasonable inference that the defendant is liable for the misconduct alleged."[6] In assessing the plausibility of the complaint, a court is to take a two-pronged approach. First, the court should identify "pleadings that, because they are no more than conclusions, are not entitled to the assumption of truth."[7] The conclusions, while they cannot be the basis for the complaint, may provide a "framework."[8] Second, after stripping the complaint of its conclusions, the court is to assess the "well-pleaded factual allegations" to "determine whether they plausibly give rise to an entitlement to relief."[9]

This radical shift in the pleading standards illustrates the Supreme Court's role in the dynamism of U.S. Civil Procedure law. The Court, in interpreting and applying

[1] *See* Wright, Charles Alan and Mary Kay Kane. 2011. Law of Federal Courts, § 68, at 467.

[2] 355 U.S. 41 (1957).

[3] 355 U.S. at 45–46.

[4] 556 U.S. 662 (2009).

[5] 556 U.S. at 678 (quoting *Bell Atlantic Corp. v. Twombly*, 550 U.S. 544, 570 (2007)).

[6] 556 U.S. at 678 (citing *Bell Atlantic Corp. v. Twombly*, 550 U.S. 544, 570 (2007)).

[7] 556 U.S. at 679.

[8] 556 U.S. at 679.

[9] 556 U.S. at 679.

Rule 8, radically altered the standard to be applied to a motion to dismiss.[10] This shift was made by judicial fiat, without following the various rule-making procedures normally required to amend the Federal Rules of Civil Procedure. The dynamism in U.S. procedure law is also reflected by the lower courts' reaction to this new pleading standard. The power of the courts allowed the Supreme Court to adopt this new standard in response to individual cases without going through the rule-making procedure required to alter the text of the Federal rule. At the same time, the power of the lower courts to interpret the new standard allowed them to moderate the impact of the new standard. Some courts adopted abroad interpretation, some a narrow interpretation, and some courts took a middle ground approach.

This chapter will start with a brief historical background on the Federal Rules of Civil Procedure and the statute that authorized the rules, the Rules Enabling Act. It will then provide a more detailed description of the Court's decision in *Iqbal* and the immediate genealogy and policy purposes behind that opinion. The third part of this chapter will analyze the reaction of the lower federal courts and the dynamism reflected in the different ways that the courts reacted.

13.2 Setting the Stage: Background and History of the Federal Rules of Civil Procedure

The Federal Rules of Civil Procedure were originally adopted in 1937 under the authority of the Rules Enabling Act, which was passed in 1934.[11] Prior to the Rules Enabling Act, the Federal courts relied on the pleading practices from the common law for legal actions. Although the Federal courts had authority to use more standardized State procedural rules that began to be adopted in the mid-nineteenth Century, the Supreme Court ridiculed those new procedures and continued to use common law pleading rules.[12] The common law system of pleading combined with the selective use of State law for issues raised in Federal court created such a complex system of pleading that practitioners had "to rely on the clerk of the court for guidance," and felt "no more certainty as to the proper procedure than if [they] were before a tribunal of a foreign country."[13]

---

[10] Although there has been some debate about this point, the radical departure from the Rule and precedent seems to be the better view. *See, e.g.* Carrington, Paul. 2010. Politics and Civil Procedure Rulemaking: Reflections on Experience. *Duke Law Journal* 60:597–667, at 651 (finding a "drastic disregard of the text of Rule 8); Note (2007). The Supreme Court, 2006 Term: Leading Cases: Federal Jurisdiction and Procedure – Civil Procedure – Pleading Standards. *Harvard Law Review* 121:305–315, at 311 (arguing conflict with text, precedent and historical sources).

[11] Burbank, Stephen V. 1982. The Rules Enabling Act of 1934. *University of Pennsylvania Law Review* 130:1015–1197, at 1097–1098.

[12] Burbank, *supra* note 11, at 1036–1039.

[13] Burbank, *supra* note 11, at 1041 (quoting American Bar Association (1896) *American Bar Association Reporter* 19:411, 410).

The Rules Enabling Act was a paradigm shift that was the culmination of a 20 year campaign to bring uniformity to Federal procedure.[14] While the act promoted uniformity, it rejected the approach in some states, such as New York, where the rules of procedure were adopted by statute (known as "code" pleading). The first bill introduced in 1912 simply gave the power to the Supreme Court to prescribe Rules of procedure.[15] This raised concerns, however, about the relationship between the rules and existing Federal statutes.[16] A second bill introduced in 1917, and supported by the American Bar Association from 1919 to 1924, addressed this concern by providing that the rules adopted under the act would supersede all conflicting laws.[17] This would have given very broad authority to the courts to supersede substantive law. A later iteration proposed by Chief Justice Taft added the use of a commission of judges and lawyers to propose rules and amendments to be approved by the Supreme Court and then submitted to Congress for its review to become effective in 6 months if the Congress took no action.[18] The next version of the bill was introduced in 1924, and was identical to the version that was ultimately passed in 1934 (except for one word).[19] The bill enacted gave the U.S. Supreme Court the power to prescribe rules of procedure, but limited that power by declaring that the rules "shall neither abridge, enlarge, nor modify the substantive rights of any litigant."[20] Although this version did not explicitly include the use of a commission, it provided that rules would "take effect 6 months after promulgation" and that they would not take effect "until they shall have been reported to Congress by the Attorney General at the beginning of a regular session and thereof and until after the close of such session."[21]

While not explicitly required by the Rules Enabling Act when adopted, consultation with expert committees "has been the cornerstone of civil rulemaking in the Federal courts since the adoption of the Rules Enabling Act."[22] The Judicial Conference, which was created by statute and to which all Federal judges belong,[23] has authority to recommend changes to the rules.[24] It oversees a Standing Committee on Rules of Practice and Procedure whose members are appointed by the Chief Justice of the Supreme Court.[25] Various advisory committees are accountable to the

---

[14] Burbank, *supra* note 11, at 1024.

[15] H.R. 26,462, 62nd Congress, 3d Session (1912); S.8454, 62nd Congress, 3d Session (1912).

[16] Burbank, *supra* note 11, at 1052–1053.

[17] Burbank, *supra* note 11, at 1066 and n.228.

[18] Burbank, *supra* note 11, at 1069–1070.

[19] Burbank, *supra* note 11, at 1097. The word that was added was "civil" in the first section to make it consistent with the second section. *See ibid.* at 1097 n.375.

[20] Public Law No. 73–415, 48 Stat. 1064 (codified at 28 U.S.C. § 2072).

[21] Public Law No. 73–415, 48 Stat. 1064 (codified at 28 U.S.C. § 2072).

[22] Bone, Robert G. 1999. The Process of Making Process: Court Rulemaking, Democratic Legitimacy, and Procedural Efficacy. *Georgetown Law Journal* 87:887–955, at 888.

[23] 28 U.S.C. § 331.

[24] 28 U.S.C. § 2073.

[25] 28 U.S.C. § 331.

Standing Committee, including an Advisory Committee on Civil Rules.[26] The members of that advisory committee are judges, lawyers and law professors.[27] Before a proposed rule change is adopted by the Supreme Court, it is considered by the Advisory Committee, the Standing Committee, and the Judicial Conference.[28] Once a rule change has been adopted by the Supreme Court, it must be reported to Congress which has about 7 months to reject it.[29] If it is not rejected by Congress, the change takes effect.

Over time, the process for adopting and amending the Federal rules of civil procedure has become more formalized and more like procedures used to adopt or modify administrative rules. For about the first 40 years under the Rules Enabling Act, until 1973, the judiciary made and modified civil rules without interference from Congress, which did not exercise its veto power.[30] Around this same time, various challenges were being made to judicial rulemaking on ideological, theoretical and practical grounds.[31] As political challenges to the rules increased, the rulemaking procedure became more formal. In 1988, as part of the Judicial Improvements and Access to Justice Act, Congress amended the Rules Enabling Act to mandate open meetings, minutes to be maintained and made available to the public, advance notice of meetings to be given, explanatory notes for proposed changes along with a written report explaining the committees' actions and including any minority or separate views.[32] Thus, by 2009, when the *Iqbal* opinion was issued, there was a fairly elaborate system in place for amendment of the Federal Rules of Civil Procedure.

The notice pleading requirement in FRCP 8 was adopted with the original federal rules according to the rule-making procedures in 1938, and have not be substantively amended. In the federal courts, prior to *Iqbal*, "the courts agreed that a claimant did not need to set out in detail the facts on which the claim for relief was based, but only needed to provide a statement sufficient to put the opposing party on notice for the claim."[33] The most commonly cited judicial authority in support of notice pleading was *Conley v. Gibson*,[34] decided in 1957 and confirmed unanimously by the U.S. Supreme Court in cases in 1993[35] and 2002.[36]

---

[26] 28 U.S.C. § 2073.

[27] Bone, *supra* note 22, at 892.

[28] 28 U.S.C. § 2073.

[29] 28 U.S.C. § 2074(a).

[30] Bone, *supra* note 22, at 893. Congress exercised its veto power to block the proposed Federal Rules of Evidence and adopted a statutory version instead. *See ibid.* at 902.

[31] *See* Bone, *supra* note 22, at 900–902.

[32] Public Law No. 100–707, 102 Stat. 4642 (1988), codified at 27 U.S.C. § 2073(c)-(d). Although the Advisory had customarily "circulated drafts to bench and bar and invited input," it "never seemed to treat participation as a requirement of legitimacy." Bone, *supra* note 22, at 903 n. 86.

[33] Parness, Jeffrey A. Moore's Federal Practice – Civil. 2015. 2–8:8.04.

[34] 355 U.S. 41 (1957).

[35] *Leatherman v. Tarrant County*, 507 U.S. 163 (1997).

[36] *Swierkiewicz v. Sorema N.A.*, 534 U.S. 506 (2002).

13.3 Dynamism at the Supreme Court: The Pleading Revolution

Rather than using the elaborate, statutorily mandated system to change the standard for pleadings in the federal courts, the Supreme Court in *Ashcroft v. Iqbal*[37] adopted radically new pleading requirements by judicial fiat.[38] That case involved a so-called "*Bivens*" claim (a claim brought directly under the U.S. Constitution rather than under a statute or common law claim) made by Javaid Iqbal, a Pakistani Muslim who has been arrested and detained after the September 11, 2001, terrorist attacks. Iqbal alleged that he was the victim of racial and religious profiling and that he was detained and treated in ways that violated his rights. He alleged that Attorney General Ashcroft was the "principle architect" of the policy, and that FBI Director Mueller was "instrumental" in its adoption.[39]

The Supreme Court held that Iqbal's complaint was not sufficient to state a legal claim. Although the trial court and Court of Appeals found that the complaint was sufficient, the Supreme Court found that the complaint was not plausible after stripping it of improper conclusions. The Court concluded that that the bare allegations that Ashcroft was the "principle architect" and that Mueller was "instrumental" were "conclusory" and therefore were "not entitled to be assumed true."[40] The remaining allegations did not establish that Ashcroft and Muller acted with discriminatory intent. Because the September 11 attacks "were perpetrated by 19 Arab Muslim hijackers who counted themselves as members in good standing of al Qaeda … it should come as no surprise that a legitimate policy … would produce disparate, incidental impact on Arab Muslims."[41] The only allegations of intent against Ashcroft and Mueller were that they adopted "a policy approving 'restrictive conditions of confinement' for post-September 11 detainees until they were 'cleared' by the FBI."[42] But such an allegation did not establish that the policy was "purposefully adopted" because of the detainees' "race, religion or national origin."[43] Because of the

---

[37] 556 U.S. 662 (2009).

[38] Although many commentators agree that *Iqbal* adopted a new pleading standard, *see, e.g*. Bone, Robert G. (2010). Plausibility Pleading Revisited and Revised: A comment on *Ashcroft v. Iqbal. Notre Dame Law Review* 85:849–885; Clermont, Kevin M. and Stephen C. Yeazell (2010). Inventing Tests, Destabilizing Systems. *Iowa Law Review* 95:821–861; Gressette, Thomas P., Jr. (2010). The Heightened Pleading Standard of Bell Atlantic v. Twombly and Ashcroft v. Iqbal. *Drake Law Review* 58: 401–455; Miller, Arthur R. (2010). From Conley to Twombly to Iqbal: A Double Plan on the Federal Rules of Civil Procedure. *Duke Law Journal* 60:1–130, some do not, *see, e.g*., Steinman, Adam N. (2010). The Pleading Problem. *Stanford Law Review* 62: 1293–1360.

[39] 556 U.S. at 669.

[40] 556 U.S. at 681.

[41] 556 U.S. at 682.

[42] 556 U.S. at 683.

[43] 556 U.S. at 682.

"'obvious alternative explanation' for the arrests," an inference of discrimination was "not a plausible conclusion."[44]

The restriction on "conclusions" was a creation of *Iqbal*, but the plausibility standard came from a previous Supreme Court case, *Bell Atlantic Corp. v. Twombly*, decided 2 years earlier.[45] That case involved a putative class action alleging that incumbent telephone companies violated the Sherman Antitrust Act by conspiring to restrain trade. The complaint alleged that the companies "engaged in parallel conduct" to inhibit the growth of upstart competitors and that the incumbent companies refrained from competing with each other.[46] The trial court dismissed the complaint for failure to state a claim, but the Court of Appeals reversed. The Supreme Court agreed with the trial court and held that the complaint was not sufficient because its allegations stopped "short of the line between possibility and plausibility."[47] The allegations of parallel conduct and refraining from competitive behavior were not enough to establish a conspiracy; there was "an obvious alternative explanation" that the incumbents were acting in their individual interests to "sit tight, expecting their neighbors to do the same thing."[48]

Although the Supreme Court described issue in *Twombly* as "the proper standard for pleading an antitrust conspiracy,"[49] in *Iqbal* the Court held that "the decision was based on [the] interpretation and application of Rule 8" and applied to "all civil actions."[50] Moreover, the Court in *Twombly* specifically rejected the applicability of the "no set of facts" standard from *Conley*. The plaintiff in *Twombly* argued that it met the *Conley* requirements, but the Court reasoned that "many judges and commentators" had "balked at taking the literal terms of the *Conley* passage as a pleading standard."[51] The Court suggested that the "no set of facts" language "should be understood in light of the [*Conley*] opinion's preceding summary of the complaint's concrete allegations, which the court quite reasonably understood as amply stating a claim for relief." To the extent that lower courts might be tempted to continue to use the "no set of facts" language from *Conley*, the Court concluded that the phrase had "earned its retirement" to be "best forgotten as an incomplete, negative gloss on an accepted pleading standard."[52]

These Supreme Court cases show dynamism in Federal civil procedure that reflects the common law tradition and the strength and independence of the judiciary. The Court, while citing to Federal Rule 8, made little effort to tie the new standards to the particular text of the rule. Instead, it simply stated the new standard as it would a common law rule. Remarkably, the Court used this common law

[44] 556 U.S. at 682.

[45] 550 U.S. 544, 570 (2007).

[46] 550 U.S. at 550–551.

[47] 550 U.S. at 557.

[48] 660 U.S. at 566–568.

[49] 550 U.S. at 553.

[50] *Iqbal*, 556 U.S. at 684.

[51] *Twombly*, 550 U.S. at 561–562.

[52] 550 U.S. at 563.

approach instead of its explicit administrative authority to amend the text of Rule 8.[53] This may have been instrumental (i.e. more effective and quicker), ideological (i.e. the majority may not have had sufficient influence through the administrative process), or perhaps both. For years prior to *Iqbal* and *Twombly*, the administrative process had considered changes to the pleading rules, but "rulemakers repeatedly expressed the view that more rigorous pleading requirements were unwarranted and would be unsound as a matter of policy."[54] The majority of the Supreme Court did not agree; it wanted to tighten up pleading standards "to filter out hypothesized excesses of meritless litigation, to deter allegedly abusive practices, and to contain costs."[55]

13.4 Dynamism in the Lower Courts: The Reaction to *Iqbal* and *Twombly*

The dynamism in the U.S. system of civil procedure is not limited to the Supreme Court. Lower courts also enjoy significant power and independence, and are fully immersed in the common law tradition. While the legal hierarchy makes the decision of the U.S. Supreme Court binding on all lower Federal courts, those lower courts are adept at limiting, distinguishing or interpreting Supreme Court opinions. The lower Federal courts consist of trial courts in 94 districts in the U.S. and appellate courts in 13 circuits. Judges in these courts have life-tenure appointment, resulting in substantial independence, and are adept at interpreting the law to meet their policy objectives. Splits between the circuits and the districts are common. In the exercise of their independence and their common law powers, the lower courts have the power to choose how closely to follow *Iqbal* and *Twombly*, or, to the extent they disagree, may find ways to avoid doing so. This is precisely what has happened in the wake of *Iqbal* and *Twombly*. Some courts have followed in letter and spirit and have applied a heightened pleading standard that has made it more difficult for plaintiffs to get past the motion to dismiss. On the other hand, some courts have limited the application of the standard, or have applied it in a way that has not significantly increased the pleading burden for the plaintiff.

There has been a remarkable amount of empirical research about the consequences of *Iqbal* and *Twombly* on motions to dismiss, but the data has been

---

[53] The Supreme Court has "the power to prescribe general rules of practice and procedure and rules of evidence for cases in the United States district court (including proceedings before magistrates thereof) and courts of appeals." 28 U.S.C. § 2072. These rules must go through the administrative procedures outline above.

[54] Hoffman, Lonny. 2013. Rulemaking in the Age of Twombly and Iqbal. *U.C. Davis Law Review* 46: 1483–1558, at 1511.

[55] Miller, *supra* note 38, at 53. *See Twombly*, 550 U.S. at 557–560 (discussing the use of pleading standards to screen out meritless cases and to avoid *in terrorem* effect of expensive discovery); *see also Iqbal*, 556 U.S. at 685–686 (rejecting case management techniques as insufficient to avoid the consequences of discovery).

interpreted in a variety of ways.[56] One thing that everyone can agree on is that the lower courts have recognized their significance by citing to them. *Iqbal* has been cited by the lower courts more than 30,000 times.[57] That being said, there is significant disagreement about the extent to which *Iqbal* and *Twombly* have affected outcomes in the lower courts. The most comprehensive study was conducted by researchers for the Federal Judicial Center.[58] It showed that defendants moved to dismiss 50 % more often after *Iqbal*.[59] However, after efforts to control for different dismissal practices among different courts, variations based on type of case, and whether the motion involved an amended complaint, the study "found that there was no 'statistically significant' increase in the likelihood that a motion to dismiss would be grated after *Iqbal*."[60] This suggests that lower courts have resisted the Supreme Court's directive to use motions to dismiss filter out meritless cases and to reduce the cost of litigation and discovery.

The Federal Judicial Center study has been criticized as focusing too much on judicial outcomes, and for failing to account for party selection effects.[61] Measuring the success rate on motions to dismiss fails to account for other negative affects based on party behavior. Faced with heightened pleading standard, defendants will be more likely to make a motion to dismiss rather than filing an answer, requiring the plaintiff to respond to the motion before moving to the discovery phase. On the other side, plaintiffs faced with the heightened pleading standard will be less likely to file a complaint or may drop the complaint, and will be more likely to settle to avoid the risk of dismissal. Using the Federal Judicial Center data, Jonah Gelbach calculated the lower bound of negative effects of the change pleading standard and found negative effects in at least 21.5 % of cases other than those involving financial instruments, civil rights and employment discrimination, and negative effects in 15.4 % of employment discrimination claims and 18.1 % of civil rights cases.[62]

---

[56] For a summary of the literature, see Glelbach, Jonah. 2012. Selection in Motion: A Formal Model of Rule 12(b)(6) and the *Twombly-Iqbal* Shift in Pleading Policy at 5–8. http://papers.ssrn.com/sol3/papers.cfm?abstract_id=2138428. Accessed 20 November 2014.

[57] Kuperman, Andrea. 2011. Memorandum to Civil Rules Committee and Standing Rules Committee on Review of Case Law Applying *Bell Atlantic Corp. v. Twombly* and *Ashcroft v. Iqbal* at 1 n. 2. http://www.uscourts.gov/uscourts/RulesAndPolicies/rules/iqbalmemo_112311.pdf. Accessed 5 September 2014.

[58] Cecil, Joe S., George W. Cort, Margaret S. Williams and Jared J. Bataillon. 2011. Motion to Dismiss for Failure to State a Claim after *Iqbal*: *Report to the Judicial Conference Advisory Committee on Civil Rules*. http://www.uscourts.gov/uscourts/RulesAndPolicies/rules/Publications/motioniqbal.pdf. Accessed 31 January 2015. This study considered cases from 23 Federal distinction courts that collectively accounted for 51 % of litigation for two nine-month periods, one before *Iqbal* and one afterwards. *See ibid.* at 5.

[59] Hoffman, *supra* note 54, at 1533–1534 (relying on data from the Federal Judicial Center report).

[60] Hoffman, *supra* note 54, at 1535 (financial instrument cases were an exception to this but were considered an outlier because of the financial crisis near that time).

[61] Gelbach, Jonah B. (2012). Locking the Doors to Discovery? Assessing the Effects of *Twombly* and *Iqbal* on Access to Discovery. *Yale Law Journal* 121:2270–2345.

[62] Gelbach, *supra* note 61, at 2338. Cases involving financial instruments were excluded because of a sharp rise in such cases after the 2008–09 financial crisis.

These estimates suggest that the parties perceive that at least some of the lower courts will apply a heightened pleading standard after *Iqbal* and *Twombly*, but these estimates do not establish actual judicial behavior or show a perception that all courts will apply a heightened standard. Anecdotal information suggests that lower courts may not be applying a heightened standard as the Supreme Court intended. The committees involved with recommending changes in the rules of civil procedure have failed to act in part because they believe that "the lower courts are adapting" to the changed doctrine.[63] A review of lower court opinions by the Chief Council to the rules committees concluded that "case law to date does not appear to indicate that *Iqbal* has dramatically changed the application of the standards used to determine pleading sufficiency."[64] Consistent with a common law customs, the review found that lower courts "are taking a context-specific approach," and "that *Twombly* and *Iqbal* are providing a new framework in which to analyze familiar pleading concepts, rather than an entirely new pleading standard."[65] The appellate courts "have reversed dismissals where district courts failed to presume the facts to be true or the plaintiff to plead with too much particularity," and "appear to apply the analysis more leniently in cases where pleading with more detail may be difficult."[66] Another commentator found that some "courts insist that the ordinary pleading standard continues to be a liberal one focused on notice, with some courts even going so far as to apply the repudiated "no set of facts" test to scrutinize the sufficiency of claims."[67]

Decisions from the Seventh Circuit provide examples of lower courts that have substantially limited the scope of the *Iqbal* and *Twombly* pleading standard. When considering the plausibility standard articulated in *Twombly*, the Seventh Circuit, while recognizing that the Supreme Court had "retooled federal pleading standards," noted that *Twombly* "made it clear that it did not, in fact, supplant the basic notice-pleading standard."[68] It then reversed the trial court's dismissal of plaintiff's claim of sexual discrimination because the allegations that she was paid less than similarly situated male employees because she was a woman and would not cooperate with the governor's office were sufficient to state a claim.

A subsequent Seventh Circuit opinion conceded that the Supreme Court had "set the bar" higher, but it suggested that it was an open question about how much higher.[69] The Court noted that this did not require "fact pleading" and that pleading still only required "fair notice."[70] The Seventh Circuit interpreted the *Iqbal* standard to require "that the plaintiff must give enough details about the subject-matter of the

[63] Hoffman, *supra* note 54, at 1531.

[64] Kuperman, *supra* note 57, at 4.

[65] Kuperman, *supra* note 57, at 4–5.

[66] Kuperman, *supra* note 57, at 5.

[67] Spencer, A. Benjamin. 2009. Understanding Pleading Doctrine. *Michigan Law Review* 94:873–935, at 7 (citations omitted).

[68] Tamayo v. Blagojevich, 526 F.3d 1074, 1082–1083 (7th Cir. 2008).

[69] Swanson v. Citibank, N.A., 614 F.3d 400, 403 (7th Cir. 2010).

[70] Swanson, 614 F.3d at 404–405.

case to present a story that holds together."[71] Applying this interpretation, the Court found that the trial court had erred in dismissing fair housing claims based on allegations that defendants' actions prevented her from getting a loan and were motivated by her race. While this standard may be slightly more demanding than the "no set of facts" standard prior to *Iqbal*, it is still sufficiently liberal to reach the opposite result in *Iqbal*. A court could find the allegation that immediately after the September 11 terrorist attacks Attorney General Ashcroft was the architect of a program to detain and mistreat Arab Muslims was a "story that holds together."

The approach of the Tenth Circuit represents a kind of compromise interpretation of the *Iqbal* standard. Unlike the Seventh Circuit, which began with the premise that the Court had not abandoned traditional notice pleading, the Tenth Circuit started from the premise that court did not mean to impose "heightened fact pleading" but instead sought a "middle ground" between that and a complaint that contained only a "formulaic recitation of the elements of cause of action."[72] In finding that middle ground, the Tenth Circuit noted that the standard should "weed out claims that do not (in the absence of additional allegations) have a reasonable prospect for success" and should "inform defendants of the actual grounds of the claim against them."[73] Applying this standard in light of the identified purpose, the Tenth Circuit held that the district court should have dismissed the complaint. The plaintiff had alleged that the Department of Human Services personnel had directed them to use a childcare provider where their daughter was killed. This allegation was insufficient because the government employees were protected by qualified immunity, and the allegations failed to "isolate the allegedly unconstitutional acts of each defendant, and thereby [did] not provide adequate notice of the nature of the claims against each."[74]

The Ninth Circuit's approach was one of the most aggressive in favor of dismissals. Its analysis started from the premise that *Twombly* held that a plaintiff "must plead a set of facts 'plausibly suggesting (not merely consistent with)' a Sherman Act violation to survive a motion to dismiss."[75] After describing the *Twombly* and *Iqbal* opinions, the court's interpreted the standard to emphasize this factual element: "In sum, for a complaint to survive a motion to dismiss, the non-conclusory 'factual content,' and reasonable inferences from that content, must be plausibly suggestive of a claim entitling the plaintiff to relief."[76] In applying this interpretation, the court found that the allegations did not contain enough facts. Plaintiffs, anti-Bush protestors, alleged that the Secret Service had violated their First Amendment rights by forcing them to relocate away from President when pro-Bush protestors were allowed to stay. In order to state a claim, the "critical question" was

[71] Swanson, 614 F.3d at 405.

[72] Robbins v. Oklahoma ex rel. Department of Human Services, 519 F.3d 1242, 1247 (10th Cir. 2008).

[73] Robbins, 519 F.3d at 1248.

[74] Robbins, 519 F.3d at 1250.

[75] Moss v. United States Secret Service, 572 F.3d 962, 968 (9th Cir. 2009).

[76] Moss, 572 F.3d at 969 (quoting *Iqbal*, 129 S. Ct. at 1949).

whether the relocation was "*because of*" their anti-Bush viewpoint.[77] The court found that the "bald allegation of impermissible motive" was not entitled to any weight because it was conclusory, and that the remaining facts did not provide any basis for impermissible motive. The complaint alleged that after allowing the protestors to be close enough to be heard, when the President was ready to leave that "all persons" at the location occupied by the anti-Bush protestors were to be moved out of handgun or explosive range. Because the protestors were in hearing distance of the President before being moved, the court found the assertion that the Secret Service was motivated by their point of view to be not plausible.[78]

These different approaches taken by the Federal circuits show dynamism in reaction to the Supreme Court decisions in *Iqbal* and *Twombly*. While the Supreme Court sought to impose a significantly more stringent pleading standard to screen out non-meritorious claims and to reduce the burden of discovery, the lower courts, using their independence and interpretive powers within the common law tradition, have adopted their own versions of the new pleading standard. The Seventh Circuit's interpretation resulted in a liberal pleading standard focused on the importance of notice similar to the pre-*Iqbal* and pre-*Twombly* standard. The Ninth Circuit's interpretation was a stricter standard focusing on the need of the plaintiff to plead facts in support of a claim. The Tenth Circuit's interpretation sought the middle ground between heightened pleading and mere notice. The Supreme Court will likely take up future cases to resolve conflicts between the circuits, which will trigger another round of dynamic interpretation in the lower courts.

13.5 Conclusion

The Federal Rules of Civil Procedure were promulgated in 1937 by the U.S. Supreme Court though and administrative-like procedure. Rule 8(a)(2) requires that a complaint provide "a short and plain statement of the claim showing that the pleader is entitled to relief." This requirement, known as notice pleading, made it substantially easier than it had been to bring a claim in the Federal courts. In 2007 and 2009, in the landmark cases of *Twombly* and *Iqbal*, the U.S. Supreme Court adopted a more stringent pleading standard that discounts conclusions and requires plausibility. This paradigmatic shift was not undertaken through the robust and representative rule-making process over which the Supreme Court had authority, but instead was done with two case holdings. This illustrates dynamism in the U.S. system for civil procedure and reflects the powerful common law tradition in the U.S. courts. The lower courts, who also have substantial independence and embrace the common law tradition, are making their own interpretations of the new pleading standard, which illustrates additional dynamism at both the appellate and trial court levels

[77] Moss, 572 F.3d at 970.

[78] Moss, 572 F.3d at 971.

Chapter 14
What is "Covered" by *Res Judicata* in Brazilian Civil Procedural Law: The Current Law and Perspectives of Change

Teresa Arruda Alvim Wambier

14.1 The Subject

In Brazil, this topic, res judicata,[1] is currently the subject of intense debate because there is a Bill for a new Civil Procedural Code in Parliament in which the changing of the traditional rule has been proposed. Our current Civil Procedural Code was enacted in 1973. It has been amended innumerable times and therefore it became rather "patchy". Furthermore, legal writers, judges and lawyers have for a long time criticized some aspects of the prior rule.

I had the honour of having been appointed by the Senate to be the general "rapporteuse" of this Bill and this was one of my personal proposals. So, my responsibility was, besides making my own contributions, to gather, organize and give the final wording to the proposals approved by the group. In this case, after the committee finished drawing up the Bill, it was sent to the Congress (Câmara), where another committee was formed, to analyze the Bill. This month, the Bill went back to the Senate, the upper house of the National Congress of Brazil where it will be analyzed again, before being sent to the President. Once approved, it will become our Civil Procedural Code.

The traditional rule currently in effect in several civil law countries including Brazil is that only the decision (the outcome) itself is vested with *resjudicata* (*decisum*). The Bill proposes that *res judicata* be extended to the solution given by a judge or by a Court to the issues/premises of the decision.

Professor, Ph.D. and Master of Laws at PUC-SP.

[1] According to Brazilian Law, *res judicata* means the impossibility of changing a final judicial decision. In slightly different forms, this is an international concept, derived from Roman Law.

T.A.A. Wambier (✉)
Department of Civil Procedural Law, Pontifical Catholic University of Sao Paolo, Rua Monte Alegre, 984, Perdizes, Sao Paolo 05014-901, São Paulo, Brazil
e-mail: teresawambier@wambier.com.br

C.B. Picker, G.I. Seidman (eds.), *The Dynamism of Civil Procedure - Global Trends and Developments*, Ius Gentium: Comparative Perspectives on Law and Justice 48, DOI 10.1007/978-3-319-21981-3_14

For several reasons we believe this to be the best choice. Two of them deserve mention: (a) it is not logical and against common sense to admit that the same *causa petendi*[2] could be considered differently in two different lawsuits, for different consequences; (b) the current rule leaves the door open to other future lawsuits where the same *causa petendi* can be seen in another way. So, in fact, the first lawsuit did not solve completely (and forever) the underlying problem. Furthermore this can give rise to the overburdening of Courts.

14.2 The Current Rule in Brazilian Civil Procedure

The Brazilian Civil Procedural Code (CPC) of 1973, currently in effect, primarily reflected the teachings of Enrico Tullio Liebman, an Italian professor who came to Brazil fleeing from the war, though of course, it also reflected many Brazilian authorities, such as José Frederico Marques, Pedro Batista Martins and Moacyr Amaral Santos.

The very concept of *res judicata* was at that time a source of considerable debate in academic circles. José Carlos Barbosa Moreira and Ovídio Baptista da Silva[3] were among those who had the deepest interest in this matter and both manifested different opinions, in several books,[4] criticizing Liebman and his ideas on the scope of *res judicata*.

Despite the influence of Liebman on Brazilian Procedural Law, it is usually said that the concept of *res judicata* of articles 468 and 469 of our CPC was conceived by Carnelutti.[5] The first article states: "*the sentence, which resolves partly or entirely the merits, is* res judicata *in relation to the merits and to the issues decided*".

Art. 469, to a certain extent, gives the exact "definition" of *res judicata* in Brazilian law. It says what is not within the scope of *resjudicata*, and hence what can be raised again in other future lawsuits. "*I – the reasons* (*Grund-motivation*) *of the decision* (decisum) *even if they are important to determine the scope of the* 'decisum' *itself*; *II – the facts, as seen by the judge, part of the motivation of the decision*; *III – the decision* 'incidenter tantum' *of the* 'Vorfragen'[6]". Based on the

---

[2] A concept similar but not identical to "cause of action". What is important to say here is that the essence of these legal phenomena is exactly the same.

[3] These two opinions are deeply studied by Sérgio Gilberto Porto, *Coisa julgada civil*. 4.ª ed. São Paulo: Revista dos Tribunais, p. 82–83.

[4] *Vide*: SILVA, Ovídio Baptista da. Limites objetivos da coisa julgada no atual direito brasileiro, *in* RePro, v. 15, p. 45, April/1979; BARBOSA MOREIRA, José Carlos. Ainda e sempre a coisa julgada, *in* Doutrinas essenciais de processo civil, v. 6, p. 679, October/2011.

[5] ARAGÂO, Egas Moniz de, *Sentença e coisa julgada: exegese do Código de Processo Civil*. Rio de Janeiro: AIDE, 1992, p. 242.

[6] The "Vorfragen" are the issues that a judge must decide before judging the merits of the claim (the main issue – *Hauptsache* – fond du litige). A judge would be unable to solve the main issue (defined by the claimant) without firstly having decided on the "Vorfragen". In other words, "Vorfragen" are issues which must be resolved before the principal issue, because their resolution indicates how the merits will be decided.

interpretation of these provisions, legal authors say that what is within the scope of *res judicata* in Brazilian procedural law is just the *acertamento* of the dispute, i.e., the resolution of the claim and neither its logical antecedents nor the rationale used. Of course, the issue of *res judicata* can be raised to avoid the Judiciary having to decide on the same *Hauptsache* twice.

It is highly likely that a judge will deliberate on proceeding issues and these issues can be important to other future lawsuits. It is possible and it really happens in practice, that the same *causa petendi* can generate other claims, according to the doctrine of the scope of *resjudicata* which is generally adopted by civil law systems that is, doctrine according to which *res judicata* covers only the outcome, the *decisum* itself. For instance: a contract is considered valid by a judge in respect of some effect (interest) in a claim for unpaid interest. This very contract can be pointed out as *causa petendi* in any other future claim where that claimant will ask for compensation for non-compliance with the terms of the agreement, and in this second law suit the second judge is not bound to consider the same contract valid! This happens in Brazil (and in most civil law countries) because *resjudicata* affects only the *decisum, i.e.* the part of the decision which is not its reasons, but the decision itself *i.e.*, the judgment. That means that in the decision given by the first judge, the only part which is "touched" by *res judicata* is the interest payable, no judge can depart from that in future lawsuits.[7]

On the one hand, Brazilian legislation renders possible the existence of contradictory decisions, from a logical point of view.[8] On the other hand, the Brazilian CPC contains a device whose goal is to avoid this possibility which is called *ação declaratória incidental* (*Zwischenfeststellungsklage*, § 256, ZPO): the parties – claimant(s) or defendant(s) can ask a judge to extend the "authority" of "res judicata" to the "reasons" of his or her future decision, if one of these "reasons" corresponds to a legal rapport which had been the object of debate between them. If they do that, the result is that this decision shall also be respected in all other future lawsuits. It is said that in this case the judge's decisions will be made *principaliter*[9] and not *incidenter tantum*.[10]

Exactly because of that this subject is regulated by art. 470 of our CPC, which provides the *ação declaratória incidental*, among other articles on the *res judicata* regime in Brazilian law. This article is a kind of counterpoint to the Brazilian *res judicata* regime, limited to the *decisum*. In fact, these limits depend on the initiative of the parties, who may use the *ação declaratória incidental*. This possibility creates a balance in our procedural system.

[7] WAMBIER, Teresa Arruda Alvim. A sentença e a coisa julgada, *in RePro*, v. 41, p. 177, janeiro/1986.

[8] It is interesting to remark that these contradictions exist on a theoretical level, not in the practical world.

[9] DINAMARCO, Cândido. *Instituições de direito processual civil*, p. 543.
Principaliter: as the main object.

[10] *Incidenter tantum* is the opposite of principaliter.

Nevertheless, the application of this technique is not common in Brazil. The causes are unknown, but I suppose it is rather refined and not well known by the average lawyer. Of course the exclusion of *reasons* (generally considered) of the scope of *res judicata* does not mean that for the Brazilian legislator reasons are not important. On the contrary, it is said in art. 468 of the CPC that reasons identify and render clear the scope of the decision and define to which extent the claimant won or lost.

Legal authors say that what is "covered" by the authority of *res judicata* is only the *decisum* because a judgment (or a sentence) is the expression of the State's will. So its reasons, although important, are not what validates an act of the State. The *decisum* itself is in a way more significant because **it awards something to somebody** and it has to be done in a definite fashion, solving a real problem, assuring the concrete and practical results of the proceedings.[11,12]

Also the *Dispositionsmaxime* (*principe dispositif*) can be seen as one of the reasons why *res judicata* does not encompass motivations (especially "Vorfragen"): according to this principle the claimant has the role and the task of creating limits to a judge's *cognitio* and to the correspondent decision. It is said that a judge cannot decide with *resjudicata's* "force" (Rechtskraft), in a definite way, what the claimant did not ask him or her to do.

Nevertheless, over the last 200 years, civil procedure is being seen less and less as a *Sache der Parteien*, *i.e.*, matter for the litigating parties. This means, for example, that the role of a judge has changed from that of a mere spectator to one of the actors of the proceedings. This approach leads to "conclusions" that maybe the scope of *resjudicata* should not be left entirely to the initiative of the parties. There are reasons connected to this public approach which would perhaps recommend the changing of this strict regime, favouring procedural effectiveness.

14.3 The Prospects of Changes in Brazilian Civil Procedural Law

In 2009 I was appointed to serve as the general reporter of a Bill for a new Brazilian CPC. The committee consisted of a group of 11 jurists: Professors, Judges and Lawyers etc. It was in fact a very heterogeneous group. As previously mentioned our CPC is 41 years old and had been amended several times. The need for change was felt by the legal community as a whole.

We proposed, among other things, the changing of the *res judicata* regime. This Bill was openly inspired by the desire to draw from proceedings far reaching results.

[11] TALAMINI, Eduardo. ***Coisa julgada e sua revisão***, p. 82, and: ARAGÃO, Egas Moniz. ***Sentença e coisa julgada***, p. 247.

[12] Chiovenda always said that the role of civil procedure is to render concrete the State's will (CHIOVENDA, Giuseppe. ***Instituições de direito processual civil***. V. 1. Campinas: Bookseller, 1998, p. 18–19). The *decisum* is therefore considered an expression of the legislator's will and it is directly related to the civil law *res judicata* doctrine.

Proceedings should be rendered more effective. In sum: the underpinning social conflict or dispute should never be brought before the Courts more than once.

We did not go far enough to say that no other *petitum* (claim) should be extracted from the same *causa petendi*. No. According to the proposed regime, a claimant could ask for compensation through a first lawsuit and years later ask for punitive damages, arising from the same *cause of action*. But in the new regime, which was originally proposed by the commission, we created a rule saying the decision on the legal relationship whose existence and validity is logically presupposed by the decision itself is also "covered" by *res judicata*, even if it is a decision *incidenter tantum*.

Despite the differences among the members of this heterogeneous commission, all of us agreed in the sense that there is no reason to restrict the authority of *res judicata* to the *decisum* itself, because the level of *cognitio*[13] of these antecedent questions are deep enough to generate a decision on the merits. Other future lawsuits would be avoided if based on the same legal relationship, on what there is already a decision *incidenter tantum*. So the scope of *res judicata* is broadened. The new legal provision says that *res judicata's* strength/authority/power covers the part of the decision on a legal relationship on which the decision of the *petitum* depends.

Let us analyze under which conditions it could happen:

First of all there has to be a disagreement between claimant and defendant on the existence or the validity of this relationship, which has to be taken into account prior to the decision of the *Hauptsache*.

Issues technically considered (*questões*, *Fragen*, questions) are matters in relation to which claimant and defendant do not agree (contentions issues). That means that there may be matters which will never become *questions*, issues, or *Fragen* because both parties agree on their legal existence or validity.

So, the first condition is the contentions nature of the issue. It is said that these issues which are prior because they have to be considered before the following question (which can be the merits), can be classified as belonging to two groups: preliminary and *prejudiciais*.

Preliminary issues are those which have to be solved before the merits. The possibility of a judge solving the dispute depends on the prior decision. Good examples are standing, competence, the existence of a lawyer representing the parties. In fact, if the judge is not competent (has no jurisdiction), if one of the parties has no standing or no lawyer, the *Hauptsache* cannot be decided.

How a judge decides the *petitum* will depend on the decision of the *prejudiciais*, for example: if A is the son of B the former is entitled to support; if the contract exists and if it is valid, it has to be complied with.

Preliminary issues interfere in the possibility of a judgment taking place; *prejudiciais* determine how the merits will be decided.

So it is the relationship with the following *issue* which identifies an issue as a preliminary or as a *prejudicial* one. An issue is neither preliminary nor *prejudicial* by itself.

[13] Knowledge, cognizance.

So, the second condition is that this issue must be previously decided. Nevertheless, legal writers point out other criteria for an issue to be considered *prejudicial*. As was said before, the main condition for an issue to be considered *prejudicial* is that its judgment is absolutely necessary for the decision on the logically subsequent issue, normally the merits, *Hauptsache*.[14] Some legal writers say that these issues must theoretically be the object of an independent lawsuit.[15] Of course, this possibility does not exist in relation to facts, which in certain circumstances, play the role of *prejudiciais*. Facts, by themselves, cannot be the object of a judicial declaration, *covered* by the *authority* of *res judicata*. Good examples would be a flood or the fact that some medicine damages health.

If the Bill passes and becomes our new civil procedural code, in the version delivered to the Senate in 2010, and still pending, the *prejudiciais* will be the object of a decision with *resjudicata*, independently of the filing of the *ação declaratória incidental*, that will not exist anymore. In future lawsuits, a judge would be bound by what was previously decided on these issues, as, for example, paternity, maternity, contracts, validity of a trademark and so on.

The current version of the Bill still contains a provision in this sense.

This option avoids: (1) the possibility of logical contradiction (although not practical) between sentences/judgments/decisions (2) and that an issue which was discussed by the parts and decided by a judge, on which the solution of the merits depends, be re-discussed and decided differently in other future lawsuits.

14.4 Reasons Which Would Recommend the Broadening of the Scope of *ResJudicata*

It shocks the common sense, as I said before, to allow two judges to decide differently the same issue. Even if this issue is not the main issue (merits, fond du litige, Streitgegenstand), the shock is almost the same. It compromises the credibility of the Judiciary and generates a lack of tranquility in society. Furthermore, if the impossibility of a reopening of issues (discussed by the parties and expressly decided) becomes the rule (and not the exception, as it is today) proceedings will be faster.

It is interesting to notice that recently European (continental) case law offers various examples of cases in which it was understood or considered that *res judicata* would encompass not only the *decisum* but reasons, under certain conditions.[16]

---

[14] ARAGÃO, Egas Moniz de. ***Sentença e coisa julgada***, p. 256–257.

[15] GRINOVER, Ada Pellegrini. ***Ação declaratória incidental***. São Paulo: RT, 1972, p. 41–46.

[16] DALLA BONTÀ, Silvana, Una benefica inquietudine. "Note comparate in tema di oggetto del giudicato nella giurisprudenza alla luce delle tesi zeuneriane", Eine "heilsame Unruhe". Rechtsvergleichende Anmerkungen zur Bestimmung der objektiven Grenzen der Rechtskraft in der jüngeren Rechtsprechung im Lichte der Thesen Zeuners, in ZZP, Zeitschrift für Zivilprozess, 125. Band. Heft 1–2012, p. 93 to 123. Certainly, this jurisprudence has nothing to do with the common law *collateral estoppel* or *issue preclusion*, but with ideas of Albrecht Zeuner, analyzed by Silvana Dalla Bontà, in this brilliant article.

Not only in Europe but also in Japan, case law draws special attention concerning this specific subject. Japanese case law recognizes the need for coherence and for different reasons it has avoided those situations in which a judge decides again the previously necessary parts of the conclusion of an earlier lawsuit. The main reason cited in Japanese decisions is that this would be a clear violation of the good faith principle (Konzept von Treu und Glauben).[17]

Also in Brazilian tax law jurisprudence there is a clear trend towards considering that even not being part of the decision *stricto sensu* (*decisum*) the judgment of *elements* (= necessary steps) which remain the same (= permanent) should be respected in future cases. In these cases, obviously the strict doctrine of *res judicata's* scope is abandoned.

14.4.1 The Influence of "Common Law" Regimes?

It is said that the proposal made by the commission who drafted a Bill for a new CPC is similar to the common law *res judicata* regime, at least to a certain extent. However, it is not entirely similar, as I will try to demonstrate in the following.

Res judicata in common law countries has two dimensions.[18] It avoids the same claim being analyzed a second time by the Judiciary – same parties, same cause of action (*causa petendi*) – and this dimension is very similar to the *res judicata* regime in civil law countries.

There is a clear relationship between the scope of *res judicata* and the possibility that the parties have of changing *causa petendi* and *petitum* during the proceedings. In fact, a wider scope of *res judicata* corresponds to greater flexibility in terms of the possibility of changing what in civil law countries is called *perpetuatio libelli* (stability of *causa petendi* and *petitum*).[19] In this regime after the judgment has been given the dispute between the parties is understood to have been entirely and definitely solved. Nothing is left behind. In fact, all the *petita* that could have been drawn from the *causae petendi* are covered by *res judicata*, even if the claim was not expressly filed.[20] This is what civil law countries call claim preclusion. The parties have a single "Day in Court", i.e., a sole opportunity or occasion to formulate their *petita* and defenses, which stem from the same situation.[21]

[17] DALLA BONTÀ, Silvana, *op. cit.*, p. 915, 6(b).

[18] SOARES, Marcos José Porto. O *collateral estoppel* no Brasil. In: ***RePro***, v. 211, p. 115, setembro/2012.

[19] Commenting deeply on this problem in Spanish law, Cintia R. Guedes, A estabilização objetiva da demanda, Rio de Janeiro, 2012, not yet published.

[20] GIDI, TESHEINER e PRATES say that *claim preclusion* means that the claimant has to make all the *petita* in the same lawsuit. This is because this is the only possibility for him to do so (Limites objetivos da coisa julgada no projeto de Código de Processo Civil: reflexões inspiradas na experiência norte-americana. *In*: ***RePro***, v. 194, p. 99, abril/2011).

[21] LOPES, Bruno Vasconcelos Carrilho. *Limites objetivos e eficácia preclusiva da coisa julgada.* São Paulo: Saraiva, 2012, p. 23–24.

The other dimension of the *res judicata* regime in common law systems is *collateral estoppel* or *issue preclusion*. This phenomenon renders undisputable[22] the resolution of an issue which is considered essential for the resolution of the claim (itself *petitum*). This issue, on what the parties cannot debate any more in the future, in no other lawsuits, is said to be a *necessary step* for the resolution of the main question.[23] Something very similar to the *questões prejudiciais*, I should say.

For an issue to be touched by collateral estoppel there has to be (1) debates on it between the parties, (2) a judge's decision about it has to be explicit, and (3) it has to be qualified as a necessary reason for the conclusion (the decision itself).[24]

English legal writers say that estoppel by *res judicata* are of two types: cause of action estoppels and issue estoppel. Identity of cause of action, parties and subject of the lawsuit gives rise to cause of action estoppels. This situation bars re-litigation completely. Issue estoppel is related to the adjudication of issues which can be considered a necessary step for the decision of the claim. It can be relaxed in more cases than cause of action estoppels. More interesting is the barring of discussions on matters which were not the object of a previous discussion, but should have been. That means that litigation can be barred even if some points were not previously decided, but could have been.

Besides these general rules, there are some other aspects of these bars on re-litigation which show that re-litigation is not easy in England. Damages should be asked for all at once. Damages stemming from the same cause of action cannot be asked in successive lawsuits.[25]

"Collateral estoppel" means that the parties have to respect prior decisions and cannot change their approach to the same issue in different lawsuits. In the light of all these observations, it becomes obvious that the estoppel clause forbids a judge to decide the same issue in a different way if ever the same issue is resubmitted to the courts. The parties' fair expectations about coherent judicial decisions are therefore fulfilled.

The doctrine of *res judicata* in England is not essentially different from the American one. The main idea is the same: it aims to avoid successive litigation on the same matters. This prohibition has two dimensions: on the one hand, it is in the public interest (in terms of costs?) that proceedings not be allowed to last forever and, on the other hand, no one should be disturbed twice regarding the same matter.

---

[22] The party has to demonstrate the identity between the two claims, as explains Artur da Fonseca Martin (Coisa julgada nos Estados Unidos. *In*: *RePro*, v. 132, p. 75, fevereiro/2006).

[23] GIDI, Antonio; TESHEINER, José Maria e PRATES, Marília Zanella. *Op. cit. Passim.*

[24] LOPES, Bruno Vasconcelos Carrilho, *op. cit.*,, p. 37–38.

[25] ANDREWS, Neil. *The modern civil process: judicial and alternative forms of dispute resolution in England.* 2ª ed. São Paulo: Revista dos Tribunais, 2011.

14.4.2 The Res Judicata *Regime in Spain*

The Spanish *res judicata* regime deserves to be mentioned separately because it was recently reformed (or altered) and its current features[26] may be considered peculiar if compared to other European civil law systems.

Art. 400 of the new LEC (Ley de Enjuiciamiento Civil Española of 2000) says that when the claimant asks for something (makes a *petitum*) that can theoretically be based on several facts or legal reasons, those facts or legal reasons should be alleged, for the claimant will not be allowed to allege them in a subsequent lawsuit. Of course this *duty* only concerns facts which are known at the time of the claim, and not those which take place afterwards.

Those facts and legal reasons even if they are not effectively alleged are taken into consideration for *lis pendens* and *res judicata* effect. Hence, Spanish law considers *touched* by *res judicata* even *reasons* (*causae petendi* + facts) which theoretically could generate other claims in the future. It is true, on the one hand, that technically facts are not covered by *res judicata*, but on the other hand this article forbids any future allegation of facts that could have been alleged in a previous lawsuit. In civil law vocabulary, the right term to describe this solution would certainly be fact *preclusion* (preclusión).

Spanish legal writers say, rightly it seems to me, that this article can generate a great deal of *transcendence*.[27] The fact is that *res judicata* extends its effects to the allegations that could have been made, but were not.[28] Of course, a judge does not take decisions on these facts or reasons (which have not been alleged) but they cannot be made in a future lawsuit.

It should be stressed that the suggestion made by the commission for the new CPC has nothing to do with this regime: we proposed that necessary steps, only if they consist in the result of the analysis of a legal relationship, around which there was a discussion between the parties, should not be discussed anymore in any other future lawsuit.

This new Spanish *res judicata* regime is being heavily criticized by legal writers. Some say this new rule (art. 400) is unconstitutional.[29] Others say that this rule creates a virtual *Streitgegenstand*.[30]

[26] Related not to the *juicio verbal*, but to the *juicio ordinario*.

[27] RAMOS, Manuel Ortells, Preclusións de Alegaciones y peticiones en la primera instancia, los procesos declarativos, *in* Cuadernos de Derecho Judicial, p. 15 a 69, especially p. 37.

[28] RAMOS, Manuel Ortells, *op. cit.*, p. 66.

[29] Ramos Mendez, quoted by Joan Picó I Junoy, Los princípios del nuevo proceso civil español, *in* RePro, v. 103, p. 59, 2001.

[30] PICÓ I JUNOY, Joan, *op. cit.*, p. 59.

14.5 What Makes the Proposed Brazilian Regime Better?

14.5.1 Choices Made by the Legislator Must Respect Common Sense

The current *res judicata* regime in Brazil allows the same issue (whose decision determines the judgment on the merits) to be decided in two different ways in two subsequent lawsuits. Even if these decisions are taken to be the basis (necessary step) for the *decisum* (= decision of the *Hauptsache*), it cannot be denied that they are logically contradictory. This possibility does not favour legal predictability. Neither does it improve consistency or promote uniformity.

In our CPC there are several provisions creating devices to avoid contradictory decisions. *Lis pendens* is, of course, forbidden (in the sense of two identical lawsuits taking place at the same time); *Praeclusio pro judicato*, lawsuits have to be reunited, if there is the danger of contradictory decisions. However, surprisingly our legislature maintained the aforementioned *res judicata* regime.

Furthermore, there are specific rules saying, for example, that the motivation of a criminal judgment binds the civil judge in a claim where the claimant asks for compensation stemming from the crime. We can also cite the influence that class action decisions have on individual lawsuits.[31] Coherence thus appears to be a goal of the Brazilian legislature.

Nevertheless, the *res judicata* regime in Brazil is heading in the "opposite direction", for it really does not favour uniformity, predictability and consistency.

14.5.1.1 Procedural Speediness

In civil law countries we speak of the "procedural" economy principle.

This principle means that procedural rules shall be interpreted in such a way as to obtain greater results from a smaller number of steps. It provides guidance to increase the efficiency of proceedings, sometimes reducing duration. In part, the lengthy duration of proceedings in Brazil is caused by an overload of cases in court. So, lack of efficiency results directly from the excessive number of pending cases in Brazil.

So, if you restrict the aspects of a decision which can be later contested, it follows that there is a tendency to reduce the number of potential new suits.

Let us clarify it further.

Admittedly, several claims may stem or derive from a legal relationship. The judge has to decide the *res in judicium deducta*, and nothing else. In Brazil, the *elements* of a lawsuit are fixed in the claim form and cannot be changed afterwards:

[31] A provision that applies not only to class actions related to consumer law but also to other types of class actions. WAMBIER, Luiz Rodrigues. *Sentença civil: liquidação e cumprimento*. 3ª ed. São Paulo: Revista dos Tribunais, 2006, p. 355.

causae petendi, *petita* and *parties*. Parties cannot be changed (*perpetuatio legitimationis*), the claim cannot be changed (*perpetuatio libelli*). It is then rather obvious that a lawsuit very often does not solve entirely the parties' dispute. Sometimes one and the same cause of action does generate several claims. Our current *res judicata* regime thus may not lead to efficiency. All the doors are open for each and every issue to be reargued, except for the main question: the divorce, the annullment of the contract, the compensation itself.

If the new *res judicata* regime is actually enacted, within the future CPC, what can be discussed in future lawsuits ceases to be an extensive list of issues, and so, it seems to me, naturally proceedings will be faster. And this is because there will be fever lawsuits to be dealt with by the Courts.

Some legal writers say that the new *res judicata* regime, proposed by the commission, limits a judge's right to decide. However, I consider this argument to be very weak. There are more important values that should be favoured by the judicial system: consistency, uniformity, coherence, and finally speediness.

The necessity of efficiency has been inspiring (now and in the past) many rules in Brazilian civil procedure. *Borrowed* evidence (from another lawsuit) is commonly used; unnecessary or useless evidence should not be produced – a judge should not allow its production; appeals dealing with the same issue of law should be reunited and decided all at once, and so on. All these tools or devices are a clear sign that there is some concern with harmony and effectiveness of civil justice in Brazilian law. A simple question can be posed: why then do we still adopt the restricted version of *res judicata*? And the answer is; how is this linked to the rule in the next paragraph?

The rule proposed by the Commission appointed by the Senate in 2003 favours harmony, predictability and hence efficiency.

14.6 Peculiar Situations Where Necessary Steps for the Final Conclusion (*Decisum*) Cannot be *Res Judicata*

14.6.1 When the Necessary Step *is a* Fact

It is possible that a *fact* plays the role of a *necessary step* (*Vorfrage*) for the decision of the main question. A claim can be brought before the Judiciary based on a car accident, or on harm caused by a medicine, on a flood.

According to the prevailing opinion of legal writers, even if the assessment of these facts is really a necessary step to the decision of the main question, which in both examples could be the compensation, a *conviction* of the judge of the first lawsuit could never bind future claims deriving from the same facts.

As was already said, our procedural rules admit the borrowed evidence and it can also be seen as a tool to avoid contradictory decisions, useful in cases like those which were cited as examples.

The situation which led the judge to have this conviction in the first lawsuit also has to be taken into account. Sometimes a fact is considered to be true or to have happened in a certain way not because evidence was produced, but because evidence was **not** produced. There are several situations in which law allows a judge to consider facts to have happened just because of the omission of one of the parties (v.g., default judgment). In these situations, the parties cannot be denied the right to produce evidence on the facts that could be considered material (= important) in a second lawsuit.

Furthermore, admittedly in civil law regimes facts (raw facts) cannot be the object of a claim, i.e., one cannot ask from the Judiciary the mere declaration that a fact existed. So, it is really nonsense, in the context of a civil law system, to extend *res judicata* to *necessary steps* of a conclusion (*decisum*) if these steps are raw *facts*.

14.6.2 Small Claims and Protective Relief Provisions

There is an undeniable relationship between the degree of *cognition* and the stability of the decision. Usually, decisions which are based in *fumus boni iuris*[32] are not *resjudicata*. The price to be paid for the possibility that a judge decides when he or she is not yet sure whether the claimant has the right he affirms to have is that these decisions are not *res judicata* in Brazilian civil procedure.

Almost the same can be said about situations where the cognition is, for some reason or another, limited, as, for instance, in the Brazilian small claim proceedings. Small claims proceedings are, all over the world, a way of improving access to justice, with the reduction of costs, bureaucracy and duration. Sometimes the parties dispense with traditional courts and let their dispute be decided by a small claims court. These proceedings are more simple than the traditional ones, less formal, faster and above all, oral.[33] Complex litigation cannot be brought before small claims courts or judges and some of the judges who work in this field are laymen. In this situation, it seems to me, *res judicata* should be limited to the *decisum*.

14.7 Conclusions

It seems to me that the *res judicata* regime proposed by the first version of the Bill for a new CPC delivered to the Senate in 2010, which is now being discussed by the *Câmara dos Deputados*, is *between* the broad *res judicata* regime, usual in common law jurisdictions, and the very narrow scope of *res judicata* that exists now in Brazilian law.

---

[32] *Fumus boni iuris*: Decisions based on *fumus boni iuris* are preliminar and based on evidence of lower degree of persuasiveness. These decisions are subject to further and deeper analyses.

[33] DINAMARCO, Cândido. *Instituições de direito processual civil*, V. III, p. 770–772.

In my view, there is not any sensible reason to consider that necessary steps to the decision – when there has been enough debate between the parties on the subject, could be differently considered, judged or decided in subsequent lawsuits.

Nowadays, the only part of the final decision which is *res judicata* (= cannot be rediscussed in a future lawsuit) is the decision itself. So, every other aspect of the reasoning on which the decision is based is, according to the current regime, subject to future discussion.

This system seems to me rather archaic: it favours neither uniformity, predictability, stability nor efficiency of civil justice.

Index

C.B. Picker, G.I. Seidman (eds.), *The Dynamism of Civil Procedure Global Trends and Developments*, Ius Gentium: Comparative Perspectives on Law and Justice 48, DOI 10.1007/978-3-319-21981-3

CPSIA information can be obtained at www.ICGtesting.com
Printed in the USA
BVOW09*0736141115

427136BV00013B/50/P

9 783319 219806